The Rise of Democracy in
Pre-Revolutionary Russia

THE RISE OF DEMOCRACY
IN PRE-REVOLUTIONARY RUSSIA

Political and Social Institutions
Under the Last Three Czars

by

JACOB WALKIN

FREDERICK A. PRAEGER
Publisher • New York

BOOKS THAT MATTER

Published in the United States of America in 1962 by
Frederick A. Praeger, Inc., Publisher
64 University Place, New York 3, N.Y.

This book is Number 115 in the series of
Praeger Publications in Russian History and World Communism

Manufactured in the United States of America

To
ALLAN A. SEGAL

Without whose influence on my life
This book could not have been written

Preface

The relation between the Soviet regime and its Czarist heritage has long been debated in the West and has evoked a variety of opinions and theories, probably only slightly less numerous than those concerning the interpretation of the Soviet regime itself. This attempt to unravel the intricacies of the subject is based on an analysis of Russian institutions, both of the state and of society. This analysis is then followed by a further analysis of the clash between state and society, which has loomed so large for almost two centuries of Russian history. If I have given more space to the Revolution of 1905 than to the Revolution of 1917, it is only because an understanding of the first revolution of the twentieth century, relatively neglected in Western literature on Russia, is indispensable for an understanding of the second.

The institutional rather than the chronological approach is well adapted to what must be the major aim of the study of any country, namely, to explain those unique patterns of social and cultural behavior that tend to give each country its distinctive political forms. Special attention has been given in the analysis to the methods used by the Czarist state to control Russian society, thus providing the basis for maximum comparability between Czarist and Communist institutions.

In presenting a full explanation of the special features of Russian civilization, I have been guided by the wish to make them comprehensible to Western readers without prior familiarity with the subject. Limitations of space have compelled me to concentrate on the central provinces of Great Russia. Although an understanding of the problem of the national minorities is important for a comprehensive grasp of Russian politics, this problem has not been given special treatment.

vii

All dates used for the period before 1918 conform to the old Julian calendar. These are the dates found in Russian sources and used by the Russians themselves. Changing them to conform to the Gregorian calendar would throw all who work closely with Russian materials into confusion. Those readers who for any reason must convert the dates to the Gregorian calendar may readily do so by adding thirteen days to the Russian dates in the twentieth century, twelve in the nineteenth, and eleven in the eighteenth.

I am especially indebted to the late Professor Robert J. Kerner for assistance in the preparation of this study. His own experience in the broad interpretation of Russian trends helped to channel my interest into the theme of this book, and his advice and encouragement were always invaluable. Professors George Vernadsky, Gleb Struve, Leslie Lipson, and Mr. George C. Guins have read all or most of the manuscript. Professor Vernadsky's boundless knowledge of Russian history helped guide me through the complexities of a number of topics. I have greatly benefited from the personal experiences of Mr. Guins and Professor Struve, and from Mr. Guins's knowledge of Russian law. Professor Lipson, though not a specialist in Czarist politics, contributed a number of valuable criticisms.

I also wish to express special thanks to the Social Science Research Council, whose generous award helped to make the publication of this book possible. The Committee for the Promotion of Advanced Slavic Cultural Studies and the Humanities Fund have also made lesser but essential contributions.

Grateful acknowledgment is made to the following publishers for permission to quote excerpts from copyrighted materials:

The Carnegie Endowment for International Peace; The Dial Press; Longmans, Green & Co.; The Macmillan Company; Methuen & Company, Ltd.; The University of Pennsylvania Press; Stanford University Press; and Yale University Press.

JACOB WALKIN

Contents

ONE

INTRODUCTION
TO THE
RUSSIAN PAST

I

The Long-range Characteristics
of Russian Society

T HE RELATION between state and society has been a problem in
two phases of the history of the modern nation-state. For most
European states, the first phase came in the eighteenth century,
during the era of the absolute monarchy and the feudal-agrarian
structure of society. With the rise of an educated and politically
conscious urban middle class, the enormous police powers of the
absolute monarchs and the feudal-agrarian structure of society became dated, and tension between a large and vocal segment of
society and the state increased. This tension was resolved by the
French Revolution (in some cases earlier, in some later), and those
states in which the urban middle class became dominant entered
a new era of parliamentarism, equality before the law, and *laissez
faire*. The sharp division between state and society was obliter-
ated, and the state became responsive to increasingly larger segments of society capable of making their voices heard. The police
powers of the state were confined to the minimum necessary to
maintain order, leaving great scope to the activities of the many
voluntary associations that constituted society. The role of government in public life, though important, was limited, and the bureaucracy was small. Under these conditions, the over-all distinction
between state and society tended to be taken for granted, or simply
overlooked.

In the third phase of the modern nation-state—the era of the
welfare state, which began in the nineteenth century and is still
under way—government controls steadily expanded, and the question has again been raised as to what the proper limits of governmental authority should be. The importance of this question has
been underlined by the rise of the totalitarian states, in which the
attempt is made to identify society with the state through the subjection to state regulation and control of all spheres of organized

3

social activity. New interest has thus been aroused in the distinction between state and society and in the kind of relationship between them that will insure the maintenance of democratic institutions. This has, in turn, drawn increased attention to the social basis of government; for, of the many factors that condition the constitutional development of any given state, the structure of the social order is certainly among the most fundamental. The manner in which a society is organized exerts an intimate and profound influence on the manner in which a state is governed.[1]

The problem of the relationship between state and society is not a new one for Russia, and in perhaps no other country is the problem a more crucial one. Unlike most other European states, Russia never entered the stage of *laissez faire*, i.e., that stage in which the role of the government in public life is reduced to the barest minimum. Russia passed directly from the era of the absolute monarchy to the era of the welfare state; worse than that, she passed directly from a monarchical police state to a totalitarian police state. She has, therefore, encountered the problem of the relation between state and society in its worst forms. The growing antagonism between state and society during the phase of the absolute monarchy has never been resolved, and the state has for centuries played an abnormally large role in the life of the people. Since little progress can be made in understanding Russia or the Russian people until this situation is explained, this study is an attempt to furnish an explanation. Although the main emphasis is necessarily on the past, the real problems under consideration are: What is the significance in Russian constitutional history of the Soviet state? And what direction is the government of Russia likely to take in the future?

Contrasts Between the Absolute Monarchy in Russia and in the Remainder of Europe

Outwardly, the Russia that emerged in the nineteenth century was an absolute monarchy closely resembling the absolute monarchies of continental Europe in the eighteenth and early nineteenth centuries. Like those Western European states, she was governed by an autocratic monarch whose legal powers were virtually unlimited. The Russian Czar, like his Western European counterparts, had performed the useful service of creating a unified state in place of the confusing array of disunited, quarreling local overlords; like them, he enjoyed, up to a point, widespread popular support. In his struggle with local overlords, he had enjoyed and retained unlimited police powers over an unusually wide area of Russian life. The people had few, if any, rights and many duties, and were subjected to the arbitrary and lawless control of an army of bureaucrats. Behind this despotic regime was a pyramidal structure of society—a society of legally established classes with varying powers and privileges, the more privileged classes being fewer in number than the less privileged. During the eighteenth century, the aristocracy had strengthened its hold over the hereditary estates and serfs, and these landowners exercised administrative powers on their own estates. In all these respects, Russia resembled the absolute monarchies of the eighteenth century.

There were, however, very great differences that have run through the whole course of Russian history and that have endowed Russia with unique characteristics. Of immediate concern for this study are, on the one hand, the unusually great legal and real powers of the Czar and the more imposing tradition of state control and interference; and, on the other hand, the peculiar inertia and lack of initiative characteristic of Russian society. In Western Europe, there were various corporate bodies—the estates, the guilds, the churches, the universities—united by common interests, a common awareness of those interests, and a common education and outlook. These institutions acquired the right of self-government and, in general, an internal life and movement of their own. In matters of police, taxation, and general administration, they came in greater or lesser degree to fulfill duties nominally associated with the crown. These institutions, the forerunners of the much more complex system of voluntary associations, acquired rights, not only by direct grant but also by custom, that the local princes and then the absolute monarch came to respect. Whatever the theoretical legal powers of the absolute monarchs, their ability to carry out a given policy depended upon the support they received from these social groups and upon the extent to which these groups were in a position to thwart their will. In all of Western Europe, the landed aristocracy had an especially important role in keeping the power of the monarch within limits. In all of it, too, there was an organized middle class with varying degrees of influence; in some countries it ultimately won political supremacy.

With the rise of the Moscow principality in the fifteenth century, such self-governing, corporate groups played a limited role in Russia. There were many units of local self-government during the fifteenth and sixteenth centuries, but most of them were not comparable to the active and well-organized corporate bodies of Western Europe. Their existence is attributed to the extreme weakness of the Russian sense of statehood and state power inherited by the early Muscovite state and to the failure of the state to supply many essential public services. As a result, these services were supplied by the people on the basis of custom, and the custom-bound units of local society either became obedient tools of the state administration or were removed without serious opposition in the course of the consolidation of state administration during the sixteenth and seventeenth centuries.[2]

By the second half of the seventeenth century, all private persons or social groups who possessed rights and privileges that could be exercised in opposition to the power of the Czar, never strong or well organized in the first place, had disappeared, and were not to rise again until the nineteenth century. In general, the rights and privileges enjoyed henceforth by any group were received from the Czar and dependent upon him; they were not derived from independent economic power or from inherited social position. The Muscovite Empire, which emerged from the Tatar occupation at the end of the fifteenth century, was regarded by the Russians as the personal inherited estate of the ruling sovereign, who had no responsibilities to the nation for its operation. As has been pointed out by V. O. Kliuchevsky, the nation—the Russian community—was, until the Time of Troubles (1584–1613), regarded as a kind of political accident, a group of temporary sojourners who happened to be residing on the estate of the Czar.[3] For the Muscovites, the state *was* the Czar, and it was easier for them to imagine a Czar without a people than a state without a Czar.

This conception of the state and the sovereign of a given dynasty as being one and the same naturally gave way after the Time of Troubles, and certainly by the time of Peter the Great, the Czar himself had come to recognize that his first duty was to the state and the nation, not to personal or dynastic interests. Nevertheless, the consequences, if not the traces, of the idea that the empire was the personal fief of the Czar were to remain until 1917. The existence of this idea is possible only in a society that is passive, obedient, unaware of, or indifferent to, its own rights, wanting in political and civic consciousness. The legal classes that emerged from this society, and particularly the nobility and the middle class, both of which played so powerful a role in the constitutional history of the West, were not necessarily comparable to the legal classes of the West, and, indeed, shared none of the latter's political achievements.

Why the Russian Aristocracy Could Not Become an Independent Political Force

There were many reasons why the aristocracy of the West was able to acquire great political influence. Among them certainly were its ownership of the land, the main source of wealth, at a time when the monarchy was decaying; its early development as a privileged caste enjoying great authority and prestige; and its organization as a corporate body united by common interests and a strong *esprit de corps*. These conditions were not met by the Russian nobility, and the latter's role in the Russian state was correspondingly different. The history of the Russian nobility, or *dvorianstvo*, is a long and complex subject, which need not be treated in this study; some of the main factors conditioning its development that prevented the nobility from exercising independent political power should, however, be emphasized.

The peculiar relation of the nobility to the land was certainly one of the most important of these factors. Unlike its Western counterpart, the Russian nobility failed to consolidate its hold on the land before the rise of a powerful monarchy and to acquire thereby economic wealth and political power that could serve as a check on the power of the monarch.[4] From the Moscow period on—when, as has been said, all Russia was regarded as the personal property of the monarch—the bulk of the landowning nobility comprised those who received their estates from the Czar in return for military service. These estates were not hereditary and were held only as long as service to the state was rendered. A group of titled and untitled boyars with hereditary estates did remain on the scene for a time, some of them being the former princes of the principalities annexed by Moscow, but since the Czar regarded them as a threat to his power, he undertook a campaign to destroy them by uprooting them from their hereditary estates and by outright physical extermination. After the Time of Troubles, the boyars ceased to be a political force of any consequence. During the course of the seventeenth century, those of them who retained their hereditary estates became obligated for service on the same basis as the serving nobility. This merging of the hereditary estates and the service estates took place also in a reverse direction, and during the first half of the eighteenth century, the former service estates came to be regarded as hereditary in the families of the existing owners, with the obligations for service being gradually curtailed and then abolished altogether in 1762. As will be seen, this development did not change the position of the nobility as a political force. In accordance, moreover, with former traditions, the nobility failed as a group either to value its land or to take a serious interest in agriculture.

In addition to the lack of a territorial base and a firm hold on the land, the course of the Russian nobility was strongly influenced by the tradition of dividing the land equally among the male heirs. In the West, some form of land entailment, generally primogeniture, played an important part in maintaining the integrity of large estates, whose owners, the great land barons, have been prominent political figures until relatively recent times. This is strikingly illustrated by the practice in England, where only one man can hold both land and title simultaneously, and where even the eldest sons are legally considered commoners until the death of their fathers. In Russia, entailment of the land did not take root, and the landowner was free to dispose of his estates as he wished. The custom was to divide the land equally among the male heirs, and the title of nobility was freely acquired by all heirs, male and female. The result was the disintegration of the great estates and a tendency, in the long run, toward the leveling and impoverishment of the nobility. According to Paul Miliukov, the fall of the boyars was at least as much a result of the freedom of testament they enjoyed as of the leveling policy of Ivan the Terrible.[5] This is almost certainly an understatement. With the succession laws as they were, no real aristocracy could ever have been formed in Russia. The opinion of Kliuchevsky, that, with or without Ivan, the course of the Muscovite Empire would not have been any different from what it was seems much more valid.[6] After association with the nobility of Western Europe made clear its differences from the *dvorianstvo*, Peter the Great, in 1714, issued a ukase decreeing that landed estates were to be passed undivided to a single heir, the choice of heir being left to the discretion of the father. Because of the resistance of the nobility, accustomed for centuries to an equal division of the land, the ukase was revoked in 1730.

The tendency toward the impoverishment of the nobility, observed by the Englishman Giles Fletcher as early as the sixteenth century, was accompanied by a tendency toward the debasement of the title. With the title passing freely to all members of the family, the successive multiplication of the various branches of the family conferred the title on a large number of individuals whose interrelationships were obscure and many of whom had little means of support. In the colorful language of Leroy-Beaulieu:

By dint of branching out, several of these princely families, and sometimes the most illustrious, have formed a dense bush whose entangled branches choke and hide one another. . . . In these numerous families sprung from the same trunk, alongside those branches that spread in the sun, flourishing and full of sap, there naturally are branches deprived of air and stripped of foliage.[7]

The contrast with England, where both the title and the family fortune are passed on to one member of the family, is again very striking.

The princely families were mainly the descendants of Rurik, the Varangian founder of the Kievan dynasty, and of Gedymin, founder of an ancient royal Lithuanian family that at one time ruled western Russia and gained fame and power in Europe by a union with the Polish dynasty. These families, of very high royal lineage, with names distinguished in Russian history, and whose ancestors were the rulers of the separate principalities that constituted Russia before their annexation by Moscow, bore the only indigenous hereditary title known in Russia—*kniaz*, or prince. The number of these families was relatively small (about sixty), but the number of individuals within them was large, and, for the reasons stated, these families, as such, lost all influence and authority. Other hereditary titles in Russia, such as count or baron, were borrowed from Western feudalism and, beginning with Peter the Great, were conferred by the Czar on a comparatively small number of individuals. The bulk of the *dvorianstvo*, which, as we have seen, absorbed the princely families, had neither name nor title nor pedigree to distinguish them from the mass of the nation. From the time of Peter the Great, this class was accessible to anyone who achieved a certain rank in military or civil service, regardless of origin. From the time of Peter the Great, at the beginning of the eighteenth century, until 1845, during the reign of Nicholas I, even the lowest-ranking officer automatically became a *dvorianin*.

This heterogeneous group, which constituted the Russian nobility, could not, under the circumstances, acquire either *esprit de corps* or a feeling of equality, and this was as true of the rapidly multiplying princely families as it was of the ordinary serving nobility. Without *esprit de corps* and a feeling of equality, it was impossible for them to act as a group, and no checks could be placed on the Czar unless they did so act. The failure of all attempts to establish aristocratic rule in Russia can, in fact, be traced in part to the internal jealousies and mutual antagonisms of the nobility. Since, furthermore, in their formative period, they lacked hereditary group interests that they shared and were ready to defend in common, they could be picked off one by one by the Czar, who, at any given time, was always far more powerful than any individual boyar or *dvorianin*—or even any combination of members of these two groups.

Their traditional helplessness before the Czar was intensified by the fact that, in their own eyes and in the eyes of the community, their status in society was acquired not from anything they inherited, but from their position in the hierarchy of service. This interest in service, rather than noble blood or birth, was discernible among the boyars at the height of their influence in the fifteenth and sixteenth centuries, when holding on to the rank in the service of the Moscow prince inherited from their fathers was one of their dominant aims.[8] With the absorption of the boyars by the more humble *dvorianstvo*, and with the establishment of the Table of Ranks by Peter the Great, rank in service acquired a more orderly, institutional, and democratic form, and ascending the ladder of service became a primary goal of the serving nobility. Although they were to be relieved of the obligation for service in the eighteenth century, they were so attached to the idea that only service gave them their social position in the state that they could not at all understand their emancipation, and for some time they regarded it suspiciously.[9] This peculiarity of the Russian nobility, as well as the lack of corporative spirit, was to show striking results at the height of their influence under Catherine.

Imitations of the Western Aristocracies
in the Eighteenth Century

In the eighteenth century, the *dvorianstvo* became a privileged estate superficially resembling the Western aristocracies. As has already been stated, their obligation for service to the state was abolished and their estates became their hereditary property. Although the institution of serfdom in Russia had originally been justified by the obligation for military service of the *dvoriane*, their rights over their serfs, who became hardly distinguishable from slaves, were now increased. State lands and state serfs were generously distributed to court favorites by the Czars.[10] Most of the legal privileges of the gentry were granted to them at that time.

The privileges acquired by the gentry in the eighteenth century were mainly derived from the new political influence exercised by them by virtue of their service in the St. Petersburg guard regiments. Several times during the eighteenth century, the nobility in the guard regiments took part in palace revolutions, unseating legal heirs and sovereigns and installing as monarchs individuals without firm legal rights to the throne (including, of course, Catherine II). In 1730, they frustrated an attempt of the higher nobility to place constitutional limitations on the power of the Czar. The outcome of the increased power enjoyed by the nobility in the eighteenth century affords perhaps the best illustration of the defects—common to this class and to Russian society as a whole—that made possible the continuation of an unlimited autocracy through the nineteenth century.

In 1775, Catherine II reorganized the provincial institutions of Russia and established, for the first time, corporate institutions for the nobility. All the rights that had been granted piecemeal to the gentry were brought together and systematized in the Charter of the Nobility issued by Catherine in 1785. With these reforms, Catherine was continuing a trend, strongly in evidence from the time of Peter the Great, of imitating Western forms. What Catherine sought was the organization of Russian society into separate estates, each with its own corporate institutions and some measure of self-government, and each participating in the local administration of the state. The governmental institutions established by Catherine in the provinces included some staffed entirely by bureaucrats, some by a combination of bureaucrats and elected representatives from the various estates, and some entirely by elected representatives. A majority of the personnel consisted of elected representatives, and the nobility, as the most privileged estate of the realm, predominated in the election of these representatives (judges, police chiefs, etc.).

In thus creating corporate institutions for the nobility and investing them with strong influence in local government, the autocracy neither established self-government in Russia nor did it limit its own power. Only the external forms of Western Europe had been adopted; the political situation remained as before. Despite Catherine's reforms, real power in the provinces remained in the hands of the governors, and, through them, orders from St. Petersburg continued to be enforced. This situation did not particularly concern the nobility, who remained devoid of political consciousness and public spirit and as devoted as before to their own narrow personal interests. In the eyes of the nobility, any rights acquired in elected service that would permit their upward movement in the Table of Ranks were of far greater importance. The elected positions were included in the Table of Ranks by the Law of 1775, but once it was revealed that there would be no free transfer from elected service to state service, and that elected service would not serve as a preliminary qualification for state service, then the nobility sought to avoid elected service, and the intellectual and moral qualifications of those elected began to decline. Evasion of elections and elected positions came to be treated by the state as a crime for which punishments were prescribed.[11]

For the nobility, participation in local administration became a new form of state service, one which was avoided by the wealthiest and most influential of them. Those who did serve were as obedient and docile to the central authorities as the directly appointed bureaucrats. The *dvorianstvo* had no traditional views or class spirit to bind their elected representatives, and the judges, police chiefs, assessors, and other local administrators showed no sense of responsibility toward their electors. In the absence of an inner feeling of solidarity and cohesion, the grant of corporate institutions to the nobility was unable to change the situation. The provincial and district societies of the nobility met every three years, as they were required to do, and conducted their elections and other necessary business without endangering either the Czar or the bureaucracy.

After the emancipation of the serfs in 1861, and after the establishment of genuine, though limited, self-government in Russia, the societies of the nobility steadily declined in importance, and their activities steadily lost any public significance they may have had. There is no more striking illustration of the basic passivity of Russian society than the failure of the *dvorianstvo* to modify existing centralization or autocracy, even when enjoying some of the advantages of Western aristocratic societies and occupying strategic positions in local administration.

Backwardness of the Urban Population

The nobility was the only class in pre-nineteenth-century Russia that might have been expected to place any limits on the power of the Czar. The Russian middle class and urban population did not have the same significance as their counterparts in the West, and their situation concerning what the Russians call "self-activity" and self-government was even more dismal than that of the nobility. Neither before nor after the nineteenth century did the urban population, or, more specifically, the city institutions, play anything like the role in peaceful political development (but not necessarily revolutionary development) played by the rural population and its institutions. From 1864 to 1917, the city Dumas were always overshadowed by the rural zemstvos.

The growth of the middle class in the West was the result of a chain of events leading from the revival of learning and the growth of trade and commerce in the Middle Ages, through the Renaissance and Reformation, into the industrial revolution. A spontaneous movement in the life of feudal Europe brought to the cities lower elements of the feudal population who there gained their freedom and then grew in power and self-assertiveness. The inhabitants of the cities—the bourgeoisie—organized into self-governing corporate bodies—the guilds—to manage and defend their interests against outside enemies. Their liberties and rights of self-government were frequently guaranteed by written charters granted them by feudal princes; sometimes these rights were gained by force. The subsequent influence of the bourgeoisie on the constitutional history of Western Europe was enormous. In the democratic states, it was their ideology and concepts of government that became dominant.

Geography, physical separation, and the Mongolian occupation played a role in cutting Russia off from the source of these developments: the revival of learning and the growth of commerce in the Middle Ages. Literacy was virtually nonexistent there before the eighteenth century, and cities and commerce grew only very slowly before the late eighteenth century. At the time of Peter the Great, economic Westernization, like almost everything else, was undertaken not through vital forces in society acting on their own initiative, but through the initiative and in the interest of the state. Although a native capitalist class with some degree of initiative and independence did emerge in Russia toward the end of the nineteenth century, the state continued to play a major economic role until 1917.

Russian cities were, as Miliukov has pointed out, necessary for the government before they were necessary for the population.[12] Initially, they were primarily military and administrative centers, with the military element predominating. The commercial-industrial element, small in size, came later, and it was even less capable than the *dvorianstvo* of asserting and defending its own rights. The city population was first distinguished from the rural population and organized by the government for purposes of taxation, in a pattern resembling that of the peasant villages. During the seventeenth century, the urban population was "frozen" in their occupations and places of work. The need for a mass infantry caused the government to add the burden of military service to that of taxation.

In 1785, Catherine, motivated by a desire to create a self-governing third estate modeled on the West, granted a charter to the city population freeing it from immobility (but not military service and taxation) and giving the various elements of the population self-governing corporate institutions. These institutions took the form of guilds and workshops, which had originated during the Middle Ages in the West and were already in decline there. A common city government composed of elected representatives from the various guilds and workshops was also established. Like those of the *dvorianstvo*, these institutions remained lifeless forms. The elected representatives had no independent sphere of activity and were quickly converted into ordinary bureaucrats, equipped with uniforms and ranks and oblivious of the interests of their electors. Interest in the elections declined, and frequently elections were not held at all. Since the cultural level of the townsmen was lower than that of the nobility, and the unskilled-labor–small-craftsmen groups outnumbered the commercial-industrial groups, this lack of interest emerged more quickly and more thoroughly than it did among the nobility.

Some Lost Opportunities to Limit the Power of the Czar

These illustrations from the eighteenth century are not the only ones to suggest the inability and unwillingness of Russian society to rise up in its own behalf against the omnipotence of the Czar before the nineteenth century. It should be remembered that, juridically, the omnipotence of the Czar was not established until Peter the Great, when, for example, the Military Statute proclaimed that "His Majesty is an autocratic Monarch who is accountable to none for his policies, but has power and authority to govern his states and lands as a Christian ruler according to his will and understanding." [13] Before the time of Peter, neither the position of the Czar nor that of the various social groups and institutions was precisely defined legally, and the latter had many opportunities to assert political rights and privileges enjoyed but failed to do so.

There was, for example, the situation in the first half of the sixteenth century, when titled boyars were entrenched in the central government, in local government, and in the army. Being the descendants of the suzerain and appanage princes who had only recently been displaced from their principalities, they still regarded themselves as hereditary rulers of Russia, independent of the Moscow Czar. There was the existence of the Boyar Duma, which, during the seventeenth century, had to be consulted by the Czar on essential matters of government and administration, and which, at times, gave opinions that were binding on the Czar. There were the examples set during the Time of Troubles by the written agreement granted by the boyar Czar, Shuisky, and, even more important, by the agreement signed by King Sigismund of Poland on behalf of his son Wladyslaw, chosen Czar in 1610, an agreement that would have made Russia a constitutional monarchy on the Polish model. There existed, until the end of the seventeenth century, the *zemsky sobor*, a national assembly similar to the estates of Western Europe, which in moments of monarchical weakness exercised legislative powers, and which, for about ten years after the election of the Romanov Dynasty in 1613, sat in continuous session, providing both taxes and army recruits to the government.

There was the presence of the well-organized and wealthy Orthodox Church, enjoying great prestige and authority among the people and, as in the West, with a sphere of activity not precisely separated from the secular. The Church was headed by a patriarch, who, during and following the patriarchate of Nikon (1652–1666), asserted the superiority of the ecclesiastical over the secular and who, in the seventeenth century, shared with the Czar the title of *Velikii Gosudar* (Great Sovereign), until, under Peter the Great, the patriarchate was abolished and the Church was administered as another bureaucratic department. After Peter the Great, there was the abortive attempt to obtain a constitutional charter from Empress Ann in 1730. Under Alexander I, a whole series of constitutional plans, inspired by the Czar himself, was drawn up, all of them in the end unrealized, mainly, according to the historian Svatikov, because of the "sometimes conscious and sometimes even purely instinctive resistance of the whole mass of the gentry, among whom the most politically conscious segments were not strong enough to put into practice an aristocratic constitution." [14]

These examples show, then, that the failure of Catherine's corporate institutions was the result of a long historical process during which Russian society, for deeply rooted reasons, showed no inner life and movement that could serve as a check on the autocracy. When the state, inspired by the example of the West and by its own interests, sought to give society the organization, cohesion, and self-government that it lacked, the population showed no interest in diverging from its traditional course. That which in the West was considered a jealously guarded right and privilege, to be won and defended by force if need be, became for the Russians just another form of state service to be avoided, and the artificially created organs of self-government were quickly converted into simple organs of administration, deprived of any independence. There is no better illustration of the inefficacy of institutions that are not rooted in the traditions and customs of the people. Where there is no inner vitality, no unity, no common aim, they cannot be created through imperial ukase.

Political Implications of a State Without a Society

The unusual concentration of power in the hands of the Czar was largely the product of the unique traits of the Russian social structure. It would be a grave mistake to regard this concentration as the result solely of force; force played no greater role in the emergence of the Russian autocracy than it did in the emergence of the absolute monarchies of Western Europe. The Russian autocracy, like the absolute monarchies, was made possible by popular support of the Muscovite princes' drive to eliminate a confusing array of local sovereigns and to establish a strong national state. If the powers of the Czar were wider than those of the Western monarchs, it was in large part because Russian society was not organized to exercise and, in the long run, did not want to exercise, powers that in the West were arrogated to more active and self-assertive private groups. Nor should it be overlooked that the autocracy was supported by a mythology, deeply engraved in the minds and hearts of the people, that was as effective as was the doctrine of natural rights in the support of democracy. It was a mythology appropriate for a primarily agricultural and illiterate people to whom the spirit of caste or class was deeply repugnant.

The Russia that emerged in the nineteenth century was in a sense a state without a society, a state, that is, in which voluntary associations operating apart from the state to satisfy some need of the population were virtually nonexistent. Except for the Orthodox Church, which was administered at the top by a part of the bureaucracy, and possibly the peasant commune, which, whatever its origin, was heavily influenced by the fiscal and administrative needs of the state, social organizations were created by the state for purposes of the state. Only in the latter half of the eighteenth century do we find the beginnings of a spontaneous organizing impulse in the Russian people, and, as we shall see, the emergence of social organizations with a life and movement of their own was to have an enormous impact on Russian politics. Until the nineteenth century, the basic organizational principle in Russian society was service to the state, and official rank constituted the foundation of social status and privilege. For social status, therefore, as well as for political power, all were dependent on the Czar. No person or group had any rights and privileges that did not emanate from the Czar, and if, in practice, he could not actually withdraw them at his discretion, they also could not, under the circumstances, become a source of independent authority or serve as a base from which he could be challenged. Russia did not possess any of the bases of democracy or limited government, namely, organized groups conscious of their rights and ready to defend them, if need be by force, against all encroachments. Neither the nobility nor any other class showed an interest in any but the narrowest class or personal aims. There was no tradition of self-government in any sphere. Printing and literacy were virtually nonexistent until the eighteenth century; so also was that most potent of all modern forces—public opinion— before which in the long run all governments must bow. There was no intellectual or literary tradition to speak of before the eighteenth century, and consequently creativeness in any field was sharply limited. Aside from the Orthodox Church and the peasant commune, there were no deeply rooted social institutions the state had to consider. The effects of limited social intercourse and social organization on the community were, in short, deep and widespread, and in the circumstances surrounding the emergence of modern Russia, it was perhaps inevitable that a strong state should have been formed and that it should have stepped into the gap left by the community. Leroy-Beaulieu has written:

Today, as at the time of Peter the Great, this traditional and monarchical government with a centuries-old past can still proceed with great strokes of the ax in a revolutionary fashion, destroying and razing existing institutions in order to build anew at its convenience and on a clear field. In Russia, the government is neither fettered by tradition nor restrained by precedent, and feels free to try any innovation, to improvise and experiment at its discretion, as on the day after a revolution that destroyed everything. The reformer does not encounter those barriers that stop him elsewhere: institutions grown old, defective, and antiquated, but hallowed by age, habit, or prejudice, respected by the people. Except for the Orthodox Church and the rural commune, nineteenth-century Russia did not possess any institution rooted in the customs or affections of the people. In this respect, the social status of Russia was not unlike the soil; the nation, too, was like a flat surface, even and smooth, on which nothing remained standing by itself, and on which the lawgiver was free to construct anew, according to the rules of science, as on a *tabula rasa*.[15]

This is not the place to begin a systematic discussion of what the state can or cannot do in molding social and political institutions. Exception, however, must be made to Leroy-Beaulieu's implication that the Russian people, or for that matter any people, constitute a *tabula rasa* on which their rulers may move in any direction. Aside from this exaggeration, he has brilliantly portrayed the relative force of the state and the relative feebleness of society in Russia up to the time of the Great Reforms. Whatever the influence of the Mongolian occupation or the Byzantine tradition, or the military needs of a state exposed to attack from east, west, and south, or the effect, direct or indirect, of all these on Russian society, it must be recognized that the inertness of that society was an indispensable condition for the rise of an all-powerful monarchy. Only Russia's exposure to attack can conceivably rank in importance with the inertness of her society. If the Mongolian occupation and the Byzantine Empire could influence Russia, it was because these two factors had prepared a fertile soil for such influence. The emergence of the autocracy in its historic form and, even more so, its maintenance for more than four hundred years are inconceivable without a society that was scattered, isolated, and lacking in organizational vitality.

Russian Society Awakens: The Influence of Westernization

If this were the whole story of Russian society, then the outlook for the future of Russia would be gloomy indeed. It has often been mentioned, however, that this picture of Russian society does not apply beyond the eighteenth century. In the nineteenth century, vast changes took place that gave society a new direction, opened a fissure between it and the state, and ultimately led to the Revolution. Two major influences brought this about: Open frontiers made Russia subject to attack from all directions, and the dominant aim from the fifteenth century on was to unify the state, to make it impregnable to attack, and to secure for Russia viable national frontiers with access to the sea. Russia, therefore, was in a state of permanent mobilization, straining to marshal her resources to provide the troops and finances required to meet her military obligations. It was under these conditions that service to the state became the dominant influence in society. Military service was exacted from the *dvorianstvo*, and it was in order to help maintain them that serfdom was introduced by tying the peasants to the soil. The peasants also were made to bear most of the crushing burden of taxation required to finance the state and, later, the burden of military service. The town dwellers likewise were fixed to their occupations and to the spot on which they lived, and made to pay taxes and to perform military service. This mobilization of the entire population and the country's resources on behalf of the military needs of the state was characteristic of Russia from the emergence of the Moscow Principality in the fifteenth century until the eighteenth century.

In the eighteenth century, Russia reached the Baltic Sea on the west and the Black Sea on the south. The strong states to the east and south with which she had been in constant conflict either disappeared or ceased to be military threats. At that time, therefore, there began the slow process of restoring freedom of movement to the various classes and of releasing them from their more onerous services and assessments. The proportion of the national budget devoted to military expenditures began to decline. The protection of the national territory and territorial expansion ceased to be the dominant, all-embracing aims of the state, and problems of the national welfare moved to the foreground. This demilitarization of the state appears to have been an essential condition for the conflict between state and society that was to follow in the nineteenth century.

Perhaps even more important than demilitarization was Westernization on a hitherto unprecedented scale. The influence of Westernization was felt as early as the fifteenth century, soon after the expulsion of the Mongols. It was to grow in importance during the seventeenth century and, after the impetus given it by Peter the Great, was to move forward with increasing intensity during the eighteenth and nineteenth centuries. By the latter half of the nineteenth century, Russia was beginning to overtake the West in every sphere—economic, intellectual, and social.

The impact of Westernization on Russian society was enormous. Cities began to grow, and urban life as it had developed in the West became more common. A network of communications—railroads, highways, telegraphs, and telephones—began to cover the country. Trade and industry expanded steadily, and, while industry remained dependent on state orders rather than mass consumption, a native industry and capitalist class took root. Educational institutions—elementary, secondary, and higher schools—multiplied, and the rate of literacy increased. The professional classes—lawyers, doctors, teachers, engineers, etc.—made their appearance and they, too, grew in number. Russia acquired her own literature, music, arts, and sciences. Newspapers and periodicals grew up and reached an ever-wider audience. Public opinion became an active force that the Czar could ignore only at the risk of precipitating revolution. Russia was still a predominantly peasant country in 1917, but fundamental changes had been introduced, and these changes were to have far-reaching political implications.

We have seen that the monarchy in Russia arose in response to conditions very similar to those that obtained in the West and that the Russian monarch possessed unusually wide powers primarily because social groups were unable and unwilling to organize and exercise the rights that are the essential condition of any kind of limited government. However great the role of force in a military state in which heavy burdens were placed on all segments of the population may have been, the survival of the autocracy for more than four hundred years was assured only because it enjoyed the support, passive or active, of an overwhelming majority of the population. In the eyes of the Russians, the services of the autocracy to Russia had been very great, but, by the nineteenth century, this same autocracy had in effect become an anachronism, able to retain the veneration of its subjects only by instituting a peaceful and orderly transition to constitutional government.

The reasons for this transition were widely understood both by the intelligentsia, who led the fight against the autocracy, and by the more enlightened members of the bureaucracy.[16] An all-powerful Czar and bureaucracy, operating without legal guarantees for Russian citizens, may have been suitable as long as Russia was an agrarian state with an illiterate population pursuing primarily military aims, but they could only serve as a destructive deterrent once the influence of the industrial revolution had made itself felt and the welfare of the inhabitants had become the primary aim of the state. With civilization becoming more complex and the activities of the state multiplying—phenomena of the nineteenth century that neither Russia nor any other modern state could avoid—the autocracy became incapable either of maintaining Russia's position as a great power or of satisfying the elementary needs of the population without enlisting the initiative and the active cooperation of society. The autocracy's inability to maintain Russia's position as a great power could alone have brought it down, because the very existence of Russia as an independent nation was threatened, and it is, of course, no accident that failure in war brought on either drastic reform or revolution in Russia. On this account alone, the fumbling and inefficient autocracy with its old-fashioned ideology, its senseless illusions of grandeur, and its large doses of irresponsibility was doomed. It was doomed if it did not seek the assistance of

society, and it was doomed if it did, for as both the Czar and the
Communists understood so well, the development of what the Russians call "social self-activity" was bound to lead to an informed and
politically conscious population that would demand a voice in the
making and the administration of national policy.

At the same time that the development of modern civilization
made traditional bureaucratic government in Russia obsolete, society shook off its centuries-old lethargy and, for the first time in its
history, exhibited a genuine and sustained organizing impulse. The
causes of its former lethargy were unquestionably complex; historical perspective suggests, however, that illiteracy was one of the chief
causes, for the leadership in organizing social groups and emanci-
pating them from bureaucratic domination was taken by the newly
founded intelligentsia. Before the eighteenth century, organized
schools in Russia existed only in the Church, which, unlike the
Western churches, made no attempt to educate laymen. The first
secular schools were established by Peter the Great at the beginning
of the eighteenth century for the purpose of training the gentry for
government service. During the course of that century, education
and culture came to be accepted as part of the equipment of the
privileged classes; during the nineteenth century, increasing numbers of children from the nonprivileged classes were drawn into the
expanding school system. After a hundred years of lay education
of a small but ever-growing segment of the population, literacy had
come of age in Russia, bringing in its wake a remarkable creativeness in literature, music, the arts, and the sciences.

In a country that had hitherto lacked an intellectual and a strong
social tradition, it is not surprising that the creative civilization of
the West should have exercised a powerful attraction for the growing intellectual class. Then as now, the future of Russia depended
on the successful absorption of the most important elements of
Western civilization, and at first the most ardent Westernizers included monarchs such as Peter the Great, Catherine the Great, and
Alexander I. All these Russian rulers were inclined to imitate the
politics of the West, and even as late as the reign of Alexander I
(1801–25), the government was subsidizing liberal periodicals and
the translation of Western political classics. With the coming of
the French Revolution, however, and the gradual democratization
of the political institutions and the prevailing ideology of the West,
Western models became a strong corrosive for the autocracy, re-

viled by the apologists of the autocracy and cited with approval by the liberals. Improved means of communication and transportation, as well as an unceasing flow of Western literature, served to make Western institutions and thought a paramount influence in shaping the minds of the Russian intelligentsia, spurring on the demand for reform.

In this demand for reform, which at times became almost universal in Russian society, the Slavophiles were no exceptions. Although they insisted on the superiority of Russian civilization over that of the West, this alleged superiority in the political sphere was based on a misinterpretation of Russian history; for they believed to have seen, in the historic relations between state and society in Russia, something that simply had not existed—freedom, democracy, and self-government. Consequently, most of the Slavophiles, though devoted to the autocracy and to the Czar, joined the advocates of reform in calling for more freedom for society and were ardent defenders of the system of local self-government established after 1864. They were also to be represented in the liberation movement of the early twentieth century by a small but able group of men led by D. N. Shipov. It should be noted, in any case, that the controversy between the Slavophiles and the Westernizers was dominant in Russian thought mainly in the early nineteenth century. In the second half the pace of Westernization became so rapid and its advantages so apparent, that this issue naturally gave way to the question of what kind of reforms were best suited to Russia. On the whole, therefore, the intelligentsia was solidly in favor of reform, and it is not surprising that by the time of Nicholas II, the Czar preferred not to have the word "intelligentsia" uttered in his presence.

The truth is that the aspiration for freedom and democracy, humanitarianism and individualism, is common to all mankind, and tends to manifest itself in any country with the first appearance of individuals whose vision is broader than that of illiterate peasants tilling the soil in time-honored ways. What happened in Russia happened also in other parts of Europe, and it is happening today in Asia and Africa. We need not be blinded to the truth of this by the existence of apparent exceptions; in dealing with mankind, there are few, if any, universal truths. Neither the Russians nor any other people will indefinitely tolerate an arbitrary and lawless rule that crushes without scruple free opportunity for the development of individual potentialities. In appropriating the symbols of democracy, the present rulers of Russia have shown a shrewd understanding of the nature of man. The day has probably passed when any ideology that does not make use of these symbols can expect to win many adherents.

Although the Westernization of Russia deprived the last Czars of any real choice as to whether or not to maintain intact their traditional powers, they nevertheless continued to believe that autocracy was the only possible form of government for Russia, that it had brought glory to Russia in the past and would continue to bring glory to Russia in the future, and that the disturbances in society were fomented by misguided intellectuals who could be brought to book by more stringent police measures and by stricter control of the social organizations through which they expressed themselves. The history of nineteenth-century Russia thus presents the amazing spectacle of a series of modern rulers who regarded themselves as the only reliable executors of policy. In a state in which the intervention of the government in the social and economic life of the country was traditionally great, they preferred to see governmental projects undertaken either by the bureaucracy or not at all. In the initiative of society they saw a dangerous threat, which, if it could not be entirely exterminated, must at least be kept within the narrowest possible bounds. Yet, to the thinking part of the population, whose numbers grew steadily during the nineteenth century, it became generally apparent, at least as early as the 1860's, that government by bureaucracy was not only unjust but also hopelessly inefficient, and must inevitably bring Russia to ruin.

The result was a clash between the state and society that manifested itself permanently, with greater or lesser intensity, from the era of the Great Reforms until 1917. Between the bureaucracy and the public there grew up mutual hatred and suspicion that were bound to end either in reconciliation or in revolution. Since the policies of the last Czars proved to be inflexible, the end was revolution and disaster. The purpose of this book will be to examine the course of the clash and to show why it led to the Revolution of 1917. But before doing so, it will be necessary to examine in greater detail the institutions of state and of society and to see what advantages and disadvantages were enjoyed by them in their mutual conflicts.

TWO

INSTITUTIONS OF THE STATE

2

The Czar, the Ministers,
and the Rule of Law

The Czar as the Guardian of the People's Interests

"THE ALL-RUSSIAN Emperor is an autocratic and unlimited monarch—God Himself commands that his supreme power be obeyed, out of conscience as well as fear." Thus did Article I of the Fundamental Laws of the Russian Empire, as issued in 1892, define the legal status of the Czar, a status that obtained up to the Revolution of 1905.[1] To begin with, it is important that non-Russian readers understand the spirit in which the enormous powers of the Czar were accepted by the Russians themselves. It would be a grave misreading of Russian constitutional history for Western readers to inject their own values into the situation and to assume that these powers were obtained by force alone and for more than four hundred years were so maintained, in opposition to the wishes of the majority of the Russian people. As pointed out in the preceding chapter, the concentration of power in the Czar reflected, in part, the peculiar qualities of Russian society and was, on the whole, approved by that society. In point of fact, the prestige of the monarchy remained high up to World War I, and the real target of Russian society through most of the years of its conflict with the state was less the Czar than the bureaucracy. In the eyes of the peasants particularly, but also in the eyes of a considerable part of the liberal and conservative intelligentsia—at least prior to the Revolution of 1905, when revolutionary ideas began to penetrate more deeply into Russian society—the Czar was a guarantor of democracy, not, of course, in the sense of restraints on power or of the guarantee of civil liberties, but in the sense of equality, justice, and the responsiveness of government to the people.

To understand this seeming paradox, upon which, incidentally, Russian historians are in agreement, it is necessary to give some attention to another paradox: the strong opposition among the Russian people to manifestations of caste or class. If we consider that legal classes were maintained in Russia through the nineteenth century, at a time when they had disappeared in the West, such opposition to a caste spirit may seem incredible. Nevertheless, its existence is beyond dispute. The corporate class institutions and the legal definition of classes were imitations of the West, imported into Russia only in the late eighteenth century, and were not indigenous to Russian life. Neither corporate institutions nor the idea of class was known in Russia before Peter the Great; even the Russian word for class (*soslovie*) did not appear until the eighteenth century. As we shall see later, the reforms of Alexander II dealt a fatal blow to the imported class structure, and its real significance in the life of the people declined steadily thereafter.

That group of the population before the eighteenth century whose collective name can be translated as the "nobility" was composed of men who had received their lands and certain privileges in return for military service. Only those few among them who were descendants of a small group of the original reigning princes of Russia had a title. Titles derived from the feudal hierarchy of the West, such as count, were imported into Russia during the eighteenth century. With the exception of a few old princely and boyar families, Russia had no aristocracy that derived hereditary status, prestige, authority, or privilege independent of the state. Rather, these were derived, after the destruction of the boyars, entirely from service to the state, which overshadowed high birth as a source of social distinction. The nobility were themselves aware that their property had originated from service, and they were concerned about its future when they were released from military service in the eighteenth century. If they in time began to believe that the property was their own and subject to civil rather than public law, this idea was not accepted by the overwhelming majority of the population, the peasants, who regarded both freedom and the land as rightfully theirs, once the nobility was released from military service. The lack of an *esprit de corps* among Russian social groups is certainly based in part on a strong aversion to the spirit of caste on the part of the Russian people. This fact also enters into the failure of aristocratic government, for, even if the nobility had been able to agree among themselves and had not on the whole opposed such a government, the aristocracy could never have won the support of the peasantry.

The repugnance of the Russians to the spirit of caste is the key to the concept of the Czar as the guardian of democracy, for his enormous popularity was partly based on his position outside and above all classes. With the *dvorianstvo* he had no tie other than that of service. The theory of the monarch as the first among the peers is alien to the Russian tradition. For the peasants particularly, the Czar was the representative of God on earth, dedicated to the welfare of his people, a bulwark against the depredations of the immediate enemies of the peasants, the landlords. The Russian peasant did not have the reverence for birth or high station so widespread among the peasantry of Europe. He recognized the right of his landlord to the land only as long as the landlord was performing military service for the Czar. Once the landlord was freed from military service, the peasant regarded freedom and the land as rightfully his own, to be granted without payment, by act of the Czar.

The idea of equality was deeply rooted in the traditions of the peasantry and was strikingly illustrated by their behavior during the peasant disorders. When looting the estate of a landlord, the spoils were divided with scrupulous equality, and large objects, such as pianos, were sometimes dismembered and the parts distributed equally, without regard to their utility. Even during the famine of 1891, as Prince V. Obolensky has pointed out, the grain brought into a stricken district had to be distributed equally, without regard to need. Only by secret collaboration with a literate peasant was it possible to divert grain to those who needed it, and had this collaboration become known, that peasant would have been in great physical danger.[2] Despite the cultural differences between the nobility and the peasantry, and despite the privileges enjoyed by the former until the second half of the nineteenth century, the idea of a hereditary privileged class could find no support in the traditions and customs of the Russian people. The peasants had to accept serfdom as a matter of necessity, but they looked to the Czar for protection against the abuses of their landlords and for the ultimate restoration of their rights. If they were actually being oppressed by their landlords, it was only because the Czar did not know about it and was being deceived by his advisers, who were themselves landlords. For the peasants, the Czar was the source of justice, equality, and democracy; the problem was only to reach him. It is for this reason that the great peasant revolts of Russian history were accompanied by the rise of Czarist pretenders.

This view of the Czar was not confined to the peasants alone. It was one of the prime articles of faith of the Slavophiles and was shared to some extent by many conservatives and moderate liberals, at least up to the end of the nineteenth century. In their view, however, the enemy of the people was not the landlord but the bureaucracy. If the autocracy was not working well, it was only because the Czar had lost touch with the people and was surrounded by irresponsible advisers from the bureaucracy. For such men, the reforms of Alexander II constituted a model of how much could be accomplished in the Russian way by an enlightened Czar in close touch with the needs of his people.[3] There seems little reason to doubt that had Alexander continued his reforms, the monarchy would have retained its prestige among a large segment of the intelligentsia. When he and his successors chose, instead, a policy of repression, the educated class became increasingly embittered against the monarchy. However repugnant the institution of Czarism may have become to Russian society in the twentieth century, it seems unquestionable that, for most of its long history, it reflected the ideals and purposes of a largely peasant society free of caste spirit.

Are Authoritarian Administrations Efficient?

There has long been a tendency to assume that authoritarian administrations are more efficient than democratic ones. Where one man has broad legislative and administrative freedom of action, it would appear that the prompt and single-minded dispatch of business would be the rule, as opposed to systems in which the separation of power prevails and in which there is a constant need for the delicate adjustment of conflicting group interests. This assumption cannot, however, survive the test of a concrete study of authoritarian administrations, and it is likely that, from the standpoint of efficiency as well as of justice, there is no substitute for the interaction of a democratically controlled bureaucracy and the free expression of public opinion. The example of Czarist Russia fully bears out the superiority of democratic government, for, despite the concentration of legislative and executive power in the person of the Czar, the operation of the governmental apparatus can justly be described as chaotic.

The root of the difficulty was the hereditary handing down of the enormous powers of the head of the government from one individual to another, regardless of whether or not the heir to the throne had any desire to govern, or any capacity to do so. Upon him fell the sole responsibility for the operation of a government that, in Russia as elsewhere, was becoming increasingly complex and that required statesmanship of the highest order. At any given time, there was little expectation that the average individuals likely to succeed to the throne would be sufficiently gifted to give Russia even a moderately good administration.

It was to be fateful for the Russian people that, at a time when the conflict between state and society was reaching its climax, the throne was occupied by a man pathetically incapable of dealing with the complex and pressing problems confronting the state authorities. For Nicholas II, the obligations of the throne were a burden well beyond his native capacities. Lacking both the will to give orders and the intellect to make the most important decisions of state, he was open to influence by anyone, whether or not in an official position, who happened to please him at any given moment. The person closest to him, the one who naturally exercised the greatest influence over him, was his wife, Alexandra, whose will was as strong as his was weak. A basically unbalanced person, colossally ignorant of the world about her, she nevertheless had supreme confidence in her own judgment, and from the beginning of their marriage, but especially after 1905, she exerted unyielding pressure on him to maintain his unlimited autocratic powers. There is some evidence to suggest that in the last stages of their rule, when they were moving irresistibly toward destruction and when the most important decisions were in effect being made by Rasputin, the Czar might have been open to saner advice. However, failure to heed the importunities of his wife would have meant the certain destruction of his domestic happiness, and domestic happiness was the main comfort he enjoyed in a life otherwise overburdened with the wearisome cares of state.

The Problem of Coordination in Administration

As Russia entered the era of the modern industrial state, a government headed by a Czar was a bizarre one, capable, as in the past, of great achievements, but subject to serious weaknesses, and in these weaknesses may be found one reason for the widening chasm between state and society in the course of the nineteenth century.

Outstanding among these weaknesses was the lack of coordination between the ministries, which, far from cooperating voluntarily with each other, were frequently engaged in bitter rivalry. Even though the Czars themselves were incapable of acting as head of the state, they showed no desire to encourage collective ministerial action, to appoint a prime minister, or to permit the emergence of a strong minister, for fear that he may deflect attention and authority from themselves. They sought, rather, to play off one minister against another, so that none could become predominant.[4] Among the histories of the great states of Europe, that of Russia up to the twentieth century is the only one not graced with the names of famous prime ministers, although, at various times, individual ministers, such as Arakcheiev or Loris-Melikov, acquired unusually great influence for varying reasons. The possibility of effective coordination of administration did arise in 1905, when a Council of Ministers, headed by a prime minister, was established, but constitutional government did not last long enough to permit new habits to take root. The testimony is virtually unanimous that the Czar consciously tried to continue to deal separately with individual ministers, bypassing the prime minister whenever it suited his purposes.[5]

Since there was no real head of the state, attempts by ambitious ministers to gain control of state policy and to enlarge the sphere of their jurisdiction were common from the middle of the nineteenth century. Such attempts, in a sense, were necessary, since a strong minister, even if he had the backing of the Czar, could not always count on the cooperation and assistance of other ministers with overlapping jurisdiction. If they differed in their points of view or were otherwise hostile, they could expect active opposition and intrigue. As a well-known professor of economics at the University of Moscow put it:

The representatives of the separate departments resemble belligerent powers, who not infrequently plot against each other, but sometimes conclude a truce, make concessions, etc. As hostile camps, our ministries conclude alliances among themselves to conduct defensive and aggressive wars against other ministries, and strive to cut down or mutilate any measure originating in a ministry hostile to the alliance. Consequently, there emerge from the Petersburg chancelleries legislative monstrosities, worthless measures.[6]

Apart from the hostility of other departments, ministers faced other hazards deriving from the Czar himself. It was, for example, the view of Nicholas II that the responsibility for the fate of Russia lay on himself, that he was answerable to God alone, and that he could best fulfill the Divine Will by following solely his own personal inspirations. Not only was the surrender of any part of his powers to persons without Divine guidance unthinkable, but his own ministers, he believed, laid claim to too great an influence on the state, and their initiative, when not in accord with his own intentions, was inadmissible.[7] The result of this outlook was that Nicholas bypassed his ministers on many occasions, and he frequently found his "inspirations" in an array of disreputable adventurers who were welcomed to the Court (Rasputin was only the best known and most influential of these). The ministers might, at any given time, find their projects disapproved because of the unknown and irresponsible influence of "backstairs" advisers, and they might even be kept in the dark on major decisions made by the Czar concerning their departments. It was, therefore, an odd feature of this authoritarian government that the ministers tended to work at cross-purposes with each other, and one or more of them might be working at cross-purposes with the Czar himself.

The "Wall" Between the Czar and His People

Regardless of the extent of irresponsible behind-the-scenes influences, the Czar did, in the main, have to rely on his ministers for information and advice about the affairs of the empire, and this fact was anything but comforting for Russian society. The Czar, upon whose decisions alone rested the government and the welfare of the people, lived in isolation at his court, unaware of the real currents of opinion among his subjects, unaware on the whole of what was going on even in the bureaucratic circles through which he ruled. His ministers, however honest, were themselves cut off and reviled by society, holding views and interests colored by the bureaucratic medium in which they operated. This situation was widely discussed in Russia and was a source of great concern, even to the more intelligent bureaucrats. For most of the population of Russia, as has been pointed out, the defects of the autocracy lay not in the Czar but in the bureaucracy through which he governed. Standing between the Czar and his people was the *sredostenie,* or wall, in the person of the bureaucracy, to which most of the abuses were attributed.

There was, indeed, such a wall, the danger of which is common to all authoritarian governments. In the preconstitutional period, state policy was determined mainly through the medium of personal reports by the ministers to the Czar. In making their reports, the ministers obtained decisions that were not bound by the law and for which the ministers could not be held answerable. How they interpreted the circumstances and the facts of a given problem and the laws pertaining to it was unknown to any third party and could not be so effectively countered by a third party. As in the democratic states, the ministers were specialists, assisted by other specialists, all beyond the view of the public. For all except the broadest political problems, the Czar had no other sources of information, and he could be overwhelmed by the technical arguments the ministers could adduce. For the more unscrupulous ministers, there were the possibilities of failing to bring out the true significance of any given problem and of distracting the attention of the Czar by presenting, at the same time, other and seemingly more interesting problems, so that a detailed examination would not be undertaken. Worse still, the decisions of the Czar were not, as a general rule, written by him personally; they were instead certified by the signature of the minister on the ministerial report, and nobody could say with certainty that the contents of the report had actually been transmitted to the Czar or that he had actually approved of the reasoning of the minister. In those cases in which the Czar had made an inscription on the report with his own hand, the minister could deliberately obscure the point of it and could put it into practice in a sense not actually approved by the Czar.[8]

Broad legislative policy was generally considered by one of two institutions—the State Council or the Committee of Ministers. The State Council, formed in 1810, consisted of an indeterminate number of persons appointed and dismissed at the discretion of the Czar (until its transformation into an upper legislative chamber in 1906). Its function was to examine laws proposed by the ministers, but its opinions were not binding on the Czar. Despite the high average age of its members, who were appointed generally at the end of many years of bureaucratic service, their spirit was surprisingly liberal. In order to avoid the certain opposition of the Council, unpopular measures were examined by the Committee of Ministers or dealt with in other ways.[9] Although the Fundamental Laws provided that all laws (as distinguished from administrative orders) must be examined by the State Council, this provision was frequently ignored. The Committee of Ministers (abolished in 1905), although designed originally to promote collective ministerial action, ceased to serve that purpose not long after its establishment in 1802. It came to include persons other than ministers, and its main functions consisted of the consideration of unpopular laws not likely to be approved by the State Council and of administrative orders and dispensations not founded on the laws. Its chairman was not a minister, nor, usually, an influential figure; he merely presided at its meetings.

Even when laws were considered by the State Council or the Committee of Ministers, the privilege of personal and private access to the Czar enjoyed by the ministers was an enormous advantage, and if their proposals were rejected, it was possible for them to persuade the Czar to approve their own decisions, not those of the Council or Committee. Nor must it be overlooked that there were times when a minister particularly interested in a matter before the State Council could obtain an imperial command from the Czar, which, when transmitted to the Council, predetermined its decision and cut off debate on those aspects resolved in the command.[10] Although the Council of State performed a useful function in checking the reactionary tendencies of the ministers, it should be noted that representatives of the public were almost never invited to present their points of view. This privilege was normally extended only to the directors of the departments within the ministry that had submitted the legislative project being discussed.[11] Nor were the deliberations of the four departments of the Council (in which the fate of a project was usually determined) and of the Committee of Ministers made public. In general, it may be said that, until the rise of the modern totalitarian states, there had been few governments in history that operated with so great a disregard of the needs and requirements of society, and in so great an isolation from it.

Part of the difficulty lay in the defective education and understanding of the men who staffed the bureaucratic apparatus, particularly of the older men who tended to predominate. Their education had been completed at a time when the full implications of the economic and social changes stimulated by the peasant reform of 1861 had not yet become clear. They had little understanding of the real significance of the institutions and the economic and social

development of the West. Although not all were representatives of
the noble and landowning classes, a majority of them were, and
some of them shared that class's tendency to disdain productive
labor. They were well trained in administrative techniques, but they
did not realize that the perfection of administrative techniques,
the manipulation of the governmental mechanism, had ceased to
have its old significance and that a primary need had now become
a constructive economic and social policy. In the era of the industrial revolution and the welfare state, the most important ministry,
that of the Interior, remained little more than a police department.
Economic policy, until the coming of Witte, amounted to little
more than balancing the state budget, and Witte, in his memoirs,
speaks of the resistance he encountered in introducing his economic
reforms. If Russia was to remain a great state, the productive energies of society had to be released and given full scope. Since this was
inconsistent with the preservation of the autocracy, the Czar and
many of his ministers preferred to maintain—and to some extent
increase—police controls. A defective education and background
helped, in part, to blind them to the utter folly of such a policy.
By 1914, the Russian bureaucracy, once a significant constructive
force in the nation, had become largely sterile and obstructive.
Urgent reforms were attended to slowly or not at all. The worst of
the ministers submitted few, if any, projects of reform to the Duma
and took office without any policy at all except to obey the will of
the Czar and to maintain the autocracy; the best of them, such as
Witte and Stolypin, accomplished a great deal, and were prevented
from accomplishing more by the resistance of the Czar, the Czarina, the court camarilla, and the other ministers.

Administrative Confusion as an Advantage for Society

It may seem paradoxical that many Russians should now look
back to a regime such as this as an era of relative liberty and prosperity. Nevertheless, an examination of what was happening to
Russian society proves them right. Only one phase of this subject
need be treated at this point. In discussing the Czarist state, it is
important to recognize that the friction, wasted effort, and at times
incompetency in high places had their advantages as well as disadvantages. Since the ministers were the main political force in Russia, they could, if united, have carried out almost any policy they

pleased, and reactionary tendencies might have had full sway. Since, in fact, each conducted his own policy independently of the others, the resistance to reaction that could not be offered by society arose within the government itself, and the more liberal ministers, along with the State Council, were able to obtain concessions to public opinion that would not otherwise have been possible. Lack of co-ordination and outright inefficiency might at times paralyze the state apparatus, but they could, at the same time, save the individual from being crushed by an all-powerful state. Society, and in particular the liberal and revolutionary movements, acquired a scope that they could not otherwise have obtained.

The "Rule of Law" in an Absolute Monarchy

An account of Czarist government is not complete without some comment on the extent to which Russia had made progress in achieving the rule of law, the foundation of any satisfactory evolution toward democracy. The answer is not a simple one, for here, as in many other areas of Russian life, the backward and the forward-looking existed side by side. After centuries of unlimited rule by an autocrat over an illiterate and inert society, it was hardly to be expected that the conception of the rule of law could have made startling progress. Nevertheless, the Czars were not unmindful of their responsibilities in this field, and at least two major steps were taken during the nineteenth century to improve the situation. One was the codification of the laws in the early nineteenth century by the great Russian statesman Count M. M. Speransky, so that it became possible for the first time for anyone, government administrators included, to acquire a knowledge of the legislation currently in force.[12] The second step was the establishment, in 1864, of an independent judicial system that proclaimed the equality of all before the law and asserted the principle that no Russian subject could be deprived of his liberty or of his rights except through the established judicial proceedings, including trial by jury.

However great the progress signified by these two steps and by the principle proclaimed in the first *Code of Laws* that the "Russian Empire is administered on the firm foundations of positive laws, statutes, and regulations, emanating from the Autocratic Power" (Article 47 of the Fundamental Laws), the rule of law was far from being achieved. The most basic remaining difficulty was

the continued concentration in the person of the Czar of the supreme legislative and executive functions, so that in practice it was
still impossible to distinguish between a law and an act of administration. Every order of the Czar on administrative affairs was, by
the letter of the law as well as by the very nature of his position as
an unlimited autocrat, a superlegal act that set aside prior edicts and
acquired the force of law.[13]

The situation was little better with regard to ministers and subordinate officials. Legal proceedings or even protests against the illegal acts of officials directly subordinate to the Czar were in fact
virtually impossible, because such officials were supposed to be acting in accordance with the instructions of the Czar and a protest
against their actions could easily be construed as a protest against
the Czar himself. Consequently, to take any action, whatever the
law might say, a minister had only to obtain the approval of the
Czar, and this he could do by means of a personal report to the latter, in which he could explain the facts and the law as he pleased,
often without any other person being in a position to refute him.
In practice, furthermore, the laws governing the actions of the ministers were so interpreted that a minister who acted illegally, without prior authorization, could escape all responsibility by later obtaining the approval of the Czar.[14]

Bureaucrats below the rank of minister were protected by provisions of the criminal code stating that officials could not be prosecuted for criminal acts without the permission of their superiors.
The result was that any official, regardless of rank, could commit
any act in violation of the law, secure in the knowledge that he
would not be prosecuted so long as he was fulfilling an order of his
superior, who might himself be involved if he gave his consent to
prosecution.

Administrative justice was not, however, totally absent in pre-
Revolutionary Russia. Where personal criminal responsibility was
not involved, and where any administrative institution had exceeded its powers without obtaining the approval of the Czar (a
step, needless to say, that was not always feasible, even for a minister), it was possible to obtain relief by appealing to the highest
administrative court, the Ruling Senate. The organization and proceedings of the Senate were exceedingly defective, but it is, nevertheless, a fact of considerable significance that, during the course of
the nineteenth century, the Senate consistently handed down de-

cisions setting aside the orders of the administration as arbitrary and illegal.[15] Unfortunately, senators were neither independent nor irreplaceable, and by the end of the nineteenth century, the membership of the Senate had been filled with men who could be counted upon to support the views of the government.[16]

The satisfactory evolution of the Russian state depended largely on the readiness of Russian society to insist on a given reform. In the light of the actual evolution of Russian society, it is no surprise that public concern over arbitrary bureaucratic action had become sufficiently acute in the years before the Revolution to lead to a fundamental reorganization of the Senate. The law of December 27, 1916, provided for the appointment of senators for life and otherwise improved the Senate sufficiently to create the beginnings of a genuine system of administrative justice.[17]

However, it was not this act but the establishment of a constitutional order in 1906 that marked the chief turning point in the evolution toward the rule of law. The significance of the Constitution of 1906 has been too little analyzed in English, and it is beyond the scope of this book to undertake such an analysis. The provisions of the Fundamental Laws of 1906 cannot, of course, be compared with the constitutional provisions of the advanced democratic states, which, in Western Europe, did not spring full-blown from absolute monarchy but were generally the outcome of a long evolution. All the defects of the Fundamental Laws of 1906 must be granted. But, in evaluating them in the light of Russian conditions at that time, they must be recognized as representing an important and fundamental step forward—a step that meant the possible end, or the beginning of the end, of all the deficiencies of the state order discussed in this chapter.[18] The Czar now ceased to be an unlimited autocrat; legislative power passed into the hands of the State Duma and the State Council, over whose acts the Czar retained veto power. The Czar could now issue only administrative orders, and then only in conformity with laws that he could no longer change unilaterally.[19] The legislature was furthermore given the right of interpellation, that is, the right to question ministers concerning administrative abuses in their departments. Of course, the ministers remained responsible to the Czar alone and were not compelled to resign if censured by the Duma, but it would be a grave mistake to suppose that, in the atmosphere that prevailed from 1906 to 1914, ministers were always prepared to view with equanimity the exposure of illegal acts committed by them or by their subordinates, or their condemnation by members of the legislature and by the press.

Even if significant progress toward the rule of law had indeed been made after 1906, the powers of the Czar continued to be great and many old habits of political action continued to survive. Whether the new constitution was to be strengthened and improved or whether the new pattern of government was to be destroyed depended on the attitude of society. If society was indifferent to illegal changes, then such changes were bound to be made. If, on the other hand, attacks on the constitution aroused the people and if the people were sufficiently well organized to resist such attacks and to demand improvement, then Russia was bound to follow the course of the constitutional monarchies of Western Europe.

3

The Police State — Czarist Version

The Police in European and Russian History

I T IS popular in some quarters to refer to Russia as having always been a police state, as if the equivalent of the MVD had always played a prominent role in Russian life, and as if the Russian people would not consider their lives complete unless ordered about at the discretion of an apparatus of unbridled force. It is, of course, true that, from the Moscow period on, some form of political police has existed almost continuously in Russia. It is nevertheless also true that comparisons between the Czarist police and the Communist police are superficial and meaningless unless the historical setting, the details of organization, and the purpose of police action are taken into account.

The meaning of the word "police" has not always been the modern one of the enforcement of law and order. The word is of Greek origin and as first used in Western Europe at the time of the Renaissance, meant a well-organized community. When taken over from the city-states by the absolute monarchies, the word referred also to the means used to bring about a well-organized community and, finally, to the administration as a whole, with the exception first of foreign and military affairs, and later also of finance and justice. The first books on administration written by French and German writers were treatises on the "police," meaning the institutions designed to insure the health, morals, prosperity, and safety of the people. Police regulations protected not only public order, but also the spiritual and material welfare of the subjects of the state. Force was used to insure the latter as well as the former, and the legal rights of the people were subordinated in greater or lesser degree to the all-embracing tutelage of the state. "It is necessary to show the people, as one shows a sick child, what they must eat and drink," Frederick the Great once said.[1] The distinction between the security and the welfare functions of the police grew up gradually, as it became recognized that the use of force did more harm than good for the public welfare, and ultimately the police were confined to the maintenance of law and order. The former meaning of the word "police" has, however, survived in the expression "police power," in whose name state interference in the social and economic life of the people is still justified. In Russia, the police retained by law their administrative and welfare functions down to 1917, but in practice they were ill-fitted to execute them and, in fact, Russian police were primarily concerned with the application of force against the population.

Russia was not, therefore, unique among the states of Europe in having passed through the phase of either absolute monarchy or all-embracing state control over the lives of the people; this phase was characteristic of most of the European states in the transition from medieval rule by warring local overlords to modern rule by a unified, national state and, for a time, was accepted and supported by the people. Where the European states did differ, however, was in the extent to which the traditional legal rights were overridden by the Crown, the extent of the personal power assumed by the Crown, and the length of time during which that personal power was exercised. In general, as one moves across Europe from west to east, the powers of the Crown were greater and were exercised for a longer period of time. In Central Europe, by the middle of the nineteenth century, the post-Napoleonic reforms and the *octroyed* constitutions of 1848–49 had led to breaks from the eighteenth-century police state.[2] In Russia, basic reforms were not made until 1861, and an *octroyed* constitution was established only in 1906. True, Russia's transition from a monarchical police state to a legal order had been delayed, but only delayed; underlying factors similar to those operating in other parts of Europe were inexorably bringing it about. Even as late as the middle of the nineteenth century, it is doubtful that Russian police practices differed very markedly from those of Napoleon III during the first decade of his rule in France. Until that time, Russia had no monopoly on arbitrary police rule. Although important underlying social differences could be discerned by keen observers, particularly during the period of harsh repression under Nicholas I, until the middle of the nineteenth century there existed no basis for the widespread belief that the secret police was an institution uniquely indigenous to Russia.

The nineteenth century was an important turning point in Rus-

sian history. After the Great Reforms of the 1860's, the social base
of an unlimited autocracy disintegrated more rapidly than ever, and
the maintenance of the autocracy required that society be placed in
a permanent state of siege. As the demands of society for political
reform became more insistent, an ever-larger police force was required to hold that society in check. With the spread of the
Okhrana at the beginning of the twentieth century, and the multiplication of police spies, the Russian political police deservedly
acquired world-wide renown, all the more so because the last remnants of the police state in Western Europe had been steadily
giving way to the rule of law and the spread of democracy. Western
Europe, too, as a result of the industrial revolution, had been making vast strides economically and socially, which Russia did not
make until the close of the nineteenth century. By the beginning of
the twentieth century, therefore, Russia did differ markedly from
the rest of Europe. These differences, although important and subjected to scrutiny in this study, have elsewhere been blown up to
proportions far beyond those justified by the historical record. Police abuses should properly be ascribed to the defects of Russian
society but not to the inclinations of the Russian people. Of all the
officials of the Czarist bureaucracy, none was more thoroughly
hated than the police, and, as we shall see, it was one of the prime
purposes of the two revolutions of the twentieth century to put an
end to arbitrary police rule.

- Neither in Russia nor elsewhere has the police always been a
separate and distinct branch of the administration. Before the
growth of specialized bureaucracies, the police power was exercised
by ordinary administrative units. This was true of Russia until the
time of Peter the Great, when the idea of the police as a special
branch of state activity entered Russian law for the first time
and elements of a separate police administration were first introduced into some of the larger cities. (A separate police force was
not established in Britain until one hundred years later, in 1815.)
It was at this very time that regulatory police power reached a new
peak. As mentioned earlier, all potential opposition to the Czar
was broken under Peter, and Russia became legally, as well as in
fact, an unlimited autocracy. Under the harsh absolutism of Peter,
Russia was run like a gigantic military machine, in which every class
had its assigned duties to carry out—the nobility to perform public
service, the peasants to till the soil, the merchants to carry on their

trade, and the priests to administer the Church. The administrative tutelage imposed by Peter was similar to that in force in the West at that time, the purpose of which was, in part, to make of the nation a unified, independent, and great state. This was also Peter's purpose, but he sought, in addition, to bring a whole new civilization to Russia, to change even the daily habits of the people. It was beyond the power of any Western monarch to have undertaken any such task; in Russia, the weakness of social tradition and the absence of corporate groups moving under their own power in their own direction expanded the scope of administrative action to a point far beyond that possible in the West.

The resulting minuteness of police regulation in Russia is well illustrated by the Regulations of the Chief Magistrate, issued in 1721, three years after the establishment of the first police office in St. Petersburg. According to the Regulations, the police:

promote law and justice; generate good behavior and moral teaching, offer security to all from bandits, robbers, thugs, impostors, etc.; drive away disorderly and obscene persons; force everyone to labor and honest industry; make good citizens, diligent and good servants; create in an orderly way cities, and in them streets; prevent high prices; bring satisfaction for everything needed in human life; ward off all diseases; bring cleanliness in the streets and houses; forbid excesses in house expenditures and in all obvious sins; take care of the beggars, the poor, the sick, the lame, and other needy persons; protect widows, orphans, and aliens, according to the commandments of God; educate the young in chastity and honest skills; in short, the police are the heart of citizenship and of good behavior, and the fundamental prop of human security and comfort.[3]

According to a ukase issued in 1807, only persons of high social station could ride through the cities in their own carriages. A merchant of the first guild could travel with a team of four horses, one of the second guild with two horses, and one of the third guild with no more than one. It was prescribed that excess horses be unharnessed on the spot and that the carriage be returned to cabmen, but the horses of the culprit were to be sold and the money sent to some charity. A ukase of Nicholas I, issued in 1835, prescribed that eating houses were not to serve such "aristocratic dishes" as turkeys, capons, pullets, chickens, or game birds of any kind, nor such fish as sterlet and sturgeon, to people in customary peasant dress (peasant's overcoats, kaftans, and uncovered sheepskin coats). Article

122 of the Regulations for the Prevention and Suppression of Crimes, inserted in the early nineteenth century, stated that "the police see to it that the young respect their elders, children obey their parents, and servants their lords and masters." [4]

Russian law was filled with such anachronistic provisions as these even down to 1917. They reflect a time when the police and police power were concerned with the whole of administration and when the state regarded it as necessary to teach the average citizen how to eat, drink, dress, live, and, of course, how to think. The assumption was that the subjects of the Crown were immature and that police supervision was in the subject's own interest. This assumption tends to be a characteristic of all despotisms. It was the one idea that even so ignorant a person as the Empress Alexandra could utilize to justify the autocracy. Today the Communists proclaim their totalitarianism as "educative" for the Russian people. Then as now, however, the evidence is overwhelming that the real concern of the despotic state is not so much the education of its citizens as the maintenance of their docility and obedience. Manifestations of self-reliance and political and social consciousness, far from being greeted with enthusiasm, are ruthlessly suppressed. As the Russian jurist Elistratov has pointed out, the citizen of a police state is "of interest first of all as an object, which it is necessary to render harmless, in the same way that animals and elemental forces of nature have to be rendered harmless." [5] Elistratov quotes the Austrian police specialist Sonnenfels to prove this point, indicating that the latter's work on the police was, until the 1840's, considered the official guide in Austrian universities.[6] Had he not been hindered by censorship, Elistratov could have quoted the words of Pobedonostsev to the same effect, using illustrations from much of Czarist policy in the nineteenth century. It was the misfortune of Russian society, for reasons already explained, that it was less capable than Austrian or German society of resisting the repressive governmental measures intended to insure docility and obedience. The result was the growth of an elaborate police force and elaborate police powers, which it is now necessary to analyze.

The Ordinary Police and the Gendarmerie

Characteristically, the police apparatus was composed mainly of three different types, each with a separate and inadequately coordinated chain of command. There was, first, the ordinary police, headed in each province by the governor.[7] The ordinary police remained part of the general administrative structure of the Empire until 1917, and the functions imposed on it by law were correspondingly large and all-embracing, in accordance with the old concept of police.[8] In practice, the welfare functions assigned by law to the ordinary police were left to the units of local self-government. Apart from its concern for the personal and property security of the population, the ordinary police tended to compete with the political police in upholding the existing order. Since it was overshadowed in this sphere by the political police, it sought to win the plaudits of its superiors primarily by zealously enforcing the laws against social intercourse. (The right of assembly will be discussed in detail in Chapter VI.) In the investigation of crimes other than political, the ordinary police, as elsewhere, was under the supervision of the district attorney and the courts, and this supervision was fairly effective.[9] However, in all its other functions, the ordinary police was subordinate to its own superiors, and it shared with other branches of the administration a wide scope for illegal action.

The more notorious political police of nineteenth-century Russia were of two kinds: the Corps of Gendarmes and the Okhrana. The Corps of Gendarmes was organized early in the nineteenth century as a part of the army, and it retained this connection until its demise in 1917. It was subordinate to its military commander in matters concerning appointment, promotion, transfer, reward, discipline, and punishment. Since it performed primarily police, not military, functions, it received its operational instructions from the Minister of the Interior and his principal police subordinate, the Chief of the Department of Police.[10] This division in the command of the Corps of Gendarmes led to great confusion.

Gendarmes were military personnel who wore distinctive blue uniforms. One section of the corps, the railroad gendarmes, was quartered at the main railroad stations and served to keep order on the railroads. The remainder of them were distributed in detachments throughout the provincial capitals, and their main purpose became the maintenance of state security. The provincial gendarme administrations were one of several local institutions over which the governor had no control; they received their orders direct from St. Petersburg.

From 1826 to 1880, the gendarmerie constituted the main force of political police under the notorious Third Section of His Majesty's Own Chancellery (replaced in 1880 by the Police Department of the Ministry of the Interior). From the very beginning, its powers were vague. The story was popular among the Russians that, when the first Chief of Gendarmes, Count Benckendorf, asked Nicholas I for instructions, Nicholas gave him his handkerchief, saying that it would serve as a symbol of the activity of the gendarmes, who were called to "dry away the tears of the grieved and the oppressed." Since the suppression of the Decembrist revolt ended, for the time being, any serious threat to the state, the main efforts of the gendarmes up to 1848 were directed toward the improvement of the social and administrative order of Russia. Included among their activities were a study of the peasant problem, a study of the condition of the workers in the two capitals, the receipt of requests on family problems arising out of disagreements between husbands and wives, and the study of the defects of the old (pre-1864) court system.[11] A balanced view of the political police in Russia requires that this aspect of the Third Section be taken into account. It was designed to be the eyes and ears of a dynasty that had ruled for centuries; it was not created for the purpose of governing by systematic terror.

With the introduction of a new judicial system in the 1860's, the Corps of Gendarmes appeared to have lost all reason for existence, for the Judicial Regulations of 1864 guaranteed to the Russian people freedom from punishment for any crime, political or otherwise, except after judicial investigation and a court decision. However, once the autocracy had decided to maintain itself at all costs, in the face of an opposition in society that had become permanent, it was inevitable that the judicial guarantees of inviolability of the individual would be chipped away and that administrative punishment, unregulated by law before the reform, would once again become normal practice. On May 19, 1871, only five years after the new judicial institutions had been opened, a law transferred the investigation of political crimes from the courts to the gendarmerie. The functions of the gendarmerie, which was by then almost certainly concerned solely with the futile attempt to suppress "sedition," otherwise remained obscure. According to Lopukhin, "not one instruction is given by law for the guidance of the activity of the gendarmes." [12] An anonymous Russian, writing in a German publication, has said:

The activity of the gendarmerie is performed under the protection of an impenetrable secrecy according to the instructions of the highest governmental levels which reach only the police; and no Russian is able, no matter how much he tries, to draw any conclusions about the rights and duties of the gendarmes from the published laws open to the scrutiny of all.[13]

Since the Czarist government was frequently incapable of keeping any secrets from the opposition, there is available an interesting statement of how the gendarmes themselves defined their functions. A circular of the Chief of Gendarmes, dated February 14, 1875, and not intended for publication, stated:

The activity of the personnel of the Corps of Gendarmes at the present time appears in two forms: in the prevention and suppression of various categories of crimes and violations of the law, and in a universal surveillance.

The first of these forms of activity rests on existing legislation. . . . The second form does not differ in its character and necessary methods of operation from those of the prosecuting attorney and the police. However, since it serves general state aims, it cannot be subordinated to strictly defined rules, but requires rather a well-known scope and alone finds its limits when material, acquired by surveillance, crosses to legal ground and is subjected to evaluation, i.e., appears as an object of activity of the first form.[14]

The powers of the Czarist police need not be belittled, but it is interesting to note that the gendarmes assumed the existence of a well-established legal system and seemed to regard themselves as outside the law only in acquiring evidence.

The Okhrana and the Role of "Provocation"

The Okhrana consisted of special sections of political police established by law to operate solely in the capital cities of St. Petersburg, Moscow, and Warsaw in 1881, at the same time that certain emergency powers (soon to be discussed) were given to the police. The Okhrana's full name was *otdeleniia po okhraneniiu obshchestvennoi bezopasnosti i poriadka* (sections for the protection of public security and order), shortened to *okhrannyia otdeleniia* (protective sections), and in foreign languages simply to Okhrana (guard). With the intensification of the revolutionary movement at the beginning of the twentieth century, the Police Department, without legal authorization, extended the Okhrana units to other large cities in Russia in 1902, generally the provincial capitals. About 1907, the Okhrana units in the provincial capitals were replaced by several regional Okhrana units, likewise without legal authorization. The regional units were abolished in 1913, but their duties were taken over by special bureaus established in the gendarme administrations of the larger cities. These reorganizations did not, of course, affect the Okhrana in St. Petersburg, Moscow, and Warsaw. The Okhrana was reputedly established to permit the local administrative authorities to carry on their investigations of political crimes with reduced dependence on the independently administered Corps of Gendarmes, but it is clear that its responsibility to the local governor was purely nominal and that, in practice, it reported directly to the Police Department. Alexander Gerasimov, a former chief of the St. Petersburg Okhrana, explained in his memoirs that his job became easier once he was able to bypass even the Police Department and report directly to the Minister of the Interior, Stolypin.[15]

The Okhrana did not share with the Corps of Gendarmes the right of conducting a formal investigation into political crimes, so that its function, in theory, was limited to uncovering such crimes. The line between the uncovering and the investigation of a crime is, of course, a shadowy one, and both police organizations tended to be concerned with the same basic task of suppressing "sedition." However, in those localities in which Okhrana units were set up, they did assume the primary role of detecting revolutionary activity. To the gendarme administrations was left the secondary role of conducting formal inquiries on the basis of the evidence collected by the Okhrana. If the case was not important enough, or the evidence not sufficient, to warrant court proceedings, the case did not go to the gendarmes at all but was dealt with by administrative proceedings. To the Okhrana, too, went most of the funds for the operation of the network of spies and secret agents that grew up on a large scale in the twentieth century. In the last years of the empire, the Okhrana therefore bore the primary responsibility for dealing with the revolutionary movement and thus acquired worldwide notoriety.

The Okhrana operated through two sets of secret agents: (1) the agents of external observation (called in Russian *filyor*, or, roughly, "secret agent"), who were what we might call plain-clothes men, and who observed and shadowed revolutionaries on the streets and

performed other detective duties; and (2) the agents of internal
observation (*sotrudnik*, i.e., "collaborator"), who penetrated revolutionary and other organizations under observation, and, while
professing sympathy for the aims of these organizations, were secretly in the pay of the police, to whom they furnished information.
There is nothing surprising about the use of the latter agents. The
policy of the government being what it was, Russia was filled with
conspiratorial revolutionary organizations, some of them preparing
attempts on the lives of high officials, including the Czar, and if the
police were to cope successfully with these organizations, they had
to find some method of finding out what the organizations were
doing. Employing spies within conspiratorial organizations, whether
their purpose be smuggling, rumrunning, or revolution, is normal
police practice in any country. Obviously, the wisest course the
Russian government could have taken would have been to adopt a
sensible policy and thereby to obviate the necessity for conspiratorial organizations and spies. Given the policy it did adopt and the
responsibilities that thereby fell to the lot of the Police Department, one must, in principle, acknowledge that the use of spies was
justified.

At the Communist trial in New York in 1949, it was disclosed
that some trusted members of the Communist Party had for some
time been in the pay of the FBI. The Communists applied a long
string of epithets to these members, including "stool pigeon,"
"*agent provocateur*," and other, unmentionable, terms, but the attitude of society toward the methods and aims of the Communists
being what it is, they did not succeed either in casting doubt on the
validity of the testimony of these secret agents or in creating a public scandal. The situation was, however, otherwise in Czarist Russia;
"provocation" became a *cause célèbre* in its last years, for which
the government was roundly condemned on several occasions in the
Duma. The reasons are not difficult to discern. The police possessed
very broad powers, which they constantly abused, so that they were
hated by society as few police forces in any country have been. The
sympathy of society tended therefore to be extended to the revolutionaries rather than the police, and terms like "stool pigeon" could
be used effectively. Furthermore, both the revolutionary movement
and the scale on which spies were used were relatively large, and several scandalous cases had come to light.[16] Finally, it became known
that Okhrana agents were not averse to manufacturing the revolu-

tionary manifestations they "uncovered" in order to give proof of their efficiency.

It is apparent that Russian society exaggerated the extent to which the secret agents were used by the police to "provoke" illegal activity, either for the purpose of securing evidence to convict revolutionaries or for the purpose of justifying their existence. It is unquestionably true that provocation as such did take place, but Russian society was not therefore justified in assuming that the guiding hand of the Okhrana could be detected behind every revolutionary manifestation. Despite the many pages of testimony on secret agents in the record of the Extraordinary Investigating Commission of the Provisional Government in 1917, that record does not bear out the charge that provocation constituted the chief, or even a significant, part of the Okhrana's purpose. Particularly significant is the testimony of S. P. Beletsky, one of the worst of the former police officials, who told the Commission he would reveal anything he knew and, it would appear, actually did.[17] In his memoirs, Gerasimov clearly explains how he tried to use his agents to obtain the maximum of information, without which he was "blind," while at the same time maintaining the safety of the agents and continuing their usefulness.[18] Since society on the whole sympathized with the revolutionaries rather than with the Okhrana, and the task of the police was in the long run hopeless, the police unquestionably played a dangerous game, and several officials lost their lives. Nevertheless, in the mid-twentieth century, it is difficult to ignore the plea of one police official after another that, without informers, they were helpless and could not successfully fulfill their obligations.

Even if the word "provocation" has been loosely used, there is no need to overlook the essential ugliness of a state in which all of society was overrun with spies and informers. These had been used in Russia for a long time, but in the twentieth century, as the revolutionary movement grew in intensity and the difficulties of maintaining the outmoded autocracy increased, they were employed on a scale far exceeding that known even as late as 1905. As the revolutionary movement moved underground after the Revolution of 1905, so did the Okhrana, but both the Okhrana and the gendarmerie also maintained a growing number of spies and informers to keep all sides of Russian political and social life under surveillance. When General Dzhunkovsky became Assistant Minister of the Interior in 1913, he was shocked to discover that there were spies in the upper grades of secondary schools and among the enlisted men in the army. Being a man of integrity, he ordered them removed—in the case of the army, with the concurrence of the Commander in Chief and the Minister of the Interior—but pressure from army officers brought their prompt return after his departure from office.[19] Surveillance over both officers and enlisted men, a good sign of large-scale disaffection in the population, had been undertaken by the gendarmerie at least as early as the reign of Alexander I.[20] Spies were, for the most part, volunteers, but there is no doubt that some officials, by intimidation, recruited them from among those who happened at one time or another to be arrested by the Okhrana.[21] The largest number of involuntary agents of the police were, of course, house janitors, who checked on passports and were required to report to the police all suspicious-looking persons entering their buildings, as well as any unusual events.

Legal Powers of the Police

Unusual powers of arrest and punishment were normally exercised by the monarchical police states of Europe, and Russia, of course, was no exception. Before the judicial reform of 1864, there were no legal guarantees protecting the rights of the individual and there was not even the embryo of a true system of justice. However, during the era of the Great Reforms after the Crimean War, when the government, with the enthusiastic support of society, undertook a radical reorganization of the state, a new judicial structure, remarkably advanced for Russia, was approved by the Czar and put into practice. A modern system of courts was set up, with judges appointed for life, public prosecutors to represent the state in the prosecution of crimes, and an independent bar to represent the accused. So responsive did the government become to public opinion that it authorized public trials, and juries drawn from all strata of the population were to sit in criminal cases. This reform represented only the beginning of a transition to a legal order after centuries of arbitrary rule; it needed many improvements and, above all, time for consolidation so that both the government authorities and the population could adjust to new and constructive habits.

Like the zemstvos, the new judicial structure was incompatible with autocratic government, the general design of which continued to pervade Russian political and social life. Since the last Czars were intent on maintaining the autocracy intact, in opposition to the whole course of Russian life after the reforms, the result was the gradual whittling away of those aspects of the new judicial system that were most in contradiction with autocratic principles. Although the guarantees of personal liberty were among the weakest parts of the new judicial system, they were nevertheless swept away in a vain effort by the state to keep the Russian people in a state of subjection and obedience that they could no longer tolerate.

All states make some provision for the arrest of a person by the police without a court order—in the democratic states under circumstances strictly defined by law. The most drastic safeguard in behalf of the individual is, of course, the *habeas corpus* used in Britain and the United States, which was much discussed and admired by Russian jurists. The Russian police could make a preliminary arrest before the appearance of the examining magistrate in order to prevent a suspect from evading investigation and trial, but within twenty-four hours after being brought before the examining magistrate, the suspect was to be examined. However, the law was silent on the length of time the police could hold him before bringing him before the examining magistrate.[22] The police could also make a preventive arrest, i.e., take a person into custody for disturbing the public peace and order. The law did not regulate this form of arrest at all; nothing was said either about the length of time such persons could be held without judicial proceedings or about any special procedures to be followed in making the arrests. It is characteristic, too, that there was no special procedure for appealing police arrests; a person subjected to arbitrary arrest could seek the punishment of the guilty policeman, but policemen, like all state officials, could be brought to trial only with the consent of their superiors.

In addition to police arrests, common to all states, the Russian police had two other principal powers, required not so much for the immediate purpose of maintaining peace and order as for the long-range purpose of holding society in check. These were police surveillance and administrative exile. A person placed under police surveillance had to live in a specified place and could not leave at any time, even to travel within the district, without the special permission of an appropriate authority. He was subject also to a number of other disabilities, all designed to enable the police to keep

watch over him and to keep him isolated from the general public.
If, as a result of these restrictions he was deprived of his means of
livelihood, he was given assistance by the state treasury. Recom-
mendations from the local authorities on the establishment of
police surveillance over a given person were considered by a Special
Council within the Ministry of the Interior, with the maximum
sentence being five years.

Administrative exile was regulated by the emergency statute of
1881. It was, however, in use before the passage of that statute and
should be classified under the normal powers of the police. There
were two forms of administrative exile. One, known as *vysylka*,
consisted merely of the banishment of a person from a given locality; the second, *ssylka*, consisted of the deportation of a person to
a given locality, where he was automatically subject to police surveillance and from which he could not, therefore, leave without
permission. *Vysylka* was wholly within the power of the governor
general or governor, but could be exercised by these officials only in
localities in a state of emergency. *Ssylka* was initiated by the local
authorities and considered by the same Special Council used for
political surveillance. Action could be taken in any locality, whether
or not a state of emergency existed, and the maximum sentence
was five years.

These, then, were the principal normal powers of the Russian
police. On the surface they seem formidable. The police could
make arrests, presumably for an indefinite period, with a minimum
of judicial interference. It disposed of great powers of administrative punishment, before the emergency statute of 1881, without a
five-year limit. It was little trammeled by judicial restraints in behalf of the liberties of Russian subjects. It had a special procedure
for dealing with state crimes, with the notoriously uncontrolled and
independent Corps of Gendarmes collecting the evidence, though
under the supervision of the prosecuting attorneys. It had great
powers over the right to organize and the right of free speech. It
became apparent, however, that the powers of the police were not
great enough, because it failed to suppress the revolutionary movement and, in 1881, the police and the administration were equipped
with even greater emergency powers. The perspective given by the
comparison between the normal powers of the police and the emergency powers it had to assume suggests that the new judicial system,
though seriously defective and constantly regressing, had a more

favorable restraining influence on the police than the bare examination of the rights of Russian subjects leads one to assume.

Most commentators are agreed that the supervision of the prosecuting attorneys over the preliminary investigations conducted by the gendarmerie in political crimes was not adequate. Nevertheless, a close reading of Lopukhin's work on the police and of the memoirs of a gendarme officer like A. I. Spiridovich gives some clue as to why the emergency statute of 1881 was necessary. Lopukhin, after heatedly explaining that the gendarmes were above the law, finally gets around to explaining that the law did require that there be sufficiently sound evidence of the commission of a state crime to permit the gendarmes to conduct their unrestrained inquiries, and that, on the ground of the "ethical and logical interpretations of their methods," the prosecuting attorneys did place obstacles in their path that the statute of 1881 was designed to remove.[23] This point is fully confirmed by Spiridovich in explaining a mission he undertook to Siberia to investigate an illegal printing press operated by the Socialist Revolutionaries. While the investigation of ordinary crimes by the ordinary police was under the supervision of the examining magistrates, who had the qualifications of judges and were supposed to be appointed for life, the investigation of state crimes by the gendarmes was placed under the supervision of the prosecuting attorneys, presumably because, as subordinates of the Minister of Justice, they were closer to the administration. But Czarist Russia was not a totalitarian state and it did not have a totalitarian administration. Spiridovich writes: "In political matters, the prosecuting attorneys (outside the two capitals), forgetting the purpose of their existence, in the majority of cases sought to free the accused and assumed the role of defense attorneys." [24]

The State of Emergency: Extraordinary Powers of the Police

However slender the guarantees of individual freedom in the ordinary laws of the Russian Empire, the government manifestly regarded them as hindering the maintenance of public order, and in 1881, administrative discretion, already very broad, was further increased by the establishment of a series of emergency powers.[25] Two forms of emergency rule were established: *usilennaia okhrana* (literally "reinforced protection," best translated as "state of emergency,") and *chrezvychainaia okhrana* (literally "extraordinary protection," best translated as "extraordinary state of emergency").

Especially noteworthy among the provisions of emergency rule was the addition of a third form of police arrest to those already described under the general laws. The police authorities, both regular and gendarme, could place under preliminary arrest for a period of not more than two weeks all persons inspiring a "well-founded suspicion" of having committed or of having participated in a state crime or of having belonged to an illegal society. By written order of the governor, the time could be extended to a month. The police could also conduct searches and seizures in any building, private or industrial, at any time, thereby removing the already inadequate guarantees against abuses under the permanent laws. The effect of these provisions was to remove whatever restraints the public prosecutors exercised against unfounded arrests, and the police now made arrests not because it had any evidence or even any suspicions that could reasonably be called "well founded," but because it hoped, by making the arrests, to collect evidence.

Nor did the police confine itself to political crimes, as was required by the law; arrests, and searches and seizures, were made also on the suspicion that other crimes had been committed. In Vilno, in 1902, fourteen-year-old girls were jailed under the Statute of 1881 for refusing to work in a local workshop. There were known cases of the use of police arrest solely because of the unfriendly feeling of some police official toward a local inhabitant. According to a statement of Assistant Minister of the Interior Durnovo before the Committee of Ministers in 1905, no local resident could be sure that he would be arrested or searched only for apparent cause. And the result was increasing unrest and bitterness against the government, without yielding essential data for police investigation.[26]

Another illustration of the enormous discretion granted the local authorities under emergency rule is to be found in the provision empowering the local authorities to issue obligatory decrees on matters concerned with the suppression of violations of public order and state security; any person failing to obey these decrees could be punished without court proceedings by imprisonment of up to three months and a fine of up to 3,000 rubles. Although the law specifically mentioned that the decrees must be connected with the suppression of sedition, the local authorities began, in practice, to issue decrees on all matters affecting the locality, including public welfare, so that administrative punishment, instead of regular court proceedings, was used for such offenses as the violation of speed laws on the streets or the failure to observe sanitary regulations. A March, 1889, decree of the Committee of Ministers ordering the local authorities to stop this abuse improved, but did not entirely remedy, the situation. Another unfortunate result was the tendency of local officials to decree taxes and other obligations not provided for by law.

The statute of August 14, 1881, was intended as a temporary measure, to remain in effect only until "sedition" had been eradicated. It was passed for a term of three years, but was renewed in 1884, 1887, 1890, 1893, 1896, 1899, and 1902. In 1905, when the whole subject of emergency rule was under examination, it was renewed by the Committee of Ministers for one year only; thereafter, the statute continued to be renewed every year by the Council of Ministers until 1917. In some areas, a state of emergency (or an extraordinary state of emergency) continued without interruption from 1881, through the Revolution of 1905, and up until 1917. In those localities in which a state of emergency had not been proclaimed, the law provided that some emergency powers could be granted to the administrative authorities, and when the statute of 1881 was promulgated, these powers were actually extended to all of Russia.[27] Consequently, this statute, although intended as a temporary measure, in effect displaced in part the permanent laws from the time of its promulgation until the Revolution swept away the old regime.

Emergency rule was one of the ugly consequences of the attempt of the Czarist government to maintain its power without the consent of the people. By widening the discretionary activity of the administrative authorities to a point well beyond the possibility of effective control, it introduced a reign of arbitrariness and checked the development of respect for the law on the part of both government and governed upon which the peaceful evolution of Russia necessarily rested. This price was paid, furthermore, without the statute's having achieved its objective, as the two revolutions of the twentieth century showed and as the government itself readily admitted in 1905. Indeed, the bitterness engendered by arbitrary rule at the discretion of local administrative authorities promoted rather than checked the revolutionary movement. In the permanent and universal operation of emergency rule, one government

commission in 1905 saw the main reason for the "rise of revolutionary ferment, criminal propaganda, and even armed revolt in a
whole series of cities and villages." [28] Despite this critical attitude
of the government, it did not produce a new statute acceptable to
the State Duma, and the law of 1881 remained in effect until 1917.

Defects in the Organization and Functioning of the Police

Clearly, the subject of the Czarist police is not exhausted by the
above discussion of the formal structure of its main branches and
their legal powers, ordinary and extraordinary. The fundamental
question still remains: Why is it that the Czarist government was
unable to suppress either the liberal opposition or the revolutionary
movement, despite its possession of a formidable police mechanism
and formidable police powers, despite, indeed, its possession of all
the advantages that an organized state with a monopoly of force
has over an unorganized society? Why is it, as official government
bodies admitted, that excessive police repression stimulated rather
than suppressed the revolutionary movement?

It is certainly true that, at the climaxes of the revolutionary movement in the latter half of the nineteenth century and in the twentieth century, society, not the state, was the victor. Concerning the
first climax, at the end of the 1870's, Leroy-Beaulieu has written:
"Two or three dozen resolute young people, having made 'a com-
pact with death,' held at bay for several years the government of
the most extensive empire in the world." [29] A small group of revolutionaries constituting the organization "The Will of the People"
(Narodnaia Volia) set out to kill Czar Alexander II, and, in fact,
hounded him to death. They fired several shots at him just outside
his palace. They blew up a train on which he was traveling. They
even succeeded in blowing up a section of the Winter Palace just
as he was about to enter. Finally, they mined a street on which he
customarily traveled, and when his carriage avoided that street,
they tore him to pieces with a hand grenade in broad daylight in
St. Petersburg. At the end of the second climax, in 1905, the government was in a state of complete confusion and paralysis, and the
police were thoroughly cowed. The government was finally overthrown in 1917, with a minimum of bloodshed, as a result of a
spontaneous and essentially unorganized and leaderless movement
on the part of the population. This outcome of the conflict between

state and society is all the more surprising if it is borne in mind that Russian society was still meagerly organized, compared to the societies of the West. Since the conditions under which a state can maintain its control over a rebellious society constitute one of the main themes of this study, a complete analysis of the reasons why the Czarist state could not hold its enormous advantages over Russian society will be reserved for a later chapter. In the pages that immediately follow, some of these reasons, in so far as they concern the organization and operation of the police, will be discussed. Not all the points raised are of equal importance, but all contribute essential data toward an appraisal of the Czarist police.

The Czarist police may be said to have resembled an alien army of occupation rather than the police of such modern democratic states as the United States and Great Britain. Its main job was repression; it was the immediate executor of an administrative policy that blocked the natural aspirations of a talented and vigorous people ready to give full scope to their faculties for the first time in their history. Low pay and extreme unpopularity brought into its ranks men with correspondingly low intellectual and moral qualifications, and many of them were called upon to perform delicate work of detection and investigation well beyond their capabilities. Both the Kakhanov commission on local government of the 1880's and the Special Conference of Count Ignatiev called attention to this situation and to the need for "decisive" measures to raise the quality of police personnel, but there was no hope of accomplishing anything as long as the police remained instruments of lawlessness and arbitrariness rather than servants of the people.[30]

The several varieties and chains of command were strongly emphasized as a cause of constant confusion among the police. The chief point of friction seems to have been between the staff of the Corps of Gendarmes and the Police Department. "The staff," writes Spiridovich, "was always at war with the Department."[31] This is fully confirmed by Lopukhin, a former Chief of the Department, who charges with great bitterness that the staff paralyzed the Department's activity. "It was sufficient," he writes, "for the commander of the Corps or the chief of staff to say several words during meetings with his subordinates in order that any order of the Police Department remain a dead letter. However urgent its instructions may be, they are destined never to be fulfilled if they are not in agreement with the views of the immediate gendarme superiors. . . ." [32] The difficulty, of course, lay in the quite incomprehensible division of functions between the two organizations, the Department being responsible for the operating orders of the gendarme units in police matters, and the gendarme staff being responsible for matters of discipline, promotion, and reward.

The absurdity of the situation is further revealed by Spiridovich's disclosures of what was happening on the side of the gendarmes. The Corps was part of the army, and no attention was paid to its need for special preparation in police functions. It had only one school, in which the gendarmes were briefly trained in a portion of their future duties; of the revolutionary movement and methods of dealing with it they learned nothing. The men appointed as commanders of the Corps were primarily soldiers, some of whom had no notion of what the police and the gendarmes were supposed to do. One "poor general," insists Spiridovich, observing that the gendarmes had spurs and cartridge pouches, assumed that the gendarmes were front-line cavalry units and ordered the railroad gendarmes to spend their time learning how to use the sword. "This is not an anecdote," he writes, "but a real fact." [33] Another general, "who knew in general only how to be pleasant," and who did not like the work of detection, set about abolishing this phase of the Corps' duties in the belief that he was accomplishing "a remarkable public deed." "These are sad facts," mourns Spiridovich, "for which Russia paid very dearly. There were, of course, exceptions, but very, very rarely." The chiefs of staff appointed were not much better. In general, the staff was "an enemy of detection (rozysk), which it thought a dirty business. . . ." The Police Department, naturally, valued detective work and tried to promote officers trained in it, but these were not favored by the Staff. As for the gendarme officers, they had to maneuver and play the diplomat in order not to ruin themselves in one institution while serving another.

An excellent indication of the faulty training of the gendarmes and their resulting ineptness has been provided by I. I. Petrunkevich, a zemstvo and Cadet Party leader who was banished from his home for twenty-five years for political unreliability. In January, 1881, while living in Smolensk, he was secretly visited by the chief of the Smolensk gendarme administration, one Colonel Yesipov. Yesipov, it seems, had been accustomed to writing his annual report on conditions in his province in accordance with a primitive stereotype full of inaccurate information, and Loris-Melikov, Alexander

II's liberal and influential Minister of the Interior (1880–81), in that year of intense revolutionary ferment, had demanded a change to genuine analysis. Feeling totally at a loss, Yesipov turned to Petrunkevich, who, he rightly suspected, knew a great deal about politics, and proposed that he write the report. Petrunkevich agreed to do so, provided that he could write as he pleased about anyone or anything, including the Governor. Looking over the gendarme material sent him as a result of his agreement with Yesipov, he was impressed by the useless and silly information it contained. As for the report, he naturally wrote it in the spirit of an ardent liberal singled out for punishment by the government, and asked for greater freedom for the public and the end of arbitrary state administration.[34]

Leroy-Beaulieu describes how, in the days when the Third Section was still in operation, the police of the Third Section and the police of the Ministry of the Interior, acting independently of one another, threw each other off the track and wasted their time chasing each other. Their agents were not known to each other, and they naturally thought their respective behavior suspicious, and so they watched and shadowed each other. Finally, according to a former minister of Alexander II, in the very middle of the crisis of the revolutionary movement the police of the Third Section made what they thought were important arrests, only to find that they had captured some of their colleagues of the Ministry of the Interior.[35] Although similar incidents have not so far been reported for the later period, they cannot be ruled out, since the duplication of secret agents continued.

It has already been mentioned that Gerasimov succeeded in bypassing the Police Department and reported directly to the Minister of the Interior; his successors continued this practice. Gerasimov became, in fact, the *de facto* head of all political investigation in the empire, giving orders to the Police Department rather than receiving them, and consulting with and giving orders to other Okhrana heads, all under the direct supervision of Stolypin himself.[36] Whether there was any effective coordination of political investigation after Gerasimov's departure in 1909 seems doubtful. Spiridovich, like Gerasimov, showed little respect for the chiefs of the Police Department, charging that, with very few exceptions, they did not understand political investigation.[37] Beletsky complained to the Extraordinary Commission that "the political section [of the Police Department] was so set up that no one could know what was happening there." [38]

Limits to the Use of Force

Probably the most important single reason for the failure of the Czarist state to maintain effective control over Russian society was its unwillingness to use unlimited force. While it is, of course, true that modern weapons of mass destruction give the state a great advantage, the advantage is lost if the state is not prepared to use them. Moreover, if the state is to avoid actual mass murder, it must keep the population in a permanent state of terror. The Czarist government was a traditional, monarchical government composed of many honorable men; it was neither organized to rule by terror nor willing to do so. Contrary to the general impression, moreover, the taking of human life is repugnant to the Russian spirit. To those who know only Communist rule in Russia this may seem unbelievable, but this is only one of the ways in which the Communists diverge from the national traditions of Russia. The fact is that capital punishment was abolished in the ordinary criminal courts of Russia as early as 1754. Its abolition was a fiction as long as corporal punishment, particularly if administered with the knout, was in force, but when the knout was abolished as an instrument of corporal punishment in 1845, and when other forms of corporal punishment that could have fatal results were abolished in 1863 and 1871, it became a fact as well.[39] In nineteenth-century Russia, execution was an exceptional measure of punishment, imposed mainly by military courts.[40] "If the civilization of a people were to be judged by the mildness of its penal laws," writes Leroy-Beaulieu, "Russia could have claimed first place in Europe." [41]

Capital punishment under the permanent laws was permissible in civil courts only for the most serious state crimes, including attacks on the imperial family and some forms of state treason. It was one of the purposes of the statute of 1881 to increase the repression against the revolutionary movement, and that statute added to the list of offenses subject to capital punishment armed resistance to the authorities and murderous attacks (regardless of whether wholly successful or not) on troops, police, or officials while they were fulfilling their duties. Because these acts were not punishable by death under the permanent laws, the statute of 1881 gave to the governors general of regions in a state of emergency the right (not hitherto mentioned) to transfer individual criminal cases to military tribunals for judgment according to the laws of war. Such transfers could be made at the discretion of the governor general when he regarded them as necessary for the protection of public order and peace. The chief purpose of the transfers was to secure the death sentence under Article 279 of the code of military punishments.

The transfer of a criminal case to a military tribunal was intended as a hard measure and its significance should not be overlooked. Those alleged to have committed crimes punishable by death under Article 279 of the code of military punishments (including ordinary cases of murder, rape, robbery, and arson) or under Article 18 of the statute of 1881 (armed resistance or an act of terrorism, whether or not it resulted in death or injury to the official), if found guilty by a military tribunal, had to be executed. The tribunal did not have the power to ease the punishment; it could always hand down a verdict of not guilty, but if its verdict was guilty, the sentence had to be capital punishment, and only a higher authority could change the sentence. The result was, of course, that the life of a defendant was not in the hands of the court but in the hands of the administrative authorities. By using his discretion to transfer a criminal case to a military tribunal, the governor general frequently predetermined the fate of the accused. Whether or not a sentence could be reviewed and reduced by the highest military tribunal likewise rested with the governor general, who had the right to confirm the sentence and prevent the appeal of the case.

Despite all this, it remains true that the military tribunals were not drumhead courts, invariably finding defendants guilty. The military courts were composed of military judges; the cases were tried by military prosecuting attorneys; the accused had their own civilian attorneys who could present defense witnesses and cross-examine prosecution witnesses. If it could not be conclusively proved that the accused had committed crimes punishable by death, he was sentenced to hard labor or imprisonment; if he was not proved guilty of any crime at all, he was acquitted. The mere fact of belonging to a revolutionary organization, even if it had dynamite or an arsenal of weapons in its possession, was not sufficient to condemn a person to death if he was not implicated in the attempted assassination of an official. It is common knowledge that some prominent Bolshevik leaders did not face any court at all, but were dealt with through administrative proceedings, because the evidence that could lead to a court sentence was lacking.

It should be noted, furthermore, that these provisions of the statute of 1881 were not widely used until the summer of 1905, when the Revolution of that year was already in progress. Between 1881 and 1902, political trials, whether before military or civilian tribunals, were relatively rare, the government having found it sufficient to deal with most political crimes by means of administrative proceedings, i.e., exile and police surveillance. Beginning in 1902, political trials were gradually restored, probably for the purpose of handing out more severe penalties than were possible under administrative proceedings. Not until 1902 was any civilian actually executed for a political crime after sentencing by a military tribunal, and only after 1905 did such executions become common.[42] In none of the courts, civil or military, were the defendants "prepared" for trial; nor did they make abject confessions. On the contrary, many of the defendants used the occasion to make inflammatory speeches explaining their revolutionary credo and denouncing the government. Whatever the status of freedom of speech for society as a whole at any given time, it was maintained in the courtroom without serious interruption from the time an independent bar was established in the 1860's.[43]

For a brief period, however, there *were* drumhead courts in Czarist Russia. These were, of course, the field courts-martial introduced by a decree of the Council of Ministers on August 19, 1906, under Article 87 of the Fundamental Laws. In localities in an extraordinary state of emergency or under martial law, the governor general could, at his discretion, transfer to such field courts-martial civilians guilty of crimes so obvious that there was no need for investigation. Field courts-martial were composed only of front-line officers; neither judges nor attorneys participated. The accused was to go before the court immediately after the perpetration of the crime, within twenty-four hours if possible, and the examination of the case was to be concluded within forty-eight hours. The sentence, invariably the death penalty, had to be carried out not later than twenty-four hours after it was handed down. The government did not seek to perpetuate the decree and did not introduce it into the Second Duma when that body convened in February, 1907. Consequently, field courts-martial ceased to operate after April 20, 1907.

With the coming of the Revolution of 1905, capital punishment, formerly so rare in Russia, became an everyday occurrence. But acts of terror also became an everyday occurrence, and there is no reason to expect any government, even a bad one, to remain idle while its citizens are being assaulted in the streets and in their homes. Whatever the precise number of alleged criminals executed by virtue of a court sentence after 1905, the number of persons killed or wounded by terrorists was at least comparable, and for some years apparently far exceeded it.[44] As Maklakov has pointed out, the Czarist government is to be condemned not because it took steps to suppress the revolutionary movement but because it took them at the discretion of the governors general and without due regard for the law.[45]

Details on the mass movement leading to the Revolution of 1905 will be given later, as will those on the regulations governing the right of assembly. It is, nevertheless, desirable at this point to give some concrete illustration of the failure of the government to use unlimited force, of its policy of irritating society and of playing into the hands of the radicals without resorting to firm measures to maintain, at any cost, its conception of "order." Petrunkevich, in his memoirs, relates two incidents which are quoted below. They took place in Moscow in July, 1905, when Russian society was rocked by the defeats of the Russian armed forces in the Far East and when the discontent long brewing among all segments of society began to be manifested more and more openly and more and more boldly. The focal point of the opposition was the zemstvos, which, beginning in November, 1904, openly met in long-forbidden congresses. To reduce friction with the government to a minimum, the congresses and their organizing bureau met in private homes. Nevertheless, the government had the legal right to prevent meetings even in private homes, and since it correctly saw in the zemstvos its most dangerous opponents, it sought to disperse the July congress, with the result described by Petrunkevich:

I recall an instance when, from the home of Golovin, situated inside a big open courtyard, where the permanent bureau of the congresses was in session, we saw the uniforms of policemen as they entered the courtyard, and then we heard their ring. In a few minutes, the Chief of Police, Noskov, entered into the room, where a group of twenty was sitting. He . . . demanded that we disperse. It goes without saying that we resolutely and categorically refused to obey. We declared that we were in private quarters, where it was not forbidden for anyone to be when he pleased and do what he pleased; that we considered such an in-

vasion of the police and such a demand on his part an illegal violation of
our rights, and that therefore we would not yield to him and would not
disperse. If he wished, let him use force on each of us. The chief of
police was puzzled and apparently did not know what to do. After a
brief silence, he declared that he would not leave until we dispersed.

"In that case," objected F. A. Golovin, "you will have to wait for a
long time; be seated, and we will continue our business."

The chief of police was even more disconcerted, and declared that he
would ask for the cards of all of us and would bring charges against us in
court. We all gave him our cards and he withdrew. It goes without saying that we were never brought to court. Such attempts of the Moscow
police were repeated many times, each time giving the impression that
they were on the alert and carried out their duties, but not seriously,
since they were in doubt as to who would be the master of the situation
the next day—the existing government or one composed of the participants of the congress. Sometimes the appearance of the police took on
an amusing character; it was always amusing when they were headed by
Police Chief Noskov. Thus, at a large assembly at the home of Prince
Dolgorukov, Noskov turned to the chairman, Count Peter Alexandrovich Heyden, with the demand to disperse, and Heyden, without moving from his place, insisted that the assembly would not disperse willingly as long as it had not finished its regular business. At that very
moment, a photographer with his big apparatus appeared in the room,
and having constructed a kind of tower from the tables standing
behind the members of the assembly, he took a picture of the wrangling
chief of police and the chairman. Noskov turned his face toward the
photographer, momentarily was fixed, and then flew into a rage. He
threw himself at the photographer, but the crowd blocked his path, and
while he tried to force his way through, the photographer disappeared
without a trace. The incident was concluded, as usual, by the handing
over of the cards of all present.[46]

In the above incidents are reflected the main characteristics of
life under the Czars that caused Czarist authoritarianism to break
down at decisive moments. The men who attended the zemstvo
congresses were intellectuals, scholars, and practical politicians
working in behalf of social rather than state interests. They represented the cream of Russian society. Many, probably the majority,
were hereditary nobles, among them princes of such distinguished
families as the Dolgorukovs, the Trubetskois, and the Lvovs. They
were, for the most part, moderates who had sought concessions by
appealing to the Czar and not by appealing to the people, i.e., they
did not call for revolution. The government had, of course, the
material means with which to disperse the congresses, but it did not

have the moral means, for dispersal by force of a group such as this meant resorting to Bolshevik methods, and at no time were the Czar and his ministers prepared to use such methods. It is apparent now, and will become even more apparent later, that the gap between the Czarist siege of society and the Communist siege of society is enormous and that it could not be bridged by the Czar without drastic changes in his mental and moral outlook and in his methods of government.

Prison Life and Exile in Practice

Life in Czarist prisons and in exile is a vast subject, well beyond the scope of this study, but aspects of it revealed by the biographies of revolutionary leaders are worthy of mention because they bear directly on the problem of why the revolutionary movement could not be suppressed. Conditions in Czarist prisons varied; there was unquestionably much brutality, and in some prisons, foul and inhuman conditions prevailed. As Isaac Deutscher has pointed out, however, Czarist prisons seem "mild, almost humanitarian," compared to the concentration camps of modern totalitarian states.[47] Political prisoners were segregated from common criminals and given more privileges and better living conditions. Once they were in prison, an active community life, accompanied by vigorous debates and the interchange of ideas, grew up among them. Where communication was prohibited, they developed techniques for circumventing the prohibition. They were permitted to have books, both from the prison library and from the outside, and also pencil and paper. Since they had no work to perform, they had ample time to read—even Marxist works could be smuggled in, for inspection methods were superficial. More amazing still, Lenin wrote the whole of his *Development of Capitalism in Russia* while in jail or in Siberian exile. The book was then published legally in 1899, during his last year in exile. According to David Footman, Kibalchich, the explosives expert of Narodnaia Volia, the band of terrorists that assassinated Alexander II in 1881, studied modern explosives intensively during the last months of a three-year stay in prison (1875–78).[48] Under conditions like these, police campaigns against the revolutionaries could actually benefit their cause, because, as Footman shows from the lives of the leaders of Narodnaia Volia, the prisons became a breeding ground for full-fledged revolutionaries. "It was in the prisons," he writes, "and nowhere else in nineteenth-century Russia, that extremists could spead their propaganda at their leisure and convenience and in complete security among the most susceptible of listeners." [49]

Life in exile was harder, depending on the term of exile and the locality to which the person was sent. For political unreliables not connected with the terror and against whom no evidence of wrongdoing could be found, administrative exile under automatic police surveillance was the rule. This form of punishment was meted out several times to the Bolshevik leaders, and their biographies again provide some picture of what exile in Siberia was like.[50] The exiles were assigned to a definite village but were not jailed and could live anywhere in the village where they could find a home. They were not, of course, required to work; those who had no independent means of support received a small government allowance. They were permitted to work if they could find work, within the limits described above for those under police surveillance. Their families were permitted to join them. Neither Lenin nor Stalin worked while in exile. Both were men of leisure and engaged largely in hunting, fishing, and reading. Neither lacked the books and newspapers they required; Lenin was especially well supplied with these and wrote many articles, which he sometimes sold for considerable sums. Neither man could, of course, move freely, but permission nevertheless could be obtained to visit other comrades in exile and to be visited by them in turn. Stalin lived in a more northerly, colder, and more desolate spot than Lenin and spent his time in greater isolation. Both carried on extensive correspondence; neither appears to have been hindered by police censorship or searches. Whether this was typical for most of the political exiles in Siberia it is difficult to say; it is sufficient to note what the treatment was of those who, in later years, established a system of exile that had little more in common with the Czarist system than the name. Conditions undoubtedly varied and for some exile became a great personal tragedy. Those sentenced to hard labor probably suffered more, but not much more, if Leroy-Beaulieu's account of life in penal servitude is accurate.[51] Escapes were relatively easy.[52] Both Stalin and Trotsky escaped from Siberia twice; Stalin did not escape for a third time in 1914, partly because of increased police surveillance, but mostly because, with the outbreak of the war and the proclamation of martial law in Russia, the exiles, Stalin included, preferred to stay where they were.[53]

The Loophole in Finland

The subject of Finland is a curious one in any discussion of the effectiveness of police control in Czarist Russia. Finland enjoyed special rights of autonomy from the time of its annexation in 1809, and the Russian police was not authorized to make arrests there. Since Finland was very close to St. Petersburg, it became a convenient haven for the revolutionaries, with whom the Finnish police sympathized and hence did not molest. Gerasimov even complained to the Czar, in his sole private audience early in 1906, that Russian police administrators on official business in Finland, when pointed out by the revolutionaries, were expelled by the Finnish police.[54] Early in 1906, when the "Battle Organization" of the Socialist Revolutionary Party decided to resume its attempts on the lives of high government officials, it made Finland its base of operations. There its plans were discussed and adopted in comparative freedom, and weapons and explosives prepared. When the plans were carried out or thwarted, as the case might be, the separate groups returned to Finland to draw up new plans. Escapes to Finland were sometimes precipitate, as, for example, when a group discovered that it was obviously being trailed and in danger of arrest. For a brief period, Lenin, too, was able to work in Finland without being disturbed. His wife, Krupskaya, acted as courier, departing for St. Petersburg each morning with articles, proofs, and instructions, and returning in the evening with news, arrangements for appointments, and questions to be resolved.[55] Eventually, the Russian government succeeded in curtailing the revolutionaries' freedom of movement in Finland, presumably as a result of the law of 1910 limiting Finnish autonomy.

All this throws an interesting light on the extraordinary difficulties involved in keeping under control a society that is ready to demand its freedom. Faced at the beginning of the twentieth century with an increasingly dangerous mass movement, the Czarist government adopted harsh measures of repression—but they were not harsh enough. The government ordered those who participated in armed uprisings to be shot without investigation, but its own

officials were assassinated and even terrorized. It succeeded, by
means of a network of spies, in partially disorganizing the revolutionary movement, but it was itself partially disorganized by unknown traitors in its own midst. The police and the administration
were given broad powers to act without regard for existing laws, but
the government-dominated prosecuting attorneys and judges could
not be compelled to forget their legal training and the requirements
of a fair trial. In the end, the state's seemingly solid administrative
apparatus, backed by what was then the most extensively organized
police system in the world, collapsed virtually without a fight under
the determined onslaught of a society still in the beginning stages
of its organization.

THREE

SOCIETY AND ITS
INSTITUTIONS

4

Pre-Revolutionary Trends
in Russian Society

THE SOCIAL changes in the nineteenth century that reacted so profoundly on state institutions represented a new departure in Russian social history and ultimately led to the Russian Revolution. Although the Revolution was both social and political in character, it is unlikely that the social trends on the eve of the Revolution wholly lost their significance in 1917. A knowledge of the nineteenth-century social base throws light on the present and future politics of Russia, as well as on its past.

The survival of legal classes, or estates, in Russia during the nineteenth century, at a time when they had long since decayed in the West, may give the impression that the caste spirit was strong in Russia and that it was perhaps associated with political absolutism. But such an impression would be erroneous: Actually, the caste spirit was repugnant to the Russian tradition, and that very repugnance was, in part, responsible for Russian absolutism. Moreover, Western literature on Russia has not stressed sufficiently that the legal class system was introduced only in the eighteenth century, largely in imitation of the West, and that, from the time of the great reforms in the 1860's, the legal privileges of the upper classes were steadily diminishing in scope and significance. Russia was moving inexorably toward civil equality and had virtually attained it by 1917.

The Nobility: Legal and Social Status

The Russian word for estate (*soslovie*) implies the existence of separate groups of citizens who are by law distinguished from each other by various hereditary rights and obligations. Each person belonged to only one of the established classes, generally the one into which he was born, and could change his class (and therefore his rights and obligations) only under specified conditions, which

73

could be quite independent of any change in his economic status. In the West, a system of estates grew out of the life of the people before the rise of unified national states and absolute monarchs, and state, law, and monarch were compelled to adapt themselves to the already existing system. In Russia, legal classes were a deliberate creation of the state, and both their rights and obligations grew out of state interests and state initiative.

It is characteristic of the Russian social tradition that even the nobility was a creation of the state. Such organization as it had and such privileges as it enjoyed were granted by the state in accordance with state needs. Russia had no aristocracy based on blood or contract. Before the eighteenth century, only the family of the Czar merited the designation "highborn" (*blagorodnyi*); all other members of society were servants (*kholopy*) of the Czar.[1] There were families of distinction, but that distinction, with the exception of the titled descendants of such dynastic founders as Rurik and Gedymin, was based originally on service to the state and rank acquired in state service. These did not, furthermore, constitute a privileged class; they were known collectively as "high-ranking men of the Czar" (*tsarskie chinovnye liudi*) and were subdivided into various ranks that had little in common with one another. The rights that they exercised in common, e.g., the possession of land and serfs, were in most cases temporary benefits granted to them by the Czar as an aid in performing military service for the state, and these rights were exercised only as long as they performed military service. There were, in the Moscow state, not classes but ranks, not rights but obligations, accompanied by unequal benefits designed to assist in the performance of those obligations.[2] All this, of course, was a consequence of the external dangers threatening Russia, which served as the driving force both in the unification of the state and in the organization of society.

The transformation of Russian society from a series of highly fragmentized ranks without organization, and, in their relation to state power, without rights, into organized groups with hereditary class privileges and obligations was a long and complex process reaching its culmination in 1785. The emergence of some conception of class rights was to some extent inherent in the various ranks of Moscow society itself, but there is no question that the entire process gained new impetus in the eighteenth century as a result of the familiarity acquired with Western societies and the desire of both the Czars and the nobles to emulate them.

The most important aspect of the process was the transformation of the serving nobility into a privileged class. At the beginning of the eighteenth century, the nobility was subject to burdensome state orders in the same way that other groups were, although the tasks it performed were, of course, different from those performed by the peasants or merchants, and gave them a higher rank. The nobility enjoyed, as has been said, only those benefits required for the fulfillment of its obligations to the state, and its members could be flogged as mercilessly for minor offenses as were the serfs. In dress, manners, and morals, the nobility was not very different from the remainder of the population. By the time it had been granted its charter by Catherine in 1785, all this had been changed; it had become Europeanized and in manners, morals, and external appearance was sharply differentiated from the rest of the population. Its members had acquired not only the external appearance of the European feudal classes but also their historical prejudices, for they now regarded themselves as highborn and the remainder of the population as lowborn. To emphasize the distinction, they had been provided with a series of privileges not available to the baser elements of the population. Although there had certainly been no equality before Peter the Great, a sharp class demarcation had grown up that was unknown in the Moscow period.

This structure, later defended so ardently by the reactionary wing of the nobility, suffered from one major defect that was to prove insurmountable: It happened to be contrary to the national tradition. The nobility formerly had had some rights, but it also had obligations, the burden of which was attested to by the extent to which it had been trying to avoid them and by its pleas to have them removed. In 1762, it was in fact freed from state service and then showered with rights not accompanied by any obligations. Historically, the serfs had been attached to the land only in order to enable the nobility to perform military service. Yet at the same time the nobility was being relieved of the obligation of service, the peasants were being converted into virtual slaves, bought and sold apart from the land. Enough has been said already to indicate why, in the long run, a movement to remedy the injustice that had been done to the masses of the people in the eighteenth century became irresistible. Once the nobles were relieved of obligatory service, neither the peasants, nor, in the long run, the majority of the nobles themselves, could understand why they should be treated differently from anybody else.

One circumstance probably helped to prolong the privileges of the nobility for a somewhat longer period than would otherwise have been possible. The "right" of self-government granted to the nobility by Catherine II in 1775 was, in fact, regarded by the nobles as a new form of state service, justifying in their eyes the continuation of serfdom.[3] Accordingly, once the requirement that elected representatives of the nobility must serve in local administration was ended in 1864, there is nothing surprising about the rapid extension of the former privileges of the nobility to the remainder of the population. "Never and nowhere," wrote Miliukov, "did the privileges of a noble estate rise so quickly, exist for so short a time, and crumble so completely as with us." [4]

Before turning to a more detailed consideration of the privileges of the nobility, a few remarks should be made about the method by which the status of nobility could be acquired. It could be acquired by a grant from the Czar, which was very rare, or by service. Hereditary nobility was automatically conferred on those holding the rank of colonel in military service, Rank IV in civilian service, or orders of a certain degree won for meritorious service (known in those days as St. Stanislav, St. Anne, St. George, and so forth). From 1722, when the Table of Ranks was first established, until 1845, hereditary nobility could be acquired at lower ranks in both military and civilian service.[5]

Class restrictions were never placed on entrance into military service. It is true that entrance into state service was, as a general rule, restricted to the nobility, but anyone, regardless of his origin, automatically became eligible if he completed a course of higher education or graduated from a gymnasium with honors. The nobility was never, therefore, a closed caste, and the bureaucracy was not entirely under its domination. When all class restrictions for entering state service were abolished by the ukase of October 5, 1906, the ultimate extinction of the nobility as a class and the end of its virtual domination of the bureaucracy became certain.

The privileges enjoyed by the nobility in the period before the Great Reforms were, as has been said, considerable. The most important of them was the sole right to possess serfs, with the concomitant administrative and judicial powers on their own estates. In addition, the nobility was not subject to obligatory service, corporal punishment, and personal taxes. Two positive rights of great significance were their right to the unconditional ownership of property, and to the protection by law of their status, life, and property, which could be taken away from them only if they committed certain specified crimes and were tried in a court, and if the punishment meted out to them was confirmed by the Czar. The elected representatives of the nobility filled the most important positions in local administration assigned to the various estates under Catherine's reorganization of local government in 1775, and the system of justice was heavily weighted in their favor.

Although the privileges of the nobility were not morally justified, it is curious to note that they did represent a landmark in the development of Russian citizenship. Romanovich-Slavatinsky writes of Catherine's Charter of the Nobility:

For the first time, there appears in our state order, which rested on the assessments and duties to the state of our social classes, a class of people whose personal rights are recognized and guaranteed by law. For the first time, there appears in our society a person and not a bondsman [kholop], a person whom it is impossible to subject to punishment without court proceedings, whom a court may not subject to corporal punishment, from whom it is impossible to take away, without court proceedings, property unconditionally in his possession.[6]

The conception of personal rights for the nobility, the very term (lichnyia preimushchestva), was introduced into Russian legislation by the Charter of the Nobility. Property, until then held as a condition of state service, came into the complete possession of the owner, who could now exploit its timber and subsoil minerals without interference by the state. It was desirable, therefore, not that these rights be taken away from the nobility, but that they be extended to all other classes. For reasons already explained, virtually every reform (with the exception of certain futile "palliative" measures adopted during the reigns of Alexander III and Nicholas II) from the 1860's on moved inexorably in that direction. Along with the steady reduction in the privileges, personal and group, of the nobility and of other privileged classes, a strong trend toward the extinction of the class principle in Russian public life was observable.

The emancipation of the serfs in 1861 was a necessary first step.

There followed, in 1864, a reorganization of the local government under which Crown officials, with some exceptions, replaced elected class representatives in local administration and all-class units of self-government were established in town and country. The judicial reform of 1864 proclaimed the principle of equality before the law for all citizens, and the class peculiarities of the old courts, while not completely destroyed, were limited to a few minor details.[7] The juries that sat in criminal cases after 1864 were all-class juries, and it was possible for former serfs to sit on a jury with their one-time masters.[8]

The main privileges left to the nobility and other privileged groups after the era of the Great Reforms were based on the distinction made in the law between the taxable and nontaxable classes, a distinction introduced at the beginning of the eighteenth century with the establishment by Peter the Great of a poll tax, i.e., a direct tax on individual heads. A small, privileged group, including the nobility, was exempt from the payment of this tax. But the differences between the two groups were not based solely on the payment or nonpayment of the tax. The nontaxable classes were also exempt from military service and corporal punishment. Neither of these exemptions should be underestimated. Military service lasted for twenty-five years and was generally considered equivalent to hard labor. Corporal punishment involved the use of the rod and, until 1845, of the knout. If the Russian penal system could be called mild in the last fifty years of the Empire, it was only because corporal punishment had been abolished as a general punitive measure in 1863.

The significance of these privileges is further underscored by an examination of the position in which the members of the taxable classes, principally the peasants and the small tradesmen and artisans of the towns, had been placed. In levying the poll tax, in conscripting recruits, and in exacting other less-important "natural obligations" from the taxable classes, the state placed the responsibility for the proper fulfillment of these obligations not on individual persons, but on the class societies to which they belonged. It was the peasant commune, not the individual peasant, that paid the poll taxes and redemption taxes to the state, and in order to guarantee to the commune the possibility of exacting the taxes from its peasant members, the law granted to it broad powers of control over these members. Members of a taxable society, whether peasant or burgher, could not withdraw without the permission of the society; they could not even travel to another city or district without permission. On the other hand, there were no restrictions on the freedom of movement of the nobility and other privileged classes, who received passports valid for an indefinite period. From a person not a member of the privileged classes who did not belong to a taxable society, the law demanded that he "choose his way of life," i.e., that he find a taxable society, peasant or burgher, that would agree to accept him.

The privileges of the nobility in the period following the emancipation of the serfs were made up, in the main, of freedom from these limitations on the taxable classes. To these privileges should be added their legal preference in the state service. It is a striking fact that little more than fifty-five years after the emancipation, the limitations imposed on the taxable classes had been largely removed and that the distinctions between the taxable and privileged classes had virtually disappeared. Although corporal punishment was abolished as a general punitive measure in 1863, peasant courts retained the right to administer corporal punishment for minor offenses until 1904. In 1874, the recruiting system was reorganized and universal military service for a term of six years was imposed equally on all classes of the population. The obligation for service was borne directly by the individual and was no longer a joint responsibility of any class society. The poll tax was abolished for the burghers (*meshchane*) in 1866, for the majority of the peasants in 1885, and for the remainder of the peasants in 1906. Joint responsibility for taxes and other public obligations was abolished for the majority of the peasants by 1903, for the remainder by 1906. The ukase of October 5, 1906, granted to the "former taxable classes" the same passport rights and freedom of movement formerly enjoyed only by the privileged classes. It also abolished all class restrictions on entering state service, and, in general, eliminated all the onerous controls exercised by the taxable class societies over their members. The ukase, too, by permitting the peasants and burghers to remain members of their class societies while they were acquiring the rights of a higher class, virtually removed all meaning from the existing class order.[9]

However, the distinction between the former taxable classes and the privileged classes was not entirely removed. The members of the former taxable classes were still personally responsible for compulsory work in the public interest in extraordinary circumstances, e.g., a railroad accident or snowdrifts on the roads or a forest fire. Some differences in punishment for the same crime likewise remained between those formerly subject to corporal punishment and those exempt, even though corporal punishment itself was abolished. As for the privileges of the nobility itself (as distinct from the privileges of the nontaxable classes, which included groups other than the nobility), they were now limited to such matters as the right to establish entailed estates, the right to mortgage property in the Noble Land Bank, a predominance guaranteed by law in elections to the zemstvos, the right to occupy the position of land captain, and an active participation in local administration through the Marshals of the Nobility.

Since the reforms affecting the class order were made from above and by evolution rather than revolution, it is characteristic that the structure of the class order was retained in the law even though it had lost its meaning and only remnants of the former privileges and obligations of the various classes remained. It is characteristic, too, that a century of belief in hereditary class distinctions had left its mark on some segments of society and that time was required to enable the manners and morals of those segments to catch up with the law. On the whole, however, it may be said that educational and property qualifications influenced the status of any given person in the last years of the Empire far more than did his class origin. Hereditary class distinctions could find no firm root in the Russian social traditions, and there can be no doubt that Russia was moving inexorably toward civil equality and the virtually complete extinction of the nobility as a class.[10]

The Nobility: Economic Decline

Partially influencing both the legal and the social status of the nobility and its political significance was the steady decline of that class as landowners and, in general, as an economic force within the country from the time of the emancipation to 1917. Unlike the British and German gentry, who prolonged their influence by retaining their land and becoming first-rate farmers, the Russian gentry unquestionably hastened its decline by displaying no serious interest in agriculture and scientific farming and by losing its land holdings at a steady rate.

The causes are not difficult to discern; they arose from the tradition of the nobility as a service class not firmly attached to the land in any locality. Another contributing factor was the custom of dividing the land equally among the male heirs. Before the eighteenth century, the landed gentry were necessarily "temporary guests" on their estates, until called to military service. After their release from obligatory service, they continued to be more impressed by the advantages of a higher rank in service than by the advantages of successfully cultivating their estates. In sharp contrast, therefore, to the landed gentry of the West, the Russian nobility took no interest either in the land or in the locality in which it was located, and absentee landlordism was fashionable for those who could afford it. So little did the nobles value the land that, in the era of serfdom, the value of an estate was determined not by its size but by the number of serfs on it. Such capital as they possessed was wasted, sometimes on senseless luxuries, instead of being applied to the land, which they failed to realize had become an important foundation of their power. Estates that remained in the hands of one family through several generations were rare, for in the absence of primogeniture, the retention of an estate by a family, so typical of the Western landed aristocracies, was virtually impossible in Russia. In any case, the Russian pomeshchiks (i.e., landowners, from *pomestie,* the name of the estate awarded to the nobility for military service), often did not value their family estates particularly and readily sold them. There were, of course, some exceptions, principally, according to Romanovich-Slavatinsky, among those aristocratic families that sought to imitate the methods of Western aristocracies. The average holdings of the pomeshchiks were steadily declining.[11] (The huge estates with hundreds of thousands of serfs, which sometimes astonished foreigners before 1861, had not been zealously built up through several generations, but rather had been granted by the Czar in the eighteenth century.)

When the serfs were emancipated, the nobles were not prepared to cope with the vast new problems that now faced them. Their debts, already heavy, continued to mount, and their land began to pass into the hands of others better able to utilize it. The nobles had 78 million dessiatines in their possession after the emancipation; in 1906, only 52 million were left, a loss of about one third of their holdings in forty years, with most of the loss taking place after 1877.[12] Although no definitive figures are available for the period after 1905, the frightened gentry was known to have been disposing

of its land at an even faster rate after the agrarian disturbances of
1905–6.[13]

The importance of the social and economic decline of the nobility should not be underestimated. The autocracy was confronted by
a situation that could not help but alarm its partisans; the most
solid citizens of the Empire, upon whose support the regime could
formerly rely unquestionably, were in irretrievable decay. They
were losing their social status and their economic power, and a good
part of them were merging with the growing intelligentsia, who had
no stake in the existing order and whose oppositional tendencies
had been manifest for some time. When the trend became clearly
evident in the 1880's, a debate arose as to what was to be done, and
those reactionary bureaucrats and nobles who believed that a return
to the past should be undertaken had their way. In an atmosphere
of general political reaction, a series of measures was adopted between 1885 and 1904 designed to restore the class principle to Russian life.

It is indicative of the extent to which the privileged position of
the nobility had deteriorated that four of the five privileges retained
by the nobility after 1906 were granted at this time, and that the
fifth (the active participation of Marshals of the Nobility in local
administration) was greatly strengthened because of the necessity of
creating new local institutions. On the economic front, a Noble
Land Bank was created in 1885 to furnish the hard-pressed gentry
with cheap credit; the policies of the bank were so liberal that it became, in effect, a device for subsidizing the gentry.[14] All the palliative measures adopted were, of course, insufficient to halt a trend so
deeply rooted in the life of the people, and, by obscuring the real
reform needs of the Empire, the government was in effect laying the
foundation for its later downfall. The disintegration of the nobility
went on, and, as we shall see, the government succeeded only in temporarily postponing the fundamental question of what elements of
the population could be counted upon to furnish support for the
existing order.

The Peasants: Legal Status

The very nature of Russian society led the reactionaries, including the Czar and the Czarina, to pin their hopes on the peasantry,
and in view of the undoubted popularity of the Czar among the

peasantry, their hopes had some foundation. Yet, in judging the mood of the peasants in the manner of Pobedonostsev,[15] the reactionaries completely misinterpreted their needs and delayed—as it proved, fatally—the measures necessary to transform them into a bulwark of the state. Only after the Revolution of 1905, when some hard lessons were driven home and a minister of the stature and authority of Stolypin appeared on the scene, were effective measures taken, but by then time had almost run out. Although the Stolypin land reforms were opposed for various reasons by a large segment of Russian society, there is now overwhelming evidence that they were the proper reforms for Russia, which, if given time to become consolidated, would have made Russia a more stable and prosperous state. It is important, therefore, in discussing the peasants to find out exactly what the situation was that the Stolypin reforms were designed to remedy. Without such clarification, neither the agrarian problem in Russia nor the subsequent revolution can be understood.

Western Europe—France and Germany, for example—affords illustrations of peasants who, as a group, were and are conservative. But the Russian peasants were a chronically dissatisfied element in the population who had borne the heaviest share of the obligations placed by the state on its citizens and who, more than any other class, had been subjected to centuries of arbitrary and lawless rule. The converse side of this situation was the peasants' tendency to break out into violent and destructive disorders, which could be put down only with the sharpest punitive measures. Although a professional revolutionary like Lenin could applaud this situation, it is clearly not a healthy one for any state. The peasant disorders could have had no constructive end, and they solved no problems, not even the peasants' economic problems. Ultimately force had to be applied and maintained to restore and keep order. The revolt led by Stenka Razin in the seventeenth century, the Pugachev rebellion in the eighteenth century, and the agrarian disorders of 1905–6 and 1917 were essentially alike in their origins and could have only one outcome: lawless and destructive anarchy rather than a healthy democratic state.

The problem for Russia, therefore, was to convert the peasants into responsible and mature citizens, endowed with rights that they could cherish for themselves and for others, respectful of the law, and capable of active participation in a sound and democratic government. At the same time, it was necessary to solve the agrarian problem, and this could only be done by the creation of conditions favorable to the introduction of advanced and scientific farming, and not, as the peasants thought, through the seizure of their former masters' land. The emancipation of the serfs was only the first step in the right direction. For 100 years, half the peasant population had been the personal property of their noble masters, without rights, without even any direct relation to the state. For centuries before that, they had, through an evolutionary process, been converted from relatively free and equal citizens into virtual slaves of their masters. The emancipation could not, in one stroke, wipe out the effects of their past. Partly because of the fiscal needs of the state, partly because the liberal designers of the reform feared that the peasants would again fall under pomeshchik influence, and partly because the adjustment of the actual conditions of peasant life to the general civil laws required considerable time and effort, the peasants remained a distinct group with their own institutions, their own continuing heavy obligations to the state, and a new form of outside tutelage. They were governed by their own special laws and customs and were isolated from daily contact with other classes and groups. In effect, they remained second-class citizens until 1906, with heavier obligations and less freedom than other citizens. The problem of the peasants was both a legal and an economic one.

The land received by the peasant as a result of the act of emancipation did not become his personal property but the property of the commune to which he belonged. The peasant was entitled to cultivate an equal share of the land, and the equality of his share could be maintained in most communes by periodic redistribution, based, for the most part, either on the total membership of the peasant household or on the number of its male workers. The commune was, in turn, jointly responsible to the state for the payment of the taxes of its members and the discharge of other obligations. The obligations of the commune to the state after the emancipation included redemption dues, i.e., yearly payments to be made over a forty-nine-year period covering the cost to the state of the act of emancipation. Since the burden of the redemption payments was very heavy—in the beginning payments exceeded the income that could be derived from the land—and since the peasant might find it more profitable to renounce his land and leave the commune rather than stay and attempt to meet the payments, the commune was given broad powers of control over its individual members. The conditions under which a peasant could leave the commune were so restrictive that they could rarely be met; and even if they could be met, the commune authorities, and in most cases the provincial authorities, could refuse permission to leave. In effect, therefore, the peasant, until October 5, 1906, remained attached to the land.[16]

The control of the commune extended also to actions of the peasant that might lead to his acquisition of a higher status and, therefore, to his automatic exclusion from the commune. Consequently, before a peasant could enter state service, enter a monastery, take an ecclesiastical position, or enter an educational institution,[17] he likewise required the permission of the commune. Also at the discretion of the commune was the right of the peasant to a passport to leave the district in which the commune was located. Apart from any difficulties he might have with the commune or with the police over arrears in taxes or redemption payments, a peasant could be recalled at any time at the demand of the head of the household or upon election to a post in peasant administration. At times, the recalls were not meant as such, the real purpose being the desire of the head of the household or the commune to extort "excess" earnings from the peasant. Most of these restrictions, as has already been pointed out, ended with the promulgation of the ukase of October 5, 1906, by the Stolypin government. (Redemption payments were reduced in various stages beginning in 1881, and were finally canceled outright, starting January 1, 1907, by the ukase of November 3, 1905.) The granting of equal rights to the peasants was one phase of Stolypin's program of converting the peasantry from an elemental and revolutionary force into a conservative bulwark of the state.

The subjection of the peasants to discretionary and arbitrary rule was not confined to the limitations placed upon their personal liberties by the system of joint responsibility (*krugovaia poruka*). They were, in addition, organized into local class units—in theory self-governing, in practice without any independence whatsoever. Peasant institutions were of two kinds: the commune, which was primarily an economic unit; and the volost, which was primarily an administrative unit composed of one or more villages.[18] The commune made decisions on a wide variety of matters of common interest, including the distribution of taxes and other obligations to the state, the redistribution of the land, and the cultivation of the soil.

The result was that the initiative of the individual peasant was hobbled and he was subject to extortion and other forms of arbitrary action by the village assembly. The volost, an administrative unit created after the emancipation, despite its self-governing features, became in effect part of the Crown administration and performed state functions of no interest to the peasant.[19] Government supervision of peasant institutions, quite extensive from the very beginning, was drastically increased in a manner reminiscent of the days of serfdom by the creation of the office of land captain (*zemsky nachalnik*) in 1889. The land captains were local landowning nobles, appointed by the Minister of the Interior. They were endowed with administrative and judicial powers that placed the peasants at their mercy, since the punishments they could inflict were not subject to appeal. Thereafter, the last vestiges of peasant self-government disappeared, and the affairs of the peasants subject to their self-governing institutions (including land rights enjoyed by individual peasants) were managed in a manner satisfactory to the government.[20]

A noteworthy feature of this system of self-government was the physical isolation it enforced on the peasants. Only communal allotment lands were subject to the jurisdiction of the volost. Other private property within the vicinity of the volost was outside its control, and such property owners took no direct part in the affairs of the volost administration. Within the peasant class itself, those peasants who managed to get through secondary school or a university were entitled to the rights of a higher status and, until 1906, were automatically excluded from the peasant societies and deprived of their allotment land, thus perpetuating the low cultural level of the peasant class. There is little doubt that, in the West, the advance of democracy was made possible by the opportunities given the lower classes to observe and imitate the upper classes. In Russia, this possibility was killed by the pseudo system of self-government set up after the emancipation, which confined most peasants to their own world, cut off in the main from outside stimuli that could have helped dissipate an outlook conditioned by centuries of bondage.[21] Finally, it should be noted that the peasant institutions were performing general state functions in behalf of the entire local community and that these functions were supported by taxation imposed on the peasants alone.

Besides being isolated in their own governmental institutions and subject to the virtually unlimited discretionary authority of the commune, the peasant officials, and the administration, the peasants did not enjoy civil rights similar to other citizens and were, in general, excluded from the operation of the civil laws of the Empire codified in Part 1, Volume X of the *Svod zakonov*. Partly through the specific terms of government statutes and partly through extensive decisions of the Senate, the peasants were, in their relations among themselves, governed instead by custom. While the peasants were endowed with land by the Statute of Emancipation, they were not free to dispose of it as they wished; the commune, not the individual peasant, was the legal owner of allotment land.[22] To the difficulties thereby created in the transfer of the land others were later added by the law of December 14, 1893. Even if a peasant's allotment land was fully redeemed, he could sell it only to another peasant. By a series of Senate decisions, allotment land was construed to include the remainder of the peasant's property necessary to cultivate the land, including buildings, agricultural implements, and livestock. The holder of the limited rights to allotment land was not an individual peasant but a peasant household (*krestianskii dvor*). The complex families that usually constituted a household cultivated the land in common and held their property in common under the direction of the head of the family, who also controlled the movement of individual members. Upon the death of the head of the household, a new head took his place. Since there was no single holder of allotment land, there was, by Senate interpretation, no right of bequeathing or inheriting the land. The word inheritance (*nasledovanie*) could be used among peasants who held no property other than allotment land and its accessories (i.e., among the vast majority of them) only in the sense of a family division (*razdel*), i.e., a decision on the part of one or more members of the family to establish a separate household. It is indicative of the callous determination of the administration to halt individualistic trends that, between 1886 and 1906, such divisions of family property could take place only with the agreement of two thirds of the village assembly, which could normally act only with the approval of the head of the family. Nevertheless, family divisions, which had been increasing steadily from the time of the emancipation, continued to take place on a large scale, the vast majority of them in violation of the law.[23]

As has been pointed out, in their relations with one another, the peasants were governed not by the civil laws of the Empire applicable to all other classes, but by the unwritten law of custom. Although there were some ardent defenders of the peasant law of custom, most Russian jurists were agreed that, apart from peasant practices concerning the household and inheritance, peasant customs varied greatly from locality to locality; there was no advanced uniformity of custom that could merit the designation of "law." Since the circumstances of peasant life were such that the civil laws were not applicable to them, and since adequate separate legislative norms were not established, much of peasant civil life was in a state of complete anarchy, subject to the whims of the commune, the volost courts, and the administration.

Like the other peasant institutions, their class courts—the volost courts—were established by the authors of the emancipation to protect them from unfavorable outside influence, in this case that of the corrupt prereform courts, which were not reorganized until 1864. The courts were to be readily accessible to the peasants and were to be composed of their own elected representatives, who were familiar with, and were to apply, local peasant customs. After a period of transition, it was intended that the class character of the courts should be ended and that they should be fused with the general judicial system. However, in 1889, the volost courts were reorganized in the opposite direction, so that their disadvantages were enormously multiplied and such advantages as they had had were lost. The judges (four in number) were appointed by the land captains (from among eight candidates elected by the village assemblies) and were subject to their disciplinary power without formal procedure. The jurisdiction of the volost courts was widened to include almost all disputes arising between peasants, thus forcing the peasants almost entirely out of the general courts. The field of legal relations regulated by unwritten law, i.e., by custom, was also expanded. The types of criminal offenses subject to the jurisdiction of the courts were increased, as was the sphere of application of corporal punishment. As before, the peasants could be punished for acts not treated as crimes for other classes and not included in the penal code.[24] This situation, in which peasants were tried for almost all civil cases and for minor criminal cases by other impoverished and ignorant peasants completely under the thumb of the land captains and without the guidance of written law, continued without major change until the reorganization of the local courts in

1912 (law of June 15), when the volost courts were substantially improved but not eliminated.[25]

The Peasants: Economic Problems

The economic problem of the peasants need not detain us long. It has been treated in various English-language studies;[26] furthermore, it was not specifically a Russian problem, but one applicable to any country in which scattered strips and communal land tenure had survived. The main difficulty with Russian agriculture was the inability of the peasants to cultivate their holdings more intensively, and significant progress in that direction could not be made so long as these holdings were divided into scattered strips and the methods and timing of cultivation remained under the control of the commune. The strips of land allotted to the individual peasant by the commune were both narrow and scattered, and all were compelled to cultivate the land in the same way and at the same time. The result under these circumstances, both in Russia and, earlier, in Western Europe, was the compulsory rotation of crops—a system from which no deviation was possible. About one third of the land was allowed to lie fallow at any given time. If an individual peasant became aware of the value of a greater diversification of crops and a more complex rotation (the three-field system was most commonly in use), he was nevertheless powerless to change the prevailing methods. The use of machinery on the narrow strips was out of the question. In those communes in which the strips were subject to periodic redistribution, the possibility that they would be assigned to someone else discouraged any attempt to improve them. Expensive improvements were, in any case, limited by the lack of capital. There was no room, in general, for individual initiative, and without individual initiative, technical progress was bound to be limited.

The problem posed by primitive methods of cultivation and poor productivity was enormously intensified by the very rapid growth of the peasant population in the latter half of the nineteenth century. Here, too, the role of the commune was unfortunate, for in those communes in which periodic redistribution was the rule,[27] and particularly in the black-earth zones, where the soil was naturally fertile, raising a large family seemed advantageous to the peasant, because he thus became entitled to a larger share of the communal allotment. It was, in fact, in the black-earth zones where the repartitional commune was prevalent that the rate of growth of the population was fastest.

The Russian peasants were not, of course, familiar with the problems of intensive and extensive cultivation. The way out of their impossible situation they could find only in the acquisition of more land. Furthermore, the tradition of serfdom, the manner of the serfs' emancipation in 1861, and the maintenance of remnants of serfdom after the emancipation strengthened the peasants in their belief that they had a right to the land of their former masters. For obvious tactical reasons, the revolutionary and liberal opposition to the autocracy accepted the peasant view that land would solve the agrarian problem, and, in one form or another, the opposition demanded that all private property be expropriated and distributed to the peasants.[28] Since the Russian agrarian problem is paralleled in many other countries, and since easy solutions have been and still are being offered, it is especially worthy of note that the weight of the evidence does not support the peasants' approach to the solution to the agrarian problem. There is hardly a writer dealing with Russian agriculture who has failed to point out that the average allotment given the peasants by the Act of Emancipation far exceeded the average holding of the peasants in Western Europe. Yet the smaller holdings of Western, Europe yielded much more produce than did the larger Russian allotments.[29] There was not enough land to solve the agrarian problem with the existing methods of cultivation, and, even if there had been, the high birth rate would have created a new crisis within a short time.[30] Furthermore, the expropriation of such successfully run large estates as there were would have damaged the national economy and lowered the standard of living of the peasants themselves, because those estates were a significant source of agricultural products for the domestic and foreign market.[31] Finally, another consequence of the equal division of all private land among the peasants would have been to strip Russian industry of its workers, thus handicapping its development and depriving agriculture of the lucrative urban market necessary for its prosperity.[32] As we shall see presently, most of the Russian workers were peasants who retained their ties with the land and moved to the cities only because they could not earn their subsistence from the land.

In any case, it is important to note that the problem of providing more land for the peasants was steadily declining in importance. It was they who were the most persistent buyers of the land being sold so rapidly by the nobles. Definitive figures on landholding are not available for the period from 1906 to 1917, but if the estimates made by Antsiferov are even approximately correct, on January 1, 1917, the situation in the fifty provinces of European Russia was as follows: 47 per cent of all the land suitable for cultivation (including forests) was in the hands of the peasants; if the forest lands are subtracted, so that the holdings of the peasants are expressed as a proportion of all the land actually under cultivation, the percentage in their hands rises to 82; if account is taken of the fact that the peasants were already renting a good part of the privately held nonallotment land, then the amount of new acreage that actually passed into their hands in 1917 was exceedingly small.[33] Even if these figures are only estimates (and they are probably accurate), the general trend was unmistakable: Privately held nonallotment land was passing into the hands of the peasants by peaceful means. If the privileges granted by the government to the nobility enabling them to hold their land had been withdrawn, and if the government had adopted a more vigorous policy in favor of the peasants, there seems no reason to doubt that the transfer of the land could have been completed peacefully within a relatively short time and without the senseless destruction that took place in 1917.

The Stolypin Reforms

After the emancipation of the serfs, the prosperity of the Russian Empire depended on the successful assumption by the peasants of the economic role formerly played by the nobility. The political stability of the Empire depended upon the emergence of a free, equal, and prosperous class of peasant landowners, who, as in the West, could be expected to become conservative supporters of the state. The circumstances under which the peasants were emancipated did not, however, assure the Empire of either economic prosperity or political stability. The peasants were left as an isolated and inferior class, a kind of "state within a state," doomed to virtual cultural and economic stagnation. They continued to perform the same obligations for the state that they had performed as serfs, they could not own property as did other classes, they were excluded from the operation of the laws of the Empire applicable to all other classes, and they were subjected to arbitrary interference on the part of the administrative authorities and the communes into virtually every phase of their lives. Their energies were directed, in the main, toward a grim struggle for mere subsistence, and they remained, as before, a potentially revolutionary force, incapable on the whole of playing a responsible and constructive part in Russian public life.

There is no doubt that the authors of the emancipation wanted the peasants to become free citizens and wanted to confine the disadvantages they suffered to a temporary period. But after the assassination of Alexander II, reactionary influence at the court prevailed, and, instead of proceeding with the completion of the reform, Alexander III retreated from its basic principles. In the disabilities of the peasants, the reactionaries saw not a danger to the state, but the essential foundation of the absolutism of the Czar. They sought, in effect, to stop the course of history and to restore to Russia the patriarchal class society that they regarded as essential for a flourishing autocracy. They counted on the unqualified support of a primitive, insulated, bureaucratically dominated peasantry, uncontaminated by excessive education and sophistication. The warning provided by the famine of 1891 went unheeded. The urgent pleas of Witte, who alone among the ministers recognized the real extent of the danger, likewise went unheeded.[34] The final and complete collapse of the fantasies on which government policy was based did not come until 1906, when the violent peasant disorders inspired a sense of direct physical fear and when the elections to the First Duma revealed that the peasants were not, after all, unqualified supporters of the autocracy. It was then that P. A. Stolypin was appointed Prime Minister. He not only understood the situation clearly, but also recognized the extreme urgency that decades of delay had created and had the vision to undertake a thoroughgoing reorganization of peasant life.

In seeking to liberate the peasants from the control of the commune, Stolypin's objectives were both political and economic. Both these objectives were symbolized in his famous statement to the Third Duma that the government "has placed its stake not on the beggarly and the drunk, but on the sturdy and the strong." Regardless of what one may think of Stolypin's politics or of the ultimate solution to the agrarian problem, it seems hardly open to question that the dissolution of the commune was an essential next step for Russia. The commune was not unique to Russia; it had been well known in Western Europe when it, too, was still a primitive agrarian society in which the dominant problem was to insure a liveli-hood for all. In an expanding exchange economy, it was essential not only that the initiative of the individual peasant be released, but that the land be placed in the hands of those best able to use it.[35] On the legal side, it was plainly necessary that the peasants be freed from the tyranny of the bureaucracy and the commune and that they be given the elementary individual rights out of which could grow a respect for the law and a legal order. In his speeches to the Third Duma, Stolypin made it plain that he regarded the de-mand for constitutional guarantees of freedom as the demand of the upper classes only, a demand the peasants could not value so long as they remained slaves of the commune—ignorant, poverty-stricken, and without rights. He saw in the liquidation of the com-mune an indispensable prerequisite for the success of the Constitu-tion and for the salvation of Russia.[36]

Two laws issued under Article 87 of the new constitution contain the main elements of the Stolypin reforms. One, the ukase of Octo-ber 5, 1906, has already been discussed. The other, the ukase of November 9, 1906 (subsequently made permanent by the passage in both legislative houses of the laws of June 14, 1910 and May 29, 1911), has been extensively treated in English.[37] The ukase of No-vember 9 permitted an individual peasant to withdraw his allot-ment land from the commune with or without commune consent and to take permanent and hereditary title to it. The land became the property not of the peasant household, but of the head of the household, who could, if he wished, sell it to other peasants. The law also provided that a peasant who had acquired separate title to his land could at any time demand that his scattered strips be con-solidated in one place; again the commune was obliged to comply, whether it was in favor of consolidation or not. There were, there-fore, two major aspects to the Stolypin land laws. The peasant could acquire his strips of land as his private property and sell them, thus relieving him of the threat of periodic redistribution and en-abling him to part completely with both his land and the commune if he so desired. If he retained his land, he was still subject to the disadvantages of scattered-strip-farming and would be forced to co-operate with the commune in the old routines of tilling the soil. On the other hand, if he elected also to consolidate his holdings, he was emancipated from the commune economically.

From 1907 to the end of 1913, more than 2.5 million households applied for the withdrawal of their lands from the commune; the withdrawal was actually effected for 2 million households by January 1, 1916. Because of various other provisions for withdrawal, including the forced legal dissolution of communal tenure for whole communes, the number of households affected is estimated by Robinson to have exceeded 4.3 million.[38] By the end of 1916, approximately 1.3 million peasant households holding allotment land—or approximately 10 per cent of the total number of such households—had been provided with consolidated holdings; millions more had made application for consolidation.[39] For both types of adjustments, the government Land Settlement Commissions received far more applications than they were able to process.

The Stolypin agrarian reforms were carried out against the opposition of a large part of Russian society. Among the main reasons for such opposition were partisan politics, the general custom of society to oppose any measure undertaken by the government, a predisposition in favor of the commune, and general ignorance of the nature of the agrarian problem. Although the reforms operated for too short a time to effect the overturn in the villages for which they were designed, the evidence indicates that they were proceeding satisfactorily and in time would have achieved their objectives. It is, of course, true that the law and its implementation by the Land Settlement Commissions exercised considerable pressure, direct and indirect, on the peasants to dissolve the communes and to consolidate, but the extent of the transformation made within ten years amid unusual calm and prosperity in the countryside indicates that the peasants were offering little or no resistance and that force alone cannot explain the success of the reforms.[40] The Russian peasants were at last moving along the path taken long before by their Western European counterparts, and the probabilities are that they would have duplicated both Western prosperity and Western conservatism. Had there been sufficient time for the reforms to become consolidated, it is probable that the radical revolution from the left could have been avoided. This, at any rate, was the opinion of the one man whose forecasts on the prospects of revolution in Russia it would be rash to question—V. I. Lenin.[41]

The Evolution of the Merchants and Industrialists

Although Russia was not at first affected by the spontaneous commercial and industrial revolutions that transformed the West, she did develop a considerable domestic and foreign trade, as well as a small merchant class with sufficient capital to carry on that trade. The merchants were not organized into corporations that could defend their interests, and they never became strong enough to displace the landowning nobility as the leading class. Like all other classes, they were subject to state service, their rank in service depending on the capitalization of their enterprises. The richest merchants, known as the *gosti* (literally, "guests"), were given the most responsible undertakings, with the capital of their own enterprises serving as security for the proper discharge of their responsibilities to the state treasury.[42] The merchants were not liberated from state service until the latter half of the eighteenth century; it was then, too, that Catherine II attempted to create a corporately organized, self-governing middle class in imitation of the middle class in the West, with the mournful results already noted.

The rank of the merchants was lower than that of the gentry in military service, and their privileges were not as great. When the poll tax was introduced at the beginning of the eighteenth century, the merchants were included in the taxable classes. However, as observation of the West led to an increasing awareness of the importance of the cities and the commercial classes in maintaining the power and prosperity of the state, the privileges of the richer merchants were increased. After 1785, the merchants of the first guild were provided with privileges similar to those of the nobility (but excluding, among other things, the right to own serfs).

By the beginning of the nineteenth century, the process of Westernization, speeded by Peter the Great, created an enormous cultural gap between the nobility and the peasants. During most of the nineteenth century, the merchants were closer to the peasants than to the nobility. For the most part, they were illiterate and could be distinguished in the cities by their peculiar, old-fashioned garb. They were poorly organized, docile in their relations with the central government, generally conservative politically, and did not aspire to play an important role in public life. After the emancipation of the serfs, their ranks were swelled by large numbers of former serfs who took advantage of the emancipation and the subsequent commercial expansion to become large-scale businessmen. Toward the close of the nineteenth century, a marked change became evident among the merchants as a group (excluding the small traders called the *meshchane*, who outnumbered the merchants). The new generation of merchants was Europeanized and educated;

the rapid growth of industry and commerce was making them richer, more influential, and more disposed to exercise their own initiative. Culturally, the merchants were merging with the intelligentsia and like the intelligentsia, the margin of their tolerance toward a bureaucratic-police order that was plainly both unjust and incompetent was steadily diminishing.[43] The new type of merchant is well symbolized by the well-known Octobrist leader A. I. Guchkov, the grandson of a serf and the son of a Moscow merchant.

The industrialists have a much shorter history in Russia than do the merchants, but their social, economic, cultural, and political development is similar. Many merchants later became factory owners, but the most powerful of the twentieth-century industrial magnates were the descendants of serfs who bought their way to freedom at the beginning of the nineteenth century and established advanced, machine-operated factories. As mentioned earlier, large-scale industry did not develop spontaneously from urban handicraft and small industries, as it did in the West. State initiative in the promotion of industry was great and received a considerable impetus at the beginning of the eighteenth century through the efforts of Peter the Great. Peter founded the factories required for the army and navy and turned many of them over to private entrepreneurs, or granted large subsidies to would-be entrepreneurs, providing them with tools and labor. Down through the nineteenth century, the development of Russian industry remained chiefly dependent on state orders and state subsidies. Clearly, the peasants were in no position to buy factory-made commodities on a large scale, but some industries (notably textiles, rubber goods, and other minor ones) were, to some extent, based on a domestic mass market. Beginning with the 1890's, a combination of favorable circumstances, including extensive state orders for railroads, the growth of the railroad network, a high protective tariff, and a great influx of foreign capital, led to the rapid development of Russian heavy industry, at a rate far surpassing the then-current rate in the West.[44] By 1914, within a period of less than twenty-four years, production of coal, pig iron, and steel had increased four to fivefold. Industrial organization and technique, while still relatively backward, were improving, and capital requirements, while still dependent on importation from abroad, were being met in an increasing degree from native resources. A good indication of the firm roots being acquired by Russian industry is the progress made under unfavorable conditions during World War I in the very industries that had been most backward: the machine tool, metalworking, and chemical industries. Left to their own resources by the War, Russian technicians succeeded in little more than a year's time (between the summer of 1915 to the end of 1916) in overcoming the munitions-supply problems of the Russian army and navy against odds immeasurably greater than those faced by the technicians of any other belligerent country.[45] Since prosperity in the countryside had also reached unparalleled heights in the period just before the war, the expectations were favorable, had there been no war and revolution, for the further expansion of Russian industry and for the final elimination of its dependence on government orders and the state of the harvest.

Like the merchants, the new generation of industrialists at the beginning of the twentieth century had been Europeanized and educated. Like the remainder of Russian society, their initiative was growing, and they were becoming increasingly critical of the autocracy. Formerly very submissive in their attitude toward the central government, they took a firm stand in favor of reform in 1904–5, and, in the constitutional era, supported the Octobrist and Cadet parties, later the Progressive Bloc.[46] Some industrialists contributed to the support of such opposition journals as Osvobozhdenie (Liberation), which was printed abroad and then smuggled into Russia between 1902 and 1905.[47] Oddly enough, some even supported the revolutionary parties, including the Bolsheviks.[48]

It is important to note that while the relationship between the commercial-industrial class and the government had been close, it was never close in the Western sense. The merchants and industrialists were not strong enough to displace the nobility as the dominant element in the government, and Russia was not, therefore, destined to go through the laissez-faire stage. The callousness exhibited by the majority of the British industrialists and by the British government toward the brutal exploitation of the workers at the beginning of the nineteenth century had no precise parallel in Russia. There the landowning nobility, like the landed aristocracies of the West, had a tradition of protectiveness toward the lower classes that was never shared by the Western middle classes, with the result that the state stepped in to protect the Russian workers in ways unknown to the former laissez-faire states of the West.[49] In this respect, Czarist Russia and Imperial Germany were alike; neither had a strong middle class that became politically dominant, and both retained strong traditions of state intervention in social and economic affairs.

The whole history of labor legislation and of the labor problem in Russia is marked by constant clashes between the government and the industrialists, although the Social Democratic writers who predominate in this field have done their best to obscure the significance of these clashes. Workers' disorders, common in Russia from the 1880's on, were a great danger to the autocracy; it was necessary, somehow, to stop them. Although it is true that the government preferred not to encourage illegal strikes by making concessions to the workers, and bloody repression was not infrequent, in the long run it did not matter to the police-minded officials of the Ministry of the Interior at whose expense the disorders were stopped. Nor was the government so blinded by middle-class interests and prejudices that it could not see the desperate position of the workers and the need to improve it, if the strikes and disorders were to be stopped. Factory legislation in Russia, developed relatively slowly because of the administration's belief that there was no labor problem in Russia, but by 1912 it had achieved impressive proportions and was inspired by police considerations.

The point is further illustrated by the Czarist government's experiment with "police socialism." Although unions were forbidden by law, some unions were organized in the larger cities at the beginning of the twentieth century under the tutelage of the Okhrana for the purpose of competing with the revolutionary parties in winning the allegiance of the workers. They were not company unions; the police was concerned not with the economic interests of the industrialists but with the political interests of the autocracy, and it encouraged the workers to demand better working conditions from their employers. The industrialists, needless to say, bitterly denounced the police unions. In thus parting with the autocracy, the industrialists were not parting with a government that unfailingly protected their interests. It was a government that stood apart from both capital and labor, concerned in the main with perpetuating itself.

The Workers

Since Russian industry did not develop organically from the small industry and handicraft in the cities (much of the handicraft was carried on in the villages by the peasant), it had to recruit most of its labor from the peasants. It is a point too frequently overlooked that, until 1917, the overwhelming majority of the workers remained peasants, registered as such in a village society, and possessors of allotment land. Not free to sever their ties with the village and reside permanently in the cities until 1906, they did not, in any case, understand the advantages of city life and came to work in the cities only out of dire necessity. A significant part of them remained seasonal workers, returning to the land for field work during the harvest season. Another part, apparently the majority, remained in the cities the year round, but left their families behind in the village and sent them part of their wages. Only a small minority had completely severed their ties with the land and lived permanently with their families in the cities.

Only a brief description of the future "rulers" of Russia can be given here.[50] Those among them who returned to their communes for field work were unskilled laborers, not tied to any single industry. Upon getting their passports each year and setting out for the cities, they did not necessarily return either to the factory or the industry in which they had worked the year before. On the whole, the Russian workers did not work in the factories willingly, and they were more interested in their land than in the machines. As a general rule, their wives and children remained behind in the commune, cultivating the family land. Even if the wives did join their husbands in the cities, they frequently returned to the commune when pregnant, and the children remained there until old enough to work. Wages were very low, particularly in the winter; the average wage of the workers was not high enough to support a family in the city. Productivity was also low. Russian workers were unorganized and virtually at the mercy of their employers. Many of the factories were built outside city limits, and the workers lived in crowded, poorly equipped barracks provided by the employers. In the cities, there was an acute housing shortage, and the workers often could not rent more than a corner of a room. In isolated communities, the factory owners had to provide living quarters, schools, hospitals, churches, playgrounds, and other facilities on factory grounds.

Although Russia was changing rapidly in the years before the Revolution, the Russian workers were still quite different from their Western European counterparts, whom they could match neither in organization, cultural level, material wealth, nor influence. Lacking these gains, they lacked also the latter's growing interest in evolution rather than revolution. Like the peasants, they were excellent material for the spread of the most irresponsible demagogy. Since the government did not permit political agitation among the workers, the underground Social Democratic organizations acquired a virtual monopoly in the dissemination of political propaganda among them. Beginning with the last decade of the nineteenth century, the Marxist-Leninist message that political freedom and parliamentarism were bourgeois prejudices, and that the workers were to become a new, privileged ruling class, was spread among the Russian workers by enthusiastic and self-sacrificing youths who had been won over to social democracy. These ideas, although unrealistic in the advanced capitalist countries in which they arose, did at least make a certain amount of sense at a time when it was becoming increasingly clear that freedom was not enough. In Russia, however, where the first essential for a sound future development was the release of the energies of society from oppressive controls by the state, and where the workers were a small, primitive, semi-peasant group incapable of managing their own affairs, much less those of the entire state, these ideas were utterly ridiculous and were bound to cause great harm. Their acceptance by even a part of the intelligentsia is indicative of the unhealthy position into which the autocracy had forced that emerging group.

From the point of view of those interested in revolution at any price and under any circumstances, these ideas did, of course, prove their ultimate value. Even before the advent of Marxism, the Russian workers proved susceptible to chaotic mass action. What, after all, did they have to lose through a general strike, when most of them had no families in the cities to be concerned about, and risked no material comforts? They were, in addition, bound to be captivated by the idea that they were a privileged class, the only group capable of ruling the state. Egged on by Social Democratic agitators, they proved to be lacking in any sense of responsibility, any understanding of the rights of others, any conception of self-imposed discipline; and no government, whatever its ideology, could, in the long run, accede to all their demands. Like the peasant disorders, factory disorders, once set in motion and left to run their course, could lead only to anarchy and destruction. In the end, order would have to be restored by force and the problem of converting the workers into responsible citizens with respect for the law and a stake in a stable government would remain, handicapped by the loss of ruined plant facilities and murdered technical personnel.

The Intelligentsia

By far the most important group in Russian society from the political point of view was the intelligentsia, a group of diverse origin not easily classifiable under the system of legal classes. The appearance on the scene in the nineteenth century—for the first time in Russian history—of a class engaged in intellectual professions was to have momentous political consequences. Its appearance was, of course, conditioned by the systematic dissemination of lay education begun during the reign of Peter the Great. If Russia, prior to the nineteenth century, failed to produce giants in the fields of literature, the arts, and the sciences, it was only because she did not possess a sizable, well-educated group permanently devoted to intellectual pursuits.

Once the dissemination of lay education had begun, there was no turning back, despite its obvious dangers to the autocracy. The government might seek to control education and frequently to limit access to it for the lower classes, but it could not check its advance without committing national suicide. At all levels—higher, intermediate, and elementary—Russian education made significant progress in the nineteenth and early twentieth centuries. After the Revolution of 1905, a series of laws was passed providing for the gradual introduction of universal primary education. The attempt to limit the access of the lower classes to education, never entirely effective in the first place, was breaking down, like the old system of legal classes itself, and, by 1914, the children of the gentry and of government officials were in a minority even in the universities.[51] Census figures show that 27.8 per cent of all inhabitants of the Empire above the age of ten were literate in 1897; that figure has been estimated to have increased to 40.2 per cent by 1914.[52] It should not be overlooked that the remarkable aptitude for education shown by peasant children was a significant factor in this achievement.

The Russian word "intelligentsia" came into use for the first time in the 1860's, and not without good cause, for the modernization of

Russian life in the era of the Great Reforms gave considerable impetus to the development of the intellectual professions—journalism, teaching, medicine, the law, engineering, etc. The definition of the word varied with the definer, but most commonly it referred to the educated opposition to the autocracy, a politically-minded group with liberal or revolutionary views devoted to the interests of the people rather than those of their own class. In its social composition, the intelligentsia consisted of two main groups, the *raznochintsi* (literally, "men of mixed ranks") and the nobility. *Raznochintsi* originally was a legal term used to designate those who did not belong to any of the legal classes. In popular usage, it referred to an educated person who did not belong to the traditional social groups (e.g., the landowning nobility, the bureaucracy, the clergy, the peasantry, or the merchants; most, if not all, could end their nonclass status by becoming honorary citizens). The *raznochintsi* consisted of sons of priests who did not want to remain in the Church, sons of small civil servants who did not want to enter state service, sons of merchants who had no desire to be merchants, sons of impoverished nobles, and peasants or *meshchane* who had received an education and were expelled from their respective class societies. As a result of the increasing democratization of the school system and the growth of the intellectual professions, the *raznochintsi* appeared on the scene in increasing numbers after the 1860's, and with their appearance, the intelligentsia as a group became much more radical than it had been in the generation before, when it consisted almost entirely of noblemen.

Although, in the present context, the intelligentsia refers to the educated, politically minded opposition to the autocracy, regardless of class status, it is apparent that the nobility constituted one of the most important social components of the intelligentsia. It was they who made up the majority of the students in the universities in the nineteenth century, and the students, as a group, were strongly opposed to the autocracy. It was the nobility, too, who, more than any other group, were streaming into the ranks of the newly opened professions, and the professional men, as a group, were likewise strongly opposed to the autocracy.[53] Unlike in the West, adherence to liberalism and radicalism in Russia was not determined by either class status or wealth; instead, the Russian followers of liberalism and radicalism were those most resistant to bureaucratic rule and most aware of its dangerous consequences for the Empire—in short, those who were best educated—and up to the twentieth century, that meant, above all, the nobility.

The intelligentsia became a permanent, self-perpetuating group in the second half of the eighteenth century with the appearance of such men as Novikov, Fonvizin, and Radishchev. Virtually all were landowning nobles, but their class interests were sacrificed to their ideals: the welfare and liberty of the Russian people.[54] The same is true of the Decembrists, who, in December, 1825, sought to stage a revolution; the political leaders of the generation of the 1830's and 1840's—men like Herzen, Ogarev, and Chaadaev—were also, with some exceptions (e.g., Belinsky), landowning nobles. The middle class (*raznochintsi*) became numerous in the 1860's, but swelling their ranks in espousing the radical doctrines of nihilism and populism was a large noble element, the "repentant" or "conscience-stricken" nobles. The idea became dominant among the latter in the 1860's and 1870's (it was present in more subdued form also among earlier generations of noblemen) that they had acquired their wealth and their privileges at the expense of the people and that the time had come to repay their debt to them. They therefore abandoned their wealth and social position and joined the famous "movement to the people." Conscience was undoubtedly a prominent motivating factor, but heroic self-denial on so large a scale was unquestionably influenced also by the progressive impoverishment of the nobility after the emancipation of the serfs.[55] Nevertheless, cases of wealthy nobles who distributed their land and money to the peasants and went to live among them were not "uncommon" in the era of the movement to the people.[56] Although no statistical studies are available, the number of such noblemen was unquestionably large. So, also, was the number of those who espoused radicalism in general.[57] The overwhelming majority of the nobility outside the bureaucracy was in the moderate opposition that demanded either more liberty and a voice in policy-making and administration, or the reorganization of the autocracy as a constitutional monarchy on Western European lines. Therefore, the reactionaries who placed their hopes on the maintenance of the class privileges of the nobility and on the maintenance of its class primacy could not have been more blind; not only was the nobility in irretrievable social and economic decay, but it was also the natural source of the leadership of the opposition.

The men and women of all classes who were emerging in increasing numbers from the secondary schools and universities during the nineteenth century found themselves in a position unique among the educated classes of Europe, and the characteristics they acquired were likewise unique. These men and women were, as has been indicated, well trained and, in many cases, exceptionally gifted. Opportunities for self-expression were, however, very limited; the circumstances of Russian life almost automatically thrust them into the opposition. A few could, of course, enter state service; even they were for the most part conservative or liberal, not reactionary. Whatever the remainder did, they were expected not to think too much or to organize too assiduously in behalf of the public welfare. It is conceivable, of course, that an educated class might meekly accept tutelage from above. There is, however, no evidence to suggest that this was or is true of the Russian educated class. Badgered at every turn by the police and the bureaucracy, they were forced into a constant preoccupation with politics and reform, regardless of what fields of expression they had chosen and regardless of whether they were men of wealth or of extreme poverty. Many, of course, turned to that now well-known group, unique to Russia among all the states of Europe—the professional revolutionaries.

It has long been observed in the West that the responsibilities of power have a sobering influence on those who had previously been indiscriminately critical. Legislative work on national problems, free and open discussion of national issues, practical work of various kinds in units of local government and in private associations—all serve both to create a pool of statesmen who can be called upon to accept heavy responsibilities without previous experience in state administration and to keep public discussion within reasonably realistic grounds. Even in the West, there is frequently occasion to marvel at the immature and impractical policies advocated by distinguished public figures with long years of practical experience, not to speak of the host of lesser figures in all walks of life who believe they have the correct formulas for solving all national and international problems. In Russia, the situation was infinitely worse, and the consequences were to prove disastrous. Russia was a highly centralized state in which the educated class was virtually excluded from responsible public activity. Self-government and private associations were limited, and initiative was discouraged. A national legislature in which persons outside the bureaucracy might possibly learn to frame a sensible law was not established until 1906. Public discussion of national and local issues was kept within narrow bounds. Even the curriculum of the schools was controlled in order to prevent the students from probing too deeply.

However oppressive the controls of the autocracy may have been, they were not oppressive enough to prevent the intelligentsia from formulating and discussing their ideas for a new political and social order. Direct attacks on the autocracy were, of course, out of the question, except in the underground, but theoretical discussions of social and economic problems were not, and if illustrations could not be drawn from Russian life, they could at least be drawn from that of Western European. As a result, their theories and ideals acquired for them overriding significance, untempered by the reality from which they were so effectively sealed off. The conception of politics as the art of the possible was foreign to the intelligentsia outside the bureaucracy. For them, politics was a matter of acquiring a neat and consistent set of theoretical principles, for the most part those that they regarded as the latest and most advanced in Western Europe. At the appropriate time, which was sure to come, Russia would somehow be reconstructed in accordance with these principles. The limitations imposed by Russia's past, as well as the practical consequences of their theoretical principles, they necessarily ignored. All this was to be clearly revealed in the Revolutions of 1905 and 1917. The consequences of these defects were to prove tragic to the intelligentsia in 1917, for those of them who entered the Provisional Government in that year were not nearly adequately prepared for the responsibilities of governing a great state.

The political propensities of the Russian intelligentsia were also conditioned by their relationship to the people. During the eighteenth and nineteenth centuries, the upper classes had been Europeanized, while, as we have seen, the mass of the peasants had adhered to their traditional customs, manners, dress, and, on the whole, had remained ignorant. Consequently, when a Russian intellectual referred to the people (*narod*), it was in no way comparable to a Western intellectual's reference to the "common man." Between the intelligentsia and the people stretched a vast, and for the time being, unbridgeable gulf. The attitude of the intelligentsia as a whole toward the people was similar to that of the "conscience-stricken" nobility, except that after the 1870's the self-sacrificing movement to the people ceased to be so widespread, and the welfare of the masses became merely one of the cardinal principles of the intelligentsia's political aspirations.

The peasants, of course, had no understanding of, or interest in, the theoretical doctrines of the intelligentsia; nor, for that matter, as has already been indicated, did the intelligentsia have any understanding of the real needs of the peasants. The gulf between them remained; the Revolutions of 1905 and 1917 were to reveal how deep was the potential hatred of the lower classes for the educated and propertied classes. Caught between an inflexible autocracy above and an uncomprehending mass below, the intelligentsia nevertheless needed the masses to fight the autocracy. The tendency was strong among them, therefore, to speak in the name of the masses, whether the masses specifically approved of their program or not. If the masses were not wise enough to appoint them their saviors, then they quite honestly assumed that role for themselves, for their faith in their own doctrines tended to be absolute. It was not an accident that, alone among the Marxists of Europe, the Russian Social Democratic Party (or, rather, the Bolshevik wing of it) developed the theory of a conspiratorial middle-class elite leading to revolution a working class that, when left to its own devices, sought only the usual economic gains. This was Lenin's reaction to specifically Russian conditions. Apart from the Social Democrats, the combination of unlimited flights of theoretical fancy, lack of practical experience, an intolerable *status quo*, and arbitrary assumptions about the will of the people produced revolutionary movements in Russia that must be counted among the most bizarre in the political history of the world.

Summary and Conclusion

Summarizing some of the changes in Russian society during the nineteenth century and the beginning of the twentieth, we find that the legal class system, established in the eighteenth century in imitation of the West, from the very beginning possessed peculiarities differentiating it from the estates of medieval Europe. After the emancipation of the serfs, each successive reform tended toward the equalization of the rights and obligations of the various classes. Despite attempts on the part of the government to reverse the trend, the system of legal classes had, by 1906, lost most of its former meaning. Although the laws dividing Russian citizens into various classes remained on the books, the differences between the legal rights and obligations of the classes had diminished markedly, and all the essential characteristics of a legal class system had disappeared. The trend was in accord with a marked tradition in Russian social history militating against the establishment of hereditary privileges based on blood or high birth alone.

The last Czars failed to realize, until it was too late, that the social basis of the autocracy was disappearing and that none of the changing classes could provide a reliable support for the existing order. The reactionaries assumed that the nobility and the peasantry were solid classes that would remain devoted to the autocracy, but the assumption proved to have no foundation whatsoever. The nobility, in addition to losing its privileges, was losing the economic basis of its power, the land; its disappearance as a distinct class was well under way. Most of the individual nobles were being absorbed in a new and rapidly rising group, the intelligentsia, which was known to be unalterably opposed to the autocracy. The peasantry was an impoverished class, isolated from the remainder of the population and governed by special laws. It was bound to remain a potentially destructive and anarchic force until the individual peasants were made equal citizens, free from arbitrary control by the commune. The Stolypin reforms might have succeeded in converting the peasants into prosperous and conservative citizens, but they were initiated too late to affect seriously the situation in 1917. The merchants and industrialists were a small group, largely of peasant origin, who were illiterate and politically inactive until their Europeanization toward the close of the nineteenth century. After the Revolution of 1905, the manifest incompetence of the bureaucracy, its inability properly to promote the economic interests of the country, its continuing bias in favor of the landowning gentry, and its interference with the free play of Russian social forces drove the merchants and industrialists into the ranks of the opposition. The workers were still half peasants, largely illiterate, unskilled, and badly paid, who were easy targets for irresponsible demagogy and, like the peasants, could be converted into a destructive and revolutionary force.

Russia did not develop a middle class similar to the powerful middle classes of the West. Those concerned with trade and industry in Russia were small in number, largely illiterate until the end

of the nineteenth century, and dependent on the state. It is characteristic that the state itself attempted to create an organized
middle class and urban self-government, but without success. It
was the educated class that was most sensitive to the oppressive
controls of the autocracy, and in Russia it replaced the Western
type of middle class in demanding constitutional and social change.
Composed at first almost entirely of the landowning gentry, it became, after the modernization of Russian life in the 1860's, a group
of diverse origin, constantly growing in numbers and influence. Dis-
trusted by the autocracy and cut off by it from responsible public
activity, the intelligentsia tended to think along highly theoretical
and utopian lines. In 1917, it was to be catapulted to power before
it had learned how to govern.

5

Censorship and the Press

THE VITALITY of any society, political or otherwise, is intimately connected with the extent of its freedom of speech and freedom of organization. A knowledge of the manner in which the Russian people enjoyed these rights is therefore an essential prerequisite for understanding the relative significance of state and society in the period before the Revolution. Although it has been customary in the past to stress freedom of speech and press as primary conditions of a healthy democracy, it is now being increasingly recognized that freedom of organization is of even greater importance. No society is likely to be granted the right of free speech unless there are organized groups ready to demand it, and, if necessary, fight for it. Nor can anything come of the free exchange of views unless there are organized groups ready to put their views into practice.

It has already been shown that before the eighteenth century neither a press nor a spontaneous and independent organizing impulse was to be found in Russia. Their subsequent rise and development were to have fateful consequences for the autocracy. With them appeared also an independent public opinion, which not even the draconian measures of Nicholas I could suppress and which, during the era of the Great Reforms, for the first time in Russian history, played a direct and decisive role in a large-scale reorganization undertaken by the state. It is possible, of course, for a state to control what the Russians call "social self-activity," the press, and public opinion to such an extent that they are reduced to impotence of a greater or lesser degree. It is important to note that in Czarist Russia the degree of impotence was lesser, not greater. While the controls of the Czarist state were indeed restrictive, they were not restrictive enough to prevent an agitated public from shaking them off and bringing the administrative mechanism to a virtual standstill in 1905, and from destroying the administrative

mechanism completely in 1917. At critical moments, it was the
Russian state and not Russian society that was reduced to impotence. Some of the reasons for this situation come readily to light
from an analysis of the kind of controls placed on the press and
voluntary association.

Attitude of the Public Toward Government-Subsidized Journals

One obvious and basic defect was the fact that the press remained
in the hands of the public, with the government standing aside and
giving orders not to print that which it regarded as harmful to its
interests. The government, as we have seen, had no positive program; it was forced, in effect, to admit that it could not trust the
people to think too much, and this, as it acknowledged in 1904–5,
was one of the reasons why public opinion became so inflamed
against the autocracy. The prohibitions against public discussion
did not, of course, leave an intellectual vacuum. An independent
public opinion existed continuously from the late eighteenth century on and found means of expression even during the worst
periods of reaction. As the government continued to delay reform,
and as public opinion became more mature and more hostile at
the close of the nineteenth century, in short, as the gulf between
state and society widened, any newspaper supporting the autocracy
and supported by it lost influence and circulation.[1] The most
widely read and influential newspapers in Czarist Russia were antigovernment. The government, naturally, was aware of this, particularly after 1905, and its only recourse was to appropriate large
sums of money to subsidize a rightist press.

The government's attempt to create a favorable press through
large-scale subsidy proved a ludicrous failure.[2] The best writers were
in the opposition camp; the poorly educated "dregs of society"
who constituted, on the whole, the reactionary right yielded no
journalistic talent. The best of the reactionary writers was Prince
Meshchersky, who had great influence over the Czar and was at
liberty to write scathing attacks on the government in his newspaper, *Grazhdanin*. According to Harold Williams, "the Liberal
journals . . . frequently quote from Prince Meshchersky's organ
strong remarks about the government, which would involve fines or
imprisonment if their author were a declared Constitutionalist."[3]

The newspapers created with government subsidies after 1905 (e.g., *Russkoe Znamia* and *Zemshchina*) were organs of the radical right, and were constantly filled with scurrilous abuse, the target of which was frequently government officials.[4] Apart from the curious fact that the government-subsidized journals attacked the government, they had almost no readers. Newspapers of the extreme right could please only the pathetic pair who headed the Empire; the military commanders would not even permit them to be circulated among the troops.[5]

Legal Powers of the Government Over the Press, 1865–1905

The rise of organized censorship in Russia paralleled the growth of a secular press in the second half of the eighteenth century. Censorship regulations reached extreme proportions under Nicholas I (1825–55), but, with the obvious failure of Nicholas' paternalistic system at the end of the Crimean War and the growth of the reading public, a more liberal set of regulations was issued in 1865, which, with important later modifications, remained in effect until 1905. The censorship regulations of 1865 exempted certain kinds of publications from precensorship. These included magazines and newspapers, provided the Minister of the Interior gave his consent (for the most part, only those journals published in the two capitals could get this consent), original works of more than 160 printed pages, and translations of more than 320 printed pages.[6] These publications were sent to the censorship authorities during or after the course of printing.

The partial end of precensorship did not mean, however, that anything like freedom of the press had been introduced or even that violations of the law could be punished only through judicial proceedings. Actually, the administration, primarily because of modifications made in the law of 1865, remained endowed with administrative powers that enabled it to determine at its discretion which publications could be issued and what they could say. As concerns books, the most important of these powers was that of outright prohibition (by the Committee of Ministers), frequently after printing, since books were not subject to precensorship. As concerns newspapers and periodicals, the government's main weapon was the right to suspend publication, either temporarily (by the Minister of the Interior) or permanently (by a group of four ministers). A significant subsidiary power was the right of the Minister of the Interior to prohibit newspapers or periodicals from discussing any question of state importance; if his order was disobeyed, he could suspend a publication for a period of up to three months.

In general, the press of the capitals (the provincial press will be discussed later) was largely free from precensorship, but no publisher or writer could be certain what action would be taken by the administration upon the publication of a book or article, even if the content had nothing to do with politics or with contemporary life. It would be superfluous to dwell upon the resulting deficiencies in the Russian press. New newspapers and magazines appeared and disappeared in rapid sequence; the editors of those that managed to remain open were constantly being punished for transgressions of the law, hypothetical or real, or simply for showing a "harmful tendency"; books printed at private expense could be arbitrarily confiscated by the state; and whole areas of Russian life could not be discussed at all. All too frequently, thoroughly loyal citizens were subjected to arbitrary and unfair reprisals simply because they exercised their patriotic duty of proposing government policies that would best serve the interests of the state. Neither the Czar nor key figures in the bureaucracy took the trouble to distinguish between those who advocated moderate and reasonable changes and those who sought revolutionary overturns. It is characteristic that most of the organs of such devoted partisans of the autocracy as the Slavophiles were closed; and even such reactionary and government-subsidized sheets as *Grazhdanin* and *Moskovskiia Vedomosti* were sometimes subjected to administrative punishment. Russian society under the last Czar was being confined by a narrow tutelage that it had long since outgrown. It does not take much imagination to realize how painful this must have been to an enormously talented people, endowed, beyond any shadow of a doubt, with unusual powers of creative thinking.

Loopholes in the Censorship Prior to 1905

Czarist control of the press suffered from the basic defect that the state stood apart from society, exercising merely preventive controls. These controls were not total and could not have succeeded in creating an intellectual vacuum. Basically, Russian public opinion remained independent, even in the worst periods of reaction, and grew in vitality and influence.

One reason for the incompleteness of the Czarist controls over the press lay in the defects of the state apparatus. Official policy toward the press varied from Czar to Czar and was devoid of both interdepartmental and intradepartmental uniformity.[7] An important influence on the Russian press was the liberal spirit that permeated the legislation of Alexander II in the era of the Great Reforms. There was involved not merely the emancipation of the serfs, but a whole series of far-reaching reforms—the introduction of self-government, the establishment of a modern and progressive judicial system, the grant of autonomy to the universities, and the press regulations of 1865—all of which, if continued and perfected, would have converted the autocracy into a constitutional monarchy. The policy of the government thereafter was directed toward whittling away the most progressive features of the reforms, but it was not necessary for the press to applaud these reactionary movements. On the contrary, the conservative and liberal organs, i.e., those publications that had the greatest influence in society, took it upon themselves to discuss the practical working of the reforms, to condemn violations of the law, and to criticize severely reactionary changes in the law. In the darkest days of reaction under Alexander III, when it became virtually a sign of unreliability to uphold the reforms of the reigning Czar's father, the most liberal journals continued, at very great risk, to attack the government for deserting the liberal principles of the 1860's. "Every leading article of *Russkiia Vedomosti*," writes the historian A. A. Kizevetter, "and every 'internal survey' of *Vestnik Evropy* contained firm criticism of the policy of counterreform, with constant references to the fact that only the logical development of the interrupted reorganization program of the 1860's could lead the country to internal prosperity and avert future terrible social storms."[8]

The intellectuals found an important loophole in that the censors were less concerned with academic theories designed for a few specialists than with concrete criticism and calls for action printed in pamphlet form and designed for mass circulation at a low price. This approach to censorship explains why, beginning in 1898, *Pravo* (*Law*), a weekly legal review, could appear without precensorship. This publication called attention to violations of and the need for improvement in the law, without encountering any significant administrative punishment.[9] It explains, also, why all three volumes of Marx's *Capital* could be translated and published legally. Upon the appearance of the first volume, in 1872, one censor wrote:

However strong and however sharp Marx's opinions concerning the relations of the capitalists to the workers, the censor does not think that they can be really harmful, since they are, so to speak, drowned in the huge mass of the abstract, partially obscure, political-economic argumentation that constitutes the content of this book. One may say positively that not many will read it in Russia, and even fewer will understand it.[10]

Nevertheless, shorter and less theoretical works of Marx were prohibited, both before and after 1905.

In the 1890's, there arose a fierce dispute between the Marxists and the Narodniki on the path to socialism to be followed in Russia, a dispute that had repercussions among wide circles of the intelligentsia. Although the dispute was, in essence, concerned with the problem of how best to overthrow the existing political and social order, it was nevertheless conducted in part in the open, and the Marxists acquired one or another legal newspaper or journal, which gave them a continuous but precarious legal outlet until 1906. Well-known Marxists, including Lenin and Plekhanov, contributed either unsigned or pseudonymous articles to these publications. Reports published by the Soviet government indicate that the language in these publications was often surprisingly explicit.[11]

That which could not be printed legally was printed illegally, either in Russia or abroad. In either case, the printed materials received wide, clandestine circulation inside Russia. The most common form of contraband literature was the leaflet, placed surreptitiously wherever it was likely to be found and read, but newspapers, magazines, and, of course, books were also circulated illegally.[12]

Where the use of neither the illegal press nor the hectograph was feasible, Russian society resorted to the pen. Despite the censorship and police terror of Nicholas I, which so impressed a casual traveler like Custine, an independent public opinion remained and was nourished by handwritten memoranda and reports passed from hand to hand. There was nothing surprising either about the emergence of liberalism on the death of Nicholas in 1855 or about the influence of public opinion on the Great Reforms that followed.

Subsequently, the pen was to play a prominent role again in the victory of public opinion over the government at the time of the famine of 1891.[13]

Thus, in pre-1905 Russia, there existed an independent and, for the most part, an opposition press, which could at times go surprisingly far in condemning the existing order and in printing material distasteful to the government. Nevertheless, it was a severely restricted press, emphasizing generalizations and abstractions rather than concrete facts, free to discuss foreign, but not Russian, life and institutions in detail. The political education of Russian intellectual youth was consequently one-sided and distorted and was to have the baneful influence noted previously. Unable to analyze adequately concrete facts and institutions, they turned to the realm of theory, where the only limit to the construction of the wildest fantasies was their imagination. The Russian censorship, by encouraging a preoccupation with theory unrelated to practice, was a primary influence in the molding of doctrinaire radicals and revolutionaries.

The Press in 1905

With the coming of the Revolution of 1905, the government was compelled to revise radically the existing press laws, and a new era began, one in which the press was relatively free. For the second time within fifty years, it was admitted that strict censorship was a complete failure. Meeting late in 1904 to discuss the fulfillment of Point 8 of the ukase of December 12, 1904, the Committee of Ministers, which had been responsible for most of the powers of administrative punishment granted to the Minister of the Interior after 1865, condemned the confusion into which the press had been thrown by its excessive dependence on administrative discretion. It found that the discussion of many problems had been pointlessly prohibited and that the state could have benefited from the illumination of these problems by public opinion. It admitted that the strict censorship had failed to achieve its purpose and had merely generated hostility toward the government. Every government that believes it can profit from muzzling the press should take special note of one of the Committee's strong statements:

The Committee . . . finds that excessive and aimless strictness, as the experience of our history as well as the history of Western Europe has shown, arouses strong discontent in society, and for the most part does not achieve its aim: Ideas find ways for getting around the laws, spread to the public, and their effect is the more powerful, the more severe the prohibitions.[14]

A year later, the conditions of censorship were radically changed by the press laws of November 24, 1905, and April 26, 1906.

The circumstances leading to the promulgation of the new laws will not be examined here. It is important to note, however, that, for a time, any censorship exercised in the capitals was exercised by society and not by the state. As the defeats of the Russian armed forces in the Far East multiplied, the press became bolder. Finally for forty days—from October 22, 1905, to December 2, 1905, known as "the days of freedom" (*dni svobody*)—the censorship was completely ignored in the capitals and reduced in effectiveness in the provinces. The underground press emerged into the open and the most radical appeals were freely printed. On the other hand, the printing workers refused to permit the most reactionary newspapers to appear and announced that such words as "Constituent Assembly," "the Soviet of Workers' Deputies," and "the Union of Unions" must be capitalized.[15] During these months, it is claimed that Russia led the entire world in the number of titles and copies of books published.[16] Not until the dissolution of the First Duma in July, 1906, was anything like a normal situation restored, but the severe restrictions of the earlier period were ended for the duration of the Czarist regime.

Government Controls After 1905

The new laws governing the press abolished precensorship for newspapers, periodicals, books, and pamphlets throughout the Empire.[17] Abolished also were all the administrative punishments discussed above, and the right of the Minister of the Interior to prohibit discussion in the press of any problem of state importance. The press was now subject to regulations defined by law, and violations could be punished only through judicial proceedings. Judicial control of the press did not, of course, leave the hands of the administration completely tied; nevertheless, the enormous abuses inherent in the old methods of administrative punishment were eliminated (primarily in St. Petersburg and Moscow), and sufficient loopholes were left in the new regulations to permit the legal publication, beginning in 1912, of the well-known Bolshevik newspaper *Pravda*.

In the end, the government found it expedient to restore some form of administrative control. This was done in June, 1907, through the right given the local authorities in areas in a state of emergency to issue obligatory decrees and to fine or imprison through administrative proceedings those who violated these decrees. The press was thereafter exposed to the financial risk of arbitrarily imposed fines, or, as an alternative, a jail sentence up to three months for the "responsible" or "sitting" editor, usually a peasant or a worker especially hired to face the hazard of imprisonment, thereby permitting the real editors to continue their work without interruption.

Relative Freedom After 1905

Despite the fact that publishing was still attended by many hazards, the atmosphere, in so far as the press was concerned, had changed radically. Russia was now a constitutional monarchy with a popularly elected lower house in which political parties of all shades, including the Bolsheviks, were represented. Although the immunity granted the Duma deputies was defective by Western standards, it nevertheless represented a considerable advance for Russia, and the deputies were free to mount the tribune of the Duma and air their revolutionary views. The proceedings were not subject to censorship (until the outbreak of World War I), and, because of the widespread interest in public affairs aroused by the Revolution of 1905, they were widely printed and read. It is even claimed by Bernard Pares that there were peasants who learned to read from the Duma debates, a claim that would seem fantastic were the country involved not Russia.[18]

The radical temper of the First and Second Dumas and their savage attacks on the government, in conjunction with the great popular interest in the new legislative institution, created serious difficulties for the government in its attempt to halt the revolutionary movement during the years 1906–7. The Duma had, furthermore, the right of interpellation, and government ministers were constantly being queried about abuses by the censorship. There is considerable justice in the remarks of the St. Petersburg press committee that "it is an odd circumstance that the Social Democrats of the State Duma, in presenting in the Duma interpellations on the persecutions of the workers' press, demand explanations from the government and are indignant over the fact that the government, by its repressions, prevents the revolutionary organs of the press from undermining the state order that it is called upon to defend."[19]

Formerly, the principles of the Great Reforms had served as a kind of unofficial limit within which the government could be criticized; now these limits were set by the October Manifesto and the new constitution. However defective the latter may have been, it proclaimed in principle, as the will of the Czar, the establishment of a new and more liberal order, which automatically expanded the limits of public expression.[20] The establishment of the constitutional monarchy meant, therefore, the beginning of a new era for the Russian press, notwithstanding the restoration of administrative punishment and the continuation of arbitrary and unfair treatment of individual newspapers and magazines. It was now possible to discuss and criticize specific Russian institutions and governmental policies. Caution and prudence were still needed, particularly in the provinces, but it was no longer necessary to resort to vague hints and innuendoes, "Aesopian" language, or foreign dispatches in press discussions of current problems. Words such as "constitution," formerly banned, came into daily use, and opinions formerly regarded as seditious became commonplace. Abstract principles and generalizations, formerly so prominent, gave way to statements of the pros and cons of contemporary problems. In the years before the revolution, the Russian press to a considerable extent actually reflected the various currents of public opinion. An important advance had been made, moreover, in making it a genuine organ of public education, and the foundation had been laid for the creation of that mature and informed public opinion which is an essential prerequisite of democratic government.

The broad scope permitted Russian authors to discuss Russian institutions fully and frankly after 1905 is illustrated by many books already cited in this study, although it should also not be overlooked that the censorship committees and the courts were busy building up a new index of prohibited books.[21] In so far as newspapers and magazines are concerned, their content is illustrated by Rosenberg's *Letopis russkoi pechati*, which consists of articles on the press originally published in *Russkiia Vedomosti*. Rosenberg's attack on the government treatment of the press was consistently blistering. In retrospect, it can even be called unfair, since it makes no mention of the new freedom that had been acquired, or of the intensified radicalism of public opinion. The persistent emphasis in the liberal press on its limits, but not its liberties, naturally reached the foreign press and helped to perpetuate the myth, still far too widespread, that the Russian press was almost completely gagged. The newspaper of the Cadet Party, *Rech,* was probably an even worse offender than *Russkiia Vedomosti.*

Organs of the press reflecting the views of the opposition parties became commonplace; they included, after 1910, those of the Bolsheviks, the Mensheviks, and the Socialist Revolutionaries (published only in St. Petersburg). Once the administration had slackened its attempts to close opposition journals and resorted to the fine as its main weapon of control, the reissuing of legal revolutionary publications depended only on the availability of funds, and these were forthcoming in one way or another to all three revolutionary parties with the revival of the labor movement in 1912. *Pravda,* to which Lenin and Plekhanov, apparently unknown to the censors, were contributors, was substantially the same partisan and distorted journal that the *Daily Worker,* for example, is today, inciting the workers to class hatred, strikes, and disrespect for the government and the law. In a veiled form that was nevertheless quite obvious both to the government and to its readers, *Pravda* called also for the overthrow of the existing political and social order.[22]

The inability to discuss day-to-day events adequately caused the pre-1905 newspaper to take second place to the monthlies, the "thick journals," as the Russians called them, in which a more cautious and theoretical survey of internal developments was possible.[23] While these journals continued to flourish after 1905, a normal development of the daily newspaper was now possible. They grew with phenomenal rapidity, as shown by the following figures:[24]

YEAR	NUMBER OF NEWSPAPERS
1883	80
1898	123
1900	125
1908	800
1911	1,007
1913	1,158

An adequate provincial press also became a possibility now. Before 1905, provincial newspapers and magazines were, with two exceptions (*Kievlianin* and *Iuzhnyi Krai* of Kharkov), subject to precensorship. They were wholly at the mercy of the taste and views of the local governor and, in most cases, were virtually unable to discuss local affairs. After 1905, journals published in the provincial cities were no longer subject to precensorship. Because of the operation of the emergency laws, they were still at the mercy of the local governors, but the views of these officials differed. On the whole, such journals were increasing in number and their quality was improving.[25]

The changes in the censorship after 1905 should be viewed against the perspective of the unprecedented growth of literacy and education. The Revolution of 1905, like the Revolution of 1917, provided an enormous stimulus to the growth of public awareness and to the thirst for education. Schools were established at a greatly accelerated rate. Nonschool education likewise progressed very rapidly; the extraordinarily rigid censorship on books available to the masses was removed after 1905, and various restrictions that had effectively checked the growth of adult education were either removed or alleviated.[26] Professors who in the 1880's rarely had ventured outside the university classroom began, after 1905, to give public lectures and participate in the growing number of people's universities.[27] Book production, despite the numerous confiscations, reached unprecedented proportions.[28] It is apparent that the face of Russian society was changing and that an elemental social movement was under way that Czarist methods of control could not check. This situation, as well as the new constitutional conditions, explains the extraordinary freedom acquired by the Russian press after 1905. The success of the censorship under Nicholas I, like the success of the police measures of the 1880's, was based as much on public inactivity as on the extraordinary efforts of the censors and police.[29] Less than a hundred years later, Nicholas II was powerless to stop the press campaign against Rasputin, much less to tamper with the press laws in general, or, as he so ardently desired, to return to autocratic rule.[30] After 1905, the failure to submit to public opinion led inevitably to revolution.

6

The Role of Voluntary Association
in Czarist Russia

I N AUTOCRATIC states, there are no political parties, and normal channels of political expression are blocked. Yet, the more restrictive and irritating the controls placed on a society, the greater the desire for political agitation; and the greater the attempt to suppress such agitation, the fiercer its tendency to seek an outlet. Thus suppression helps make politics the dominant concern of every citizen, finding its way into all activities—literature, art, science, and everything else normally regarded as nonpolitical. From the point of view of the controlling state, the greatest danger lies in those activities, regardless of their purpose, in which two or more citizens act together. In an autocratic state trying to hold down a seething populace, there is no such thing as a harmless form of association. No era furnishes a better illustration of this than the last years of the Czarist Empire.

Laws Governing Voluntary Association

It is characteristic that, while the old fundamental laws proclaimed freedom of the press in principle, they absolutely denied the principle of freedom of association. Laws regulating the conduct of public meetings or the establishment of societies and unions were virtually nonexistent; all forms of association, temporary or permanent, were under the complete and uncontrolled authority of the administration. Even home meetings held only for amusement or entertainment were not exempt from police control.[1]

Like the old press laws, the old laws on association did not survive the Revolution of 1905. In the course of 1904, Russian society became bolder and bolder, culminating, finally, in the "days of freedom," when the administrative apparatus was paralyzed, the revolutionary underground emerged entirely into the open, and meetings were held and unions formed at will (*iavochnym poriad-kom*). The October Manifesto promised to establish freedom of association, and the Fundamental Laws of 1906 did establish it in principle (Articles 78 and 80), with the same defect noted regarding the principle of freedom of the press. The "temporary" laws of March 4, 1906, worked out to determine the legal limits of the principle of free association, constituted a considerable improvement over the earlier situation; but Russian subjects continued to have less scope in their right to organize and to speak than they did in their right to express opinions in print.[2] Nevertheless, in theory at least, political parties and trade unions could now be organized freely. Important, also, was the distinction now made between public and private meetings; only the former were made subject to police control.

The Place of the Church in Russian Society

The fact that Russian society prior to the late eighteenth century showed no disposition to organize has already been discussed. Such organizations as existed before that time arose, for the most part, out of state needs and state compulsion and did not have deep roots. It is astonishing, therefore, that at the beginning of the nineteenth century Russian society was still in the beginning stages of its organization, having no powerful organizational traditions comparable to those in the West.

The commune and the Church were two major exceptions. It has already been indicated that the commune was a drag on progress, incapable either of playing a constructive role or of serving as a base for the organizational impulse that was beginning to take root. In considering the place of the Orthodox Church in Russian history, all parallels with Western Christianity, whether Catholic or Protestant, must be set aside. Christianity, introduced into Russia in the tenth century, was adapted to Russian conditions, and the Church there did not play a role comparable to that which it played in the West. The Orthodox Church is not, therefore, a major exception to the backwardness of Russian social organization; on the contrary, the conditions responsible for that backwardness extended also to the Church, which became a ward of the state and joined Russian society in the demand for emancipation from excessive state control at the beginning of the twentieth century.

The history of the Orthodox Church is a long and complex subject, the main outlines of which fortunately are available in English.[3] Space will not permit more than a brief outline of the basic weaknesses of the Church as an organized social force. As for Russian society as a whole, illiteracy appears to have been one of the basic causes of these weaknesses. When Christianity was first introduced into Russia, the Russian people were too backward to assimilate its inner spiritual meaning; religious life became largely a matter of observing the rites and ceremonies prescribed by the Church, and even this was done only after a long evolution.[4] Although literacy until the eighteenth century was virtually confined to the Church, it was not sufficiently developed to enable Russian priests to undertake the spiritual education of the people. For the Russian Orthodox Church, as for the Eastern Church in general, dogma was fixed; no attempt was made to develop Church tenets, and there were no lively theological disputes, such as those known to the West, about the interpretation of the more obscure tenets— a situation that facilitated the establishment of national churches in the East and the subordination of Church to state.[5]

A more important factor, however, in bringing about the eventual subordination of Church to state in Russia was the indifference of the congregation. Although parish congregations were active prior to the time of Peter the Great, and even had the right to elect and dismiss priests, they, like other social organizations of that time, lacked the inner cohesion and *esprit de corps* effectively to resist the steady development of state power during the course of the seventeenth century. Parish elections continued in limited form until 1797, but in fact the bishops had gained control of the local churches by the end of the seventeenth century. Contributing to this process, and to the disappearance of the Church's independence, was the seventeenth-century schism that removed from the congregation its most ardent and zealous members. The Church probably hastened its subordination by seeking the help of the state in suppressing these schismatics (known as the Old Believers), who broke away because of disputes over ritual.[6]

As an institution, the Church, like the state, became rigidly centralized, with the most important decisions made in St. Petersburg by the Czar through the lay head, the Chief Procurator of the Holy Synod. The authority of the local bishops was slight, and even the ecclesiastics in the Holy Synod were compelled to yield to the will of the Chief Procurator.

Local religious life bore little resemblance to its counterpart in the West. There was no community life centered around the Church. The congregation itself had no voice in Church affairs. Religious education for the masses was in general neglected. Popular interest in religions was confined to the magic and beauty of the rituals, and the village priest's functions were mainly concerned with the mechanical performance of these rituals. Very few priests ever delivered sermons. The widespread mistaken belief that the priests exercised a strong moral influence over their congregation is based, apparently, on Western experience and bears little resemblance to Russian reality. The clergy was an isolated class, over-worked, impoverished, and openly abused by their superiors.[7] Being partly dependent for their livelihood on fees collected from the peasants for religious services performed, many were known for their greediness. Drunkenness was not uncommon. For these and other reasons, village priests were traditionally derided and ridiculed by the peasants. The state, of course, attempted to use the Church to keep the people in submission; undoubtedly the state had some success, but the evidence of its failure is much more impressive. Under the conditions existing in Russia in the decades before the Revolution, the close connection of the clergy with the state and the established interests, obvious enough to the people, merely contributed further to the disrespect in which the clergy was held.[8]

The abuses connected with the dictatorial control of the Church by the state, along with the sharp antagonism that had grown up between state and society, had their effects on the clergy. During the Revolution of 1905, a "significant" minority of the lower clergy was "tinged with liberalism" and supported the population against the government.[9] A strong movement arose among the clergy, high and low, including the Holy Synod itself, to call together a Church council, or *sobor*, in order to carry out a reform of the Church administration. Reactionary influences prevailed, however, after the suppression of the Revolution, and the reforms were never undertaken, although the demand for them was later revived. The maintenance of the old abuses, followed in later years by the Rasputin scandals, which affected the Church as well as the state, demoralized the clergy and brought the Church, on the eve of the Revolution, to a new low in its popular standing.[10]

The Initial Encouragement of Voluntary Association

Thus, such long-established institutions as the Church and the commune, by virtue of their close ties with the state, could not become the nucleus of an effectively organized social force. Accordingly, the tradition of "self-activity" in Russian society must be sought in the new organizations that emerged in the eighteenth, nineteenth, and twentieth centuries. The restraints placed upon the new organizational impulse were formidable. Nevertheless, it would be a mistake to presuppose rigid uniformity in the policy of the autocracy toward social self-activity or increasing repressiveness in its policy. The Russian autocracy was a traditional government which had ruled for centuries with the consent of the people and which dealt with new problems as they arose on a trial-and-error basis. At times it actively encouraged all forms of social activities; at other times it dealt harshly with the most seemingly harmless manifestations of such activities. For example, the active social movement during the reign of Alexander I and the quiet submissiveness of society during the reign of Nicholas I had little in common. A new and highly significant revival of social self-activity took place during the reign of Alexander II, only to subside again during the reign of Alexander III. The revival that followed in the 1890's proved to be irresistible and, in the long run, uncontrollable, and led directly to the two Russian revolutions. As in the case of the censorship, the success or failure of the repressive measures taken against voluntary association depended, in large part, on the temper of society, the vitality of which, at the height of its revivals, proved stronger than any controls the autocracy could impose.

The rise of voluntary association in Russia antedates the time when they became subject to strict government regulation. Government authorization of private societies was begun by Catherine the Great, but her purpose in chartering them was to encourage and not to check private initiative, and the bylaws of the societies incorporated more privileges than obligations.[11] Catherine's attitude changed after the French Revolution, and, during the brief reign of her son, Paul I (1796–1801), all public organizations were closed. The situation changed again during the early reign of Alexander I, who proved to be even more liberal than Catherine. Alexander required the confirmation only of those societies that requested special privileges or exemptions from the general laws; all other societies pursuing useful aims could be organized freely, subject only to the general laws.[12] In the early part of Alexander's reign, especially after the Napoleonic Wars, there existed a considerable number of active organizations, of which the best known were the Masonic lodges, the secret societies active prior to the Decembrist revolt, and the literary circles. The first phase of government regulation of voluntary association ended in August, 1822, when an official decree ordered the closing of the Masonic lodges and all other secret societies.[13]

The early encouragement of voluntary association was also manifested in the authority given the universities by the university rules of 1804 to spread and control secondary and elementary education in their districts.[14] This grant of administrative authority to self-governing universities, so strange for a regime frequently and inaccurately equated with a modern totalitarian state, could not, of course, last; even so, it was not until ten years after Nicholas I ascended the throne that the universities (by the law of 1835) were permanently relieved of their control over education, which was thereafter supervised strictly by bureaucratic institutions. The universities, granted autonomy in 1804, now lost their rights of self-government and did not regain them until 1863.

The promising beginning in voluntary association made during the early reign of Alexander I did not survive the decree of August, 1822, and the general reaction that followed the Decembrist revolt in 1825. Thereafter, no society could be organized without the personal authorization of the Czar. Because of the Decembrist revolt, Nicholas I was highly suspicious of voluntary association, and, during the whole of his reign (1825–55), he approved the organization of only twenty-five philanthropic, learned, and agricultural societies. Most of these were not true private societies, since their bylaws were drawn up by the Committee of Ministers, not the founders of the societies; they received the designation "Imperial," obtained financial aid from the state treasury, and enjoyed the right of free correspondence.[15]

The Significance of the Great Reforms in the Development of Voluntary Association

With the coming of the Great Reforms and the subsequent improvement of the social, economic, and political situation, voluntary associations began to grow at a rapid rate. The change has been well described by Nicholas Berdyaev, who writes: "There is something mysterious in the growth of movements in public life in Russia during the 1860's. 'Society' made its appearance; public opinion began to form. This was still not the case in the 1840's, when there were figures who stood alone and small circles." [16] As mentioned earlier, Russia began to move at an accelerated pace in the direction of a modern industrial society. Apart from such important factors as the growth of industry, the increase in social mobility, the growth of an all-class intelligentsia, and the emergence of the intellectual professions, the political atmosphere changed radically, and it was the conscious intention of Alexander II to encourage social self-activity. In granting such basic reforms as local self-government and a modern judicial system, he was aware that the end result would be constitutional government.

In so far as government policy toward voluntary association was concerned, the change was not very radical; a large part of the credit for the growth of social organization plainly belongs to the spontaneous internal evolution of Russian society. It was no longer necessary for the Czar personally to authorize each new society organized; authorization could now be granted by individual ministers, depending upon the field of the society's activity. The Minister of the Interior, for example, could authorize the opening of philanthropic societies and consumers' cooperatives. Under the new university regulations of 1863, the Minister of Education could authorize the universities to found learned societies.[17] A further step forward was taken in 1897, when model bylaws for types of societies whose promotion was regarded as desirable were issued; proposed societies that accepted these bylaws could be approved by the local governors.[18] The results were, in some cases, startling. In 1862, there were six private charitable organizations; in 1899, more than 7,000.[19] Six learned societies were started in the eighteenth century, of which only one, the Free Economic Society, survived. In 1856, there were not more than 20 to 25 such societies, but in 1899 there were 340.[20] By 1905, Russia had the beginnings of a network of voluntary associations—social, cultural, economic, scientific, etc.—all of them forbidden to pursue political aims and seemingly harmless. The March 4, 1906, rules on association shifted the regulation of private societies from the ministers to newly established provincial boards on voluntary association. These boards, which had both judicial and administrative functions, were dominated by the administration and were endowed with great discretionary powers, so that the legal situation did not change so radically as was implied by the text of the law. Nevertheless, as will be shown in detail later, much could now be done in the way of organization that had been inconceivable before 1905.

In addition to requiring the initial approval of a minister, the voluntary associations that grew up after the era of the Great Reforms remained by law wholly at the mercy of the police. No distinction was made between public and private meetings; even legally established societies could not hold plenary sessions without first notifying the police. The scope of their activities was defined in their bylaws, and no unusual steps could be taken without the further authorization of the administration. Undertakings such as concerts, balls, and plays, though authorized by the bylaws, could be arranged only with the permission of the local police chief.[21] The founders of a society had to be men of proved reliability who did not sympathize with "radical" causes. The society's activities had to be simple, formal, and readily subject to observation; above all, they could not involve direct contact with large masses of people. The last century of Czarist history is filled with examples of the normal, healthy development of voluntary associations that, for one reason or another, aroused the suspicion of the authorities and were either arbitrarily closed or restrained in their normal development.

Nevertheless, the rise of a variety of voluntary associations on a scale never before known in Russian history, some of them very active and issuing their own publications, is an important political fact, which, in the long run, was inconsistent with the maintenance of the autocracy. The presence of legal channels of association played an important part in society's conquest of the state in 1905 and 1917. Czarist officials sensed the danger and retained for themselves the right of absolute control through the general laws before 1905 and through the emergency laws after 1905, but, as with the censorship, their control was preventive and they acted only in special circumstances. With the growing maturity of Russian society and the inability of the state to use drastic, or, as one might say today, totalitarian measures, the initiative of the public slowly and imperceptibly broadened, and the freedom of choice left to the state slowly and imperceptibly narrowed. Consequently, a fair estimate of the attitude exhibited by the Czarist government toward public initiative must give adequate attention to the positive freedom granted society, as well as to the arbitrary limits placed upon it.

Student Organizations and the Student Movement

Of all the elements of society, the students were the least likely to submit quietly to the irritating restrictions placed upon public initiative. It is appropriate, therefore, that this brief survey of the role of voluntary association in Czarist Russia begin with the universities. The status granted them at any given time was a sensitive gauge of the basic intentions of the reigning Czar. The students, furthermore, reacted to unjust restrictions more quickly than did the rest of the population, and the rise and fall of the student movement constitutes a small-scale model of what was to follow shortly afterward for society as a whole.

It has already been mentioned that the universities were granted autonomy in 1804, lost it in 1835, and regained it in 1863. In 1884, under Alexander III, they lost it once more with the imposition of university rules even more stringent than those of 1835.[22] Under these new rules, the rectors, deans, and professors were no longer to be elected by the university council of professors but were to be appointed by the Minister of Education. The rights of the council were limited and the management of the university was entrusted to the appointed rector, who was, in turn, placed directly under the curator of the educational region (there were fifteen such regions in Russia). Upon the curator fell the ultimate responsibility for the maintenance of discipline and order. Assisting him in watching over the students was an inspector appointed by the minister, the inspector, in turn, being provided with a staff of appointed assistants.

Most curious of all were those provisions affecting the students designed to put an end to the political ferment and disorders prevalent in the universities since the era of the Great Reforms. Their history provides an object lesson in how not to treat students and how to guarantee the political radicalism and the disorders such rules are designed to prevent. The students were to regard themselves as "individual visitors to the university," to whom was forbidden "any action having a corporative character" and "any meetings or gatherings for joint deliberation on any matters whatsoever."[23] They were, in short, not to join together for any purpose—social, economic, literary, or scientific—on pain of such punishments as expulsion, fine, imprisonment, exile, and, later, recruitment into the army. Even applause after a lecture was regarded as a sign of unreliability and was forbidden.[24]

This policy toward students, which went far beyond the policy on association for society as a whole, could not, of course, be enforced, and the students formed a series of illegal organizations, apparently coordinated from the University of Moscow.[25]

Initially, the students were not politically minded. They shared with Russian society as a whole the reaction against political activity that had set in after the assassination of Alexander II in 1881. There were constant clashes with the authorities, but the students' demands were academic, not political. They were discontented with the close supervision by the inspector and the curator, the constant threat of expulsion, and the arbitrary interference of the police, and they merely demanded the modification of the statute of 1884. They consciously avoided engaging in disorders or turning mass meetings (which became common despite the official rules) into political demonstrations against the existing order. " 'Politics,' " writes the ardent Social Democrat Cherevanin with reference to events as late as 1899, "was a terrible bugaboo, which the student body could not digest for the time being." [26] At the end of the nineteenth century, the situation in the universities, as in society as a whole, changed. As Russian society became more mature and more active, it encountered an inflexible and unyielding attitude on the part of the government. In the universities, the inspectors and curators who had shown leniency toward student organizations in the early 1890's were replaced by others prepared to enforce a sterner policy. The result was a turn to the left on the part of both society and of the students. The more radically inclined students were joining the Social Democratic and Socialist Revolutionary parties. Clashes with the administration remained on a small scale until 1899, when the students throughout the Empire began to act together, using new and more radical tactics. In February, 1899, a strike begun in the higher educational institutions of St. Petersburg spread rapidly to most of the other institutions of higher learning throughout the Empire.[27]

Confronted by this new situation, the government acted in its usual blundering fashion: It resorted to increased repression. It adopted a new weapon—recruitment into the army (actually an old tactic of Nicholas I)—and continued on a larger scale its older instruments of expulsion: exile, arrest, and beatings by the police (to break up mass meetings). The assassination of the Minister of Education, Bogolepov, in 1901 brought to the post a more liberal minister, the aged General Vannovsky, who did promulgate new rules permitting some legal organization in the universities. But the concessions were too little and too late.[28] In 1900–1, two schools of thought grew up among the students, the "Academicians" and the "Politicians," the former limiting their demands to academic freedom, the latter demanding wider political reform. Although the Academicians were at first an overwhelming majority among the students, the situation changed after the publication of the Vannovsky reforms, and, as the population as a whole followed the students in an increasingly radical trend, the views of the Academicians disappeared entirely. Beginning in 1901, mass street demonstrations were organized by the students, which were joined by other elements of the population. In March, 1902, the first all-Russian congress of students was held, at a time when unauthorized all-Russian congresses of any kind were still a rarity.[29]

Turbulence in the universities (including student strikes) continued in greater or lesser degree up to the year 1905, when it reached its peak. After the events of "Bloody Sunday," January 9, 1905, the government itself closed the universities to prevent the certain student disturbances, and academic work remained practically suspended until the fall of 1906. On August 27, 1905, the government suddenly and belatedly restored autonomy to the universities.[30] By this time, the whole of Russian society was in an uproar. The student movement was being led by a group of extreme radicals, mostly Social Democrats and some Socialist Revolutionaries and others. Because of the relative conservatism of the professors, the students demanded that the management of the universities be turned over to them.[31] Overriding the liberal professors who sought a return to normal academic life, the students opened the doors of the universities to mass meetings of the workers. Since the police could not enter the universities except at the request of the university council, these meetings were held in complete freedom. Here, in closed quarters, revolutionary speeches were made and strikes organized; here the revolutionary parties made their plans without interference.

The course taken by the universities after their reopening in the fall of 1906 has been fully described in English.[32] With the students now free to organize (the bylaws of their organizations were confirmed by the university council), a large variety of student organizations sprang up, and a student press grew up for the first time. The freedom to join political parties ended the former monopoly of parties of the left among the students, and organized groups of students with moderate and conservative views appeared. Since the breach between the state and society had not been healed, a spirit of opposition remained strong among the students, and political demonstrations continued on a lesser scale. Furthermore, the government moved to the right after the suppression of the Revolution and in January, 1911, took steps to limit once more the unusual degree of autonomy granted to the universities. Once again, students were forbidden to organize and to hold meetings, and the police were permitted to enter the university grounds to break up the meetings. Once again, mass expulsions of students took place. Once again, professors were appointed and dismissed on the basis of their political views (professors dismissed from the state universities could teach in private or municipal universities). University autonomy was restored during the war by the liberal Minister of Education, P. N. Ignatiev, but government policy toward the universities as well as toward other manifestations of social self-activity goes a long way toward explaining the course of events in 1917.

Learned Societies

The rise of the universities in the latter half of the eighteenth century coincided with the rise of learned societies, which were among the first of the voluntary associations to be established with the express consent of the government. The richest and oldest of these was the Imperial Free Economic Society, founded in 1765 with the approval and financial support of Catherine II. (The word "free" was inserted with the approval of Catherine to denote its independence from the state.) The society had three main branches, but also included innumerable special sections, committees, and commissions. It had a spacious structure in St. Petersburg, a library of approximately 200,000 volumes, and a capitalization of more than 500,000 rubles. (The ruble was stabilized in the decades before the Revolution at two to the dollar.) The society rendered invaluable service in behalf of public welfare during the century and a half of its existence. Its main concern was the improvement of agriculture, but it was concerned also with theoretical problems of the national economy and with such diverse matters as the spread of vaccination and of education. It made studies of the ways in which the cultivation of crops and the production of livestock could be improved and encouraged the introduction of new crops. It made studies of soil science and other technical improvements and sought to spread information by establishing schools and distributing literature. It collected statistics, sent out questionnaires, dispatched scientific expeditions, and arranged exhibitions. From time to time, it offered prizes for the best essays on national economic problems. The first such prize in the eighteenth century was awarded to a work that proved that the economic welfare of Russia would be served by the abolition of serfdom. Its *Trudy* (*Transactions*), issued six times a year in the form of thick volumes, constitute an inexhaustible store of economic information about Russia. At various times it issued countless other periodical publications and major economic works.[33]

Except for the four years during the reign of Emperor Paul (1796–1801), when it was in effect closed, the society managed to avoid direct clashes with the government until 1900, a time of revived public activity, when the accumulation of unresolved problems and the inflexible determination of the Czar to continue ruling through the bureaucracy brought about the first major signs of mass discontent and public disorders that led to the Revolution of 1905. The specific activity of the society that incurred the government's distrust was its practice of conducting public debates on current economic questions of national importance. In the last years of the nineteenth century, masses of excited listeners had been crowding into the society's halls to listen to debates on the tariff, the vodka monopoly, the gold reform, the advantages of high and low wheat prices, the reasons for the recurring famines, and the relative merits of the Marxist and Narodnik points of view. Lively debates on national economic problems attended by vast crowds were precisely the kind of activity the bureaucracy could not tolerate, and in April, 1900, steps were taken to convert the society into a narrow technical organization. By order of the Czar, its activities were temporarily placed under the control of the Minister of Agriculture, and access to its sessions was forbidden to outsiders. A temporary commission was also established to work out new bylaws. The assembly of the society thereupon decided to suspend that part of the society's activity which was under the control of the Minister in view of its "firm conviction that the society, the oldest social institution in Russia that has sought to express the true needs of the time and serve the public interest, can fruitfully develop its activity only through the maintenance of the principles of publicity, complete independence, and freedom of scientific investigation." Since the society declined to accept the new bylaws, its activities remained partially curtailed until 1917; only its special commissions and committees continued to operate.

Of lesser importance but in the same vein, the Juridical Society of the University of Moscow was closed by order of the Minister of Education in 1899. This society had played the same role as an organized forum that the journal *Pravo* played in the press, i.e., the defects of the existing government could be publicly discussed under the guise of a learned society devoted to the study of law. The legal reports presented and discussed at the Juridical Society public sessions were naturally restrained and clothed in the proper mantle of abstractness, but political subjects were discussed there that could not be discussed under other circumstances. The Juridical Society undoubtedly played an important role in popularizing constitutional ideas among the intelligentsia.[34] The closing of the Moscow society was apparently directed against its liberal and outspoken chairman, S. A. Muromtsev, later a prominent member of the Cadet Party and President of the First Duma, but law societies continued to operate at other universities and even in a number of provincial cities that had no universities.[35] The Moscow Juridical Society was reopened in 1910.

The Bar

The establishment of a modern judicial system was incompatible with autocracy. The very nature of his profession prepared the lawyer for the battle against autocracy, but the independent bar es-

tablished in 1864 remained independent. The disciplining of attorneys admitted to the bar and the admission of new members
were controlled by an elected council, whose jurisdiction coincided
with that of the first court of appellate jurisdiction, the Judicial
Board. As elsewhere, the Judicial Board exercised supervisory powers over the elected councils. The bar did not remain unaffected by
the progressive mutilation of the judicial statute of 1864. In 1874,
the Czar ordered that the establishment of new councils in districts
in which they had not yet been introduced be suspended, since the
councils already established had not lived up to their imposed task
of "supervising the dignity and ethical purity" of their members. In
1889, it was forbidden also to open branches of the councils.[36] In
those areas in which neither a council nor branches of a council
were open, disciplinary powers over the attorneys were exercised by
the district courts. While, by 1874, elected councils had been established only in the St. Petersburg, Moscow, and Kharkov judicial
districts, it should be kept in mind that the judicial districts embraced several provinces, and there is evidence indicating that the
attorneys in the other districts were not, in any case, ready for self-
government. Despite continued attacks on the bar, its right of self-
government was not withdrawn, and in 1904, at a time when young
lawyers were appearing at political trials not to defend the accused
but to stage political demonstrations, new councils of barristers
were again being opened, thanks to the support given them by the
Minister of Justice, N. V. Muraviev.[37] Although attorneys and, to a
considerable extent, the accused enjoyed virtually complete freedom of speech in the courtroom, the arrest and exile of attorneys
participating in political trials were not unknown.[38]

The Peculiar Significance of Banquets and Funerals

The general restrictions placed on public meetings and public
speeches probably explain the great popularity in pre-Revolutionary
Russia of jubilee banquets, i.e., banquets arranged to celebrate the
anniversary of significant events or prominent persons. These banquets offered excuses for obtaining permission to make speeches,
and it was customary, in liberal circles, to include just enough of
the opposition spirit to satisfy the craving of the audience; but this
spirit was moderate enough to forestall the police from breaking up
the gathering.[39] In November, 1904, the celebration of the fortieth

anniversary of the judicial reform of 1864 started the "banquet campaign," which continued into 1905. The banquets were subsequently arranged simply for the purpose of making radical speeches and adopting radical resolutions, including the demand for the convening of a constituent assembly.[40]

Another event likely to go completely out of control was the gathering of masses of people for the funeral of some well-known figure or for the honoring of his memory. Depending upon the temper of society, such funerals were the occasions for outright political demonstrations, or, at the very least, for demonstration on the part of the crowd that they had emotions and ideals which the police could not control. Most characteristic, perhaps, is the letter Nicholas wrote to his mother on November 11, 1910, in which he boasted that the funeral of Tolstoy had passed quietly, not because large detachments of police were on hand or because the people were cowed, but because Tolstoy was buried so quickly that not many people were in time for the funeral.[41] As to home meetings, despite the theoretical right of the police to interfere in these, they appear, on the whole, to have taken place without real difficulty; at the end of the nineteenth century, there were even regular political salons in St. Petersburg.[42]

Educational Societies

A good example of what could and could not be done on private initiative is afforded by the history of the societies for the propagation of education (literally, "societies of literacy"). These societies were not necessarily concerned with the operation of private schools, although it should be noted that private schools did exist on a small scale. Their main goals appear to have been the publication and distribution of books suitable for the people, but they were also concerned with the opening of libraries, reading rooms, and other institutions of nonschool education, the precise nature and extent of their activities varying with the locality. In the two capitals, they were also drawing up plans for universal primary education. This sort of activity was, of course, very popular with the Russian intelligentsia, and the societies were enthusiastically supported. Although the two committees for the propagation of education in the capitals had been founded earlier, they did not come to life until the 1880's. In the 1890's, they were operating on a large scale throughout most of the Empire and were making plans for extending their operations still further, when, late in 1895, they were suddenly reorganized and placed directly under the control of the Minister of Education. Since nothing could now be done without the specific approval of the Minister, the reorganization and transfer were tantamount to closing.

The reason for the closing of the Moscow and St. Petersburg committees is to be found in a secret letter written in February, 1895, by the Minister of the Interior, I. N. Durnovo, to the Minister of Education, I. D. Delianov. As usual, the letter fell into the hands of the opposition, and its text is available in full.[43] Durnovo had no confidence in the loyalty either of the leaders of the committees or of the promoters of the popular literature (Mikhailovsky, Uspensky, and Tolstoy are mentioned by name). Despite the rigid censorship of books intended for the people, he did not believe that the censorship alone could eliminate from them antigovernment propaganda or that government control over the free distribution of books was adequate. He was disturbed by the part taken in this distribution by student youth; he was even more disturbed by the penetration of these youths into the villages. He regarded the whole enterprise as a well-planned attempt on the part of antigovernment elements to carry on their campaign against the government on legal grounds. Since the societies were operating on their own initiative, without appropriate "moral control," he strongly recommended their subjection to an appropriate government department, the Ministry of Education. (The two committees were parts, respectively, of the Free Economic Society and the Moscow Agricultural Society and had been operating under the vague supervision of the Ministry of Agriculture.) This was accomplished for the two capital committees in 1895; in 1902, all other societies concerned with education for the people were brought under stricter control by the Ministry.[44] Then, in 1905, they were again permitted to elect their own officers, and their activity was again broadened.[45]

It would be a mistake, however, to suppose that private initiative in the field of public education actually ceased before 1905, or that the bureaucracy ever succeeded in controlling it to the extent desired by Minister Durnovo. The movement for nonschool education reached remarkable proportions in pre-Revolutionary Russia, and the bureaucracy was never more than an irritating deterrent absorbing a large part of the energy of the movement's indefatigable leaders. A good example of what could be done has been given by Kizevetter. At the very time that the education committees in the capitals were closed, the idea of "self-education" was becoming increasingly popular in Russian society. A group of scholars and educators (among them Miliukov) decided that the time was ripe for the spread of university education modeled on the "university extension" courses of Britain and the United States. To set up an independent organization for that purpose was manifestly impossible at that time, and so a way out was found least calculated to arouse the suspicions of the authorities. Moscow housed the seemingly harmless Society for the Propagation of Technical Skills, which was under the patronage of one of the grand dukes. This society already had an educational section made up of various commissions concerned with pedagogical problems not related to technical skills, and it was decided to set up a commission for the organization of home reading within this educational section. No special permission was required to organize this commission, and its name gave no indication that it was, in fact, going to spread university education independent of the state universities. The undertaking won the usual enthusiastic support of the Moscow academic staff, and a series of correspondence courses was worked out for all branches of university education except medicine. The required aids and books were published and periodically revised, and the number of subscribers from all parts of the Empire exceeded all expectations. The correspondence courses were conducted on an increasing scale for more than ten years, until the population was distracted from such activity by the events of 1905.[46]

This did not exhaust the commission's work. Within it was formed a lecture bureau, which arranged to have professors deliver lectures in certain cities in the provinces. The arrival of a Moscow professor aroused great excitement in the provincial cities, and the attitude of the local governors, whose permission was required for the delivery of the lectures, was suspicious. It became necessary to submit the text of all lectures in advance, and the lecturer could not depart from it. There were, of course, times when the governors refused to authorize the lectures, but, on the whole, these lecture tours proved very successful.[47]

Congresses and Conventions

While the government, in some cases at least, showed considerable tolerance toward the organization and activity of primary societies, it was highly suspicious of the gathering of large numbers of representatives of these societies in congresses. In every case, these required the special permission of the appropriate minister. There was an authorized agenda from which the congress could not depart, and police representatives were on hand to insure that forbidden subjects were not discussed. In general, regional congresses were authorized first, beginning in the early 1860's; all-Russian congresses followed later—in some cases much later. The group affected before 1905 included biologists, physicians, agronomists, archaeologists, and handicraft workers (*kustari*). A congress of jurists, authorized after a three-year delay, was held in Moscow in 1875, but no such congress was ever authorized again.[48] There was a natural desire on the part of elementary schoolteachers to discuss common educational problems, and authorization for congresses was obtained with difficulty after the rise of the zemstvo schools in the 1870's. However, in 1885, Delianov, the reactionary Minister of Education, forbade the convening of teachers' congresses.[49] The authorized congresses seemed harmless enough, but they were actually being used secretly for political purposes. It should also be noted that beginning late in 1904, and lasting at least through 1905, a whole series of unauthorized congresses, principally of unauthorized societies and unions, was taking place for the express purpose of passing radical resolutions.

Since congresses were akin to public meetings, the legal situation did not change under the law of March 4, 1906. Under Section III, Paragraph 17, of the new rules on public meetings, congresses, unless established permanently by law, had to be authorized by the Minister of the Interior in agreement with other appropriate ministers. At the very minimum, therefore, authorized agenda and the presence of police representatives remained the rule. However, even if the law remained constant, the political atmosphere had changed, and congresses that could not have convened prior to 1905 were authorized, as, for example, the first congresses of writers, held in 1906 and 1910; these, however, seemed to languish, because the problem of censorship could not be discussed.[50] On the other hand, the first congress of cooperative societies in 1908 was greeted with great enthusiasm, so much so that the government closed it before it had completed its work. The second congress, held in 1912, was likewise very active. Although the leaders of the consumers' cooperatives could not participate, unofficially they took part in the work of the congress. The third congress, in 1913, which again included all cooperative societies, was greeted with even more enthusiasm than the first, although its chairman was a government appointee.[51] The first all-Russian congress of primary schoolteachers, held during the Christmas holidays of 1913, was apparently moderate in its political tendencies, but radical in the educational program it adopted.[52] Thus, most of the numerous, well-attended congresses held between the two revolutions were able to discuss live issues, including government policy, within their own fields, and all of them were bound to be political in one way or another.

The Successful Organization of the Revolutionary Movement

It need hardly be pointed out that the revolutionary propaganda being spread so freely throughout Russia in the nineteenth century was the work of revolutionary organizations, which flourished in spite of the severity of the laws on association and the zealous efforts of the police to distinguish itself by uncovering them. That the history of Russia in the nineteenth and early twentieth centuries is in part the history of a series of revolutionary movements is too well known to require any comment. However, the expression of remorse on the part of the government over the severity of the old laws and the frank admission of their failure is of interest. It was stated in the deliberations of the State Council over the law of March 4, 1906:

The obligation to request from the appropriate authorities permission for the organization of societies, causing usually no little waste of time and trouble on the part of the founders, the almost complete ban on the founding of societies pursuing political and economic aims, and the severity of the punishments for belonging to secret societies, especially those political, formerly restrained the attempts to organize societies of a political or economic character. However, the enemies of the government and the adherents of revolutionary theories suffered from no such limitations. In spite of the legal prohibitions, they covered the Empire with a network of illegal associations. These elements, representing a minority of the population, but armed with energy and means, sometimes very significant, for the struggle with the government, constituted an imposing organizational force. On the other hand, the majority of the population, inclined toward order and the peaceful solution of social and cultural problems, proved disunited. It was not only powerless before the onslaught of closely knit extreme parties, but also impotent to give active support to the government.[53]

Associations of Merchants and Industrialists

One of the most revealing developments in the organizational impulse was that shown by the industrialists and merchants in the latter half of the nineteenth and the beginning of the twentieth centuries. Since the merchants and industrialists were generally of recent peasant origin and, until the last decade of the nineteenth century, illiterate, they did not organize on their own initiative until the 1860's, and the results before 1905 were relatively meager. Up to 1905, only one third of industry (including mining) had been organized in any way, and there was only one regional association that combined representatives of various branches of industry and trade, organized in St. Petersburg as late as 1897.[54] Among the most significant organizations were those in the mining, metallurgical, and oil industries, which began to make their appearance in the 1870's. These organizations, though influential as lobbies, were under strong government tutelage. The chairmen of their annual congresses were appointed by the Ministry of Finance (after 1906, by the Ministry of Trade and Industry), and it was the chairmen who arranged the programs of the congresses. From these programs, approved by the Ministry, there could be no deviation. The congresses were obliged to consider problems in which the government was interested, and their executive organs had to supply information to the government about the branches of industry they represented.[55]

The modest role initially played by the industrialists and the growth in their power and self-assurance can be traced in the three all-Russian congresses of trade and industry held before 1905. The first two, held in 1870 and 1882, were called on the initiative of the engineers and professors who had organized the first societies for the promotion of trade and industry in the 1860's. The third congress, held in 1896, was organized and sponsored by Witte's Ministry of Finance, not without protest, it should be added, from the earlier, private sponsors.[56] To each of these congresses, the merchants and industrialists sent progressively larger and more assertive delegations, but they were nevertheless outnumbered by the intellectuals and spokesmen of agricultural interests present, and they lost the debates on the tariff issue to the agricultural interests. All three congresses were held in connection with world fairs, apparently the only time the government would allow such gatherings.[57]

As the stormy years 1904–6 approached, the ground was being laid for a new departure both in the attitude of the industrialists toward the government and in their ability to organize. The Europeanization of the industrialists and the growth of their economic power during the 1890's have already been discussed. They were still dependent on state orders, state subsidies, and the general policy of an all-powerful state,[58] and their attitude toward the state necessarily remained cautious. Nevertheless, the weakness shown by the government in 1905, together with the coming of the Duma, gave the industrialists some scope to express their increasing aggressiveness in defense of their own interests.

The grounds for their dissatisfaction were many. The bureaucracy was in the hands of an agrarian aristocracy, ill-informed on modern economic needs and still contemptuous of productive labor. The Ministry of Finance was charged with the promotion of industry but Witte, a strong pro-industry minister, has written sharply about the difficulties he encountered in carrying out his duties.[59] The traditional protective attitude of the Russian nobility toward the lower classes caused frequent clashes with the industrialists over government labor policy. So strong was the desire of the bureaucracy to favor the poor rather than the rich that a shrewd observer like Polovtsev has aptly stated that "the first socialists are —chinovniks [the Russian term for government bureaucrats]."[60] Besides all this, many industrialists by 1905 were quite aware that their dependence on state orders was unnecessary, that a market potentially far richer than the state existed among the masses of peasants, and that government by bureaucracy was a severe handicap in the proper promotion of this market. For these and other reasons, the merchants and industrialists, hitherto two of the least active and most conservative elements of the population, joined virtually all other groups after January 9, 1905, in speaking out for the end of bureaucratic rule, the calling of a representative legislative assembly, and the establishment of civil liberties.[61]

New conditions required new organizations, and these now took the same form known in the West—the trade association, organized either to include all the manufacturers of a given industry, or organized territorially to include all the manufacturers in a given region. Virtually all trade and industrial enterprises, regardless of size, were swept into the movement to organize trade associations. Since all-Russian unions of industrialists were forbidden by the law of March 4, 1906 (Section II, Paragraph 6), a special dispensation was obtained from the Czar to permit the Minister of Trade and Industry to authorize such organizations.[62] As Ermansky points out, the industrialists were petitioning the government not for organizations "of the old type," but for "independent associations"; it is not likely that the industrialists were now subject to any special government supervision, except when they organized what the law defined as a "public meeting." Since it was now the intention of the government that capital and labor should organize independently and settle their disputes themselves, the newly established associations took action against strikers on their own initiative, using for the first time such standard weapons as the lockout and the black list. In addition, they acted as lobbies, combating proposed laws, drafting new ones, and seeking to interpret old laws in their favor. For the first time, the associations maintained a permanent legal staff. For the first time, too, the industrialists did not hesitate to act in concert through their associations to reject what they regarded as illegal demands made upon them by government agencies.[63] The days of the old-fashioned, illiterate, and submissive Moscow merchants were plainly a thing of the past. Nevertheless, significant groups of industrialists, apparently because of their continued heavy dependence on state orders, resisted the trend against state tutelage, and such organizations as the annual congresses of the metallurgy, mining, and oil industries continued to accept government-appointed chairmen and government-approved programs.

Another major development made possible under the new conditions was the organization, in 1906, of the permanent All-Empire Congress of the Representatives of Industry and Trade. Before 1905, it will be recalled, the three temporary all-Russian congresses were attended by more representatives of the intelligentsia and agrarian interests than of business. Now a permanent congress was organized, headed by a permanent council and executive committee, and composed solely of business interests.[64] As to the relation of the congress to the government, the decree authorizing the congress provided merely that the local administration was to be notified in advance when the congress was to be convened (Article 27). Article 30 placed the program under the control of the congress and its permanent council.[65] According to Pares, the congress usually met during the sessions of the Duma, of which many of its participants were members, and "sometimes its debates were the more interesting and important of the two."[66] The avowed purpose of the congress was to place the views of all industry before that new and all-important force in the Russian state, public opinion.

One further point should be mentioned on the Europeanization of Russian industry. As the complexity of its organization grew, it found need for the first time for the services of the intelligentsia, who, in the years before the Revolution, were beginning to enter the employ of trade associations, industry publications, etc., in considerable numbers. P. A. Berlin claims that 1,000 intellectuals, many of them former Marxists, were in the employ of the various capitalist organizations. The industrialists' increasing interest in general economic conditions provided still more common ground with the intellectuals, and, in 1910 in Moscow, a novel development occurred: Industrialists and intelligentsia engaged in economic conversations.[67] The industrialists remained liberal in their viewpoint and joined the intelligentsia in protesting the excesses of state tutelage that were again being manifested after the suppression of the Revolution of 1905.

Trade Unions

Before 1905, trade unions were illegal and were virtually nonexistent; the characteristic form of association in the professions and, to some extent, among the workers was the mutual-aid society (obshchestvo or kassa vzaimopomoshchi). Such societies, which could be established legally, provided aid in case of accident, illness, or unemployment, furnished funeral expenses, pensions, etc. They seem to have been common among the intelligentsia, as well as among the workers and artisans of Poland and the Baltic states and the Jews of the northwest provinces; but in the central Russian provinces, they were relatively limited in number prior to 1905.[68] Despite the illegality of strikes, these were common among the Russian workers from the 1870's on, and, beginning in 1895, they occasionally reached formidable proportions. A general strike played an important part in the success of the Revolution of 1905.

The first unions of workers (apart from those supported by the police) were organized in the two capital cities after January 9, 1905. During the "days of freedom" (the six weeks beginning October 22, 1905), trade unions were organized on a large scale throughout Russia. The suppression of the unions began in December, 1905, and continued thereafter with varying intensity. Even the promulgation of the new rules of association on March 4, 1906, which legalized trade unions, did not put a stop to suppressive measures. Nevertheless, despite great difficulties, skilled workers (printing workers, metalworkers, leatherworkers, tailors, cooks, etc.) did manage to form legal unions.[69] These unions survived until the outbreak of the war in 1914, although by comparison with the years of the Revolution (1905-7) with greatly reduced membership.

Bureaucratic repression and the activities of the employers' associations alone would have made the existence of the trade unions precarious, but the apathy of the workers was equally important, if not decisive, in reducing their membership and influence. The majority of the workers, it will be recalled, were peasants still tied to the land, many of whom came to the cities in the fall and winter for seasonal work and returned to the land in time for the harvest. These "workers" could be drawn into trade unions during the special circumstances of the years of the Revolution, but in normal times it was impossible to keep them interested in the day-to-day work of the trade unions, to convince them of the gains they could make, and to subject them to discipline and organization. The labor movement experienced a revival between 1911 to 1914, and new waves of strikes broke out, but for the most part these were spontaneous and unorganized.

Nevertheless, a number of trade unions in several big cities and industrial regions survived until the outbreak of World War I. Although constantly persecuted by the administration and at times dissolved, legal means for reorganization remained, and the government was now powerless to suppress the unions completely in the face of a determined attempt to keep them alive.[70] It is indicative of the firmness of the unions' position that, when a general strike threatened in 1913, the head of the St. Petersburg Okhrana advised against liquidating the unions (at least in St. Petersburg), on the ground that to do so might only hasten the strike.[71] Some of the surviving unions were publishing their own newspapers; all

were engaged in the attempt to satisfy the workers' expanding cultural needs. The sickness-insurance law of 1912 gave the workers a
new form of organization; sick-benefit funds were established in
various enterprises and were administered by a joint committee of
labor and management. The labor representatives were elected and
had a majority of one in the committees. Aside from the interruption of war and revolution, the potential development of self-
government among the workers afforded by these committees was
disrupted by the Bolsheviks, who were interested in controlling the
workers rather than in promoting their "self-activity." [72]

Under the old methods, when disputes broke out between the
workers and the entrepreneurs, it was not unusual for the government to intervene arbitrarily, at times favoring one side, at times
the other. When, despite government intervention, the workers engaged in strikes and disorders, police and sometimes troops were
required to suppress them. The government became aware of the
favorable climate thus created for revolutionary agitators, and, in
promulgating the new rules on association of March 4, 1906, its intention was to give both sides equal opportunity to form professional organizations and settle their disputes themselves. Strikes
for economic reasons were made legal in December, 1905; in 1907,
the Senate handed down a decision permitting labor unions to
have strike funds.[73] This was an important and desirable development, even if the government continued its old practices for the
time being. (As has been pointed out, the government permitted
the industrialists to organize beyond the bounds of the law of
March 4, while suppressing trade unions.) It is also true, in part,
that the provincial boards on voluntary association closed unions
that struck and did not permit the word "strike" to be mentioned
in the union bylaws, while the police continued to exile strikers as
ringleaders of rebellion.[74] Despite all this, it seems certain that, by
the eve of World War I, a useful beginning in trade-union organization had been made. Nevertheless, it was only a beginning; on
the eve of the Revolution, the vast majority of Russian workers had
progressed only slightly toward assuming the privileges and responsibilities of organized power, and, on the whole, they remained a
primitive and essentially anarchic group.

The Cooperative Movement

If the workers' attempt to organize trade unions in the years before the Revolution met with little success, the masses were making more progress in organizing cooperatives. The remarkable intensity of the cooperative movement—a movement that affected all strata of the population, but especially the peasants—in the last years of the Empire indicates that cooperative organization is deeply rooted in the Russian social tradition. We have seen that the guild, with its hierarchical gradations, had found no active response in Russian life when introduced by ukase in the eighteenth century. The artel, on the other hand, which has been a feature of Russian life for many centuries, is essentially a primitive form of cooperation.[75] As Russia became more and more modernized at the beginning of the twentieth century, the population entered into the cooperative movement with an energy and enthusiasm which may be compared only with those engendered by the movement for education. And when the artificial brakes imposed on the cooperative movement by the Czarist government were removed in 1917, the end of that year found Russia leading the world in the number of its consumer and credit cooperatives.[76] However, the quality of the cooperatives still left much to be desired, as did the quality of many other forms of voluntary association with at most fifty, and frequently far fewer, years of working experience, whose membership had not yet attained an adequate cultural level.

There were two main types of cooperatives in Russia. The consumer cooperatives were occupied primarily with retail and wholesale marketing, but during World War I, they also entered industrial production on a considerable scale. One of the outstanding features of the consumer-cooperative movement was the dominant role acquired in them by the peasants; in 1897, only 18 per cent of all consumer cooperatives were rural societies, but by 1914, the proportion had jumped to 86 per cent.[77] Credit cooperatives were dominated even more by the peasants, with only a minute fraction of them being nonpeasant. The main function of the credit cooperatives was the furnishing of short-term loans to their members.

Cooperatives first arose in Russia in the 1860's, but they could not acquire a firm basis until the 1890's. Their growth became really turbulent after the Revolution of 1905, partly because police restrictions were relaxed and partly because the peasants, for various reasons, exhibited a new and more receptive attitude toward them. On January 1, 1905, for example, there were 950 consumers' societies. On January 1, 1914, there were more than 10,000. Because of the difficulties in obtaining consumer goods during the war years, the rate of increase accelerated sharply, and, on January 1, 1917, the number had reached 20,000.[78] A similar growth took place among the credit cooperatives. On January 1, 1905, there were about 1,400 of both types; on January 1, 1914, the number had grown to 13,000.[79]

Along with the growth of primary cooperative societies, there was a tendency toward the establishment of cooperative unions. Here, however, the obstacles created by the autocracy were so great that their growth could not commence on a significant scale until the outbreak of World War I.[80] Before 1914, only 13 credit unions and 25 consumers' unions were in operation; on July 1, 1916, there were 84 credit unions and, at the end of that year, there were more than 200 consumers' unions.[81] However, all this applies only to legal cooperative unions. The need for cooperative unions was too great to permit their complete suppression by the bureaucracy, and, before the war, many that had never been legally authorized were in operation.[82]

The most important consumers' union was the Moscow Union of Consumers' Societies, founded in 1898, which, in the years before the war, became one of the largest federations of consumers' societies in Europe. In 1917, its name was changed to the All-Russian Central Union of Consumers' Societies. A very prominent role in the Russian cooperative movement was played by the Moscow People's Bank, opened in 1912, a national bank for cooperative credit with branches in all the principal cities of Russia. Aside from their very important contributions to the cooperative movement, these two national institutions were becoming powerful contributors to social and educational causes. Despite the short history of the cooperative movement in Russia, it occupies a very prominent place in the history of "social self-activity" before 1917. The most popular and successful of the mass movements in Czarist Russia, it performed an indispensable economic function.[83] Although its organizational structure was still defective, it was improving and becoming both more complex and more unified. Its primary organizations were, on the whole, sound and profitable. Closer and closer ties were being established with such other nonbureaucratic organizations as the zemstvos and the municipal governments. Like the zemstvos and the war-industry committees, it performed indispensable supply functions for the armed forces during the war. It disposed of capital valued in the hundreds of millions of rubles, and it was becoming more independent of official subsidies. It had assumed a primary role in spreading education to the people outside the state schools, surpassing even the zemstvos in the intensity of this work.[84]

Political Parties

The establishment of a constitutional regime and the growth of political parties contributed to the promotion of a more normal system of voluntary association after 1905. Not only was it now possible to have political opinions highly critical of the government, but it was also possible to build political parties around them that could participate in the elections to the Duma. The defects of the constitutional regime established after 1905 are well known. Quite apart from the electoral law, neither the Cadets nor any party to the left of the Cadets could become fully legal, i.e., their bylaws could not be registered under the law of March 4, 1906.[85]

There still remains the problem of what was meant by "legal" and "illegal" parties under the Czarist government. The "illegal" parties were naturally subject to great handicaps in the electoral campaigns, since they could not legally organize, hold party congresses, or publish official lists of candidates. In practice, however, local party committees met openly, party lists leaving no doubt as to which parties the candidates represented were published unofficially, and even party congresses were held secretly.[86] If anything, under the conditions prevailing in Czarist society, government persecution merely added to the votes of the opposition parties. In fact, in the elections to the Second Duma under the electoral law of December 11, 1905, Stolypin, using every resource available to the government to elect government favorites, succeeded instead in electing an overwhelming majority of the representatives of "illegal" parties. Once elected, the members of "illegal" parties, the Social Democrats included, could organize their party caucuses in the Duma, and even the most extreme parties could publish their own journals legally. Here, perhaps more graphically than in any other field, is revealed the underlying helplessness of the Czarist government, the wide gap that could exist between its aims and intentions on the one hand, and the actual results of its methods on the other. The presence in the Duma of genuine (even if only "unofficial") opposition parties meant the vigorous exercise of the Duma's right to question ministers concerning administrative abuses.

The Subsidized Organizations of the Extreme Right

With the emergence of constitutional government and party politics, the question of which parties and other voluntary groups would support the government and the autocracy (these were no longer synonymous) became all-important. The government was as poorly situated regarding such support as it was in the matter of the press. The gulf between state and society was now wider than ever, and by 1907, the opportunities for reconciliation created by the Revolution of 1905 had slipped away. The government and the bureaucracy were held in such universal contempt in Russian society that any organization associated with them automatically lost popularity. A good illustration from the pre-1905 period is the fate of the Red Cross, which, in Russia as in other countries, was organized during the 1860's. In Russia, it was placed under the control of the administration, with the result that it came to share the contempt with which the public regarded the bureaucracy as a whole, although in most other countries it was held in public esteem. By and large, the Russian Red Cross received few if any voluntary contributions from society, which formed its own organizations for disaster or war relief.

For example, during the famine of 1891, the government tried to channel all relief work through the Red Cross and special government organizations. At first it entirely forbade the formation of private relief organizations, but the agitated temper of society made the enforcement of this measure impossible, and the government was finally forced to yield. Of the private organizations that arose, those headed by Leo Tolstoy and V. I. Vernadsky (a well-known scientist and liberal public figure) were the best known and won the most public sympathy. Petrunkevich points out that even when the Grand Duke Nicholas Mikhailovich wanted to contribute

40,000 rubles, he gave it to Vernadsky rather than to the Red Cross.[87]

It is not possible at this point to discuss in detail the sources of support for the government after 1905. It is only necessary to note that a share of the funds used to subsidize the press went to organizations of the extreme right, with the same mournful results. Popular public figures could easily be compromised merely by being seen in public with a minister, while to accept money from the government (it was popularly called "dark money") constituted an outrageous scandal, one that it was considered expedient to hide, if possible. Furthermore, the funds were distributed in accordance not with the tastes of the ministers but with those of the Czar. While it was possible for the Czar to set a kind of party line, contrary to appearances he had no way of compelling anyone to follow it. What actually happened after the suppression of the Revolution of 1905 was that the Czar moved steadily to the right, while society moved steadily to the left. The result was that on the eve of the Revolution, the government-subsidized organizations of the extreme right—of which the best known was the Union of the Russian People—were in irretrievable decay, constantly declining in membership, despite heavy increases in government outlays from 1912 on.[88]

Conclusion

The history of Russia from 1905 to 1917 cannot be understood without a thorough study of the enormous growth of voluntary association during those years. This growth must, in fact, be recognized as one of the most significant developments in Russian history, for in it lay—and still lies—the key to the spiritual emancipation of the Russian people and to their emergence as the democratic, respected, and genuinely powerful nation they will almost certainly become in the future. With every new association, countless numbers of people were given the opportunity to learn to manage their own private affairs, and this habit, once acquired at any level, was bound eventually to be applied to national affairs. With the growth of such complex and influential associations as the Congress of the Representatives of Industry and Trade, the Moscow Union of Consumers' Societies, the Moscow People's Bank, and the zemstvo and municipal unions, new areas of important public activity irretrievably moved from the hands of the bureaucracy to those of society. With the growth of such associations appeared powerful and influential public bodies without whose assent and cooperation important national policies could not be carried out. It was for this reason that the autocracy became reluctant, in the latter half of the nineteenth century, to admit the existence of well-known famines (1891–92, 1897–98), for famines in a great state graphically demonstrated the bankruptcy of government by bureaucracy and made necessary the assistance of social forces endangering the survival of the autocracy. It is for this reason, too, that the autocracy watched the rise of voluntary associations and public initiative in general so suspiciously and jealously. In taking a hostile attitude toward them during the war, the Empress was only being consistent, as were those reactionary ministers who regarded them as nests of sedition and potential breeders of an alternative government. Their mistake was in believing that they still had a choice in dealing with them. The persecution of these organizations during the war was perhaps the last in a series of fatal mistakes made by the autocracy during the last years of the Empire.

The implications for the future of Russia of the growth of an organizational impulse and public initiative too elemental to be checked by the autocracy are enormous. However, before considering these implications in detail, it will be necessary to analyze the place in Russian life of the most important of the public organizations, the Russian form of local self-government—the zemstvo.

7

The Zemstvos — Local Self-government in an Autocratic State

THE Russian zemstvos were not voluntary associations, but units of local self-government established in 1864, shortly after the emancipation of the serfs. Since they were genuine units of self-government, divorced from the central administration, they came to be associated in the peculiar conditions of Russian life with society rather than with the state, and they represented, along with the voluntary associations, an area of public initiative subject to the supervision of the bureaucracy. Because of the scope and importance of their functions and the governmental powers with which they were endowed, they necessarily occupy a high place in the study of social self-activity in Russia. Moreover, in the contest between the state and society, which became so sharp toward the close of the nineteenth century, the zemstvos became the natural center for political activity and political leadership. The study of the zemstvos is, consequently, indispensable for an understanding of the politics of Czarist Russia and the background of the Revolution.

The importance of the zemstvos does not, however, stop at this point. The establishment of the zemstvos in 1864 represents a unique example of an autocratic state introducing local self-government in the provinces. This attempt to encourage self-government below while maintaining absolutism at the top necessarily proved inconsistent. The study of the Russian zemstvos therefore presents an unparalleled opportunity to demonstrate clearly and concretely why it is that political and social institutions at all levels of a given state tend everywhere to operate in accordance with the same principles. It is a study in essence of the very vitals of politics.

The Influence of the Social Theory of Self-government on the Zemstvos

The zemstvos were established during the era of the Great Reforms as a part of the reorganization of local administration made necessary by the emancipation of the serfs and the abolition of the administrative and judicial powers of the landed nobility on their own estates. Thirty-four of the fifty European provinces were affected by the reform. Various reasons, among them the presence of non-Russian landlords with separatist tendencies (e.g., the Poles of the western provinces) or a sparsity of population (e.g., the province of Astrakhan), accounted for the nonintroduction of zemstvos in a given area. Certain welfare functions affecting the local population—until then virtually not performed at all—fell within the jurisdiction of the zemstvos. These functions included the promotion of education; the advancement of agriculture, commerce, and industry; public health; charity and relief; fire prevention and fire insurance; the construction and maintenance of roads; the organization of the food supply (transferred to the bureaucracy in 1900); and the provision of veterinary services.

The zemstvos were established at two levels of local administration: the province (*guberniia*) and the district (*uyezd*). At each level there was a zemstvo assembly, which met only briefly once a year, and an executive board (*uprava*). The assemblies consisted chiefly of councilors elected by the local population. The boards consisted of a chairman and two members elected by the assemblies; under the law of 1864, the chairmen of both the provincial and the district boards had to be confirmed by the government. The district councilors were elected by the local population on the basis of a curial system. The first curia consisted of individuals who possessed land outside the cities (mainly the nobility); the second curia was composed of those owning property in the cities (mainly the urban bourgeoisie); the third curia was composed of the peasant communes. The provincial councilors were elected by the district zemstvo assemblies from the councilors who composed the district assemblies.

The zemstvos were endowed with some but not all the governmental powers normally associated with local self-government. To fulfill their functions on behalf of the local population, they could levy taxes and spend the tax receipts on their own initiative. The provincial zemstvo assemblies could also issue obligatory decrees, subject to the supervision of the administration. The zemstvos lacked police powers; the police in the Russian Empire was a part of the central administration, controlled ultimately by the Minister of the Interior. The zemstvos could enforce neither decrees nor tax levies without the cooperation of the Crown administration.

While this distribution of power between the zemstvos and the Crown administration conformed to the political realities of the time, it should be noted that it also conformed to the social theory of self-government, the only theory of self-government known in Russia at that time. The social theory of self-government contrasts society with the state, i.e., the social interests of the former with the political interests of the latter. By this theory, self-government is the management by local society of its own interests, which have nothing to do with the state. The state, in turn, continues to manage its own political interests, which have nothing to do with society.[1] This obviously defective theory of self-government ultimately gave way to the state theory of self-government (just as it had earlier in the rest of continental Europe), but, in accordance with it, the zemstvos were at first considered another form of voluntary association and were regarded by theorists of public law "not as links in the machinery of government, nor as authoritative organs of public law, but as private corporate associations formed in order to satisfy such local interests as are distinct from the interests of the State."[2] The sphere of activity of the zemstvos lay, as stated in the law, in "local benefits and needs," which were regarded as primarily economic in character, the state presumably bearing no responsibility for them.

The Constitutional Aspirations of the Nobility

All this, of course, serves to emphasize the zemstvos' status as genuine units of local self-government, endowed with the authority to act in their own sphere in the interests of local society. Yet, in drafting the statute on self-government, other influences led to serious infringement of the idea that state and society had their own spheres of activity in which neither one nor the other had the right to interfere. During the era of the Great Reforms, Russian society was in a state of extreme ferment, and the demand for the introduction of a constitution was widespread. There is evidence for believing that Alexander II was fully aware that the introduction of local self-government meant the beginning of a new era in Russian political life and would eventually lead to a constitution. In his view, Russian society was as yet too immature for a constitution, but he believed that the new institutions of self-government would serve as a proving ground for the training of public initiative and that, if they proved successful, he could give the signal for new advances. Rash and impetuous steps before the situation was ripe would be not only "harmful, but even criminal."[3]

There was widespread awareness that the zemstvo reform was a fundamental change that would inevitably lead to more changes, and, for that reason, many opposed the reform. Reactionary circles at Court were strong enough seriously to influence the law on self-government as it was finally worked out, with the result that it became a compromise between those who favored the new liberal course and those who opposed it. The reactionary Minister of the Interior, P. A. Valuev, who took over the preparation of the law from the more liberal Miliutin, consciously sought to pacify the liberals by giving the zemstvos independent power and by defining their competence loosely enough to provide for their future expansion; at the same time, however, Valuev feared the consequences of an independent zemstvo power and sought to place the new institutions under the strict tutelage of the old bureaucratic institutions. The resulting compromise of two irreconcilable principles of government was an unstable one, bound to drive the zemstvo workers to despair and disillusionment and to justify the worst fears of the reactionaries. The political temper of the zemstvo workers, most of whom were nobles, also influenced this outcome of the zemstvo reform.

The numerical predominance acquired in the zemstvos by the nobility was not at first overwhelming. The nobles apparently did constitute a majority in most of the district zemstvo assemblies, but in view of the cultural and economic level of the peasants, it is not likely that many peasants sought election to the provincial zemstvo assemblies or sought to compete with the nobility in managing the affairs of the district zemstvos. With the exception of such provinces as Viatka and Perm, where the nobility constituted only a small proportion of the population, it was inevitable that the most active zemstvo workers would be the nobles—and, furthermore, those nobles who preferred to remain in their districts and have no part in the state service.[4]

In the wake of the Great Reforms, reaction against the extreme repression under Nicholas I was virtually universal, and everywhere voices were raised for the granting of a constitution. From 1858 until 1862, one provincial assembly of the nobility after another petitioned the Czar for a fundamental reorganization of the state. Included in their demands were such reforms as the reorganization of the police and the courts, the responsibility of officials before the law, local self-government, freedom of press, speech, and assembly. When, after the promulgation of the peasant reform, the liberal officials who backed it were dismissed, the assemblies of the nobility moved to the left, and in 1862, a series of them openly asked for the calling of a national assembly of elected representatives as the most basic reform so that national problems could be weighed with the full participation of public opinion.[5]

Neither then nor later was the nobility a united class. But even those opposed to the emancipation of the peasants were in favor of convening a national representative assembly, and some of the predominantly conservative provincial assemblies did not hesitate to use the terrible word "constitution." They felt that their increased influence in a national assembly would bring adequate compensation for the postemancipation loss of local privileges. The main distinction between the conservative wing of the nobility and the liberal, or "conscience-stricken," wing lay in their views of the future of class privileges. The conservatives expected to retain these privileges and to acquire a dominant influence in the national assembly. The liberals, whose opinions were most eloquently presented in the Tver address to the Czar of February, 1862, advocated immediate equality for all classes. Both groups were opposed to the bureaucratic-police rule of Nicholas I, and both were in favor of a national assembly elected by all classes.[6]

Valuev, seeking to pacify the liberal aspirations of the nobility, gave open assurances that the zemstvos, only a first step in local self-government, would serve as a "school of representative institutions." It was his hope that the widespread demands for the "crowning of the structure" would be temporarily checked by deflecting interest from national to purely local affairs.[7] Nevertheless, from 1863 to 1865, the government had under consideration a project for national zemstvo representation. This was based on the supposition that, according to Valuev, "it would be difficult for the government permanently to refuse the request" for representative participation in administration and legislation.[8] The government abandoned the project, but the idea of national representation remained strong among the nobility, and in January, 1865, after the promulgation of the zemstvo law, the Moscow assembly of the nobility adopted an address (by a vote of 270 to 36) again appealing to the Czar to establish a national representative assembly. Thereupon the Moscow assembly was ordered closed by the government, the governor general was dismissed, and the Czar angrily withdrew from the provincial societies of the nobility the right they had obtained in 1831 to petition the Czar on matters of state. Henceforth, they were to confine themselves to their class needs in the narrowest sense of the term.[9] However, with the opening of the zemstvos, the nobility had acquired a new vehicle for carrying on their fight for national representation.

The Zemstvo as a Structure "Without a Roof and Without a Foundation"

The constitutional aspirations of the nobility were nevertheless to play a major role in the clashes between the zemstvos and the central administration only later. It cannot be emphasized too strongly that these clashes were inherent in the dual system of local administration set up in 1864, and would have arisen merely as a result of the attempts of the zemstvo workers to look after their local interests.[10] The basic difficulty was the presence in the state of two contrasting principles of government: at the top, the principle that the will of the monarch is supreme and is not limited by the independent activities of representatives of the people; in the localities, the principle that the representatives of the people are to act independently of the Crown administration in local matters, which are in practice indissolubly tied to general state matters and general state policy. There was no intention at the top of abandoning the autocracy, and to ensure the safeguarding of the interests of the autocracy, the new institutions of self-government were placed under strict administrative supervision.

The jurisdiction of the zemstvos and that of the state were deliberately vague and, at times, even conflicting. The law continued to place the very same responsibilities (i.e., public health, roads, fire fighting, etc.) on the reformed local administration as had been placed on the zemstvos. However, local administration was adapted primarily to the exercise of police functions and could not actively enter the field of local welfare. As the distinguished Russian jurist A. D. Gradovsky emphasizes, in the natural course of events almost everything that could be considered an object of local administration except strictly police functions entered into the competence of the zemstvos, which became the *de facto* centers of local administration.[11] The result was a strange division of power certain to generate antagonism between society and state. The zemstvos had the power of taxation and the power to issue decrees; it was they who raised funds and planned improvements in behalf of the local population. Since, however, they were regarded as similar to private corporations or societies, their control over any given local project stopped right there. To ensure the fulfillment of the local population's obligations toward a project, they had to turn to the local police, the sole agency allowed to use force against the population. Neither of these parallel sets of institutions, the zemstvos and the Crown administration, had any right to issue direct orders to each other, but the successful completion of a project required their close cooperation. The situation was explained thus by Gradovsky: "In the hands of governmental offices and officials remained power without competence; in the hands of the zemstvo institutions was concentrated competence without power." [12]

Ignoring, for the moment, the antagonism that had already arisen between the bureaucracy and society, it is clear that, given this division of local responsibility, violent and bitter clashes were inevitable. The separation of administrative management and administrative power was both artificial and unnatural, and either side was bound to feel that the other was intruding into its own domain. Lack of cooperation on the part of the lowest police officer or an order from him contradicting a zemstvo order was sufficient provocation for bitter feelings extending up to the provincial zemstvo assembly and the governor, causing petty disputes that would have to be heard and settled by the highest administrative court, the First Department of the Senate.

Lack of cooperation on the part of the local police, a common occurrence felt most acutely in the matter of tax collection, at times caused financial difficulties for individual zemstvos. The police, naturally enough, gave primary attention to collecting state rather than zemstvo taxes, and the zemstvos could do nothing to change this priority. They tried rewarding the police for the prompt collection of zemstvo tax arrears, but the Senate found this practice illegal.[13] They made generous allowances of special travel funds to the police officers, substantially increasing their yearly income, but the situation remained unchanged.[14]

It is interesting to note, however, that the zemstvos themselves could, in turn, refuse to cooperate with the government; by no means did they become obedient instruments of the administration. The central government could regulate in detail matters falling within the jurisdiction of the zemstvos, and, in doing so, it tended to ignore the existence of a new generation of public officials who knew their business and should have been consulted. In June, 1893, the government issued a law increasing administrative control over local medical institutions, which the zemstvo officials regarded as an infringement on their rights of autonomy, and they refused to enforce the law. After arousing a great deal of resentment by insisting on enforcement, the Minister of the Interior was compelled to retreat, and the law remained a dead letter.[15] The same was true of a law issued in June, 1902, concerning veterinarians. Under pressure from the zemstvos, the government called a conference of zemstvo officials after the law was promulgated, and then issued an order suspending its execution.[16] As Witte points out, even when a law did not seriously inhibit the activities of the zemstvos and seemed to be to their advantage, the mere fact that they had had no part in drafting the law and that it did not conform to their desires led to firm resistance and to the promulgation of a new law.[17]

In delimiting the spheres of action of the two competing systems of local administration, the government naturally favored its own bureaucracy, over which it had full control. The history of zemstvo participation in education is a case in point. Although the law of 1864 specified that zemstvo participation was to be chiefly economic, the law was at first interpreted liberally, and, for a time, primary education was almost wholly under zemstvo control. After Count D. A. Tolstoy became Minister of Education, the situation changed, and, beginning in 1869, a series of measures enacted limited zemstvo participation to planning schools and supplying the funds for them, while educational policy was determined by the Minister of Education and enforced by local bureaucratic organs subordinate to him.[18] While the government tendency to favor the bureaucracy over the zemstvos was most striking in the field of education, it extended to other matters as well, including some, such as the repair of roads, that had no political significance.[19] In the period before the Revolution, when the zemstvos had proved their worth and had acquired great popularity in society, the government took the additional step of engaging in outright competition with them in an attempt to capture some of their popularity. It granted assistance to the population in such important fields as agronomy and livestock-raising, gave financial aid to the handicrafts, and sent a flood of instructors in a variety of fields into the provinces. All this, however, was done haphazardly and unsystematically; there was no real hope that the government could effectively compete with the zemstvos, much less replace them in essential matters of local public welfare.[20]

The difficulties encountered by the zemstvos in their relations with the central government and the local bureaucracy reached down into the very heart of their own localities. The district, the lowest level at which the zemstvo was established, was a large unit, remote from the local population. It had to cope with problems such as epidemics, food supply, and general economic conditions, requiring close contact and cooperation with the local population and an intimate knowledge of the circumstances peculiar to the locality. These two conditions could have been best attained if an all-class petty zemstvo unit, which the district and provincial councilors would represent and serve, had been organized at the volost level. However, such a unit was not organized, and the agitation in its behalf was not successful until after the February Revolution, partly because the reactionaries preferred that the peasants remain isolated. As a result, the zemstvos did not have their own local agents familiar with the population and with local interests and needs, but had to deal with volost and village administrations under the domination of the local bureaucracy.[21] Given the hostility of the central administration above and the lack of close relations with the population below, the zemstvo was said to be a structure "without a foundation and without a roof."

The situation might have been at least partially repaired if the zemstvos had been free to send their agents into the localities to make on-the-spot studies. However, the autocracy could not tolerate the free movement of the intelligentsia into the villages. It was especially suspicious of the executive agents of the zemstvos, the hired employees known as the "third element" (the bureaucracy being the first, and the elected councilors the second, elements)— the engineers, doctors, teachers, statisticians, agronomists, etc.— without whom the zemstvos could not carry out their work. As the activities of the zemstvos expanded in the 1890's, increasing numbers of these professional men were hired.[22] They became an indispensable technical staff, and, quite unofficially, in the view of some, quite illegally, special advisory councils and committees of these professionals were organized around the zemstvo boards. There is no doubt that they acquired an important, if not a dominant, voice in the determination of zemstvo affairs. Together with a minority of the more liberal noble councillors, they caused the zemstvos to give fairer attention to the interests of the peasants as against those of the nobility. This combination also had a strong influence on the liberal political course taken by the zemstvos.

The third element consisted of those nonclass professionals (*raznochintsi*) who had the most radical tendencies among the intelligentsia. In the eyes of the more reactionary ministers of the interior (especially Plehve, 1902–4), they were outright revolutionaries who had displaced the legally elected representatives of the people (after 1890, mainly the nobility) in the management of zemstvo affairs. There is no question that, on the whole, they were opposed to the autocracy; that was true also of almost all the dedicated zemstvo workers, elected or hired. There is no doubt, too, that they were further to the left than the bulk of the elected councilors. There is good evidence, however, that for most of the period from 1890 to 1914, the majority of them were not revolutionaries. A considerable number of them apparently did become Marxists after 1900, at a time when Russian society as a whole was moving to the left, but it is, nevertheless, highly significant that after 1907 they were influenced by the general reaction against the revolutionary excesses of 1905, and that, eschewing ideological considerations, they devoted themselves once again to the practical work of the zemstvos.[23] This "ever-increasing note of practicality" among the third element is one of many signs that, in the period between the two revolutions, the relative freedom of press and organization were beginning to have sound results.

It was partly because of this distrust of the third element that the government hampered the attempts of the zemstvos, in the absence of lower zemstvo units, to send their own agents into the villages to gather necessary information. The zemstvos by law were charged with the problem of organizing the food supply, but they could be barred from sending investigators into the villages to check on food needs and food reserves. They were charged with the promotion of the economic welfare of the population, but could be forbidden to make their own firsthand surveys of local economic conditions. They were ordered by law to evaluate landed property for purposes of taxation, and were even given government subsidies to carry on the evaluation, but the Minister of the Interior had the right to stop the work at his discretion.[24] Much of this work was done by the zemstvo statisticians, who, as Polner points out, were virtually considered "the main enemies of the government."

It should be recalled, however, that here again the policy of the autocracy was preventive, and it would be a mistake to equate individual cases of prohibition with the total destruction of the investigative work of the zemstvos. Despite all the difficulties, many statisticians were carrying on their investigations, penetrating right into the peasant households. As the state subsidies show, the work was essential, and there was no personnel other than the zemstvo employees who had the time and the training to do it. Moreover, after the Revolution of 1905, when the government ceased to regard the peasants as unspoiled bearers of the autocratic tradition who must, at all costs, remain uncorrupted by the misguided intelligentsia, there was a considerable, though by no means complete, relaxation of government policy.

Attitude of the Government Toward United Zemstvo Activity

The desire on the part of the zemstvo workers of the several provinces to communicate with each other and otherwise join together to discuss common problems was normal and natural. One province might, for example, undertake one or another project and find it unworkable. Thereafter it would have been an unnecessary waste of time, money, and energy for any other province to experiment with the same project. Or, neighboring provinces would certainly want to take concerted action against such problems as epidemics and destructive insects or animals. Since the provinces were essentially artificially delimited administrative units frequently beset by almost identical problems, it was hardly conceivable these plagues could be fought successfully without concerted action. It would have been equally senseless for neighboring provinces to attempt to build roads or lay telephone lines without coordination. There was not one field of zemstvo activity in which united action, whether the provinces were neighboring ones or not, could fail to be advantageous both to the localities and the state. The final factor predetermining the desire of the zemstvos for united action was the impossibility of drawing a sharp line of demarcation between problems of local welfare and general state interests. In Russia particularly, where the state was accustomed to act in so broad a field, it was essential that national legislation be in harmony with actual conditions in the localities. The need for some form of common consultation with the government on necessary changes in the general state laws was therefore bound to be felt from the beginning.

Although the text of the law of 1864, and the discussions concerning it in the State Council, seemed to imply that cooperation between the zemstvos would be encouraged, the government took another view of the matter once the zemstvos were actually formed. If the government took a suspicious attitude toward the union of certain voluntary associations, it had good reason to assume an even more suspicious attitude toward the union of the zemstvos. The pressure from below was stronger in the case of the zemstvos than it was for the voluntary associations, but the government, nevertheless, took firm measures to stop concerted zemstvo action throughout the half century of zemstvo institutions. The result was the irritation of the whole zemstvo world—an irritation that contributed immeasurably to the growth of the conviction among the ordinarily sober-minded zemstvo men in 1904–5, and again in 1916–17, that peaceful collaboration with the government was impossible. And here, as in other areas of repression, the government in the end failed to achieve its objectives.

In the first decades after the establishment of zemstvo institutions, the government refused to permit one zemstvo to enter into an agreement with a neighboring zemstvo, even if the proposed agreement dealt with the most practical measures having no political significance whatsoever. Petitions to enter an agreement were customarily refused (by the governors concerned) on the purely formal ground that "the sphere of activity of the zemstvo institutions is limited by the boundaries of the province within their jurisdiction." [25] One of the most striking illustrations of the government's obstinacy, even at this level of zemstvo cooperation, occurred at the time of the coronation of Nicholas II, in 1896. Minister of the Interior Goremykin then vetoed a project by the chairmen of the provincial zemstvo boards to offer, as a gift, the pooled funds of the zemstvos in place of the customary bread and salt, which involved the purchase of elaborate dishes and salt cellars by each zemstvo.

As the role of the zemstvos in internal affairs became increasingly significant, the attempt to ban all forms of joint zemstvo action inevitably broke down. Beginning in 1902, but especially after 1905, a series of interprovincial zemstvo organizations concerned with such specific matters as food, insurance, and book trade and publishing were authorized by law. From the point of view of the zemstvo workers, the difficulty still remained that these organizations were wholly dependent on the discretion of the administration, and on the eve of World War I, a bill was under consideration in the Duma to work out fixed rules for them.[26]

At no time did the government lose its sensitivity toward the ideas of a zemstvo union (national congresses, regional congresses, a common press organ, etc.) and toward the closely associated idea of national representation. Until the Fundamental Laws of 1906 shifted the center of political agitation from the zemstvos to the Duma, the movement for a zemstvo union became also a movement for the establishment of national representation and of individual freedom. The first great wave of both movements, begun in the early 1870's, ended shortly after the assassination of Alexander II, on March 1, 1881. The second wave, which was more firmly rooted and, in effect, irresistible, began with the zemstvo addresses on the occasion of Nicholas II's accession to the throne in 1894, and ended with the promulgation of the manifesto of October 17, 1905. During the course of both waves, government policy remained, on the whole, inflexible, although some concessions were bound to be made. During the course of the second wave, the government even seemed to be more afraid of the attempts of the zemstvos to unite than it was of the revolutionary movement. However, the more the government attacked public initiative, the more the zemstvo men felt the need to unite; as Shipov, the Chairman of the Moscow Zemstvo Board and leader of the movement for union, specifically points out, the zemstvo men were driven toward union by their awareness that union was essential for the successful defense of the independence of local government.[27] It goes without saying that that which was not authorized legally was accomplished illegally.

The Reform of 1890

As already stated, clashes between the units of self-government and the central government were made inevitable by the absence of strict lines of demarcation between their respective spheres of activity and by the local units' lack of police powers. The government also expressed its lack of confidence toward the units of self-government by placing them under close administrative supervision. Almost from the beginning, the government decided that its supervision over the zemstvos was inadequate, and there followed a series of new laws increasing the dependence of the zemstvos on the central administration. This process reached its culmination in the new zemstvo statute of 1890, which increased administrative supervision still further and changed the zemstvo electoral law so as to give the landowning nobility an overwhelming predominance.

The zemstvo reform was initiated by Alexander III's reactionary Minister of the Interior, Count D. A. Tolstoy (1882–89). Recognizing that the "systematic opposition to the government on the part of the zemstvo institutions" was based not on the political unreliability of any individuals but on the dual system of administration set up by the statute of 1864, Tolstoy sought to remedy the situation by converting the zemstvos in effect into bureaucratic institutions. Since the zemstvos had become the *de facto* centers of local administration, and since it was unlikely that the local population would take any further interest in zemstvo affairs if Tolstoy's project became law, strong opposition to it arose among several of the ministers and in the State Council. In its final form, the statute of 1890 increased the governor's supervision over zemstvo activities but left intact the essential independence of the zemstvo institutions.[28]

The zemstvo statute of 1890 also changed the zemstvo electoral law so as to give the nobility an overwhelming predominance. The three curiae were retained, but the first curia now consisted only of the landed nobility and the second of all other property owners, except the peasants. The distribution of seats among the three curiae was such that the nobility was now able to elect a majority in almost all of the district zemstvo assemblies.[29] Since the nobility had rapidly been losing its land, it became common in the years between 1905 and 1917 that no elections were held in the first curia at all. In the majority of districts, the number of qualified nobles who showed up for the elections was smaller than the number of councilors to be elected, so that they automatically elected not only themselves but even those who were not present, whether they wanted to serve or not. In a number of districts, the total number of qualified nobles diminished, becoming actually smaller than the number to be elected.[30]

"We" and "They"

Despite this shortsighted attempt to turn the zemstvos over to a class that was in decline—a class, moreover, that was anything but the bulwark of the autocracy it was supposed to be—and despite the strengthening of the control of the governor over the activities and personnel of the zemstvos, the latter continued on their own course. The basic independence of the zemstvo organs from the central administration remained untouched, and, as Tolstoy himself admitted, opposition to the government on the part of the zemstvo workers was inevitable. What actually happened was that the more reactionary noble landowners stayed away from the elections and the liberal wing continued to dominate zemstvo activity. In their efforts to overcome the resistance of the more conservative-minded nobles and to give the zemstvos a democratic direction, the liberals were joined by the third element, which grew steadily in number and influence during the 1890's.

The failure of the statute of 1890 was foreshadowed as early as 1894, when Nicholas II was presented with a series of zemstvo addresses requesting, in cautious and guarded tones, greater unity between Czar and people, and consultation of representatives of the people on the needs of the country. The Czar's well-known reply, in which he referred to the "voices heard in several zemstvo assemblies of people carried away by senseless dreams about the participation of zemstvo representatives in matters of internal administration," likewise foreshadowed the continuation of the severe bureaucratic repression initiated by Alexander III. Since, by the beginning of the twentieth century, Russian society was too mature to continue to tolerate the ill-conceived and senseless tutelage of the state, the mild zemstvo demand of 1894 for greater unity of Czar and people was replaced, ten years later, by the demand for the establishment of a ministry responsible to a democratically elected parliament.

Under the impact of the government's inflexible policy of hampering zemstvo activity, the fundamentally loyal zemstvo men lost all hope of obtaining constructive concessions from above and resorted to radical tactics in order to bring about a radical reorganization of the state. Every weapon in the government arsenal was used, in the utterly vain hope of compelling the zemstvo workers to submit meekly to the prescriptions from above, at the expense of the needs of the country and the localities, and to confine themselves exclusively to "local benefits and needs." The situation was described thus by Shipov:

It was possible to compare the work of the zemstvo boards with the work of a steam engine operating under unfavorable circumstances, so that the greater part of the energy developed by the machine is lost in unproductive friction and only the smaller part goes into useful work. In projecting and organizing a plan of work, it was necessary not only to have in mind that which was expedient, but also to expend much attention, time, and effort to ward off the always possible counteraction of the administrative authorities. Nevertheless, all precautions proved insufficient, and zemstvo work was doomed inevitably to prolonged, unproductive friction.[31]

The harsh and increasingly rigid policy of the government toward public initiative naturally pushed problems of politics into disproportionate prominence, forced the zemstvo men further and further to the left, and inspired them to draw closer in an illegal union in order jointly to defend their interests; but it also had the effect of deepening the chasm between state and society to a point rare, if not unknown, in the annals of any other country. The chasm was symbolized by the custom that took hold among the zemstvo men, even the most conservative of them, of referring to "we" and "they" —"they" being, of course, the representatives of the central government. State and society became two warring and irreconcilable camps between which there could be no collaboration, and, in the eyes at least of the most radical of the zemstvo workers, no peace and no accommodation. This situation explains the contempt with

which society treated publications and organizations subsidized by
the government. Those who defended the autocracy, those who
were even seen in the company of a high official, became compromised in the eyes of society and were virtually regarded as traitors.
The injection of politics into every phase of life created a situation
not unlike that of the modern totalitarian state, except that it was
society, not the state, which called the tune. On the eve of the
Revolution of 1905, the central government was in a state of virtual collapse, discredited and isolated.

After the Revolution of 1905, the position of the zemstvo as an
immediate political factor in Russian life changed. In the days
when no legal outlet for political activity existed and when social
and political discontent were rising, the zemstvos had become the
natural center of political opposition. It was the zemstvo workers
who were bearing the full brunt of government repression and who
most urgently felt the need for constitutional government. Among
them were some of the most distinguished representatives of the
nobility and the intelligentsia, with years of practical semigovern-
mental experience, which could not be matched outside the zemstvo world. In the zemstvo provinces, where large numbers of the
third element were also operating, there existed the nuclei of organizations, legal and illegal, that could serve as a base for rallying
the entire population.

After 1905, the center of political opposition naturally shifted to
the State Duma and to the political parties, whether authorized or
not, organized relatively freely and participating in the elections to
the Duma. Under Stolypin, the extreme repression of the zemstvos
was replaced by a new attitude of confidence in them and by an
active attempt to win them over to the side of the government.
Moreover, the bulk of the provincial nobility, largely indifferent to
politics, who, before 1905, had moved to the left with society as a
whole, had been frightened by the peasant disorders during the
Revolution and was now moving to the right. In the zemstvo elections held after 1905, the formerly dominant liberal element found
itself in a minority, and zemstvo work was taken over by moderately
conservative, even reactionary, nobles.[32] However, the political attitude of the conservative nobility of 1905 and after had, on the
whole, nothing to do with the nobility's attitude toward zemstvo
work, which, under its leadership, continued to develop at the same
rate as before.[33]

Indispensability of Public Initiative in World War I

The outbreak of World War I shattered the illusion of the government that the bureaucracy alone was capable of managing the affairs of the country. At the time of the Russo-Japanese War, in 1904, an interzemstvo organization had been formed with the permission of the Czar but over the opposition of Minister of the Interior Plehve, to provide relief for battle casualties. The interzemstvo organization continued to function in the field of disaster relief at the conclusion of the war, though, after the death of Prime Minister Stolypin, it had become relatively inactive. At the beginning of World War I, it was immediately reconstituted as the All-Russian Union of Zemstvos with the support of all but one provincial zemstvo. Although the official function of the Union was relief for the sick and wounded, it became the coordinating agency for the normal welfare functions of the local zemstvos—that is, it became a key factor in the organization of the entire Russian rear. Its functions embraced the placing of army orders, and it even operated its own factories. By 1916, its budget amounted to 600 million rubles a year, most of it drawn from the state treasury, and, directly or indirectly, hundreds of thousands of persons were at its service.

The enlistment of public initiative during the war did not stop with the zemstvos. Municipal self-government was overcoming its backwardness, and an All-Russian Union of Towns was organized along the same lines and with the same broadened functions as the Union of Zemstvos. As a result of the munitions crisis of the spring of 1915, the two Unions formed a joint committee for the supply of the army, known as the Zemgor (from the first letters of *zemstvo* and *gorod*, the Russian word for town).

Another result of the crisis of 1915 was the formation of two other major organization complexes to enlist public aid in organizing the rear. One complex, the central and local war-industries committees, was designed to permit the self-mobilization of industry. These committees included not only industry representatives, but also representatives of the workers, the two Unions, and the government. Unlike the other organizations mentioned, the Special Councils organized in the spring of 1915 on the insistence of the Duma were governmental institutions, but they were designed to modify the purely bureaucratic mobilization of the rear that had led to disaster. There were five of these Special Councils—for Defense, Fuel, Food, Transport, and Refugees. Although presided over by different ministers, the Special Councils also included representatives from other government departments, representatives elected by the Duma, by the State Council, by the two Unions, and by the Central War Industries Committee. The important role played by the cooperative movement in supplying the army during the war was mentioned in the previous chapter.

That public initiative had become an indispensable factor in internal administration was clear enough in 1914. It was, however, to be demonstrated beyond the shadow of a doubt during the course of the war, when the unyielding adherence to the illusions of the government spelled disaster for Russia. Never before in Russian history had the state given so wide a scope to popular initiative or permitted this initiative to manifest itself on so vast a scale. Never before in Russian history had society, as distinct from the state, exhibited the heights of creative energy reached in 1915–16. The harnessing of the vital forces of the nation could not prevent Russia's collapse in 1917; the blame for this rests exclusively on the Czar and the bureaucracy. But this mobilization of forces did solve the munitions crisis of 1915. Neither the collapse of Russia nor the Revolution can be traced to a shortage of munitions. There is not even the slightest vestige of truth in the belief that, on the eve of the Revolution, the Russian people needed more state tutelage, more pushing around by the police. What they needed, above all, was the freedom to organize the growing creative forces of society, without interference from a huge and unproductive state apparatus set in motion merely to maintain unrestricted power at the top.

The Czar, or, more particularly, the Czarina, thought otherwise, and the work of the Union of Zemstvos, as well as the Union of Towns and the war-industries committees, was constantly frustrated because of the suspicious attitude of the government. The attitude of the government had not been uniform after 1905. During the first wave of zemstvo constitutional activity—from 1880 to 1882—under Loris-Melikov and Alexander III's first Minister of the Interior, N. P. Ignatiev, the government had resorted to a policy of conciliation toward the zemstvos, and toward public opinion in general. This was now to be repeated at the end of the second wave of zemstvo constitutional activity under Prime Minister and Minister of the Interior Stolypin, who showed that he well understood the danger of the "we" and "they" division. He made an honest, albeit unsuccessful, attempt to bring "public men" into his cabinet. A reform of the local administration and the zemstvos was projected but never realized. Stolypin even went so far as to propose that the state treasury cover all those expenditures of the zemstvos and municipal dumas for which their own resources were insufficient. There were to be no limits to state subsidies, the only requirement being that the governor and a committee of the Ministry of the Interior find the expenditure "useful and necessary to local life." [34] In 1911–12, zemstvo institutions were introduced into nine new provinces of European Russia, raising the total number of zemstvo provinces from thirty-four to forty-three. Interference with the decisions and personnel of the zemstvo institutions, now managed by conservative nobles, became less frequent and was avoided by the government as much as possible. The governors were ordered by Stolypin to conciliate society, to irritate no one unnecessarily, and, in particular, to court the friendship of influential social circles.[35] In St. Petersburg, the equally wise attempt was made to end the cold, formal, and aloof attitudes of government departments toward visiting zemstvo and municipal officials and to treat them with sympathy, cordiality, and understanding.[36] The interzemstvo organization was given active, even if limited, support. However, the policy of conciliation ended with the death of Stolypin in 1911, and the government thereafter continued the hopeless warfare against the zemstvos begun in the very first years of their existence.

During the war, the Union of Zemstvos worked out plans for dealing with such problems as epidemics, the care of refugees and disabled soldiers, the supply of food, etc., but these were not destined to be realized. The Ministry of the Interior sought, instead, to assign as much of the work as possible to local bureaucratic organizations; or to the Red Cross; or to a committee headed by a grand duchess. When, as a result of this lack of planning, inefficient methods of operation, and confusion of authorities, essential work was being neglected, the Union usually managed to obtain some concessions without, however, being able to carry out its over-all plan. In special emergencies, the two Unions, and not the bureaucracy, were able to act promptly, but, as soon as the emergency was over, the government reminded the Unions that their jurisdiction did not extend beyond rendering aid to sick and wounded soldiers, and precedence was then given to a bureaucratic organization. The constant, petty, and senseless persecution of public organizations during the war, along with the manifest inability of the government properly to organize the urgent problems of internal administration, from which the public organizations were in whole or in part excluded, goes far to explain why, by February, 1917, the reigning dynasty was approaching its demise.

The hopelessness of the government's fight against the zemstvos was perhaps revealed more clearly during the war years than at any other time in their history. At the same time that the government was treating the Union of Zemstvos with such complete distrust, it was giving it hundreds of millions of rubles to ensure the performance of the most essential war functions. At the same time that the Minister of the Interior was trying to limit sharply the jurisdiction of the Union, army headquarters, under the personal command of the Czar after September, 1915, was drawing the Union into wider and wider collaboration. These facts accurately reflect the basic contradiction in which the government found itself. It could neither do without the union—it could not otherwise successfully conduct the war—nor do with it—for that would imply that the existing government was unnecessary. The government's dilemma was raised in the Council of Ministers in September, 1915, by several of the ministers, among them the Minister of Agriculture, A. V. Krivoshein, by no means a reactionary.

A. V. Krivoshein and others raised the general question of the self-abolition of the government from the time of the organization of the Special Council of Defense, which everywhere favors the public organizations; everywhere there come forward various public men, and the Zemstvo Union with Prince Lvov at its head. This prince is, in fact, becoming virtually the head of a special government; at the front, they speak only about him: He is the savior of the situation, he supplies the army, feeds the hungry, heals the sick, organizes barbershops for the soldiers. . . . But who surrounds him, who are his collaborators, who are his agents? Nobody knows. All of his work is beyond control, although hundreds of millions of state funds are poured out to him. It is necessary to put an end to this, or to turn complete power over to him. Irresponsible directors of responsible affairs and state funds cannot be tolerated. It may be impossible to remove the power already usurped by the Union, but there is no need further to expand its functions.[37]

The dilemma cited was that of a government in power that had outlived its usefulness and, by retaining power, had split state and

society into two irreconcilable camps. In this highly charged atmosphere, any accomplishment by the public organizations seemed like
an overpowering advertisement for society and against the existing
government. The more the government became conscious of its
own weaknesses, the more suspicious was its attitude toward the
public organizations. The increased persecution of the public organizations drove society to the left, and the ministers soon found
cause to become even more suspicious. The last Minister of the
Interior, A. D. Protopopov, a Rasputin appointee, in refusing to
permit the Union of Zemstvos to hold a scheduled congress in
Moscow in December, 1916, told Prince Lvov that he was aware
that the Cadets had a plan to kidnap the Czar from headquarters,
bring him to Moscow, and force him to kneel and swear allegiance
to the constitution.[38]

Ignoring, for the moment, the defects of the government as a
whole during the war, the outcome of the fifty-year struggle between the government and the zemstvos on the eve of the war's
conclusion is striking. To the zemstvo men and to society at large,
it seemed that the main interest of the government was not in
bringing about an honorable peace for Russia, but in maintaining
its power at any price. Unable to organize the country for victory,
the government sought, nevertheless, to prevent loyal and patriotic
social forces from doing the job. It seemed to be indifferent to the
fate of Russia, the real interests of the people; all its attention
seemed to be concentrated on the problem of fighting its own subjects, not the enemy. This was a lesson that every patriotic Russian,
regardless of his political views, could not fail to understand by the
end of 1916.

The Incompatibility of Autocratic Government with Local Decision-Making in Any Sphere

The February Revolution of 1917 was, in part, the inevitable result of the dual system of administration set up in Russia in 1864.
Once the principle of local self-government, and of social self-activity in general, took root, the only question remaining was whether
the ultimate reform of the principle of autocracy at the top would
take place peacefully or by force. In order to safeguard local interests, the men directing the zemstvo institutions had no choice but to
seek the expansion of their jurisdiction, the acquisition of police

power, and a voice in national legislation and administration. If the principle that the will of the Czar was not limited by the will of the people was to be maintained, the ministers had no choice but to reduce the competence of the zemstvos, to confine their activity to "local benefits and needs" in the narrowest sense of that term, and, in the long run, to destroy them completely. There is no basis whatsoever to the idea that local government represents a nonpolitical sphere, in which, in the interest of efficiency, free or partial rein may be given to individual and public initiative at the same time that the supremacy of the will of the autocrat (in modern euphemistic terms, the "party") is rigidly maintained at the top. Local government is indissolubly connected with national government, and political considerations alone determine whether or not the introduction of local self-government or any form of decentralization is feasible.[39] The primary purpose of local administration in an autocratic state is to ensure the dominance of the central authorities over all segments of the population, and the more autocratic the state, the more it disregards the wishes of the people, the smaller the leeway given local administrators.

There is evidence in the history of many other countries that autocracy and local decision-making cannot exist side by side, and that, inevitably, one or the other will ultimately triumph. As a general rule, it may be said that the French Revolution dealt a fatal blow not only to monarchical absolutism in Europe but also to centralized administration, and that the emergence of constitutional government in a given country was followed sooner or later by the introduction of local self-government. In France, the succession of liberal and absolutist regimes after the Revolution was accompanied also by changes in the institutions of local administration, until finally the triumph of the Third Republic in 1870 led to a steady trend toward decentralization and self-government. In Prussia, the granting of a constitution at the national level in 1850 led, in 1872 and 1875, to the establishment of self-government at the district and provincial levels. One of the first steps taken by modern dictatorships has been the destruction of local self-government and the introduction of extreme centralization. The movement may be from the bottom up or from the top down; in any case, national and local institutions of government tend, in the long run, to be modeled on common political principles.

However, not only institutions of government are so affected;

there is ample evidence that all institutions, social as well as governmental, constitute an integrated whole, with the various parts so functioning as to complement each other and to inculcate common patterns of behavior. Deviations from the common pattern create stresses and strains—disequilibrium—in the integrated structure and, in the long run, these tend to be resolved either by the elimination of the deviation or its absorption of the whole.[40] It is surely no accident, for example, that the United States is covered with a network of voluntary associations, almost invariably functioning on the principle that the deciding voice belongs to the group as a whole and that elected representatives are responsible to the group and act with their consent.

It would be a mistake to suppose that the traditional pattern in Russia was based on unquestioning obedience to an army of chinovniks and secret police. This was and is alien to the Russian social tradition; it is the artificially inculcated fruit of recent governments, which have sought to retain their power at any price. The traditional social pattern in Russia is similar to that of the Far East and is based on the family. The three basic institutions (there were hardly any others)—the family, the commune, and the autocracy—differed more in size than in structure; all were held together by patriarchal authority. Within each unit, the members were equal, but the head of the family—the father, elder, or Czar—had unlimited authority. The obedience exacted was more the obedience of a child than that of a slave. Equals were addressed as "brother" (*brat*); superiors, including the Czar, were addressed as "father" (*batiushka*). This conception of the Czar as the head of a vast family accounts, in part, for the unlimited power he enjoyed and for the peasants' view that "father" could be relied upon to look after their needs.[41]

With the modernization of Russia, patriarchal authority began to disintegrate—in the family, in the commune, and, ultimately, in the nation. In its place came the growth of individualism, and, for the first time, organizations other than the commune began to take root and to exhibit a sustained independent initiative. The Czars, however, continued to believe that they were entitled to absolute obedience and sought to perpetuate patriarchal relations in the village, even though their primitive social foundations were disappearing. Until the elections to the First Duma, they and their reactionary supporters continued to assume that the peasants were the

unspoiled pillars of the autocratic tradition whose devotion to the
autocracy was beyond question. When the artificially perpetuated
patriarchal relations produced results opposite from those expected,
force was brought to bear to extract the obedience and passivity
that were no longer offered voluntarily. The problem for the Czars
was not merely to ensure the obedience of the zemstvos, but also
that of organized society in all its manifestations.

It is interesting to note that Witte, in his memorandum on the
incompatibility of self-government and autocracy, shrank from this
conclusion. It is not self-government "in the broadest sense of the
word" that is incompatible with autocracy, he maintained, but only
one specific kind of self-government, namely all-class institutions
based on the elective principle and concerned with the administration of state functions in a locality in behalf of the population as a
whole. Voluntary associations of all kinds and class societies were
specifically and firmly excluded; these belong to the realm of the
"personal activity of the individual, material and spiritual," and "lie
outside the general sphere of state influence." Even to as conservative a minister as Goremykin, the consistent opposition to self-government seemed like a kind of horror, for it meant the acknowledgment that unlimited bureaucratic rule would become necessary for
the preservation of the autocracy and that the population would be
converted into an "amorphous mass" (*bezsviaznyia tolpy*, literally
"disconnected crowds"), into "human dust" (*liudskaia pyl*). In
theory, such a state of affairs seemed unthinkable to all the ministers, and Witte blandly agreed that the individual must be given
full scope under the law to pursue his private interests outside the
sphere of politics.

Only in abstract theory is it possible to imagine a state in which all
social activity would be replaced by the activity of chinovniks and the
whole sphere of private-legal interests would be regulated by organs of
government. It is possible to say with assurance that, in such a state, the
whole population would be turned into "an amorphous mass," into
"human dust." . . . For my part, I am deeply convinced that only with
a population capable of self-activity can there be a powerful state, and
that a healthy policy of an autocratic empire must be directed toward
the broadest possible development of social activity in the sphere of
private-legal interests, must treat with confidence all manifestations of
public activity not concerned directly with the state structure or its internal and external administration.[42]

These laudable sentiments on the part of Witte, shared by Goremykin and apparently by the other ministers, remained pure
theory. Once the Czar had resolved to adhere to the idea of the
Empress that the "Czar can do anything," then governmental
policy inevitably moved toward the creation of the kind of state
Witte could conceive only in "abstract theory," and the artificial
distinction he drew between self-government and self-activity in
governmental institutions and in private societies was forgotten. If
Goremykin's conception that local self-government had nothing to
do with the political order was an illusion, so was Witte's conception that organized private interests are neither a concern of the
state nor can influence it. Every organized social group is a potential
citadel of politics, exercising authority over its members and the
public which cannot be claimed by the state. In a society beset by
a rising political temper, political activity forbidden in one group
will appear in another, whether the original interest of the group
be syphilis, alcoholism, or bird watching.[43] Habits of self-government and self-reliance acquired in one field are inevitably carried
over into other fields. The truth is that public initiative in any
sphere was the deadliest enemy of the autocracy, and, as has been
demonstrated in this and the preceding chapters, it was so treated
by the government. In more recent times, this truth has been vividly
demonstrated by the Nazis, one of whose first moves on taking
power was to carry out the policy of "coordination" (*Gleichschal-
tung*), i.e., the subjugation of *all* state and social institutions to the
will of the party. The dilemma of the Czar, not encountered by the
Nazis or, for that matter, by the Bolsheviks, was that neither he
nor his supporters could face the full implications of their policy.
Bound by the traditional methods of bureaucratic rule, by the needs
of the state, and even by some vestiges of human decency, they
could resort only to ineffective half-measures.

Why Russia Was Moving Inevitably Toward Democracy

The period from 1907 until 1914 was a period of counterrevolu-
tion, but it was a period also of the consolidation of the gains made
during 1905–6. It would be a grave misreading of the significance of
this phase of Russian history to disregard the relative freedom of
press and organization then being enjoyed by Russian society. If it
is true that all social institutions are interrelated and have innate

political significance, regardless of their primary purpose, then it is inconceivable that the Czar could have continued indefinitely to move to the right, while society simultaneously continued to organize and to state its views with relative freedom. The government made some inroads on this freedom—for example, in forbidding students to organize once more in 1911, in restoring an index of forbidden books for the masses (only in school libraries) in 1912, and in persecuting the trade unions; but it had become powerless to eliminate the new press laws and the new laws on voluntary association. It has already been mentioned that a new press law was drawn up by Minister of the Interior N. A. Maklakov, but that nothing came of it. Exactly the same happened to the attempted revision of the law of March 4, 1906, on voluntary association. The revision was introduced into the Duma at the beginning of 1911, but died a natural death there, and the government did not dare to defy public opinion and act on its own.[44] Inside and outside the zemstvos, relative freedom of press and organization continued to be enjoyed, and there can be no doubt that it was undermining the power of the autocracy and the Czar's own freedom of action in ways he could only partially understand.

The war appears to have been an essential condition for the precipitation of the February Revolution. Had there been no war, there are good grounds for believing that Russian society's growing maturity and its new ways of action at the lowest levels would have forced the central government to adjust its ways of action at the top without a revolution. Given the limitations mentioned, within which Czarist policy was conducted, what the Czar and the Czarina thought about it could not have affected the result.

With or without a revolution, there can be no question that Russia was following the other major European powers in moving from absolute monarchy to constitutional democracy. The social foundations of autocracy were crumbling, and, with each day, the strains and stresses created by autocratic rule, the resistance it encountered, were becoming greater and greater. As many Russians frequently put it, change was being brought about by life itself. Probably the most fundamental misconception entertained by the outside world about Russia has been the idea that *only a violent and radical revolution* could contribute to change. A revolution was already going on, silently, it is true, and even hidden beneath the day-by-day drudgery under way in the zemstvos, the schools, the

cooperatives, and all other private societies; but it was going on as
surely and as thoroughly as any revolution known in history. It can
be said without any qualification whatsoever that, had this silent
revolution been allowed to continue in 1917, Russia would today
have been more drastically transformed than it has been transformed by more than four decades of Bolshevik rule, paid for at so
terrible a price. There is, after all, no substitute for sound evolution
in the realization of any vision of society or government. All that
revolution can do is to prepare the way for it, if it is, in fact, being
blocked.

What was needed, above all, to make Russia a thriving democracy and a great state was the organization and enlightenment of
the masses on the basis of self-government and "self-activity."
Needless to say, the much-despised gentry toiling in the zemstvos
was contributing more to this end than the "great" standard-bearers
of progress known as the Bolsheviks, who, in accordance with Leninist theory, were busy imposing their will on the trade unions and
suppressing any signs of self-government among the workers. It is
clear that the attitude of any government and any party toward
this problem of the organization and relative freedom of expression
of the masses provides a sensitive index of its real attitude toward
democracy. Here, then, is a means for judging any Russian government of the future, which in other respects is hardly likely, for a
time at least, to resemble the governments of the Western democracies. Here, too, is the basis of a program on which all future Russian
parties and Russian leaders genuinely interested in democracy can
unite.

FOUR

STATE AND SOCIETY IN CONFLICT

8

The Revolution of 1905 and the
Emergence of
Constitutional Government

The Historical Background of the Clash Between
State and Society

LIKE THE absolute monarchies of Western Europe, the Russian autocracy performed valuable historical services for the nation, and its rise was made possible by the support of the people. Its main service was the elimination of warring feudal entities and the creation of a unified national state capable of defending the national interest against outside enemies. Both the autocracy and Russian society had major characteristics distinguishing them from their Western European counterparts, but their historical course was nevertheless similar. As life became more complex and society more mature, the police-bureaucratic methods of the absolute monarchies could no longer satisfy the national interests and became intolerable to the people. Since the absolute monarchies rested on a large measure of popular support, they were compelled, in the end, to yield to the overwhelming influence of public opinion. Despite the superiority of power enjoyed by the state over society, the state in each case, Russia included, was unable to wage prolonged battle with public opinion.

In Russia, however, the state was unusually strong and society unusually weak. What primarily distinguished the Russian autocracy from the absolute monarchies of Europe was the absence, until the nineteenth century, of an organized society capable of acting independently of the state and placing limits on its powers. As Russian society began to organize, therefore, and to overcome its backwardness, it met more rigorous countermeasures on the part of the autocracy than could be employed by the absolute monarchies of Western Europe. The pace at which society could organize was, furthermore, necessarily slow. Since education appears to have been a prerequisite for organization, the movement began with a few intellectuals of the nobility, and, as society became more modernized, spread slowly to broader elements of the population. The spread of education and organization increased the capacity of society to resist repression, and, with their spread, the Czars could head off mass discontent only by making progressively more liberal concessions.

It was to be fateful for the reigning dynasty that its representatives failed to recognize this fact. Unwilling to face the necessity of relinquishing their power, and blinded by the past glories of the autocracy and the traditional support they had received from the peasantry, they preferred to believe that the signs of discontent were primarily the work of a few "noisy" intellectuals whose capacity for making trouble always seemed to be disproportionate to their numbers. The Czarist concessions tended, therefore, to come too late, and the result was an increasing feeling of distrust toward the government on the part of society, even of its moderate elements, who began to think of the government as their enemy. At the latest, this antagonism between state and society arose under Nicholas I (1825–55), whose despotic measures far exceeded the readiness of public opinion to tolerate them.

The aspiration of Russian society for freedom dominated the entire history of Russia during the nineteenth and early twentieth centuries. There was, of course, a tradition of meek submission to state authority, but it may be found in its clearest form only as far back as the seventeenth century. At the very time that the autocracy reached its peak under Peter the Great, at the end of the seventeenth century, an impetus was given to the Westernization of Russia which gradually reversed the trend and demonstrated, beyond any shadow of a doubt, that the Russian people were no longer willing to tolerate excessive and arbitrary state authority. Survivals of the older tradition necessarily remained, but what stands out after the eighteenth century is a rich tradition of revolutionary thought and revolutionary action symbolized by a galaxy of great names. Once the impoverished illiterates of the seventeenth century were converted into the educated milieu of the nineteenth century engaged in creating a modern industrial society, the creative genius of the Russian people came to the fore, as did a capacity for managing their own affairs that clashed head on with the older tradition of prescription from above. The result was the rise of a movement for freedom, known in Russian history as the "Liberation Movement." [1]

The easiest path to freedom obviously involved the cooperation of the omnipotent Czar, and it is readily understandable why the Great Reforms of Alexander II aroused so much enthusiasm among the moderate element of the intelligentsia. Even if he had not immediately granted a constitution, such measures as the introduction of local self-government, trial by jury, equality before the law, punishment only after a fair trial, autonomy for the universities, and liberalized censorship laws were all incompatible with the autocracy, and, ultimately, their consistent application meant the successful "crowning of the structure," as the intelligentsia cautiously phrased their desire for a constitution. As has already been indicated, the reforms were not carried out consistently. A shot fired at Alexander in 1866 led him to turn to the right, and, after his assassination in 1881, his son Alexander III turned to thoroughgoing reaction. To suppress the rising discontent, reliance had to be placed on police repression.

Needless to say, police repression cannot ordinarily eliminate social discontent; it can only drive social discontent below the surface, where it festers and grows, and either finds a satisfactory outlet or explodes. The success of the police repression of the 1880's under Alexander III was illusory. It was made possible by the reaction of society, outraged by the assassination of the "Czar-Liberator," against political agitation of any kind and by the fact that time was needed to enable society to digest the Great Reforms. Reaction could neither completely destroy the Great Reforms nor bring the progress of society to a halt. Fundamental changes, affecting all the classes of the population, were taking place, wealth was being accumulated, the cultural level was rising, new habits of thought and action were growing up. New and urgent problems had to be solved, but the government neither understood them nor dared to deal with them. Once it had decided to maintain autocracy at any cost and had chosen repression as a means of dealing with social discontent, it had to be ready to use more repression, its choice of policy was restricted, and it was compelled constantly to pretend that all was well.

When society awoke from its political lethargy at the beginning of the 1890's, it bore little resemblance to the society of sixty years before that had meekly submitted to the despotism of Nicholas I. Yet Nicholas's despotic measures of control had remained basically constant. The result during the next fifteen years was a sweeping social movement, which drew into political agitation every element of the population and, in the year 1905, paralyzed and disorganized a seemingly invincible administrative apparatus. Thereafter, as the events of 1905 and 1917 convincingly demonstrate, society had to be the victor in any contest between state and society.

It is important to note that the revolutionaries were not the key to the victory of society. They could neither create nor control the social movement. It was not until much later, after a complete victory had been won over the state, that the Communists were able to take advantage of that victory. The role of the revolutionaries was important, but secondary. The success of the social movement depended, instead, on the state of mind of the liberals and the conservatives, and it was their desertion of the autocracy, both in 1905 and 1917, that proved decisive. The saying attributed to Bismarck is relevant in this connection: "The power of revolution lies not in the extreme ideas of its leaders, but in that small portion of moderate demands unsatisfied at the right time." [2] The truth of this saying was to be vividly demonstrated by the social movement leading to the Revolution of 1905.

Revival of the Social Movement in the 1890's

The revival of the temper of society began with the famine of 1891, when, for the first time, Alexander III was compelled to bow to public opinion by acknowledging that a famine existed and by permitting society to organize in behalf of the hungry. Much hope was at first placed in the new Czar, Nicholas II, who succeeded his father in 1894 and who, it was anticipated, would adopt a more humane policy. At first, nothing more was expected than the support and extension of the Great Reforms, which, in the eyes of liberal society at that time were not inconsistent with autocracy. But Nicholas inherited his father's advisers, who affirmed the inconsistency, and he chose to follow his father's policy of aggressive reaction, directing his blows at the zemstvo men and other moderate leaders of society. In choosing this course, neither Nicholas nor his advisers could be aware of what is so clear now: that it was impossible to compel Russian society of the early twentieth century to remain completely passive while the bureaucracy continued to mis-manage the country, without resorting to far more ruthless methods than Nicholas was prepared to adopt. The old methods had, after all, been successful so far. The country seemed prosperous, firm, and strong—a power to be reckoned with in international affairs. The peasants, presumably, were solidly behind the autocracy.

There was, of course, no immediate change in the temper of society after Nicholas's "senseless dreams" speech. What distinguished it chiefly from the society of the previous decade was the unusual energy being devoted to self-activity, i.e., to the organization of voluntary associations and the spread of education. The government had no way of halting self-activity, and it did not attempt to do so. Although the line between political and nonpolitical activity is a shadowy one, the government was compelled to draw such a line. Interference, when it came—as in the case of the closing of the two committees for the propagation of education and the closing of the Moscow Juridical Society—was arbitrary, incomplete, and futile. New and dangerous ideas were rising in the expanding universities, but the government did all that it could do when it sought to confine these ideas to a small circle of academicians and when it prevented them from being applied to concrete conditions at home.

It was the zemstvo men who were most concerned with politics, but their views remained moderate during the 1890's. The prohibitions against discussing state affairs in the zemstvo assemblies and against holding zemstvo conferences became more fictitious than real. The marshals of the nobility presiding in the zemstvo assemblies were powerless to prevent orators from discussing problems beyond "local benefits and needs." Zemstvo conferences, repeatedly forbidden on pain of punishment, were being held secretly, and, after 1900, openly. The occasion for these conferences was the convening of zemstvo men in a given city for the purpose of attending other seemingly harmless congresses, such as those on medicine, education, and handicrafts. The zemstvo groups then took the opportunity to meet privately and adopted resolutions that were subsequently introduced at the various zemstvo assemblies.[3] It was also at these congresses on medicine, education, etc., that the intelligentsia found the opportunity to meet privately and discuss political problems. During the revival of the social temper of the 1890's, the congresses began to draw up formal petitions to the government having nothing to do with the purpose of these meetings. Typical of the petitions adopted were those demanding the abolition of corporal punishment and the right of women to enter higher educational institutions; after 1900, however, the petitions became more and more political and more and more radical.

With the exception of the zemstvo addresses of 1894, the petitions to the government openly formulated by the zemstvos during the 1890's were not directly political. They were concerned, rather, with such matters as the expansion of zemstvo jurisdiction, the need for zemstvo congresses, the publication of an interzemstvo periodical, and the abolition of corporal punishment. Moreover, the first wave of zemstvo constitutional activity at the end of the 1870's had shown that political agitation limited to the zemstvos and to the intelligentsia was not an immediate threat to the autocracy. It was only when all elements of the population acted in concert that Russian society, still weakly organized by Western standards, could prove the victor over the bureaucratic machine. Around 1900, the stage was set for a turn to the left by the zemstvo men and the intelligentsia and for the participation of the entire population in political agitation; signs of the coming revolution became unmistakable. The only war going on was the war between the bureaucracy and the people; although external war played an important role both in 1905 and 1917, it was by no means an indispensable role. The government could, with impunity, neither continue arbitrary police rule nor neglect the basic needs of the population indefinitely.

The Emergence of Mass Discontent

That this was true is indicated by the emergence of mass discontent at the turn of the century and by the open signs of a growing disrespect for the government. These developments were reflected first in the cities, where, from 1901 on, a new weapon of political agitation—the street demonstration—came into use. In 1899 the students had learned from the labor movement how to apply the strike in the universities. In 1901, the workers were to learn the value of the street demonstration from the students. These demonstrations, first organized by the university students of St. Petersburg in the square facing the Kazan Cathedral on February 19, 1901, the fortieth anniversary of the emancipation of the peasants, spread rapidly to other universities and were promptly joined by sympathetic workers and other elements of the urban population. Thereafter, whether organized by students, workers, or other groups, they became common occurrences. It was at this time that May First strikes and demonstrations also became common in Russia.

Perhaps no other manifestation of the social movement indicates so clearly how deeply the discontent with the existing order was felt not only by the intellectuals, but also by the common man. The demonstrations were chaotic affairs, with thousands of people storming through the streets of a city, carrying red banners and singing revolutionary songs. Plainly an anomaly in an autocratic state, they were usually met by Cossacks and mounted police, who made futile attempts to disperse the crowd. Whips, arrests, and exile were the chief weapons of the police; the crowds usually defended themselves with sticks, and sometimes with stones and barricades. While firing into the crowds did occur at times, it was the exception rather than the rule.

It cannot be said that the ministers remained blind to this and other forms of mass discontent. The two chief ministers concerned, Minister of the Interior D. S. Sipiagin (1899–1902) and Minister of the Interior V. K. Plehve (1902–4), were both struck down by terrorists. Although neither of these men wrote memoirs, both of them are quoted by close associates as having referred to the danger of the situation.[4] Both attempted to take action, but both were wholeheartedly devoted to the maintenance of the autocracy, and, within the confines of this sterile policy, their efforts were doomed to failure. In the end, their main weapon remained repression, and repression cannot wipe out mass discontent.

Strikes, which, during the industrial upturn of the 1890's, had sharply increased, were closely associated with street demonstrations by workers. Most of the new workers who came to the cities during that decade were peasants, closely tied to the land and with little to lose during a strike. The strike movement reached a new high in the summer of 1903, with the outbreak in southern Russia of a general strike that affected almost all the industrial centers of that region. It was the first time that the workers of the newly created heavy industries of southern Russia had participated in the strike movement on a large scale. The government had no consistent policy toward strikes. In so far as it attempted to use force to suppress both strikes and demonstrations, the atmosphere became supercharged, and the basic causes of discontent were not eliminated. Although the aims of the workers remained primarily economic, the political demands that began to be made assumed more and more importance as 1905 approached.

The most dangerous expression of mass discontent, that of the peasants, made as yet only a brief appearance. In the spring of 1902, serious peasant disturbances broke out in the provinces of Poltava and Kharkov and were quickly suppressed. But the quick suppression was illusory, for it was followed in 1905–6 by the greatest peasant revolt since the time of Pugachev, 130 years earlier.

It was in this atmosphere that the two main revolutionary parties, the Social Democrats and the Socialist Revolutionaries, were organized—the former in 1898 and the latter in 1901. Immediately relevant to the problem of the conquest of the state by society are two issues affecting these parties: the degree of their influence on the masses and the resort of the Socialist Revolutionaries to terror. With the assassination of Minister of Education Bogolepov in 1901, terror, for the first time since the 1880's, again became an important factor on the Russian scene. Its reappearance was another indication of the depth of the rising mass discontent, for, without the sympathy of society, terror could not be successful. It was precisely the strong reaction of Russian society against terror after the assassination of Alexander II that had made it so easy for the government to suppress the terrorists. The new generation of terrorists, who began their operations at the beginning of the twentieth century, had learned some useful lessons. They respected the traditional view that evil government policies were the work of the bureaucracy, not of the Czar, and no attempt was planned on the life of the Czar before 1905. The record of every candidate for assassination was carefully weighed to make sure that his demise would evoke public approval. History is not likely to quarrel with the judgments of the terrorists in this respect. Men like Bogolepov, Sipiagin, Plehve, and Grand Duke Sergei Alexandrovich were hated advocates of repression, and few mourned their passing.

Although the terrorists played some part in disorganizing the administration in 1905, their role, as well as that of the revolutionaries in general, was secondary in the victory of society over the autocracy in 1905. It was not the activities of the revolutionaries but the inflexible policy of the autocracy that raised the political temperature of all of society, thereby laying the foundation for such measure of success as the revolutionaries were able to achieve. A characteristic feature of the social movement leading to the Revolution of 1905 was the growing tolerance of a wider and wider segment of the population toward terrorist activity as the government continued its refusal to grant long-overdue concessions. In the same way, it was not the activities of the newly organized Social Democratic agitators that led the workers to participate in strikes and street demonstrations. These remained primarily economic in origin and purpose until 1905; before that time the workers, on the whole, paid no attention to the political slogans of the Social Democrats.[5] The pattern of the social movement, as it was manifested before and after 1905, shows that the disorders in the cities and the villages could have no serious political significance, and, in view of the relatively strong state apparatus, could not have reached the dimensions they did without the rise of a political agitation that drew in all classes of the population. The creation of an overpowering climate of opinion against the government in a society on the whole traditionally attached to that government was not an easy task. It was finally achieved by the last Czar, and the basis of his "achievement" was his persistent refusal to grant any concessions to the moderate liberals.

The Rebuff to the Liberals in 1902

The primary purpose of the zemstvo addresses of 1894 was to forge a closer unity between the Czar and the people, to set aside the oppressive tutelage of the bureaucratic machine. The zemstvos, in effect, were asking that Nicholas put an end to the reactionary policies pursued by his father and return to the principles of the Great Reforms. It was not until 1902 that the zemstvos were again ready to press similar demands openly. The occasion that prompted them at that time to take joint action was the convening of Witte's Special Conference on the Needs of Agricultural Industry. In order to discuss the situation created by the Special Conference, and the action to be taken by the zemstvos, representatives from twenty-five zemstvo boards met privately in Shipov's home in Moscow in May, 1902. Such meetings were, of course, strictly forbidden, but they were now taking place regularly. Characteristically enough, the meeting was projected at the All-Russian Exhibition of Handicrafts held in St. Petersburg in March, 1902, and the excuse for coming to Moscow was furnished by the congress on fire fighting being held there. Needless to say, neither handicraftsmen predominated at the exhibition nor firemen at the congress; both were convenient meeting grounds for zemstvo men, the third element, and the intelligentsia in general.

A six-point program regarded as indispensable for the solution of the agricultural problem was drawn up by the zemstvo men at the May meeting in Moscow. Again no mention was made of the autocracy or a constitution. Included were such practical problems as the legal position of the peasants (equality of rights, freedom from administrative tutelage, etc.), the need for the free expansion of primary education, the need for zemstvo reform, the need for a reform of fiscal and economic policies, and the need for free press discussion of economic problems.[6] The zemstvo men agreed to introduce these points in the local committees of the Special Conference the government was organizing.

It is apparent, in retrospect, that the Czar had reached one of the many critical points of his career. To continue with the policy of counterreform forty years after the emancipation of the serfs was beyond his power and meant courting disaster. A convenient opportunity was now open to permit public discussion of fundamental reforms in official governmental bodies and to adopt them as his grandfather had done in the 1860's, without the pressure posed by the threat of revolution. This course, however, the Czar declined to take. Around the Special Conference on the Needs of Agricultural Industry hinged a battle for supremacy between Minister of Finance Witte and Minister of the Interior Plehve. Witte strongly favored fundamental peasant reform, which automatically involved reform of the state structure also. Plehve was opposed to both. In the contest between them, it was Plehve who emerged victorious, and with his victory disappeared all hope of a reconciliation between the moderate zemstvo men and the autocracy, inside or outside the Special Conference.

When Plehve learned of the unofficial conference the zemstvo men had held in Moscow, he persuaded the Czar to issue an order censuring them and warning that, if they repeated their actions, they would be dismissed from their positions and forbidden to take further part in public activity. Although Witte had obtained broad scope for the expression of members' views for the local committees, Plehve sent a circular to the governors, and through them to the marshals of the nobility, warning them that the program of the Moscow conference was not to be discussed either in the local committees or in the zemstvo assemblies. In several of the local committees, the zemstvo men spoke in vain in behalf of a broad agenda, and when it was refused, declined to take any further part in the deliberations of the committees. Many of the zemstvo men were punished for their speeches in the committees (mainly by exile or exclusion from zemstvo activity); Plehve even removed from office some governors who, he thought, had shown too much leniency.[7]

In general, the clash between the zemstvos and the government reached its peak during the two years of Plehve's ministry; the zemstvo men were demanding more freedom, while the government, through Plehve, sought continuing obedience and used its enormous arbitrary power in vain attempts to exact obedience. Moreover, in the atmosphere of growing self-activity and the fermentation of ideas, Plehve chose to direct his main fire against the liberals, not the revolutionaries. "We are not frightened by the demands of the left," he told a well-known public man; "we can cope with them. Dangerous to us are the moderate demands, which it is impossible to refuse without the violation of elementary justice. We must satisfy them, and in growing they will, in the end, force us out of our position."[8] Since, at the same time that he was so recklessly violating "elementary justice," Plehve took virtually no decisive steps to solve pressing social and economic problems, the inevitable result was a sharp turn to the left, not only by the zemstvo men and the intelligentsia, but by all elements of the population.

New Liberal Tactics: The Union of Liberation

In the 1860's, liberalism had succeeded in inspiring the Czar to grant reforms incompatible with the autocracy, and the belief was widespread both in governmental and social circles that the reforms would eventually lead to a constitution. Throughout the nineteenth century, the tradition of the 1860's retained its hold on the liberals, the most active of whom were zemstvo nobles. Even during the period of reaction, they continued to believe in the ultimate reconciliation of state and society and frowned on the revolutionary movement, which made this reconciliation more difficult to achieve. They were aware that the peaceful evolution of existing institutions, particularly the institutions of self-government, would enable them to attain their goals, i.e., the rule of law and representative government. The retention of these views, however, required the cooperation of the government, and by the beginning of the twentieth century, the long years of inflexible reaction under Alexander III and Nicholas II began to dislodge them. A new brand of liberalism arose, one which no longer believed that peaceful evolution was possible. This new generation of liberals believed that the government's persecution of self-activity and self-government would not voluntarily be abandoned, that attempts to collaborate with the government were futile, and that the first prerequisite of constructive internal reform was the destruction of the autocracy and its replacement by a Western-type parliamentary regime. Their attention, therefore, shifted from the gradual improvement of the existing order to open warfare against it, and in this warfare, the revolutionary movement seemed to be a natural and useful ally.

Like the revolutionary parties, the new liberals had an illegal organization as well as an illegal paper published abroad. The latter, a fortnightly entitled *Osvobozhdenie* (*Liberation*), preceded the organization, first appearing in Stuttgart in June, 1902, under the editorship of Peter Struve. The Union of Liberation was planned a year later in the Black Forest region of Germany. The idea of the Union originated in the literary suppers regularly held in St. Petersburg after 1902. After the meeting in Germany in the summer of 1903, the founders came to the All-Russian Exhibition of Livestock being held in Kharkov that September under the auspices of the Kharkov zemstvo and the Kharkov Agricultural Society. At private gatherings in Kharkov, they gave reports and made plans for the organization of sections of the Union in all the zemstvo provinces and, in so far as possible, in the non-zemstvo provinces as well. The constituent congress of the Union of Liberation was held in St. Petersburg in January, 1904, in connection with the third congress on technical education, which convened at the same time. Here the organizational plans were approved, the bylaws worked out, and the Council of the Union of Liberation elected. The organization of the various local sections followed shortly thereafter.

The emphasis on the zemstvo provinces was not accidental, since strong organizational ties already existed among the various district zemstvos of a given province and among the provincial zemstvos. Furthermore, it was in the zemstvo cities that the various congresses of intellectuals, the organizational ground for the intelligentsia as a whole, were held. An illegal network of local sections of the Union of Liberation was thereby successfully created throughout Russia, but primarily in the zemstvo provinces, in accordance with the plans laid in Kharkov.[9]

The publication of *Osvobozhdenie* and the organization of the Union of Liberation were the work of two distinct groups of the intelligentsia—zemstvo men, and professors and journalists. Both were equally represented at the organizational meeting in Germany in the summer of 1903, and in the council elected in St. Petersburg in January, 1904.[10] It was, however, the professors and the journalists who were the natural leaders of the new trend in liberalism. Wholly devoid of practical experience and guided by theories having nothing to do with the realities of Russian life, they looked down on zemstvo work itself and could not conceive of any progress in Russia until the autocracy had been overthrown and replaced by a government modeled on the most advanced democracies of Western Europe. Since constructive achievement under the autocracy might reconcile the population to its existence, they regarded such achievement as positively harmful. If the overthrow of the autocracy was the first prerequisite of progress, then mass discontent must be increased and all efforts directed toward discrediting the autocracy. In pursuing these tactics, the journalist-politicians felt a natural sympathy with the revolutionaries, who pursued the same tactics, although their ultimate aims were quite different.

In the first issues of *Osvobozhdenie*, Peter Struve maintained that the liberals and the revolutionaries had much in common and that an alliance should be formed between them.[11] As society moved to the left after 1902, and the influence of the theoreticians increased in the liberal movement, the alliance became a reality. In September–October, 1904, four representatives from the Union of Liberation met with representatives of a group of other parties in Paris to discuss "coordinated" action. Present were the liberal and revolutionary parties of some of the minority nationalities, and the Socialist Revolutionaries, but not the Social Democrats, who declined to have dealings with the bourgeois parties. After extended discussions, an agreement was reached on parallel action for the destruction of the autocracy; the positive points of the agreement were deliberately couched in vague terms, permitting each party to interpret them as it saw fit.[12]

It is interesting to note that during an earlier phase of the constitutional movement, the liberals had also made contact with the revolutionaries, but for quite different reasons. In December, 1878, two zemstvo men, I. I. Petrunkevich and A. F. Lindfors, met with the terrorists in Kiev in a vain effort to persuade them to abandon their terrorist activities. It was then recognized by the zemstvo liberals that terrorism resulted in the adoption of reactionary countermeasures by the government, and that so long as terror continued, it would be difficult for the government to take the path of peaceful reform. A quarter of a century later, the liberals met with the revolutionaries to make common cause, and terrorism was tolerated even in conservative circles. The ultimate aims of the liberals still remained quite distinct from those of the revolutionaries. They sought a constitutional monarchy, not a republic; parliamentary democracy, not a violent social and economic upheaval; the rule of law, not a revolutionary dictatorship. However, their supposed devotion to compromise and peaceful evolution was virtually forgotten, and their immediate tactics hardly differed from those of the revolutionaries. What the liberals now wanted was not compromise, but complete surrender by the Czar and the calling of a constituent assembly to draft a constitution. Any concession by the Czar short of this came to be regarded by them as fraud and hypocrisy. Since the Czar plainly was not going to agree voluntarily to the calling of a constituent assembly, the liberals even began to advocate the use of force.[13] The basic social and economic reforms so urgently required, which were indeed prerequisite to the sound functioning of a constitutional monarchy, were regarded as impossible of achievement until a constituent assembly had been called.

It was apparent from the first issue of *Osvobozhdenie* that some of the zemstvo men were already in sympathy with the new trend in liberalism. The government might have halted the trend if it had used the Special Conference on the Needs of Agricultural Industry to return to the path of the Great Reforms. When, instead, it continued the policy of repression, aiming its hardest blows at the moderate liberals rather than the revolutionaries, it began to inflame an already dangerous situation and to shift all of society to the left, so that it was only a matter of time before the mood of the Liberation Movement became the mood of most of the liberals.

One of the most striking aspects of the rise of the political temperature of Russian society at the beginning of the twentieth century was the growing recognition of society that it need not fear the government. Many examples of the boldness of the population and its readiness to defy the authorities have already been cited. With the appearance of the Liberation Movement, in 1902–3, a new step forward was taken at its recommendation: the resort to boycott. A good illustration has been given by Maklakov from the behavior of the legal profession. During the course of the social revival of the 1890's, the younger lawyers began to organize for the purpose of rendering legal aid in outlying districts in which no lawyers had appeared before. Out of this grew the practice of defending persons not for individual crimes committed, but for social crimes—e.g., participation in factory or agrarian disorders, and strikes. This work, at first, was taken seriously, and one of its constructive results was the improvement of the judicial process under the statute of 1864. As a result of the influence of the Liberation Movement, however, the attitude of the attorneys changed, and they began to participate in political trials, not for the purpose of defending the accused, but in order to stage political demonstrations. They made political speeches in the courtroom not germane to the legal issues involved, and when the court declined to listen, the defense attorneys left in a body. The government, of course, punished some of these attorneys, but it could not punish all. The government not only failed to modify the self-governing councils of barristers, but actually began to open them in judicial districts in which they had hitherto been lacking.[15]

Boycott and obstruction, tactics taken up by all classes of the population, eventually came to play an important role in compelling the Czar to surrender. Their expansion, however, was a gradual process. Before the outbreak of the Russo-Japanese War, boycott was practiced in the various congresses of intellectuals, which began to emerge as pure political meetings, crowding out all considerations of narrow professional interests. A good example is the Pirogov congress of physicians, held in St. Petersburg at the beginning of 1904. Here were passed the first resolutions that, in a more radical form, became universal a year later. Characteristic for the congress was the resolution of the combined sections of social medicine, internal medicine, and tuberculosis, which stated:

The sound and proper fight against infant mortality, alcoholism, tuberculosis, syphilis, and other common diseases, representing in Russia social ills of great importance, is possible only under conditions guar-

anteeing the broad spread of information about their causes and prevention, and for this, full freedom of person, speech, press, and assembly
are necessary prerequisites.[16]

Initially, the zemstvo men were far from ready to take the advanced position of the "theoreticians" and the zemstvo constitutionalists of the Union of Liberation. Apart from the conservatism
of many zemstvo nobles, the practical nature of their work gave
them a closer grasp of the realities of Russian life than the theoreticians possessed, and it made them less susceptible to being carried
away by panaceas. The fusion of the views of the zemstvo men and
the theoreticians was to come later, when the inflexibility of the
autocracy seemed to leave no other course open to them. In 1902–3,
the zemstvo men as a group were, as yet, relatively cautious, thanks
in part to the influence of Shipov. At the end of 1903, as a result of
another of Shipov's unofficial conferences, a series of provincial
zemstvos passed resolutions asking that zemstvo assemblies be permitted to discuss legislation concerning the local population before going to the State Council; some took the additional step of
requesting that such legislation be considered by a national assembly of representatives elected by the zemstvos.[17] All of Plehve's
warnings to the governors and marshals of the nobility not to permit the consideration of such problems in the zemstvo assemblies
proved, in the main, to be fruitless.

The Significance of the Russo-Japanese War

The Russo-Japanese War began late in January, 1904. Mass discontent had arisen long before the outbreak of the war and would
have continued inexorably until the basic causes of discontent were
removed, but the news of defeat after defeat in the Far East dealt
the autocracy the last fatal blows. For society at large, the war was
final proof of the bankruptcy of police-bureaucratic rule.[18] By undermining the faith in the omniscience of the Czar, the reactionary
groups around him, and the bureaucracy in general, it was to result
in the isolation of the Czar and a readiness on his part to yield to
popular clamor. The war was not popular with society, and it had
almost no effect on the open warfare declared against the autocracy
by the intellectuals of the Liberation Movement. Instead, defeatism began to permeate large segments of the intelligentsia. The
peasants understood the significance of the war with Japan even

less than they understood the significance of World War I, but the defeats and the loss of life in the Far East, in conjunction with their own unsatisfied needs, were bound to have a profound effect on their political consciousness. In the second half of 1904, there appeared among the peasants an awareness of politics, which, for the first time, created a receptiveness to radical propaganda. The situation is described thus by the Social Democrat Maevsky:

In the recent past, out of some thousands of proclamations distributed by the socialist parties, it was to be expected that a hundred or so would reach the people and be read by them. Now, tens of thousands of revolutionary leaflets were accepted, and it is certain that nine-tenths of them not only were read, but were read eagerly until worn out. Until recently, a newspaper was considered by the broad masses—and especially by the peasantry—as a "seigneurial" matter; if one accidentally fell into their hands, it was, at best, used as cigarette paper. Now, it was carefully, even eagerly smoothed out and handed to the literate ones, and the crowd, holding its breath, avidly listened to "what they write about the war." Not only did the military units, advancing by all railroad lines, almost come to blows over a newspaper or some other printed leaflet thrown from the windows of a passing train, but also the peasants of the villages close to the railroads, from that time—and for several years after the war—continued to solicit a newspaper from travelers.[19]

The growth of political consciousness among the masses was a characteristic feature of the revolutions of 1905 and 1917, and its importance must not be underestimated. It gave even the disorders of the peasants a political complexion, and for the first time made the masses receptive to the demagogic propaganda of the revolutionaries. This continued after the Russo-Japanese War through the period of at least the first two Dumas, and no evaluation of the significance of the Duma can afford to neglect the mass interest in it.

The First Congress of Zemstvos

After the assassination of Plehve, in the summer of 1904, it was widely recognized that Plehve's policy could not be continued, and the Czar now sought, two years too late, to follow the course of a liberal autocracy. The new Minister of the Interior, Prince P. D. Sviatopolk-Mirsky, was a liberal, who, immediately upon taking office, announced that he would seek the confidence of society. Mirsky thought that he could win this confidence by revoking the most odious of Plehve's repressive measures, but neither he nor his successors could grasp how far society had shifted to the left after two years of Plehve.

The circumstances surrounding the calling of the first congress of zemstvos in St. Petersburg early in November, 1904, were indicative of the new atmosphere. Such congresses had been strictly forbidden, and only a few months before, Shipov had been refused confirmation as chairman of the Moscow zemstvo board, partly because of his efforts in behalf of united zemstvo activity. Mirsky now sought the Czar's approval for the congress, and it was given, but the Czar withdrew his approval when Mirsky informed him that the agenda consisted not of practical zemstvo affairs but of general political problems. As a result, the congress met in private quarters as a purely private affair, without any obstacles placed in its way by the government.

If the attitude of the government toward the zemstvos had changed, the attitude of the zemstvo men toward the government had changed even more. A program of eleven points was adopted by the congress. The language used was not unlike that heard among the zemstvo men many times in the past. There was the customary reference to the unhealthy split between state and society, and the need to reconcile the two by disarming the omnipotent bureaucracy, with its broad powers of personal discretion and administrative arbitrariness. On ten points of the eleven-point program, the zemstvo men were in unanimous agreement. These included such traditional demands as freedom of speech, association, press, and religion; no punishment without judicial proceedings; the inviolability of person and domicile, except by court action; the responsibility of chinovniks for violations of the law; equality of rights for all citizens of the Empire; peasant reform; and the expansion and improvement of zemstvo institutions. There was unanimous agreement also on the need for national representation, but the congress split on the question of whether the representative assembly should be advisory or legislative. The vote in favor of a legislative assembly was 60 to 38.[20]

The zemstvo men who attended the November congress had not been regularly elected by the zemstvo assemblies. They unofficially represented only the most active and liberal part of the zemstvo world, but their views at this time came closest to reflecting the general mood of the zemstvos. The eleven-point program of the congress was widely discussed in society, and Sviatopolk-Mirsky sought government action on it. The result was the already discussed ukase of December 12, 1904. In it was projected a series of reforms, which, if carried out, would have restored the spirit of the Great Reforms to the autocracy and would have gone far to meet the demands of liberal society.[21] However, it lacked one fundamental reform: national representation. Mirsky had recommended to the Czar the establishment of an advisory national assembly in accordance with the minority view of the zemstvo congress, but at the last minute, the Czar, on the advice of Witte, deleted from the ukase any reference to a national assembly.[22]

Had the reforms proposed in the ukase of December 12 been announced in 1902, they would have been enthusiastically received and would have temporarily checked the growth of the Liberation Movement. Had they been consistently carried out, both the Liberation Movement and the revolutionary movement would have been rendered impotent. Late in 1904, the situation had changed to such an extent that the promulgation of the ukase could not even make a favorable impression, particularly since on the same day a thoroughly reactionary and inconsistent government communiqué had also been promulgated.[23] With or without the communiqué, some form of national representation was now a universal demand; in the promise of reform without representation, society saw only new evidence of the government's lack of sincerity. It is difficult to say with certainty whether the promise of an advisory national assembly could have halted the Revolution. Probably it could have; there were liberals who still supported the autocracy, and the rupture of the united front of the liberals was bound to have momentous consequences. Since the ukase did not promise national representation, its immediate effect was to end the role of the loyal zemstvo movement. From then on, it was the Liberation Movement, with its program of open and irreconcilable warfare against the autocracy, that spoke for the liberals.

The Union of Liberation Takes the Field

The Union of Liberation was not a party; it was an alliance of persons and groups of diverse political tendencies. Despite the presence of the six zemstvo men in the Council of the Union, the management of the union's affairs was actually in the hands of the

intellectuals, most of whom were to the left of the zemstvo constitutionalists and later refused to join the Cadet Party.[24] The Union
did not believe that the appointment of Sviatopolk-Mirsky meant
any change in the policy of the autocracy, and it was while the latter was seeking to bring state and society together that the Union's
representatives were meeting with representatives of the revolutionaries in Paris in order to form a common front in the fight against
the autocracy. In October, 1904, the Council of the Union decided
to organize a banquet campaign on the approaching fortieth anniversary of the judicial reform of 1864. The banquets were, in effect,
to be political meetings at which more radical resolutions than
those likely to be proposed at the zemstvo congress could be
adopted. In particular, the Union sought to spread the demand for
a constituent assembly, elected on the basis of universal, equal,
secret, and direct suffrage. At the zemstvo congress, the proposal of
a constituent assembly was unanimously rejected; the word "constitution" was not even mentioned in the eleven theses of the congress. This, of course, was the proper approach for a moderate group
seeking an *octroyed* constitution and not wishing to incite the
masses. This approach was rejected by the Liberationists and the
revolutionaries, and beginning in November, 1904, the spread of
the idea of a constituent assembly was initiated at a series of banquets arranged by the intellectuals. These banquets reflected a new
liberty in arranging public assemblies, and the period after January
9 saw the open emergence of mass meetings and revolutionary agitators. The press followed suit in seizing new liberties and shaking
off the old censorship. Legal journals reported the adoption of
resolutions in behalf of a constituent assembly at some of the banquets in November, 1904, and thereafter began to report freely the
increasingly stormy developments of the year 1905, ignoring, for the
most part, the customary government orders on the suppression of
news events.[25]

The Council of the Union of Liberation also took the initiative,
toward the close of 1904, in organizing the professional intelligentsia into unions, the purpose being to spread the constitutional
program of the Liberationists to the rank and file of the intelligentsia. The unions had no real professional interests; such interests were mentioned only to point out that they could not be
pursued until the autocracy had been replaced by a constitutional
regime. Most, but not all, of the unions of the intelligentsia came

out in favor of a constituent assembly, elected on the basis of universal, equal, secret, and direct suffrage (frequently called in Russian *chetyrekhvostka*, "the four tails"); this was also the program of the Union of Unions organized under the chairmanship of Miliukov early in May, 1905. Although at first the members of the controlling group of the Council of the Union of Liberation were the chairmen of the individual unions, they were gradually displaced by revolutionaries, mostly Social Democrats, who took over the union movement of the intellectuals and used it to advocate armed revolt. After July, 1905, Miliukov remained chairman of the Union of Unions in name only.[26]

One factor making possible the organization of the intellectuals was the strange ukase of February 18, 1905, which invited private persons and institutions to submit to the Council of Ministers their views and proposals on questions "concerning the improvement of the state order and the national welfare." Since, under the existing laws on press and assembly, the formulation of proposals for the reorganization of the state was regarded as a criminal act, this ukase, in effect, created legal anarchy. The ukase did not actually authorize the organization of new societies, but it was cited by those who organized such societies without official sanction, and it was bound to confuse the police.[27] The police was, in any case, quite incapable of dealing with the mass movement of 1905; its futile attempts to do so made it seem ridiculous and increased disrespect for the law. There were brushes with the organizational meeting of the unions similar to the one with the July congress of zemstvos. When the government attempted to prosecute a few members of a union, all the remaining members came forward and asked to be prosecuted, an action resulting in the release of all.[28] The prosecution of even small numbers of union leaders had to be abandoned. In the summer of 1905, Assistant Minister of the Interior Trepov ordered the arrest of ten to twelve of them, but had them released after an outcry arose in the press. "Their indictment," he said, "would extremely aggravate our relations with society.[29]

By the summer of 1905, thanks to the combined efforts of the Union of Liberation, the Union of Unions, and the revolutionaries, the demand for a constituent assembly and universal suffrage was being raised by an overwhelming majority of the intelligentsia. In a wide variety of organizations and in a wide variety of meetings,

including street rallies, the calling of a constituent assembly on the
basis of the "four-tailed formula" was advanced as a condition of
the resumption of "peaceful cultural work." While the question of
prosecuting almost the entire population was purely academic, all
this political agitation was quite legal under the terms of the ukase
of February 18, which placed no conditions on the formulation of
proposals for the reorganization of the state.

After the failure of the November congress and the retirement of
Sviatopolk-Mirsky, the zemstvo men, too, were moving to the left,
and they remained indifferent to the further concessions made by
the government under the pressure of revolutionary ferment. On
February 18, 1905, a rescript in the name of the new Minister of the
Interior, A. G. Bulygin, promised the establishment of an advisory
duma, and on August 6 of that year, the statute of the "Bulygin
Duma" was promulgated. These measures might have been effective in November, 1904; few were ready to accept less than a legislative duma and the end of the autocracy after that.

There is no need to trace in detail the increasingly radical mood
of the series of zemstvo congresses held after November. At the
July congress (the only one forbidden by the government), it was
decided that appeals must be made to the people, not to the Czar.
As an alternative to the Bulygin Duma, the congress approved its
own draft constitution, which called for full-fledged parliamentarism and the four-tailed electoral formula. The congress did not
vote on the issue of a constituent assembly, but there was no hope
that the draft constitution would be *octroyed* (in Russian, *oktroiro-
vat*) by the autocracy; like the calling of a constituent assembly, it,
in effect, presupposed the complete destruction of the existing government. Needless to say, there was likewise no hope that Russia
could actually make a direct transition from autocracy to full-
fledged parliamentarism, with the Czar a figurehead and the government in the hands of a responsible ministry, dependent on a
parliament elected by universal, equal, secret, and direct suffrage.[30]
All that separated the zemstvo men from the intellectuals of the
Liberation Movement was the issue of a constituent assembly.
Thanks, therefore, to the inability of the autocracy to grant timely
concessions, the views of the "theoreticians" of the Union of Liberation became dominant at the zemstvo congresses and among the
future leaders of the Cadet Party. The irreconcilable attitude to-

ward the government, the tolerance of revolution, and the utopian strategy that thereby infected Russia's most distinguished liberals were to have a fateful influence on the course of events after the Revolution, down to the conquest of power by the Bolsheviks in October, 1917.

The Workers and Peasants in the Revolution

The spread of disorders among the workers and peasants was of key importance in the ultimate success of the Revolution, though the assumption of some Marxists that these disorders were in themselves of overriding importance is an oversimplification. It has already been pointed out that serious strike waves started long before 1905, but after the events of January 9, 1905—"Bloody Sunday"—when troops fired on a defenseless crowd of workers seeking to present their grievances to the Czar, the waves of strikes received a new impetus, drawing in groups of workers not involved before. By the end of 1905, more Russian workers had participated in strikes than had those of any other country in a single year up to that time. Political motives naturally played an important part in bringing about strikes on so great a scale; but the workers were not so sensitive to political problems as were the intelligentsia, and for them economic grievances were likewise important. During the first months after January 9, most of the workers turned a deaf ear to the revolutionary slogans of the Social Democratic agitators (except in the non-Russian borderland provinces). It was only at the climax of the revolutionary movement, in the fall of 1905, when the political temperature of society as a whole reached a new high and the administrative apparatus was virtually paralyzed, that the workers began to listen with approval to revolutionary speeches and that economic demands receded temporarily into the background.

A significant influence in this transformation was the sudden grant of autonomy to the universities at the end of August. Mass meetings on a scale not possible before were held without police interference within the walls of the universities, and the revolutionary underground, seizing this unparalleled opportunity to make open, direct contact with the masses, took command. The Soviet of Workers' Deputies, dominated by the Mensheviks, made its appearance in St. Petersburg (at the Polytechnical Institute) only on

October 13, after the general strike leading to the October Manifesto had begun; Soviets were extended shortly afterward to Moscow and other cities.[31]

It would be a mistake to conclude from this that the workers understood the significance of the slogans they heard or that it was the revolutionaries who had brought about their rebellious mood. Actually, the mood of the workers developed out of the circumstances of the time, independent of the influence of any party, and Social-Democratic agitators frequently had to tell them things quite different from what they had been ordered to say by the Party.[32] Only when their mood had become radical enough did they listen with enthusiasm to revolutionary slogans, and then not because they were ready to rise in revolt to carry them out, but because, as one Social-Democratic writer points out, the occasion was a festive one and the slogans seemed appropriate for the occasion.[33] The chief concern of the workers remained their economic interests, the significance of which was better comprehended than the political slogans of the day.[34] At the base of the revolution was the emergence of a primitive, elemental, and anarchistic force, the agrarian disorders of the peasants and the factory disorders of the half-peasants who constituted the bulk of the workers. After 1905, the state apparatus, though temporarily paralyzed, recovered and succeeded in putting down the disorders. In 1917, the state apparatus disintegrated along with the monarchy, and the Provisional Government was incapable of organizing a new one, so that this primitive and anarchistic force raged on unchecked. It was this situation that the Bolsheviks capitalized on in their conquest of power in 1917.

Peasant disturbances began in some provinces in the early spring of 1905, reaching their peak in the last half of 1905 and the first half of 1906, and then were gradually suppressed by force. The forms taken by the disturbances varied with the time and place. The nonviolent forms included the refusal to pay rent and taxes, labor strikes, and the illegal pasturing of livestock and cutting of timber. Violence was in evidence mainly in the black-earth provinces, where the worst abuses of serfdom had formerly taken place, and it was undertaken in some cases to discourage the return of the landlords. At best, groups of peasants, usually with an armed bodyguard, descended on the estate of a landlord and carried off the grain. At worst, the entire estate was plundered, the manor house burned, and the land occupied. On the whole, the worst forms of violence began only in the fall of 1905, after the promulgation of the October Manifesto.

If it is easy to exaggerate the political consciousness of the workers, it is likewise easy to underestimate the political consciousness of the peasants. The peasants were, of course, furthest removed from the political life of the country, and the causes of the disturbances were primarily economic. Nevertheless, as has already been pointed out, the peasants acquired a new consciousness of the problems of war and politics at the end of 1904, and there is no question that throughout this period they were following political developments attentively. The peasants were probably the chief sufferers from the reactionary and sterile policies of the last two Czars, and they were to prove that they understood this in the elections to the first two Dumas. They were to prove it also in the many political meetings being held in 1905 (more in the industrial and non-black-earth provinces than in the black-earth provinces, and again with the legal authorization of the ukase of February 18), at which the leading political demands of the day and other local problems were discussed. As Pares has pointed out, some issues, such as the abolition of class distinctions, access to education, freedom of speech, press, and association, were readily understood and accepted. The extraordinary activity in education and organization during the Duma period cannot, in fact, be explained without the great interest in both generated among the peasants by the hectic events of the revolutionary period.

Another indication that the era of patriarchal relations was coming to an end in Russia and that the peasants were becoming conscious of their rights is to be found in the manner in which the land captains and village administrations were set aside and ignored, followed, in the political meetings in some localities, by close discussions of the legal position of the village and expressions of active resentment by the peasants against outside interference in their affairs. While, therefore, the peasant disturbances were primarily economic in origin and peasant demands were above all economic demands, with the desire for more land predominating, the peasants were by no means immune from the political aspirations common to society as a whole. Like society as a whole, the fact that they had no tradition of political democracy is no justification for assuming that they were ready to accept arbitrary and unlimited intrusion into their affairs indefinitely. However, because political considerations influenced them to a lesser extent than they influenced the rest of society, and because their economic grievances arose out of their own unique way of life, the peasant movement followed its own course, independent from the movement going on in the towns. The influence of the revolutionaries on the peasants, unlike revolutionary influence on the urban population, was sporadic and, on the whole, without special significance.[35]

The Climax of the Revolution

Not one class, indeed one could almost say not one person, was exempt from the political fermentation in Russian society in the year 1905, when the mass discontent that manifested itself at the turn of the century reached its climax, and the political views of a whole society were permanently shifted to the left. As concession after concession was extracted from the government, as liberty after liberty was seized with impunity, and as the massive and once-feared bureaucratic machine ground to a halt, helpless before the onslaughts of an external enemy, but above all of an internal enemy artificially created by years of incredible blundering, the bureaucracy lost its moral support. "It is impossible to live thus any longer," was the universal cry. Although there was some difference in the interpretation of the word "freedom," it was a word that was on the lips of all. Drawn into the Liberation Movement were groups that had rarely, if ever, entered the political arena in the past. After centuries of political inertness, the merchants and industrialists began to assert themselves, and on the eve of the October Manifesto, they were in favor of a legislative Duma elected by universal suffrage. Probably unprecedented in world history were the political activities of fourteen-year-old school children. Like the university students, many went out on strike after January 9, organizing street demonstrations and political meetings at which revolutionary speeches were made.[36] Just as characteristic for that time, but far more significant, was the demand of the Church, including the Holy Synod itself, for self-government and the open revolt of about half of the bureaucracy.

The revolt of the chinovniks was not an essential prerequisite for the Revolution; even if they had been united, they would have been powerless to halt the Revolution. Their participation in the

Liberation Movement is rather another indication of the depth of the spiritual travail of Russian society and the sweep of the new climate of opinion. That there were serious defections in all ranks of the bureaucracy was revealed before 1905 by the repeated publication of secret government documents, mostly abroad, and frequently by the editors of *Osvobozhdenie*.[37] After January 9, the discontent of the chinovniks emerged into the open and was manifested among the lower police ranks by a refusal to carry out the repressive measures ordered by the government, and even by demonstrative resignations of whole groups of police officers.[38] In many cases, of course, refusals to obey orders were based on fear of the masses, but the existence of sincere sympathy for the Liberation Movement is beyond question. Whatever the convictions of individual policemen, they were also handicapped in the fulfillment of their duties by the belief they shared with society that the government was crumbling and that they might soon be subject to the orders of a new government made up of the very "public men" whose activities they were called upon to halt.

By May, 1905, the chinovniks, as a whole, were joining the others of the intelligentsia in organizing unions. The various unions of chinovniks were later united into two main all-Russian unions, the All-Russian Union of Government Employees, which was in favor of a legislative Duma elected by universal, equal, secret, and direct suffrage, and the Union of Postal-Telegraph Chinovniks, which was in favor of a constituent assembly also to be elected on the basis of the "four-tailed" electoral formula.[39] Many of the chinovniks, whether organized or not, joined the general strike that led to the promulgation of the October Manifesto.[40]

The political temperature of society reached its highest point in October; on the eighth of that month, a strike on the railroads was followed by a country-wide general strike. Since the general strike was political in origin, its proportions and effectiveness were unique in world history. It was, in fact, not so much a labor strike as a strike of a whole society (strictly speaking, only the urban part of it), and there was hardly any aspect of normal life that did not come to a standstill. Participating in the strike were groups such as the professional intelligentsia, house servants, janitors, a portion of the shopkeepers, and a considerable number of state employees. Those who did not participate sympathized with the strike; there were some capitalists, for example, who paid their employees in whole or in part for time lost during the strike, and after the strike was over, some even paid their workers for time taken to attend sessions of the Soviet.[41] Deserted by almost all his former supporters, the Czar now had no choice but to give up the autocracy. In a manifesto published on October 17, the promise was made that a legislative Duma would be established, the electoral law worked out for the now-defunct Bulygin Duma would be liberalized, and civil liberties would be granted.[42]

Although the "days of freedom" followed immediately after the promulgation of the October Manifesto, the revolutionary movement was now on the wane and was soon to be suppressed by a revived administrative machine. Nevertheless, society had won a major victory, and it is necessary to dwell further on some of the more curious aspects that have so far come to light on the relations between state and society at that time. From about August to October, the state apparatus had come to a virtual standstill. Normal legislative activity practically ceased, and the government was almost wholly occupied with its vain attempt to halt the revolutionary disturbances. At the climax of the Revolution in October, huge crowds flooded the main thoroughfares of all cities, carrying red banners with revolutionary inscriptions, and singing revolutionary songs. The police were confused and cowed, and at the insistence of the crowds, doffed their hats before processions and flags.[43]

Even more illustrative of the sad state into which the supposedly mighty police had fallen in 1905 is the story told by the former head of the St. Petersburg Okhrana, A. Gerasimov. On October 21, the government proclaimed a limited amnesty for political prisoners. Several days later, two men appeared at the headquarters of the Okhrana in Gerasimov's absence, presented a warrant from the Soviet of Workers' Deputies, and demanded that they be shown the prison quarters of the Okhrana in order to check whether the amnesty had been carried out. Gerasimov's intimidated aide, Lt. Col. Model, obligingly showed the two men through all the rooms of the Okhrana. According to Gerasimov, who questioned Model closely afterward, the men would even have been shown the papers in his desk had they so asked.[44] This incident, it should be added, is more of a reflection on the confusion of the police than the power of the Soviet. As the director of the general strike, the Soviet did enjoy considerable authority for a brief period, but in 1905, it remained little more than a general strike committee, emerging

as a rival government only in 1917, after the administrative apparatus had been completely swept away and full sway was given to
the anarchistic and irresponsible tendencies of the primitive Russian workers.

As already pointed out, the forty days beginning October 22,
1905, are called the "days of freedom." Society had been promised civil liberties by the October Manifesto. In the absence of
new legal norms or of a firm government, society seized these
liberties without waiting for government action or authorization.
In the capitals (the situation was not quite so favorable in the
provinces) censorship was suspended entirely and there was little
or no interference with the right of free association. Revolutionary
newspapers were founded and books published. Mass meetings
were held outside the safe confines of the universities, and revolutionary orators, fresh from jail or exile, freely demanded a constituent assembly or called for armed uprising. If there was any censorship operating at all during the "days of freedom," it was only that
imposed by the printers' union and the Soviet.[45]

The victory of society over the state had been achieved by an almost single-minded devotion of society to the ideal of liberty, at
the expense of normal cultural and economic pursuits. The more
the government sought to retain its power, the more society tended
to become exclusively concerned with politics and political agitation. This had its effect on art, literature, and science, which were
under the control of society and not the state, so that there emerged
a kind of socially imposed totalitarianism; just as the various voluntary associations denied that they could carry on with their normal
functions until a constitution had been granted, so artists and scien-
tists, under the pressure of the prevailing climate of opinion, were
expected to emphasize the contributions of art and science to the
fight against the autocracy, if necessary, at the expense of all their
other values. The situation was explained thus by a well-known
contemporary journalist:

The creative ability of men to form images by the combination of colors
or words, art and poetry, is valued by us only in so far as it serves to
arouse the public to the battle with the autocracy. Science, valued
abroad as the development of the intellectual power of mankind and
as an instrument for the dominance of man over nature, has lost its
huge methodological and practical significance for us, but has, on the
other hand, acquired great value for its philosophical conclusions, aim-

ing, as they do, to liberate mankind from that darkness in which the autocracy and the forces supporting it have enshrouded the mind. Abroad, this liberating, rationalizing force of science was a by-product which accompanied the development of scientific methods and the intensification of the dominance over nature. With us, on the contrary, the militant side of scientific hypotheses, since they are an excellent instrument for the fight against the ideology of the autocracy, has been advanced to prominence, and the development of methods, the study of details, without the knowledge of which general ideas lose their value, have been thrust into a distant corner and are even branded by the advanced part of society as pedantry and the reactionary "science for science's sake." [46]

The Decline of the Revolution

On the day of the promulgation of the October Manifesto, and for several days thereafter, scenes of wild rejoicing took place in the streets of the Russian cities, but the revolutionary movement had reached its peak (in urban, not rural Russia) only to decline progressively thereafter. It is true that the "days of freedom" followed, that the Soviet still enjoyed great prestige, that it issued calls for more general strikes, and that an armed uprising was attempted in Moscow in December; the revolutionary mood plainly did not die down suddenly—it would have been remarkable, indeed, if it had. Nevertheless, an obvious and marked change was detectable in the attitude of the crowds milling about in the streets; they exulted over their great victory, but they were ready now to begin the process of returning to normal life, and all the oratory of the revolutionaries and liberals proclaiming the need to consolidate the victory by calling a constituent assembly was fruitless. It was precisely because the political temperature declined after October 17 that the repressive measures of Ministers of the Interior Durnovo and Stolypin were once again to prove successful. By 1908, society was pacified, but the dangerous gap between it and the state remained. The Czar had succeeded only in winning time; either he was to make good his promise of freedom and fundamental reform, or he would inevitably face revolution again.

A remarkable aspect of both Russian revolutions was their lack of leadership; neither was the result of the actions, planned or otherwise, of any one part of the population, least of all of the revolutionaries. Both revolutions were rather elemental waves of mass discontent, which, as they grew in intensity, swept along almost the entire population, leaving the Czar isolated. It is doubtful whether Russian society was as yet sufficiently well organized to have made possible a successful assault on the formidable power of the state in any other way. By 1917, the decay of the monarchy and the dislocations caused by the war were too great to permit the survival of the monarchy. In 1905, however, the granting of a legislative Duma and the promise of civil liberties, even though late and extracted by force, achieved their purpose: They satisfied the man in the street as well as many conservatives and liberals, and thereby ruptured the united front of society. Neither workers' disorders nor peasant disorders, the main bulwark of the Revolution, had entirely spent their force, as the response of the St. Petersburg workers to the new general strike called by the Petersburg Soviet early in November, the armed uprising in Moscow, and the peasant uprisings, now reaching their peak, showed. But all these revolutionary manifestations, however impressive their proportions, lacked adequate coordination and were regarded with indifference or outright hostility by large groups of the population, the bulk of the intelligentsia, the industrialists, shopkeepers, retail clerks, domestic servants, and others formerly sympathetic, but now anxious to see a return to normal life. The evidence is impressive that no single group was capable of successfully defying the Czarist state; this achievement seemed assured only to a spontaneous and elemental movement of the entire population.

All this emphasizes anew the key importance of the role of the liberals and the changed atmosphere that would almost certainly have been brought about if the Czar, by granting adequate concessions in time, had detached the liberals from the revolutionary movement. The government, acting in the name of law and order, could probably have successfully put down the sporadic outbursts of the revolutionary movement alone. However, against an opposition that included the moderate liberals, the government was powerless, not because it lacked physical force, but because it lacked the ruthlessness necessary to take action against essentially loyal citizens who proclaimed that *they* were acting in the name of law and order and who included some of the most talented and respected figures of Russian society. With each day of indecision, moreover, more and more conservatives moved into the camp of the opposition, until finally the autocracy's last supporters abandoned the government, convinced that only the liberals would be able to halt the Revolution. There were no conservatives in Russia on the eve of October 17, 1905. All of society, from the extreme revolutionaries to the extreme conservatives, were agreed on at least one point—that it was impossible to continue with the old order. The Czar was forced to yield, but he was yielding to the solid and respected citizens who composed the loyal opposition, and not to the professional revolutionaries, who, had they stood alone, could have been suppressed, as they were suppressed when they stood alone before and after 1905.[47]

Reasons for the Success of the Revolution

In retrospect, there are two main reasons why the attempt of the Czarist government to maintain its power and keep Russian society under control was doomed to failure. One was the fundamental freedom of press, speech, and organization possessed by Russian society. The state stood by, exercising preventive controls, but these controls were haphazard and uncertain, and, in the long run, they served no useful purpose. Whether the controls at any given moment were severe or mild, society continued to move in its own direction; public life was basically in its hands, and neither ministers, ordinary chinovniks, the army, nor the police were exempt from its influence. As society grew, moreover, the government was compelled to give ground; no other course was open to it, for the government had no press of its own acceptable to society or which it could impose on society, and a modern industrial society ordinarily cannot be limited to the initiative of a centralized bureaucracy. The government could, of course, prevent society from growing, but only at the expense of Russia's national interests, and in practice it was limited to checking, as best it could, society's rate of growth.

When, at the beginning of the twentieth century, the lawless and arbitrary controls of the government and the sterility of its policy resulted in the eruption of mass discontent, and the Czar remained unwilling to abandon the autocracy, the government's only answer was increased repression, which, in turn, increased discontent. There began a vicious circle of increasing repression and increasing discontent. Ordinarily, nothing can prevent the political temperature of a whole society from rising higher and higher, thereby emboldening that society. The indefinite strengthening of a state apparatus in order to maintain unrelenting pressure on society is another matter. There were well-defined limits beyond which the Czarist state could not go in attempting to put down social disturbances. Therefore, once the vicious circle of repression and discontent had begun, and social discontent had passed the point at which the traditional methods of control were effective, the Czarist state was helpless. This leads to the second main reason for the Czar's inability to maintain his power—his unwillingness to use unlimited force.

At first sight, the victory of society over the state seems incomprehensible. The state had a formidable police mechanism. If it did not have all the weapons of mass destruction in use today, those it did have, including rifles and artillery, were quite adequate against unarmed crowds. Russian society consisted of isolated and unarmed individuals, by comparison with Western Europe as yet very poorly organized and not easily prepared for coordinated action. Yet it was the state which, in the end, capitulated, its administrative apparatus paralyzed and disorganized. Society overcame its isolation by means of electric currents, spontaneously discharged in a highly charged atmosphere, but it was an essential precondition of the growth of the necessary tension that the state's monopoly of violence remain largely an unused potential.

During the periods when society reacted against revolution, as in the 1880's, and again after 1905, the state's superior organization was quite adequate to deal with sporadic outbursts of revolutionary disturbances. However, during the periods when the agitation of society was steadily increasing, the man in the street quickly discovered that he need not fear the consequences of his boldness. If the odious prohibitions of the government were ignored, a few of the zemstvo men or the intellectuals might be exiled or jailed, some of those participating in street demonstrations might be beaten, or even wounded or killed. These possible consequences were not a sufficient deterrent for bold action in the face of the determination aroused by the hatred of the government—a determination each person knew was shared by his neighbor. The fact that those who were punished immediately became popular heroes undoubtedly contributed to the mass readiness to defy the state. There was no need for the whole population to become martyrs in order to express their dissatisfaction with the Czarist state, although it should be noted that potential martyrs were available in adequate numbers particularly among those youths passionately devoted to the Revolution ready to sacrifice their lives to strike down a hated minister, governor, or police official.

The readiness to defy the state naturally reached its peak during the Revolution of 1905. It is, in fact, one of the most remarkable aspects of that revolution that, in St. Petersburg at least, and probably in most other cities, it was conducted in the presence of reliable and fully armed troops. Yet, in most instances, the troops did not open fire, despite Trepov's order of October 14 that mass meetings were to be prohibited and that the troops were neither to use blank cartridges nor to spare their ammunition in enforcing the prohibition. Nor did the demonstrating masses show the slightest fear of the troops; rather it was the troops who were afraid of the masses.[48]

The troops could, of course, have been compelled to fire; the Bolsheviks were to demonstrate in 1917 how this could be done. But the attempt to suppress the Revolution by force meant the spilling of "rivers of blood," and any result achieved would have been purely temporary. A state that is unwilling to satisfy the demands of a society must place that society under permanent siege; it must anticipate desperate and increasing resistance, and it must be prepared to use force on any scale indefinitely. Once this course is taken, it is doubtful that there is any safe way back. The Czar was not unaware of this. On October 19, 1905, he wrote to his mother:

There were only two ways open: to find an energetic soldier and crush the rebellion by sheer force. There would be time to breathe then but, as likely as not, one would have to use force again in a few months; and that would mean rivers of blood, and in the end we should be where we had started. I mean to say, government authority would be vindicated, but there would be no positive result and no possibility of progress achieved. The other way out would be to give to the people their civil rights, freedom of speech and press, also have all laws confirmed by a State Duma—that, of course, would be a constitution. . . . There was no other way out than to cross oneself and give what everyone was asking for. . . . We are in the midst of a revolution with an administrative apparatus entirely disorganized, and in this lies the main danger.[49]

It should be noted that the Czar did not fully understand the situation, at least prior to his signing of the October Manifesto. Before signing, he entertained the naïve idea that he might be able to find a soldier sufficiently devoted to him to run a dictatorship while he himself continued to enjoy the prerogatives of the autocracy. His choice of a dictator was his cousin, the Grand Duke Nicholas Nicholaevich, later commander in chief of the Russian Army during World War I. This is the way in which the Grand Duke received the idea:

He [Baron Frederichs, Minister of the Imperial Court] had been delighted at the Grand Duke's arrival, and had told him it had been looked forward to in order that he might take the responsibility of setting up a dictatorship. At that the Grand Duke suddenly and unaccountably lost all control of himself; he whipped out a revolver and shouted: "If the Emperor does not accept the Witte program, if he wants to force me to become Dictator, I shall kill myself in his presence with this revolver. I am going on to the Czar; I only called here to let you know my intentions. You must support Witte at all costs. It is necessary for the good of Russia and of all of us." Then he went off like a madman.[50]

For a man of so little depth as the Czar, it must have seemed like a simple matter to set up a military dictatorship, and he and his advisers at first talked lightly of it. All, presumably, that was needed was a courageous soldier, and there seemed to be an abundant supply of them. The problem, however, was much deeper than that. The man who undertook the responsibility of becoming military dictator needed, above all, two main qualities: one, the willingness to assume a crushing responsibility; the other, sufficient ruthlessness to dispose without qualms of an opposition that was certain to grow, to become more desperate, and to use any available channel to strike back. Each of these qualities, taken separately, is relatively rare; taken together, they may well be entirely absent in whole generations. Assuming that a dictator could have been found, he might still have refused the job, unless he was supremely confident that he was doing what was right, whether from the point of view of his own interests or the interests of Russia. It is apparent that the Czar was not looking for another Plehve or even for a Stolypin; he was looking for a Lenin or a Stalin. The Czar did not understand either the nature of the assignment he was offering the Grand Duke or the changes in his government and in his own position that were certain to follow. He had, in short, no choices left that would have enabled him to maintain the autocracy in anything like its existing form. Once society had matured sufficiently to start the vicious

circle of increasing repression and increasing discontent, he was
bound to surrender to the liberals in one way or another. It was to
be fateful to him, but above all to the Russian people, that he surrendered under circumstances that preserved the gap between state
and society and slowed down the further inevitable constitutional
development of Russia.

9

Why the Liberals Lost and the
Bolsheviks Won in 1917

ALTHOUGH, IN 1906, the Revolution, as well as the brutal attempts on the part of the government to suppress it, had yet to run their full course, future prospects for the final emancipation of society from onerous state controls seemed favorable. The more than one hundred years of democratic aspiration had been crowned with initial success, and Russian society entered a new era of constitutional government. Society had shown that at critical moments it could break the power of the state, and it was, in fact, to repeat the process in 1917. New liberties having been won, the Russian people entered an unparalleled period of feverish organization and self-expression, which, as we have seen, was beyond effective state control and was bound ultimately to undermine the autocracy completely. Nevertheless, this and many other favorable developments were to be halted eleven years later, hard-won liberties were to be stamped out, and bureaucratic and police controls were to be tightened anew, with an intensity and scope beyond the imagination of any Czar. Why, it may be asked, should such favorable developments have ended in disaster both for the Russian people and for the world? Why, in short, should the Communists and not the liberals have triumphed in 1917?

The Views of V. A. Maklakov

The answer to these questions cannot be given solely in terms of the specific events of 1917, however greatly their juncture may have influenced the final outcome. The answer must be sought, rather, in the interaction of these events with deeper forces in Russian public life discernible for many years before the Revolution. In the analysis of these forces, the views of V. A. Maklakov easily stand out. In this writer's opinion, Maklakov's analysis now provides, and will continue to provide, the most penetrating explanation of why the February Revolution, which overthrew the Czarist regime in 1917, was followed eight months later by a successful *coup d'état* staged by the Bolsheviks.[1]

Underlying Maklakov's argument is the view that there were only two main political forces in Russia, the existing state apparatus and what he (as well as others) called the "Acheron" (the river of Hades symbolizing the nether world).[2] By the Acheron was meant principally the workers' and peasant disorders. The recurrence of these disorders was indicative of a fundamental malaise in Russian society. Essentially destructive in their purpose, they brought about temporary periods of anarchy interrupting the orderly development of society and state. If these disorders were to be suppressed, harsh measures had to be taken by a strong state apparatus. In 1905, the state apparatus, although shaken by the Revolution, remained intact, and was able to suppress the disorders. In 1917, however, the Provisional Government dismantled a key part of the old state apparatus and proved incapable of replacing it, thus giving free reign to the rampaging peasants and workers and paving the way for the seizure of power by the Bolsheviks.

Since the Provisional Government was initially composed almost exclusively of liberals, its failure was, in part, also their failure. Granted that the Provisional Government was faced by severe problems that might well have stumped the most experienced administrators, it nevertheless remains true that the liberals attempted a role for which they were inadequately prepared. For reasons pointed out previously, they were not equipped to run a state machine, and yet this was the role to which they ultimately fell heir. The situation as it actually emerged in the constitutional period from 1906 to 1917 was, therefore, virtually hopeless, given the interruption of the war. Of the two main political forces, one, the traditional ruling power, went into rapid decline because of the blindness and the blundering of its head. The liberal intelligentsia remained in opposition, unaware that, left to themselves, they could not form an effective counterweight to the bureaucracy and could not cope with the anarchy of the Acheron. If these premises of Maklakov are correct, then one way in which revolution could have been avoided was through the cooperation of society—i.e., the liberals—with sound elements of the bureaucracy, in order to make the new constitution work and to introduce the urgent reforms able to consolidate popular support behind it. Even if Maklakov's idea is regarded as a purely theoretical proposition, it is worthy of close consideration, both as a clue to what was happening in Russia at that time and as a guide to similar political problems widely applicable outside of Russia. Each side had much to offer and much to gain from cooperation; each side was indispensable to the other. The bureaucracy had the know-how of running a great state, but it was too isolated from social circles to understand fully either the needs of society or the methods of winning over public opinion. The liberal opposition knew the ways of society, but it was deficient in its knowledge of the techniques and the heavy responsibilities of governing. Working jointly, each side could have overcome its deficiencies by learning from the other.

The Mood of the Czar in 1905-6

If state and society were to cooperate under the constitution of 1906 to heal the breach between them and ward off future revolutionary shocks, then, of course, it was essential that each side be willing to work with the other and that they agree on a joint program of practical reform. There is little doubt that the liberals were unwilling to cooperate. Concerning the attitude of the Czar and the bureaucracy, there have been, and probably will be, many disputes.

Those who believe that the concessions made by the government in 1905 were not sincere and were not indicative of a change in its irreconcilable attitude toward public initiative have a strong case. From the beginning of his reign, Nicholas revered the memory and policy of his father, Alexander III. There is evidence that he was already under the domination of the Czarina and that then, as later, she was urging him to retain his unlimited powers. The Czar did not wish to grant a constitution, had consistently avoided making the concession long after it was politically wise to hold out, and had finally given in under duress. Thereafter, he persistently refused to use the word "constitution." To deputations of rightists received after the October Manifesto, he uttered mysterious phrases, such as "My autocracy remains as of old." Subsequently, he gave his wholehearted support to the most extreme reactionaries, and in the years before and during the war, he gave sympathetic consideration to various plans being drawn up to set aside the constitution.

Revab

While all this is true, those who believe that a genuine opportunity had arisen to deflect government policy into new, constructive channels likewise have a powerful case, one that is too frequently overlooked. As we have seen, the Czar was not a man of decisive action; when a crisis arose, he was inclined to take the path of least resistance. The responsibility he alone had before 1905 for the operation of the great Empire was beyond his strength; he maintained it only because he thought it was his obligation to do so. When he found that the good of Russia required that he retreat, and he was advised by those he trusted to do so, he retreated, probably even before he had exhausted all means of resistance.

It was in character for the Czar that, once having retreated, he was inclined to reconcile himself with the situation, at least as long as determined action was required to reverse his course. There is evidence that, to begin with, he was inclined to accept the new situation that arose after 1905, just as he did in 1917. This is indicated by the correctness of his attitude toward the First Duma in his address from the throne on its opening on April 27, 1906. It is also indicated by a whole series of memoir writers who had occasion to talk with him at that time, including Kokovtsov, Izvolsky, Kryzhanovsky, Witte, and Shipov.[3]

The accuracy of these writers is beyond question. They are supported by what is known about the general atmosphere then prevalent. The old policy of repression without removing the causes of discontent had clearly failed. The confidence not only of the Czar, but also of the sincere conservatives and assorted adventurers who had been urging him to maintain the autocracy, had been shattered, and society, as a whole, had moved to the left. There were few persons after October, 1905, who were not ready to support the new constitution, and those few found it expedient to remain in the background for the time being. Many ministers, and probably the overwhelming majority of the rank and file of the bureaucracy, would have welcomed cooperation with the "public men" in a joint effort to reduce the abnormal tension between state and society. In all the most important fields of public life, a new course was projected with the approval of the Czar, and liberal reforms were being discussed within as well as outside the bureaucracy.

Moreover, the Czar and the Court clique, as well as the nobles, had been frightened by the revolt of the masses and by the accompanying excesses. Although the rupture of the united front of society by the October Manifesto had broken the back of the Revolution, and the state apparatus was to prove capable of suppressing the disorders, for the time being, at any rate, without the assistance of the liberals, this was not understood until later. Meanwhile, the Czar himself was not sure what the outcome of the Revolution would be.[4] For a while, he was not even certain that it was safe to dissolve the First Duma, which was serving to promote and not to halt the Revolution. Whatever his personal predilections, he had surrendered to the respected men among the liberals, to whom he now looked for assistance in pacifying the country. The testimony is that, at the urging of some of his ministers, he had perceived, temporarily at least, the danger of governing in isolation from society and was sympathetic to the idea of appointing some of the "public men" as ministers.

There is some reason, therefore, for believing that the Czar was psychologically disposed to accept the idea of cooperation with the liberals, particularly during the first months after the establishment of a constitutional regime and shortly after the period when the old policy had brought him to the brink of disaster. It is true that he preferred to think that nothing had changed, that the October Manifesto and the Fundamental Laws of 1906 were merely new steps in the long evolution of the autocracy, and that he had not granted a "constitution." Nevertheless, he had given his word in the October Manifesto that there would be a legislative Duma, and there is good evidence that he regarded it as unworthy of a Czar to go back on his word.[5] Regardless of how he viewed his powers, he had taken the momentous, irreversible step of establishing national representation with legislative powers, thereby limiting his own powers and removing the primary obstacle to the development of the rule of law.

The Russian scene in 1905–6, therefore, was a dramatic one. The evidence suggests in retrospect that for a fleeting moment the powerful forces driving the Czar toward reaction, and ultimately destruction, were temporarily disarmed. The liberals had only to remain true to the principles of liberalism, ignore the Czar's aversion toward the word "constitution," and apply themselves with statesmanship to urgent reforms to make possible enormous gains, and, in the end, probably to achieve their fundamental aim—a sound and respected constitutional monarchy. It is true that the reactionaries were waiting in the wings for their cue, but they need never have received it. If the assumption that the Czar was ready to co-operate with the liberals is correct, and if the liberals had exhibited the statesmanship the conservatives expected of them, then Makla-kov's supposition that the reactionaries would have been discredited and the subsequent decay of the monarchy halted seems sound. Be-fore, however, testing the validity of this supposition, it will be nec-essary to examine the course actually taken by the liberals during that critical period.

The Mood of the Liberals in 1905–6

If there is any doubt about the Czar's real intentions after the issuance of the October Manifesto, there can be none about the behavior of the liberals. Thanks to the Czar's own pre-1905 policy of excluding society in so far as possible from responsible work and of prohibiting concrete discussion of internal conditions, a sense of responsibility and a sense of reality about Russian life were rare among the liberal intelligentsia. They entered what is now generally recognized as a new era in Russian history with a mentality condi-tioned by the victory they had achieved with the tactics of the Liberation Movement. As we have seen, after 1902, a part of the liberals had shifted from their traditional policy of compromise and gradual reform to an inflexible demand for the complete destruc-tion of the autocracy. Links were formed with the revolutionaries for the achievement of this common aim, and respect for the law was replaced by a belief in the utility of force. Revolutionary dis-orders, formerly regarded as a danger to liberal aims, were now seen as the means for bringing democracy, freedom, and law to Russia.

This shift was not unique to Russian liberals. There is a place for revolutionary ideas in the armory of those who prefer evolution, if evolution fails to budge an obstinate tyranny. What is peculiar to the liberals of the Liberation Movement was the failure of vic-tory to sober them. Like the revolutionaries, the liberals had become "maximalists," with an ideal concerning which there could be no compromise, and which was to be introduced in full, without delay. Their ideal was, however, not a utopian society but the most ad-vanced form of parliamentarism.

Not all of the liberals shared the views of the Liberation Move-ment, but because of the shift to the left, its tactics came to deter-mine the policy of the most important liberal party elected to the

First Duma in 1906, the Constitutional-Democratic (Cadet) Party. The victory won by the intellectuals of the Liberation Movement at the July congress of zemstvos was to be repeated at the two subsequent zemstvo congresses and at the first congresses of the Cadet Party held in late 1905 and early 1906. The October Manifesto and the promulgation of the Fundamental Laws of 1906 were thought to have changed nothing. The new Constitution was branded a "pseudo constitution," and its very issuance by the Czar was regarded as a violation of the October Manifesto. The Cadets came to the First Duma pledged not to treat the Duma as a normal institution and to hold its organic work to a minimum; it was first to assume constituent functions in order to transform the "pseudo constitution" into a genuine constitution. The most basic changes desired were universal, equal, secret, and direct elections, the abolition of the upper house (the reorganized State Council), and ministerial responsibility.

— It would be tempting, but a gross oversimplification, to view the events of 1906 and after as a duel between good and evil, between the elected representatives of the people pledged to reform, and the brutal autocracy, anxious to retain its old powers. Whatever may have been the true attitude of the Czar at that time toward the concessions he had granted under the threat of revolution, there can be no doubt that the Cadets themselves rejected the new constitution and were unwilling to make the compromises necessary for collaboration with the government within its framework. In accordance with shortcomings common to the intelligentsia of that time, they assumed that the people were ready for full-fledged parliamentarism and that their victory at the polls was a mandate to introduce it without delay and without modification. They took it for granted that they expressed the "will of the people," and, as is not unusual in times of revolution, that the will of the people was above the law. They came to the Duma with the feeling of conquerors, convinced that the beaten government would yield to their demands without a fight, and that if it did not yield, the people would rise up in their defense.

Moreover, having achieved so much with the aid of the mass movement and the revolutionaries, they failed to realize the danger from the left and continued their alliance with it. Although the Cadets and other moderates constituted a majority of the Duma, they joined with the main revolutionary group (a faction of the

Populists called the *Trudoviki*) as the "united opposition," sought to discredit the government, and, in effect, promoted the use of the Duma as a revolutionary tribune. At a time when the government was battling the violence and disorders of revolution, they refused to condemn the revolutionary terror, while demanding a general amnesty, the complete abolition of capital punishment, and the abolition of the emergency laws.

The Unbridgeable Gulf Between State and Society

The revelation in the First Duma that the liberals were more interested in condemning the government and forcing its capitulation than in applying themselves to the work of reform did not, at first, end the hope of the Czar and the liberal ministers that agreement was possible. This is indicated by the attempts made by Izvolsky and Stolypin prior to the dissolution of the Duma on July 8, 1906, and by Stolypin after the dissolution, to form a coalition cabinet or a Duma ministry by negotiation with some of the public men. (The first attempt to form a coalition cabinet had been made by Witte immediately after the October Manifesto, in 1905.) In an atmosphere that made it mandatory to conduct these negotiations in secret and in which agreement on the part of the liberals would have resulted in the charge of "treason," these negotiations were inevitably doomed. Even as conservative a man and as devoted a former follower of the autocracy as the Slavophile Shipov could no longer believe in the honesty of the ministers or conceive of the possibility of associating himself with them in the effort to put down the Revolution. The dissolution of the First Duma was followed by the dissolution of the Second Duma on June 3, 1907. (It had convened on February 20.) On the same day, the government took action to break the deadlock by illegally proclaiming a new electoral law, which shifted the choice of most of the representatives from the peasants, who had proved not to be as conservative as anticipated, to the landowning nobility.[6] As a result, the Third Duma (1907–12) and the Fourth Duma (1912–17) were overwhelmingly conservative, although groups of Cadets and various shades of revolutionaries continued to be elected.

The liberals had challenged the government with the threat of power, and their challenge had now been met with the exercise of power. They had failed to realize that the balance of power was in favor of the government. The state apparatus remained intact, and the prestige of the monarch remained relatively high. The Revolution, which most of the liberals had assumed would come to their aid, was therefore suppressed, with the same arbitrariness and brutality to which the bureaucracy and the police had been accustomed. By insisting on continuing the "war" with the autocracy, and by failing to reach agreement with the government within the framework of the new Constitution, the liberals may have lost an opportunity to cure the twin evils upon which the Revolution of 1917 and the Bolshevik seizure of power partially depended—their own incapacity to govern and the decay of the monarchy. In Maklakov's view, the Cadet Party had betrayed the principles of liberalism and had failed in the historic mission that liberalism and the Party, in the light of the talent and brilliance within its ranks, were called upon to perform at that juncture. They had, instead, undertaken the wholly unnecessary role of "clothing the revolutionary tendencies of the Duma with the appearance of constitutionality."

Although it may be useful to examine the tactics of the liberals in the light of what they should have done, the mistake should not be made of holding any of them personally responsible for what they did do. The responsibility for their defects and their failures rests ultimately with the monarchy, for it was its intransigeant maintenance of autocracy that made the liberals what they were. Their mistaken tactics were only a reflection of the virtually universal attitude of hatred and suspicion toward the bureaucracy. A mental barrier had been created that the "public men" could not breach. State and society had become two warring camps between which, in the eyes of the public, reconciliation was impossible.[7]

Maklakov himself apparently was not exempt from the effects of the mental barrier. His writings seem to indicate that his ideas were, to a great extent, the result of reflection in retrospect, after the distaste he shared with other public men for the bureaucracy and its methods had been cooled by time, and after events had disclosed both the extent of the danger from the left and the powerlessness of the liberals divorced from the Acheron and the bureaucracy. It seems probable also that his attitude toward the government was changed by a more objective study of the documents while in emigration than was possible in the heated atmosphere before the Revolution, when it was almost automatically assumed that nothing good could come from the bureaucracy.

The Czar Turns to Extreme Reaction

The disillusionment of the Czar with the loyalty and statesman-ship of the liberals did not lead to the abolition of the constitution. So bold a move would have been out of character for him. There-after, however, he showed the greatest confidence toward those who denied the constitution and demonstratively expressed their con-tempt for the Duma. This reopened the road for adventurers to acquire influence at the Court by proclaiming their devotion to unlimited autocracy. Organized into groups that proved, in the end, to be ephemeral, the so-called "dark forces" became a decisive influence in Russian official life. They had ready access to the Czar and were showered with favors. Their organizations and their press were generously supplied with state funds. To give the Czar an illusion of great popularity they flooded him with correspondence expressing their devotion to him and supporting exactly those fea-tures of the old regime that had defeated it in 1905, and that were to doom it and the imperial family in 1917.

To Nicholas, the dregs of society who made up the membership of these reactionary organizations were the true "voice of the peo-ple." In retrospect, after the Revolution had subsided, he regarded the October Manifesto as the result only of the intrigue of Witte. Liberal ministers who sought to work with the Duma, among whom, despite his many faults, Stolypin must be included, found their programs compromised and were forced from the political scene.

The slowness of reform during the Duma period can be attrib-uted also to the movement to the right of those conservatives, mainly the landowning nobility, who, frightened by the Revolution of 1905, had looked to the constitution and the liberals for assist-ance in pacification. In his espousal of reaction and in his neglect of the national interest, the Czar ultimately left far behind even this group. Liberalism and conservatism, whether in the camp of the bureaucracy or in the camp of society, remained without sup-port, and in the absence of firm organizational ties and the ability to take bold action, whether against the Czar or the Acheron, they were helpless.

The triumph of reaction was not inevitable. Had the liberals co-operated with the government in putting through reform and suppressing revolutionary disorders, a deeply felt need would have been fulfilled and the constitution would probably have continued to receive the widespread support it had in 1905. The reactionaries would have had little basis on which to attack either the liberals or the Duma, and their influence on the Czar unquestionably would have been less than it was. Once, however, the Cadet deputies revealed that they were continuing to join with the revolutionaries in dealing blows to the new legal order, the reactionaries could successfully play on the fear of revolution. A significant part of society shifted back to the right, and the Czar's sympathies for the reactionaries received the full sway that ended in his destruction.

The Intelligentsia Turns to Practical Work

If, at the same time that the government was degenerating at the highest level, Russian society was showing the enormous vitality depicted earlier, then some inkling of what might have been achieved, if cooperation between the liberals and the bureaucracy had been possible, becomes apparent. Under the constitution of 1906, the Czar permanently lost the unlimited power that put him above the law. Although the initiative in amending the constitution was his, no amendment could be passed without the approval of the two legislative houses. No new law, no new tax, no new expenditure could be made without the approval of the Duma.[8] It is true that the Czar retained many powers, and as was shown on June 3, 1907, the balance of power was initially in his favor, but there was no reason to expect that it would remain so indefinitely. Once the Duma had demonstrated its value by practical work and had acquired firm popular support, the Czar would have been powerless in any conflict with it. In the long run, the liberals could probably have had their parliamentarism, for, as in the West, the ministers were bound ultimately to look to the electors and not to the monarch for support. Russia had no need, in 1906, for an advanced constitution that would dazzle Europe. She did have need for the kind of framework for the development of the rule of law provided by the Fundamental Laws of that year, which, while limiting the power of the Czar, protected state interests in an immature society. Thereafter, hard and unspectacular work was necessary to raise the cultural level of the masses so that they would understand and successfully discharge the responsibilities of citizens of a democracy.

It is apparent that such concrete and responsible work served, at the same time, as an antidote to the preoccupation of the intelligentsia with theoretical utopias, which blinded them to the real needs of the country. Maklakov has pointed out how the atmosphere of the Second Duma differed from that of the First. The successful dissolution of the First Duma and the failure of the Viborg appeal had made the liberal deputies of the Second Duma more cautious as the futility of challenging the government without power became apparent. Turning to pressing legislative work, the Cadet deputies quickly came to understand the utility of joining with moderates of other parties and with the bureaucracy in working out practical measures. The doctrinaire leaders of the Party preferred their old tactics but were ultimately won over by the rank and file.[9] The educational effect of the Second Duma made its dissolution unnecessary. The liberal deputies were dispersed just at the point at which they were settling down to constructive effort on major legislation. Dissolution was the work not of Stolypin but of the Czar, who was, in turn, influenced by the reactionary Union of the Russian People.

Premature dissolution and the new electoral law brought about a new shift to the left of the Cadets at the same time that the Czar and many former liberals were moving to the right. The moderate parties were further estranged from each other, and their union in behalf of pressing reform on which they were all agreed became impossible until the emergence of the Progressive Bloc in the Fourth Duma, during the war. The Progressive Bloc, which did not include the parties of the extreme left and right, sought a "ministry of confidence" (but not one responsible to the Duma) with which an agreement could be formed on the basis of a concrete program of urgent reforms, without challenging the governmental structure. This new offer of reconciliation with society was refused by the Czar, who, under the influence of the Czarina, had now resolutely turned toward disaster.

The organization of the Progressive Bloc, although it came too late to affect the outcome of the constitutional experiment in Russia, was an important landmark, and its early espousal by Maklakov is another illustration of his acute statesmanship. It seems incongruous, in the beginning stages of constitutional government, for moderate parties to quarrel with one another and with the government over ideological and party problems incomprehensible to the masses, thereby paralyzing the adoption of concrete measures essential for reconstruction upon which they can, in fact, all agree. There might have been disagreements over the details and tempo of reforms, but these could have been settled by compromise, to the probable advantage of the national interest.

The revulsion from a preoccupation with radical theory and utopian dreams was evident outside the Duma among many segments of the intelligentsia in the period after 1905. Sparked, in part, by the revelation in 1905 of what revolution actually meant, and by the defeat of the revolutionary movement and the reaction which followed, it was aided also by the opportunities for practical work opened by the increasing industrialization of Russia, by the continued expansion of zemstvo activity and of the "third element," and by the burgeoning cooperative movement. The widespread preoccupation of the intelligentsia with Marxism and Populism, so characteristic of the 1890's, had subsided; both these ideologies were in decline. An intellectual calm had settled down after the Revolution of 1905, particularly among the youth, and, to some contemporary observers, it seemed as if creativeness in political ideas had virtually ceased.[10] Whatever the new social views that might have sprung up as an alternative to Marxism and Populism, they were bound to be strongly colored by the intense practical activity in which so many intellectuals were engaged. They were bound, therefore, to be less radical than those of the immediate past, to be more concerned with gradual change and democratic political institutions, and to reflect more accurately the real needs of the people and of the country.[11]

These developments had made considerable progress in the years before the Revolution, and they had their effect even on the Bolshevik movement. The Bolshevik wing of the Social Democratic Party consisted in those years of Lenin and those who at any given time chose to be his followers. Between 1907 and 1917, his following underwent great change. Most of the intellectual and idealistic youth who had been Bolsheviks during the years of the first Revolution (1905–7) had been alienated from Lenin for one or another reason, and those who succeeded them often had quite different qualities. On the eve of the Revolution, they consisted, to a great extent, of

summarily educated youth who had grown up during the previous
decade and who were uncritically attracted to the "advanced" ideas
of the Leninist brand of Marxism. Included also were "eternal
students" from the universities, who were more interested in political agitation than in serious study. "These, with numerous other
second-rate intellectuals," states one writer, "formed a kind of sub-
elite that was to provide the backbone of the Revolution when it
came." [12] It is the opinion of another writer, an eyewitness of both
revolutions and a former follower of Lenin, that the greater fanati-
cism and intolerance and the lesser moral scruples of the new generation of Bolsheviks were essential for the seizure of power in
1917. "As a witness, I can state that Lenin's victory would have
been impossible if his Party had remained as it was in 1905-7." [13]

The Origins of the February Revolution

The Revolution of February, 1917, was not different in kind from
the Revolution of 1905. Fundamentally, both were protests of a
nation ready to think and act for itself against an autocracy seeking to maintain itself long after it had outlived its usefulness. In
both cases, the final blow to the monarch came in time of war, after
he had demonstrated beyond any shadow of a doubt his inability
either to defend the national interest against external enemies or
to meet the internal needs of the people. In both, the monarch was
finally left isolated and helpless, opposed by all segments of the
population acting together spontaneously and without leadership.

There were, however, major differences, the primary one center-
ing on the role of the war in each of the revolutions. In 1905, the
war was fought on a distant front, remote from the main centers
of the population, giving rise, in consequence, to a defeatist attitude
on the part of a large part of the opposition to the autocracy. The
main features of the mass movement that brought down the autocracy were in evidence before the start of the Russo-Japanese War,
so that the causes of the Revolution plainly antedate the war. The
defeats in the Far East merely hastened a process already under
way by increasing the dissatisfaction and the boldness of the population and undermining more rapidly the self-confidence of the
Czar and the Court.

On the eve of World War I, there was no comparable revolutionary movement under way, principally, in this writer's opinion,

because the neglect of the needs of the population, the chief cause of the Revolution of 1905, was not nearly so flagrant. The slowness with which the Duma was passing essential reforms and the sympathy of the Czar for extreme reaction might, in time, have given rise to a comparable revolutionary movement, but there are solid grounds for believing that the situation might have been corrected without a revolutionary upheaval. Constitutional government, the liberties enjoyed that were nonexistent before 1905, the enormous vitality shown by Russian society, the growth of self-activity on all fronts, the unusual economic prosperity, all these suggest that a revolutionary situation was remote in 1914. Finally, the Stolypin reforms, the rapid transfer of the land of the nobility into the hands of the peasantry, and the growth of heavy industry at the same time that the rural standard of living was rising were removing the chief cause of the social upheaval of 1917—the peasant revolt. This, as we have seen, was Lenin's opinion, and on this subject he had no peer.

While the evidence seems good that the war was an essential condition for the outbreak of the February Revolution, it is indecisive on the question of the inevitability of the Revolution once the war had begun. It is possible that inherent weaknesses would have made Russia unable to withstand the strain of the war under any condition. Nevertheless, the mismanagement of the state was so great during the war that it is tenable to believe that a sound government might have enabled Russia to limp through the remaining months of hostilities without the outbreak of an uncontrollable revolt of the masses. It is, for example, Maklakov's view that cooperation between the bureaucracy and the public in 1905–6 might have avoided revolution, by preventing the decline of the monarchy in the years following and making possible a wartime government that would have commanded the confidence of the country.

This writer believes that Maklakov is right, and that in 1917, as in 1905, it was the repudiation of the incompetent and reactionary monarchy by the entire population that paved the way for revolution and in 1917 led to the outbreak of the masses. Because of the obvious effect of the war on Russian national interests, defeatism was confined to the extreme left, mainly Bolsheviks, during World War I. The intense attention of the nation was therefore riveted on the government. As we have seen, never before in the history of

Russian society had public opinion been so articulate or public initiative so creative. It was precisely at this time that the Czar's belief in the continuation of his unlimited powers reached a *reductio ad absurdum* and the government reached almost incredible heights of irresponsible folly. There is little doubt that the primary responsibility for this situation falls on the Empress Alexandra Fedorovna, who, though influential before September, 1915, became the *de facto* ruler after that time. Behind her stood the most successful and disreputable of a long series of backstage adventurers welcomed to the Court, Rasputin.

The deterioration of the government was intimately connected with the revolt of the masses that followed. The war had brought the people serious economic privations and the loss or the maiming of members of their families. Their morale had been shaken by the ignominious defeats of the Russian army. There is nothing in the evidence to suggest that they bore all this without being aware of the irresponsibility of the government in the conduct of the war. As had been the case during the Russo-Japanese War, interest in politics was sharply awakened among the masses, and in their own way, they followed events in Petrograd with great intensity.[14] Talk of the follies of the Czar, so much discussed by the intelligentsia, reached them, and on the eve of the Revolution the remnants of the traditional prestige the Czar enjoyed among the peasants collapsed. With it also collapsed the ties to authority holding together an empire otherwise lacking the organizational cohesiveness, capacity for self-government, general civic consciousness, and consensus of opinion capable of keeping some semblance of order.

The February Revolution, which began with riots over a bread shortage in Petrograd on February 23, was a surprise to the revolutionaries. It is now generally recognized that neither Bolshevik nor any other revolutionary propaganda had a significant part in the overthrow of the monarchy. Once the bonds of discipline had been snapped and the revolutionary parties were free to organize and disseminate their propaganda at will, their influence on the masses rose sharply. Nevertheless, until the Bolsheviks later created a new state apparatus capable of holding the masses in check, propaganda was effective only in so far as it conformed to the underlying moods and desires of the masses. It was the Bolsheviks who reaped the greatest advantage in the competition of revolutionary propaganda between February and October.

If the role of the revolutionaries in the February Revolution was slight, that of the liberal and conservative upper classes was correspondingly large. Whatever the part that propaganda, and the attitudes toward the state shaped by it, played in the emergence of mass riots, the upper classes were its principal source.[15] In 1917, the desertion of the Czar by the bureaucracy and the Court was even more complete than in 1905. Recognition that the end was near was widespread in these circles, and among those most insistent in urging the necessity of a palace revolution were some of the members of the imperial family. Not only were there now few reliable troops willing to quell the riots, but a large part of the army officer corps, including the high command, also approved of the Revolution. The monarchy had become a caricature of the traditional institution that had ruled Russia for centuries, and it seems doubtful that there were any honest men left ready to defend Nicholas II's government.

It is possible to argue, as some have done, that the revolt of the masses was grounded in long-existing social and economic grievances and would, therefore, inevitably have exploded, regardless of the decay of the monarchy or the attitude of the upper classes. It should be emphasized, however, that this argument, whether or not it assumes that the war was an additional indispensable factor, is based only on conjecture, the validity of which has by no means been convincingly demonstrated. In the two Russian revolutions of the twentieth century, mass revolt was, in fact, accompanied by the disaffection of the upper classes. Other mass revolts without support from above have been suppressed without serious political consequences in the history of modern Russia; it is indeed doubtful whether an uprising of the masses has ever been successful in any country against a united upper class. Moreover, the argument overlooks the key importance of the disintegration of the state apparatus in the course taken by the 1917 Revolution.

Social upheaval, as opposed to the mere displacement of an existing regime, came in October, not in February. The mass rioting in February had no purpose and no direction. There are those who question, and with good reason, that a social revolution involving the destruction of the old legal system need have ensued. February, 1917, like October, 1905, was an era of good feeling, of universal rejoicing at the downfall of a hated government. As symbols of the change, both the Duma and the Provisional Government were at

first highly popular with the mobs, and they responded as enthusiastically to patriotic speeches as to the slogans of class warfare of
the revolutionaries. February, 1917, should not be confused with
October, 1917; although the difference between them lies in part
in the underlying mood of the masses, the real key was the disappearance of state coercion.

The Liberals in Power

The first Provisional Government organized in March, 1917, by
the Duma consisted of eleven ministers, all but one of whom
(Kerensky) were moderate liberals. The validity of Maklakov's
thesis on the mistakes of the liberals rests on the fact that they
came to power under conditions comparable to those under which
they sought power in 1905, but, having achieved power, they found
events beyond their control and ultimately delivered the country
into the hands of the Bolsheviks. It is true that the war created un-
foreseen difficulties, which enormously complicated the problem
of establishing a viable new government. Nevertheless, this writer
agrees with Maklakov that their aims and attitudes were such that
they could not have coped with revolution under any circumstances.

Thrust into power in February, 1917, before the new conditions
of the post-1905 era had given them a firm understanding of the
realities of Russian life or of the essence of statesmanship, the liberals were hopelessly lost virtually from the beginning. Eager to
contrast their methods of government with those of the old order,
they failed to create a new state apparatus of control capable of
enforcing firm measures. In the place of the local administration of
the old order there appeared throughout the country in the first
days of the Revolution local committees and Soviets elected by the
population. There was no uniformity in the creation of these local
organizations and no hierarchical tie between them and the central
government. Some of them in the heart of Russia even declared
themselves independent republics.

The old police organizations were disbanded, and a new people's
militia was to be created, with chiefs elected by the people and
subordinate to organs of local self-government. A general amnesty
released all political prisoners exiled or imprisoned by the old
regime. A long-sought aim, the abolition of capital punishment,
was decreed. (It was nominally restored at the front in July.) The

political creed of the new government was expressed thus on the eve of its replacement by the first coalition on April 26:

Called into life by a great popular movement, the Provisional Government regards itself as the agent and custodian of the people's will. As the basis of political administration, it has chosen not violence or compulsion but the voluntary subordination of free citizens to the government they have themselves created. It seeks support not in physical but in moral forces.[16]

The difficulties of the Provisional Government were compounded by the existence of the Soviet, which was formed not only in Petrograd, but in all towns, in the army, and in some villages. The Soviet (the Russian word for "council") was a form of organization best understood by the Russian masses, who were almost entirely devoid of any organizational traditions. Functional groups of any size could, at a moment's notice, elect a council that was capable of taking the initiative, but which, at the same time, was automatically subject to control and placed a minimum of organizational restrictions on the membership as a whole. The Soviets, in addition to being better understood by the workers and peasantry than the Provisional Government, were led by socialists who were more in tune with the mood of the masses than were the liberals. Consequently, there were two governments in Petrograd: one, the Provisional Government; the other, the Soviet of Workers' and Soldiers' Deputies. Since the Soviet had a greater hold on the masses, and, in addition, controlled communications and the Petrograd garrison, while the liberals of the Provisional Government had no reliable police or troops at their disposal, the latter lost control of the situation and were swept from the scene.

The Bolsheviks did not gain control of the Soviets until September, after the suppression of the Kornilov revolt; until then, the Socialist Revolutionaries and the Mensheviks were in the majority. These socialists understood the elements of statecraft even less than did the liberals. Devoid to begin with of any understanding of the forces that had been let loose, and too timid to seize power themselves, they pretended to remain on the side lines safeguarding the interests of the future socialist revolution, while permitting the inevitable "bourgeois" revolution to run its course. Meanwhile, they encouraged the destructive instincts of the masses in an effort to "deepen the revolution" and increased the futility of the task of restoration faced by the Provisional Government. So inadequate were the traditional doctrines of the socialists, whether Marxism or Populism, in interpreting the new situation they faced, so confused did they become, that at one and the same time they favored continuation of the war until a satisfactory peace had been achieved and supported measures that inevitably broke down discipline in the army.

The Moderate Socialists in Power

Beginning in May, the Soviet authorized the moderate socialists to participate in coalition cabinets of the Provisional Government, and after July, they predominated in the government. Their role remained a peculiar and untenable one. As socialists, they had long sought revolution, and they hailed and apparently still hail February as a great victory. They preached the doctrine of class warfare to deepen the revolution, naturally feared the possibility of counter-revolution, and pursued that bogey long after it had any hope of resurrection. Toward the danger presented by their fellow revolutionaries, the Bolsheviks, they remained, on the whole, blind, and, despite the provocative acts of the latter, they were relatively tolerant toward them. As the Revolution deepened with the passage of time, it became apparent to some socialists, particularly those with the responsibility of a ministry, that mob violence and anarchy were not satisfactory means for realizing the ideals of the Revolution.

Events were to show that, given the attitudes of the socialists, there was no way out for them. Some, such as Prime Minister Kerensky, persisted for some time in believing that exhortation alone would suffice to restore discipline among the masses. As the trend to the left continued, urging moderation on the masses merely meant loss of influence. Ultimately, they were faced with the choice of two extremes, both of them dangerous for themselves: the Bolsheviks or a military dictatorship. When the latter choice was presented to them in August in the form of the Kornilov revolt, they joined with the Bolsheviks in suppressing it, but immediately afterward they lost control of the Soviets to the Bolsheviks. The Kerensky Government, which had sought to serve as a bridge between the left and the right, lost the support of both, and on October 25, the Bolshevik insurrection, thinly disguised in preparation, easily wrested power from it.

The Origins of the October Revolution: The Masses in Revolt

The reason for the drift to the left between February and October, for the "deepening of the Revolution," is to be found in the free play given to mass instincts in the absence of a coercive government. The collapse of the ties of authority with the decay and then the disappearance of the traditional monarchy left a void that could not be filled by the Provisional Government and opened the way to mob rule. At the top were idealistic intellectuals, divided into bickering groups with widely divergent ideas on policy, without experience in governing, and with an aversion to the measures of repression that alone could restore order. Below were the still-primitive masses, who degenerated into mobs seeking to gratify what they understood as their rights, without regard for their obligations to the law, the general interest, or the rights of others. The resulting dissolution of the state was reflected in the collapse of the army, and in factory and agrarian disorders.

Constant military reverses and disorderly retreats, immense losses and the obvious incompetence of the government had shaken army morale even before the outbreak of the February Revolution. Desertion, the hatred of officers, and the refusal to obey orders were already manifest, and the conviction was widespread that the incompetence of the government made further sacrifices useless. Disaffection seems to have been most serious among reserve units in the rear; at the front, supplies were better than at any time during the war, thanks, in part, to the efforts of the public organizations after the crisis of 1915, and most observers credit front-line units with continued military effectiveness.

Whatever fighting capacity the Russian Army still possessed was unquestionably finished with the advent of the Revolution. The snapping of the bonds of authority had an immediate effect on military discipline, and as the rear became even more disorganized and Bolshevik agitators gained ready access to the troops, the armed forces were slowly transformed into unruly mobs determined not to fight.

The desire for peace was widespread among the masses, and its urgency as a condition for pacification of the country was not fully understood, either by the Provisional Government or by most of the upper classes. Even the vast majority of the revolutionaries who regarded the war as "imperialist" could not face the prospect of Russia's complete defeat by the German Empire. Under the impact of revolution, the peasants did not appear to give this prospect much thought. Since the state was too remote for their understanding, so also were enlightened patriotism and nationalism. Under normal conditions, they had sufficient understanding of the needs of the nation to fight willingly and bravely; under revolutionary conditions, this understanding was too primitive to remain dominant, and it receded before the problems of the land, economic survival, and the general reorganization under way. The intense excitement of a revolution is plainly not conducive to a willingness to face death and privation, unless the revolution itself is regarded as in danger. Nevertheless, feelings of patriotism and nationalism did not wholly disappear overnight. Like other excesses of the Acheron, the desire for peace at any price gathered momentum slowly and became a progressively more important factor in the months after February.

Disorders in the villages were relatively mild during the first few months after the February Revolution. The peasants at first were satisfied to squeeze out the landlords by peaceful means. This slow start of the agrarian movement is attributable, in part, to the absence of the youth at the front; it was not unusual, subsequently, for deserters to incite a village to violent action. Another reason, frequently overlooked, was the expectation of the peasants that the government would order the land distributed to them. In the absence of a law distributing the land, which was to have been worked out by the Constituent Assembly, and in the absence of any effective restraints on the peasants, violence against the landowners slowly gathered momentum in the fall of 1917, and reached its peak shortly after the seizure of power by the Bolsheviks. The land was seized, manor houses were sacked and burned, and the landlords were expelled or killed. Communes usually acted as a unit against all landowners who were not members, including the individual peasant-farmers who had acquired consolidated holdings under the Stolypin laws. Bolshevik and Socialist Revolutionary propaganda played some part in bringing on this violence, but it is questionable whether the influence of propaganda was decisive.

The breakdown of discipline in the factories after the February Revolution led to a continuous and sharp decline in industrial production. The workers, whose attention was increasingly diverted from productive work, made economic demands, which, if fulfilled, would have bankrupted the individual enterprise and ultimately the national economy. Even the attempt to raise the depressed wartime wages prevalent in some industries was not economically feasible; in any case, the presentation of impossible demands was an old evil of the Russian labor movement. Everywhere, factory committees were elected by the workers, and these committees, for the most part, under the leadership of Bolsheviks, began to interfere increasingly with all phases of management, to the detriment of the enterprises' efficiency and profitability. Threats of violence frequently replaced negotiations as a means of gaining demands, and riotous workers drove away or killed unpopular factory owners and engineers. Factory disorders, like the agrarian revolt and the disintegration of the army, became progressively more violent and more destructive between February and October.

Although the strike movement had revived, beginning in 1915, Bolshevik influence on the workers was negligible until the coming of the Revolution. After February, they easily won the support of the workers, among whom the proportion of peasants with close ties to the village had increased during the war and who therefore had little stake in orderly production. Of all the revolutionaries, the Bolsheviks were the least concerned with the social consequences of the impossible demands of the workers, and they were ready to promise them anything, no matter how fantastic. Bolshevik control of the workers played a key role in their conquest of power, but in virtually all other respects, the revolutionary situation in 1917 Russia bore no resemblance whatsoever to the revolutionary situation envisaged by Marx. It should be added that the inability of the Bolsheviks to revive industry during the 1917–20 period, food shortages in the cities, and the desire to share in the seizure of land led to the wholesale return of workers to the villages. A considerable part of the proletariat melted away at the very time the Bolsheviks were seizing power in their name.

A final factor influencing the outcome of the Revolution was the release of the pent-up hatred of the lower classes for the educated and propertied classes, a hatred based on the historic gulf between the masses of the people and the elite and on the sense of injustice harbored by the former against the latter. Normally dormant, it was greatly exacerbated by the war, and its potential was revealed immediately after the February Revolution by the refusal of the peasants to elect members of the intelligentsia to the volost and village committees, even those who had worked closely with them in the cooperatives and the schools. All revolutionary parties preaching the doctrine of class warfare helped to sharpen the resentment against the upper classes after February, but it was the violence of Leninism that best expressed the mood of the common people as the revolt from below reached its peak in the fall of 1917. The Bolshevik program of exterminating the elite had the sympathy of the people and helped to sustain Bolshevik rule through the vicissitudes of the Civil War.

This is not to say, however, that the Marxist doctrine of class warfare was vindicated. The peasants of that time, the most numerous element of the population and the chief source of the hatred, are themselves classed as "bourgeois" or "petty bourgeois" by the Bolsheviks. Their hatred was indiscriminate, directed not against the mythical "capitalists," but against all who by their dress and manner of life differed from them. A radical lawyer or teacher who had spent his life fighting the autocracy and perhaps idealizing the peasants was as likely to fall under suspicion as the most ruthless landowner or industrialist. Marxist-Leninist doctrine may have been a useful tool in the Bolshevik seizure of power, but it cannot explain what happened in Russia in 1917.

Given this process of internal decay and the insoluble problems facing any government that refused to take decisive internal action and bring the war to an end, all who participated in the government inevitably lost popular favor. The Duma, the first Provisional Government composed largely of liberals, and the subsequent coalition governments dominated by the moderate socialists, all enjoyed great initial popularity, but all quickly lost it when faced with the responsibilities of power. Although Lenin's radical doctrines frightened many of his followers in April, 1917, and made him appear half-mad to his competitors on the left, the drift of events favored him. Ultimately, the popular mood temporarily caught up with his radical slogans, and, showing the keen sense of timing characteristic of all true political geniuses, he persuaded his Party to strike at just the right moment (October 25, 1917).

The results of the elections to the constituent assembly three weeks after the seizure of power show that the Bolsheviks never commanded a popular majority, but in the chaotic conditions of that time they did not need it. They enjoyed sufficient support among the poorer classes of the cities and in the army, at a time when the peasants were preoccupied with the violent seizure of the land, to win an easy victory. Their tight organization, their fanatical sense of mission, and the supreme self-confidence of some brilliant leaders proved to be decisive assets both before and after their seizure of power. Although they inherited many of the weaknesses of the Kerensky regime and quickly cooled the ardor of many of their backers as economic conditions became worse than they had been in October, they now had the advantage of holding state power and would stop at nothing to retain it. Against a divided opposition without popular support and unable to agree on a possible post-Soviet government, they managed to survive the Civil War despite their weaknesses.

Could the Victory of the Bolsheviks Have Been Avoided?

The victory of the Bolsheviks was not at all inevitable. There is widespread agreement that the Bolshevik Party was Lenin's personal organization and that its successful seizure of power, which contradicted the Marxist tenet that a bourgeois stage of development must precede a socialist revolution, was possible only because of his genius and boldness. At several points before and after October, a mistake on his part would probably have led to the destruction of the Party.

The problem as to whether a Bolshevik victory might have been staved off despite Lenin is more complex, but is nevertheless worth considering. The belief that the Bolsheviks could have been stopped presumes that there was no inevitable explosion from below that was bound to rage on unchecked. Its adherents deny that what happened in 1917 reflects a desire for anarchy on the part of the Russian people. It is argued, on the contrary, that what they sought was a strong government, which, unlike the government of Nicholas II, could fulfill their needs. The assumption is made that the Russian people, like any other people, fear unrestrained violence and disorder, and that, at the first sign of the shocks the mob rule of 1917 had in store for them, they would have welcomed strong measures to restore order. According to the Duma Provincial Section, during the first months after February, "the thirst and yearning for a strong government are such in the provinces that, if they should be put to a serious test in this respect, they are ready to follow any strong government, whatever its origin." [17] Accustomed to strong government, the peasants were prone, in the early period, to send many representatives to Petrograd for information and instructions. The report of the Provincial Section also points to the timidity and conservatism of the town dwellers and to the recognition by the peasants that, in the absence of the Czar and the old authorities, they themselves must help to maintain order.[18] Another eyewitness, emphasizing the importance of the absence of state coercion, finds that the attitude of the masses was ambivalent, ready for destruction, but also eager to obey a new authority.[19]

The possibility of checking the primitive outbursts of the masses with the cooperation of at least a segment of the masses themselves probably existed only during the first months after February, possibly as late as July. Once the revolutionary conflagration had gathered momentum, it probably could not have been checked at all until it had run its course. It was the conservatives and liberals of the Duma Committee who had the most favorable opportunity during the first days of the Revolution, when the prestige of both the Duma and the Provisional Government was still high. The retention of the monarchy, with the throne going either to Nicholas's son under a regency, or to his brother, would have been helpful, but apparently was not acceptable to the masses. In any case, there were no Lenins or Stolypins on the right, no one, that is, with the experience or the confidence necessary to undertake the responsibility of establishing a new authority. The Duma leaders were confused by the first appearance of the mob and readily yielded to the demands of the Soviet. Thereafter, the mob reigned supreme, and Lenin was to be handed his long-awaited opportunity. For the conservatives, liberals, and even the non-Bolshevik revolutionaries, the authority and the firmament of law of the old regime were indispensable.

Epilogue

Given this record of the development of Czarist institutions prior to 1917, and the circumstances under which they were destroyed during the course of World War I, what conclusions may be drawn about the relationship between the Czarist and the Communist regimes? May it be said that the Soviet state is an organic outgrowth of recent Russian constitutional history and accurately expresses the adaptation made by the Russian people to the political, social, and economic changes the twentieth century has wrought on a world-wide basis; or may it be said that the Soviet state is an aberration in Russian constitutional history bearing little or no relationship to its Czarist predecessors and finding its origin in the unique situation arising out of Russia's participation in World War I?

Since the study of both regimes is an enormously complex subject, and since the comparison between them is bound to be even more complex, it is possible for both points of view to be argued. Nevertheless, on the basis of the partial contribution to the subject represented by this work, the writer leans strongly to the second point of view. Although there are some parallels between the Bolshevik and the Czarist governments, there are even more striking differences. In general, the diverse policies of the Czars during the long period of their rule, shifting historical contexts, and fundamental changes in Russian society make facile identification of the Czars with the Bolsheviks misleading.

The parallels are derived, in part, from the fact that for long periods of Czarist rule Russian society was under the tutelage of a strong central administration. However, this tutelage arose without serious resistance and was based on the readiness of most elements of the population to accept it. Moreover, it was not unique to Russia: Except for the sweeping powers assumed by the monarchy because of the passivity of Russian society and the lateness of the demand for their disintegration, Russia followed a course not substantially different from the other powers of Western Europe. The battle mounted in the nineteenth century between a monarch resistant to change and a society insistent on change cannot fairly be cited as evidence that Russia has never changed at all. It indicates only that in the period before the Revolution, as in the period after, a stable relationship between the government and the people had not yet been established.

If a comparison is made of the Soviet regime with Russia before the nineteenth century, it seems to have validity primarily during periods of upheaval such as the reign of Peter the Great (1682–1725) or Ivan the Terrible (1533–84). Even then, the passivity of Russian society and its acceptance of the monarchy as a traditional and necessary institution ruled out any need for placing society under siege and imposing total controls (or their equivalent in view of the absence of the technological prerequisites). At no time in the period before the Revolution were such features as the Iron Curtain and the secret police wholly identical to Soviet practices; frequently, they were either nonexistent or barely developed.

Although both the last Czars and the Bolsheviks were concerned with the problem of keeping Russian society under control, the origin of the social order established by the Bolsheviks cannot, on the whole, be found in the Russian past. It is true that both were concerned with the same problem and that one succeeded while the other failed, but to conclude from this simply that one was more efficient than the other does not contribute anything to an understanding of the differences and the similarities of the two regimes. It is doubtful whether the Russian past or the past of any other country can serve as a guide to the development of the Soviet regime. That regime was built in response to immediate pressures, the most important of which, by far, was the insecurity of its leaders, and the result was a state structure and state policies probably unparalleled in the history of mankind.

Lenin's ultimate success need not obscure the danger in which his program and tactics had placed him and his followers after he had taken command of the Party in April, 1917. His advocacy of defeatism in time of total war, his demand for the overthrow of a revolutionary government that, in his own words, had made of Russia "the freest country in the world of all the belligerent powers," his virtually open espousal of civil war, his irresponsible demagogy, his calculated refusal of cooperation with all other revolutionary parties, and the label of "bourgeois" and "imperialist" he affixed to them—all this would have insured the destruction of the Bolshevik Party had any strong non-Bolshevik government come to power. From the time the April theses were promulgated, the Bolsheviks became an isolated group destined to shoot all other aspirants for power or be shot.

Once in power, the Bolsheviks had to ensure its retention at all costs. They were equipped, moreover, with an aggressive ideology almost totally irrelevant to the problems with which they were confronted. As a result of the upheaval brought about by war and revolution, there was in Russia, as there had been in 1905, an aroused peasantry, more or less conscious of the shortcomings of the old order and aware of the many things they lacked. Left to themselves, it seems reasonable to suppose that their awakened energy would have been directed toward the further organization of voluntary associations, a course with which they had already made considerable headway before the war. The revolt of the peasants had been inspired by the "bourgeois" desire to increase their landholdings and to cultivate and enjoy the fruits of their own soil; they did not have the remotest interest in the visionary schemes of a new and allegedly higher society of the Bolsheviks and other intellectuals. If, therefore, a government capable of restoring order, ready to reconcile the peasantry with the educated classes, and ready to give Russian society the leeway it needed to continue its all-embracing advances in self-activity had come to power after the Revolution, Russia might well have become a center of attention after World War I with methods of advancing an underdeveloped society differing sharply from those associated with Soviet Communism.

Spurred by the need to retain power and, despite the claims of the Marxists, blinded rather than enlightened by their ideology, the Bolsheviks proceeded in a different way and recklessly generated tensions that have never since been wholly relaxed. They set class against class, even peasant against peasant, and cited this as evidence that the class struggle was in progress. They eliminated all the liberties won at such great cost under the Czars, which the monarchy never dared to eradicate. They introduced the use of unrestricted violence and turned it against those left groups that, like themselves, had fought bitterly against the Czars. They limited and then destroyed the last vestiges of self-activity and introduced an enormously expanded version of a police-bureaucratic regime against which the Russian people had fought two revolutions in the twentieth century.

It is commonly recognized that the Bolsheviks could not have taken and held power were it not for the genius of Lenin. The difficulties involved for a small band of men, however determined, to seize power and to introduce unpopular measures over the opposition of virtually an entire people should not be underestimated. At crucial moments it was Lenin the practical politician and not Lenin the ideologist who made the key decisions that enabled the Bolsheviks to keep their shaky regime alive.

What is not so commonly recognized is that Lenin, on his death in January, 1924, did not leave behind a stable regime destined automatically to solve the dilemma raised by the Bolshevik seizure of power in 1917 by wiping out the limited area of free activity left to society. As was suggested by the disputes among the Party leaders at the time, and later in substance affirmed by Stalin, the Bolsheviks had the choice of either reaching an accommodation with the people and perhaps ultimately losing their power, or of increasing their control of public life and the level of terror to the point where popular movements comparable to those of 1905 and 1917 became impossible.

If, as some have claimed, the nature of the Russian "soul" or the primitiveness of the Russian peasant inevitably dictated the latter choice, it is not easy to understand why it was not made earlier, perhaps in 1905, when the Czar was confronted by a similar problem. At that time, the Czar shrank from the prospect of "rivers of blood." If some twenty years later it was decreed that rivers of blood must flow, it was not because the problem had changed but because a different sort of man made the decision. Despite the lack of brilliance in theory and oratory, which misled so many people at the time, Stalin was as unique a genius as was Lenin. Inheriting from Lenin a mechanism that had already proved its worth as a means of laying siege to Russian society, he perfected that mechanism to the point required to annihilate society as an independent self-governing unit and, therefore, as an independent political force. Without his demonstrated ability to manipulate men and institutions, his iron will, his infinite ruthlessness, and his willingness to accept the limited movement and the narrow conspiratorial life entailed by the supreme battle with his fellow countrymen, if not all mankind, it is questionable whether the Soviet regime would have become what it is today.

Although rivers of blood were necessary to consolidate the Stalinist regime, uninterrupted large-scale bloodletting was neither indispensable nor practical as a permanent instrument of government. Stalin, having established the principle that he was ready to liquidate anyone, regardless of the numbers involved or the position of the victims, was able to rule with the fear of the population pitched at a lower level. The key attribute of government by terror is not the number of people arrested or liquidated, but the principle that anyone is subject to indiscriminate arrest, whether or not he be guilty of any crime. The resulting uncertainty as to what was or was not punishable generated a feeling of insecurity among all citizens of fundamental importance in extracting obedience to the dictates of Party and government. The atmosphere of mutual suspicion created also served as an important deterrent to unauthorized group activity.

Government by terror was indispensable to the consolidation of the Stalinist state, but other elements have also contributed.* After the Party fell into the hands of Stalin in the twenties, and especially after the introduction of the Five-Year Plans and the collectivization of agriculture, control over virtually all phases of organized social activity steadily tended to tighten. This control was partially relaxed during the war to ensure support of the war effort, but it reached its peak in the postwar period. No sector of public life, whether concerned with music, art, sports, or any other form of organized social activity, was left free from Party and administrative control. If Stalin got from Russian society the degree of passivity and obedience the Czar had unsuccessfully sought, then it was partly because spontaneous collective action and individual initiative, the basis of effective resistance, had been rigidly chan-

* The above emphasis on the coercive aspects of Soviet state and society, although, in the opinion of the writer, justified by the evidence, does not mean that coercion alone holds together the Soviet regime or that the casual tourist in the Soviet Union can expect to find a population constantly in a state of fear and permanently on the point of revolt. Indoctrination and incentives also play important roles in the Soviet system, but they have been effective because of the universal awareness that dissent or even the outward lack of enthusiasm can have dire consequences. Neither hatred of the regime nor the formation of coherent anti-Soviet political views is very common in the Soviet Union. There are, instead, varying degrees of acceptance of, or indifference to, the propaganda stereotypes of the government, and the most common attitude toward the regime is one of apathy.

neled and controlled, at the point of contact between the masses and local authority as well as elsewhere.

In the light of the interrelation of political and social institutions at all levels, it is questionable whether in Russia, or in any other state in which a small group of men seek to perpetuate their rule, any change for the better may be expected. Genuine decentralization would appear to create tensions and conflicts between the central and local administrations that, in the long run at least, could be resolved only by the spread of local initiative or its destruction. It is significant that Stalin, despite the extraordinary control he maintained over Russian society, foresaw the necessity of further invasions by the state in the already severely limited sphere of private initiative during the alleged higher stage in the evolution of the Soviet regime envisaged by Marxist-Leninist theory —Communism. The experience of the Czars, with which he was undoubtedly familiar, suggests the soundness of his apparent objective, a mass of robotlike slaves as described by George Orwell in 1984, or by Eugene Zamiatin in the novel We, wherein the state makes certain that the happiness of the people would not be marred by any yearnings toward nonconformity by perfecting a brain operation for the removal of imagination or fancy (fantaziia), the chief source of evil.

Each step taken by Lenin and Stalin to impose their will on Russian society and to ensure their retention of power was appropriately rationalized in terms of Marxist-Leninist theory. Since the dazzling goals of Marxism remained and the Stalinist state became a ruthless police-bureaucratic regime ruling over a people impoverished by the demands of rapid industrialization, an enormous gap was opened between the Party's daily propaganda themes and the reality of Soviet life. Peaceful, confident competition with capitalist states for the allegiance of the peoples of the world was never a practical possibility. Hollow propaganda had to be fed to the Soviet peoples and to the rest of the world, and contact between the two had to be reduced to a minimum, in the best of circumstances carefully controlled. The mere existence of a free capitalist world enjoying a much higher standard of living than that of the Soviet Union must have seemed like a dire threat to the insecure Soviet leaders.

Other aspects of the internal structure of power have also contributed to the unyielding Soviet assumption that the outside world is an implacable enemy with which there cannot be permanent friendship and which must ultimately be conquered. The dictatorship itself, with all its ugly and inhuman characteristics so strongly at variance with the promises of the ideology, must be justified by the presence of a formidable enemy ready to attack. The enormous sacrifices in material well-being the Soviet people have been required to make since the introduction of the Five-Year Plans are similarly justified. Since it cannot be admitted that a serious opposition is to be found in a society that has achieved Socialism and is in process of building Communism, any internal opposition is almost always linked with the presence abroad of a hostile capitalist world. All enemies of the state *ipso facto* have no support within Soviet society and have become agents of hostile capitalist powers. A wide variety of internal ills, such as alcoholism and juvenile delinquency, incompatible with the allegedly ideal Soviet society, are also attributed, in part, to outside capitalist influence.

When the Communists seized power in 1917, their ideology led them to assume the existence of an implacable hostility between capitalist states and their infant Bolshevik state, and a war to the death between them. Since that time, they have been compelled to assume the presence of a hostile outside world for reasons that transcend mere ideology, for this other world is a key factor in the Soviet structure of power. How or when the Soviet Union will emerge from this rigid internal and external posture is a moot question.

An explanation of the foreign policy of the Bolsheviks, like that of their internal policy, must be sought in the internal structure of their power, in the siege of society they have been forced to maintain since they took over the Russian state. It has nothing to do with the alleged peculiarities of the Russian national character or with the alleged unfriendliness of the so-called capitalist powers. Ever since the end of the intervention in 1919, the Soviet Union could easily have won the friendship of the non-Soviet states had it wanted that friendship. Neither at that time nor at the end of World War II were the democratic nations seriously prepared to launch a new war for the sake of overthrowing Communism. The only real danger faced by the Soviet Union came from Japan and from Nazi Germany, but they were a threat to the rest of the world also.

The real origin of the Bolshevik regime is to be found in the dilemma the Bolsheviks faced upon seizing power in 1917, when, determined to rule although a tiny minority, they proceeded, in accordance with ideological misconceptions and the dynamics of power, to impose on Russian society a program unrelated to its needs and in defiance of its aspirations. As a result it became a regime dedicated primarily to perpetuating itself, and it has not only failed to meet the internal needs of the people, but it is also deeply repugnant to human nature. The idea that this regime, which has ruled at so terrible a cost to the Russian people, is in any sense indigenous to them has no validity.

Only the accidental emergence of two contrasting but towering geniuses made possible the creation of the Soviet regime in its present form. Like all regimes seeking to maintain themselves without regard to the needs and wishes of the people, it has become a brittle mechanism with which it is dangerous to tinker. This mechanism has inevitably fallen into the hands of lesser, in contrast to Lenin and Stalin, average leaders; and average leaders must rely on a greater measure of popular support than was previously sought by the totalitarian dictators of the twentieth century.

The habit of self-government had not manifested itself very long in Russia before it was completely crushed by the Bolsheviks, and it has not been given expression for more than four decades. It can hardly be said to be a vital factor now in the attitudes of the Russian people, particularly since the consideration of alternatives to the Soviet system under present conditions is reserved for the rare martyr rather than the rank and file of the population. Nevertheless, pre-Revolutionary traditions and pre-Revolutionary society expressed the spirit of a relatively free people, while Soviet society has been the arbitrary creation of an all-powerful state. It does not seem unreasonable to suppose, therefore, that in the long run the Russian people will find more inspiration in the pre-Revolutionary rather than the Soviet organization of society.

Notes

Chapter 1
THE LONG-RANGE CHARACTERISTICS OF RUSSIAN SOCIETY

1. For a theoretical treatment of this subject, see R. M. MacIver, *The Web of Government* (New York, 1947). For a theoretical treatment of the distinction between state and society, see Ernest Barker, *Principles of Social and Political Theory* (London and New York, 1951), pp. 1–88.

2. A. A. Kizevetter, *Mestnoe samoupravlenie v Rossii, IX–XIX st., istoricheskii ocherk* (*Local Self-government in Russia, 9th to 19th Centuries: A Historical Outline*) (Moscow, 1910), pp. 1–2 and *passim*. The comments on Russian society that follow apply only to Great Russia, and then only after the rise of the Muscovite state. Among the Great Russians, exceptions to the general lack of independent organizing ability were manifested by the Cossacks and the Old Believers, but space does not permit any discussion of the role and significance of these groups. The emphasis throughout the text is on the lack of strong organizational ties and on the resulting lack of an independent assertion of power. This does not preclude the representation of group interests to the Czar, or such spectacular expressions of local initiative as the Russian expansion to the Pacific.

3. V. O. Kliuchevsky, *History of Russia* (London, 1911–31), III, 49–52.

4. There is a penetrating discussion of the nobility and the land in Anatole Leroy-Beaulieu's *L'empire des Tsars et les Russes* (Paris, 1889–93), I, 349–55. Beaulieu (1842–1912) was a well-known French writer on national and international affairs. Between 1872 and 1881, he made four trips to Russia, after which he wrote his three-volume work on the Russian Empire. His association with high officials in Russia, his mastery of the Russian language and the Russian past, and his brilliant style have made his volumes on Russia standard references both for Russian and Western scholars. He was professor of contemporary history and Eastern affairs in L'École Libre des Sciences Politiques of Paris. Several years before his death, he became director of that institution.

5. Paul Miliukov, *Ocherki po istorii russkoi kultury* (*Essays on the History of Russian Culture*) (6th ed.; St. Petersburg, 1909), I, 229.

6. Kliuchevsky, *op. cit.*, II, 103.

7. Leroy-Beaulieu, *op. cit.*, I, 341. On the impoverishment and variation in the social position of the nobility, see also A. Romanovich-Slavatinsky, *Dvorianstvo v Rossii ot nachala XVIII veka do otmeny krepostnogo prava* (*The Nobility in Russia from the Beginning of the Eighteenth Century Until the Abolition of Serfdom*) (2d ed.; Kiev, 1912) pp. 24–26, 65–67.

8. The competition for places in the service of the Moscow prince was based on a system of defining rank, called the *mestnichestvo* (from the word *mesto*, or place). Since, as has previously been noted, the boyars retained the social prestige acquired by them before the rise of the Moscow state, high rank in the service of the Moscow prince was a symbol of high birth. Nevertheless, the use of the *mestnichestvo* reveals, in part, why high birth did not in itself carry much weight socially. The oldest princely families in sixteenth-century Moscow were

composed of so many members, and the lines between them were already so obscure, that the method they adopted of determining their order of precedence had to be based on external signs, viz., the relative position of their ancestors in the hierarchy of service. Under the *mestnichestvo*, precedence in the service of the Czar was determined not by fitness or high birth, but by the ranks held by the ancestors of the aspirants. Elaborate genealogical tables were drawn up, which enabled the boyars to determine their relative rank by tracing their relationship to individuals formerly appointed to the service. This, of course, made the boyars into a mass of competing individuals, jealously striving to maintain the service position inherited from their fathers. The competition was as much between members of a given family as between families. As long as the *mestnichestvo* lasted, it limited the discretion of the Czar in making appointments, but with the decline of the boyars, the system was abolished, and the genealogical tables were burned in 1682, without opposition. There is an excellent account of the *mestnichestvo* in Kliuchevsky, *op. cit.*, II, 45–47. The account in Miliukov, *op. cit.*, I, 230–31, though briefer, is useful in bringing out the main features. According to Miliukov, the Czars consciously made use of the *mestnichestvo* to keep the boyars divided.

9. Miliukov, *op. cit.*, III, 322. This statement of Miliukov is not contradicted by the enthusiasm with which the nobility at first greeted their liberation from service, as recorded in the memoirs of Bolotov (unlike most nobles, an enthusiastic farmer). Once the initial enthusiasm over divesting themselves of a heavy obligation had cooled, the deeply rooted tradition that status and privilege are derived only from service made itself felt at all levels of Russian society, including the nobility itself. See the comments on this point of Kizevetter, "Iz razmyshlenii o revoliutsii" ("From Reflections on Revolution") *Sovremennyia Zapiski*, 42 (Paris, 1930), 353–54. See also Romanovich-Slavatinsky's description of how a special commission established by Catherine to improve the act of emancipation was interpreted by the nobles as the restoration of obligatory service, in *Dvorianstvo v Rossii*, pp. 202–3. The Senate twice had to affirm that the Act of 1762 remained in force and that the nobles remained free from obligatory service and education.

10. The distribution of serfs ceased with Alexander I. See Romanovich-Slavatinsky, *op. cit.*, 173–74.

11. Miliukov, *op. cit.*, II, 323–24. See also Romanovich-Slavatinsky, *op. cit.*, pp. 413–21, 503–14; S. Y. Witte, *Samoderzhavie i zemstvo* (*Autocracy and Zemstvo*) (Stuttgart, 1903), pp. 55–59; and S. F. Platonov, *Lektsii po russkoi istorii* (*Lectures on Russian History*) (St. Petersburg, 1901), pp. 542–48. Platonov's work, available in an excellent French translation, gives only the general setting and does not attempt to evaluate the role of the nobility in local government. The best source in a Western language is Leroy-Beaulieu, *op. cit.*, I, 387–90, and II, 165–67.

12. Miliukov, *op. cit.*, I, 241. Again, Miliukov, I, 240–52, and Witte, *op. cit.*, pp. 55–59, are two standard references for this subject. On the organization of the town classes up to the time of Peter the Great, see Kliuchevsky, *Istoriia soslovii v Rossii* (History of Legal Classes in Russia) (3d ed.; Petrograd, 1918), pp. 170–80. A good description of the early Russian towns is available in German in Boris Brutzkus, "Die historischen Eigentümlichkeiten der wirtschaftlichen und sozialen Entwicklung Russlands" ("The Historical Characteristics of the Economic and Social Development of Russia"), *Jahrbücher für Kultur und Geschichte der Slaven*, X, Nos. 1–2 (1934), 84–87.

13. Quoted by George Vernadsky, *Political and Diplomatic History of Russia* (Boston, 1936), p. 232. The Russian text may be found in V. N. Latkin, *Uchebnik istorii russkago prava perioda imperii, XVIII i XIX st.* (*Textbook on the History of Russian Law During the Period of the Empire, 18th and 19th Centuries*) (2d ed.; St. Petersburg, 1909), pp. 244–45.

14. S. G. Svatikov, *Obshchestvennoe dvizhenie v Rossii (1700–1895)* (*The Social Movement in Russia, 1700–1895*) (Rostov-on-Don, 1905), Part I, pp. 155–56.

15. Leroy-Beaulieu, *op. cit.*, II, 294. Cf. also the well-known "Philosophical Letter" of Chaadaev.

16. In this study, many references will be made to the views of the Russians on this subject. The best single, systematic exposition is in N. I. Lazarevsky, *Lektsii po russkomu gosudarstvennomu pravu* (*Lectures on Russian State Law*) (St. Petersburg, 1908–10), I, 69–85.

Chapter 2
THE CZAR, THE MINISTERS, AND THE RULE OF LAW

1. This and subsequent quotations from the Fundamental Laws of 1892 have been taken from *Svod zakonov rossiiskoi imperii* (*Legal Code of the Russian Empire*), I.

2. V. Obolensky, "Vospominaniia a golodnom 1891 gode" ("Recollections of the Famine of 1891"), *Sovremennyia Zapiski*, No. 7 (1921), pp. 272–73. The inclination of the peasants to divide large objects equally was mentioned in the Council of Ministers in 1905. See V. I. Gurko, *Features and Figures of the Past* (Stanford, Calif., 1939), p. 411.

3. See, for example, the rapturous terms in which B. N. Chicherin discusses Alexander II while simultaneously demanding the end of the autocracy: "The Statute of February 19 [the day the serfs were emancipated in 1861] is the greatest legislative monument of Russian history. . . . A country that has completed such an internal reorganization deserves the respect both of those who witnessed it and of their descendants. And the name of the Czar who executed it remains blessed in eternity." *Rossiia nakanune dvadtsatago stoletiia* (*Russia on the Eve of the Twentieth Century*) (3d ed.; Berlin, 1901), p. 13. Chicherin, an eminent professor of law and philosopher, published this book anonymously outside Russia in 1900. It attracted a great deal of attention because it was obviously the work of a strong conservative who had reluctantly come to the conclusion that a legislative assembly was necessary to save society from the evil influence of the bureaucracy.

4. Leroy-Beaulieu, *op. cit.*, II, 84, 87.

5. Of the many references available on the relations between the Czar and his ministers during the constitutional period, the following three are representative examples from men independent of Rasputin: Witte (Prime Minister, 1905–6), *Vospominaniia* (*Memoirs*) (Berlin, 1922), II, 70–71, 77, 96–99; V. N. Kokovtsov (Prime Minister, 1911–14), *Iz moego proshlogo* (*Out of My Past*) (Paris, 1933), II, 129–31, 134–35, 321–22; testimony of Prince N. B. Shcherbatov (Minister of the Interior, June–September, 1915), in *Padenie tsarkogo rezhima . . .* (*The Fall of the Czarist Regime . . .*) (Moscow, 1924–27), VII, 213–19.

6. I. Kh. Ozerov, *Politika po rabochemy voprosu v Rossii za poslednie gody* (*Recent Policy Concerning the Labor Problem in Russia*) (Moscow, 1906),

p. 244. There is a more judicious statement of the problem in Lazarevsky, *op. cit.*, II, 178. One of the best illustrations of what the "war" between the ministers meant in practice may be found in the government's treatment of the peasant problem from 1902 until 1906.

7. For contrasting expressions of these views of the Czar, see "Dnevnik A. A. Polovtseva" ("The Diary of A. A. Polovtsev"), *Krasnyi Arkhiv*, III (1923), 151, and S. S. Oldenburg, *Tsarstvovanie Imperatora Nikolaia II* (*The Reign of Emperor Nicholas II*) (Belgrade and Munich, 1939–49), I, 39. Polovtsev, a member of the State Council with more than fifty years of service in the bureaucracy, was in close touch with the ministers and the highest circles of the government, and makes many interesting remarks in his diary about the St. Petersburg scene. Oldenburg's volume is a publication of the Society for the Propagation of Russian National and Patriotic Literature, a pre-World War II monarchist organization based in Belgrade. Oldenburg makes an able, if shortsighted and vain, attempt to uphold Nicholas and the autocracy.

8. Lazarevsky, *op. cit.*, II, 168.

9. The State Council played an important role in amending some statutes, such as those of 1864 and 1890 concerning the zemstvos, in a liberal direction. Other statutes, such as the one establishing D. A. Tolstoy's system of classical education (1871), or the one establishing the land captaincies (1889), became law only when the Czar approved the opinion of the minority of the Council. Laws most objectionable to society, such as the police statute of 1881, the university regulations of 1884, and the statutes limiting the rights of Jews, Poles, and other non-Russians, could not be put through the State Council at all because of the known opposition of a majority of its members.

10. In his diary, Polovtsev refers scornfully to the ministers who "run to the Czar and ask for special imperial orders in order to protect themselves by force from the free expression of opinion in the Council." Polovtsev, *op. cit.*, III, 112.

11. Gurko, *op. cit.*, pp. 26–27.

12. Speransky's work of codification led to the publication, in 1833, of two major sources of Russian law. One was the *Svod zakonov* (*Code of Laws*), which encompassed within a series of fifteen (later sixteen) volumes current legislation on specific subjects culled from a mass of conflicting laws issued by successive Czars through the centuries. The second was the *Polnoe sobranie zakonov* (*Full Collection of Laws*), which consisted of a chronological tabulation of all the laws that had been issued between 1649 and 1832. Thereafter, the *Svod zakonov* was periodically revised and kept up to date. The chronological tabulation of the laws was likewise continued, and two additional collections of laws were published prior to 1917.

13. Cf. Article 53 of the Fundamental Laws: "Laws are issued in the form of codes, regulations, statutes, charters, decrees, instructions, manifestoes, ukases, opinions of the State Council, and reports honored with imperial approval." Also Article 70: "An imperial ukase dealing with a particular case, or composed especially of any category of cases, for this case or category of cases sets aside the action of the general laws."

14. Lazarevsky, *op. cit.*, I, 44–45.

15. See, for example, V. M. Gessen, *Iskliuchitelnoe polozhenie* (*The State of Emergency*) (St. Petersburg, 1908), p. 257. Gessen, a vigorous critic of arbitrary bureaucracy, writes: "Entering into a discussion of administrative orders, even if founded on discretionary authority, the Ruling Senate, in many of its decisions, developed a theory fully analogous to the theory of the French Council

of State *de l'annulation pour détournement de pouvoir:* An administrative act, adopted within the limits of discretionary powers, is subject to annulment if the official has made use of his powers for purposes other than those for which they were granted to him."

16. G. B. Sliozberg, *Dorevoliutsionnyi stroi Rossii (Pre-Revolutionary Regime of Russia)* (Paris, 1933), pp. 19, 148; Witte, *Vospominaniia,* I, 191.

17. Because of the Revolution and the press of other events, references to the reformed Senate in the literature on Russia are relatively rare. It is, however, discussed at length in the 1917 edition of A. I. Elistratov's *Osnovnyia nachala administrativnago prava (Fundamental Principles of Administrative Law)* (2d ed.; Moscow, 1917), pp. 272–83.

18. The main provisions of the Fundamental Laws of 1906 have been summarized by P. P. Gronsky and N. J. Astrov, *The War and the Russian Government* (New Haven, Conn., 1929), and by Michael T. Florinsky, *Toward an Understanding of the U.S.S.R.* (1st ed.; New York, 1939), chap. i. Readers of Russian will do well to study the analysis of V. A. Maklakov, *Vlast i obshchestvennost na zakate staroi Rossii, vospominaniia (State and Society in the Decline of Old Russia, Memoirs)* (Paris, 1936), pp. 556–99. The laws themselves may be consulted in volume I of *Svod zakonov,* as issued after 1906.

19. Article 11 of the Fundamental Laws of 1906 stated: "The Emperor, in proceedings of supreme administration, issues, in conformity with the laws, ukases for the organization and operation of the various parts of the state administration, as well as orders necessary for the execution of the laws."

Chapter 3
THE POLICE STATE—CZARIST VERSION

1. Quoted by P. Sheimin in his article "Politsiia," *Entsiklopedicheskii Slovar* (Brockhaus and Efron) (St. Petersburg, 1890–1904), XXIV, 321. The history of the concept of police is discussed also in Otto Mayer, *Deutsches Verwaltungsrecht (German Administrative Law)* (Munich and Leipzig, 1924), I, 203–9.

2. W. F. Willoughby has distinguished four different ways by which modern states have acquired their constitutions: (1) by grant, (2) by deliberate creation, (3) by a process of gradual evolution, and (4) by revolution. An *octroyed* constitution falls into the first category, i.e., it is a constitution granted by a reigning autocrat, usually under the threat of revolution, whereby he surrenders his position as autocrat and is pledged to rule in accordance with newly promulgated principles and institutions. *The Government of Modern States* (rev. and enl. ed.; New York, 1936), pp. 118–23.

3. *Polnoe sobranie zakonov,* 1st series, VI, No. 3708; quoted by Elistratov, *op. cit.,* p. 11.

4. All these laws are quoted by Elistratov, *op. cit.,* pp. 11–12.

5. *Ibid.,* p. 12.

6. *Ibid.,* pp. 10–11. Elistratov's book, first published in 1914, is one of many illustrating the comparative freedom enjoyed by Russian writers despite censorship.

7. The local units of administration in imperial Russia were composed of the province (*guberniia*) and of its subdivisions, the districts (*uyezd*). The head of the province was the governor, an official appointed by the Czar. The head of the district, a police official called the *ispravnik,* served also as the chief administrative official of the district.

8. These functions were listed in Articles 81–84 of the *Obshchee uchre-zhdenie gubernskoe* (volume II of the *Svod zakonov*), which, as issued in 1892, contained seventy-three separate points.

9. A. A. Lopukhin, *Nastoiashchee i budushchee russkoi politsii (Present and Future of the Russian Police)* (Moscow, 1907), p. 42. Lopukhin was head of the Police Department from 1902 to 1905. Although he had been high in the police hierarchy, his work, a savage indictment of the then-existing police system, called for the ultimate transfer of control over the police from the central government to local institutions of self-government.

10. The text offers only the very briefest outline of the top management of the police between 1905 and 1917. The Police Department became the managing center of all police forces in the Empire in 1880, when the Third Section of His Majesty's Own Chancellery, which controlled the political police, was abolished. The Chief of the Police Department became the primary police official only in 1905, after the post of Assistant Minister of the Interior and Director of the Police became a supervisory instead of an executive one. The Assistant Minister had, until then, invariably held the title of Commander of the Corps of Gendarmes. Thereafter, the two positions were separated, although it was not unusual for the Czar to appoint one person to both. For the very complex history of the top management of the police, the following sources may be consulted: *Ministerstvo Vnutrennykh Del, 1802–1902, istoricheskii ocherk*, pp. 110–11, 173–74 (an official publication issued in connection with the centennial of the ministry in 1902); ukase of September 22, 1904, *Polnoe sobranie zakonov* (3d series), XXIV, No. 25,123; ukase of May 21, 1905, *ibid.*, XXV, No. 26,254; ukase of November 10, 1905, *ibid.*, No. 26,892; testimony of I. M. Zolotarev, in *Padenie tsarkogo rezhima* . . . , V, 52, 128–29. (Zolotarev was Assistant Minister of the Interior from 1911 to 1915; he was supervisor of the police from 1911 to 1913.)

11. A full account of the varied activities of the Third Section may be found in *Ministerstvo Vnutrennykh Del* . . . , pp. 97–101. This document indicates that there were exactly forty employees working for the Third Section in 1855. This figure does not include the gendarmes, who were carried on the budget of the War Ministry.

12. Lopukhin, *op. cit.*, p. 13.

13. Moskwitsch, "Die Polizei," in J. Melnik (ed.), *Russen über Russland, ein Sammelwerk* (Frankfurt-am-Main, 1906), p. 430.

14. Peter Struve, "Rossiia pod nadzorom politsii" ("Russia Under the Surveillance of the Police"), *Osvobozhdenie*, No. 20 (April 18, 1903), pp. 357–58. This was the first installment of six articles on the police by Struve. The others appeared in Nos. 29, 30, 33, 35, and 43, respectively. The circular quoted was part of a systematic summary of the laws and instructions governing the operations of the gendarmes, prepared for the information of the provincial gendarme administrations by a Col. Dobriakov.

15. Alexander Gerasimov, *Der Kampf gegen die erste russische Revolution (The Fight Against the First Russian Revolution)* (Frauenfeld and Leipzig, 1934), pp. 11, 87–88. Gerasimov was head of the St. Petersburg Okhrana from 1905 to 1909.

16. The most sordid of these cases was that of Bogrov, an agent of the secret police, who assassinated Prime Minister Stolypin, apparently with the complicity or tolerance of high government officials. Probably the best-known case was that of Azev, who unquestionably deserves to be ranked with the most celebrated

spies of history. While in the pay of the police, Azev became the head of the "fighting organization" of the Socialist Revolutionary Party, successfully organized the assassinations of Minister of the Interior Plehve and of Grand Duke Sergei Alexandrovich, the Czar's uncle, took part in other assassinations and attempted assassinations, and at the time of his exposure was making plans for the assassination of the Czar. He nevertheless became a highly valued agent of the police, betraying many of his colleagues and frustrating their terrorist plans, and through Gerasimov was a trusted adviser to Stolypin on the revolutionary movement. For the story of his career, see Boris Nicolaevsky, *Aseff: The Russian Judas* (London, 1934).

17. Testimony of Beletsky, in *Padenie tsarskogo rezhima* . . . , III, 327–83, especially 275–76. Beletsky was Assistant Chief and Chief of the Police Department from 1910 to 1914.

18. Gerasimov, *op. cit.*, pp. 89, 126–27.

19. Testimony of V. F. Dzhunkovsky, in *Padenie tsarskogo rezhima* . . . , V, 70–71; testimony of S. P. Beletsky, in *ibid.*, III, 269–71. Dzhunkovsky was Assistant Minister of the Interior in charge of the police from 1913 to 1915.

20. M. T. Florinsky, *Russia: A History and an Interpretation* (New York, 1953), II, 739, n. 11. For excerpts from a circular of the Police Department dated May 21, 1887, giving instructions on army surveillance, see Struve, "Rossiia pod nadzorom politsii," *Osvobozhdenie*, No. 29 (August 19, 1903), pp. 86–87.

21. On the recruitment of spies, see Gerasimov, *op. cit.*, pp. 86, 206; Beletsky, in *Padenie tsarkogo rezhima* . . . , III, 269, 271–72; A. I. Spiridovich, in *Arkhiv russkoi revoliutsii*, XV, 123–25; A. T. Vasiliev, *The Ochrana: The Russian Secret Police* (Philadelphia, 1930), pp. 54–57. Gerasimov flatly denies using intimidation at any time; he also doubts its utility and points to its danger for the police. Spiridovich describes Zubatov's method of recruiting spies over a cup of tea from among those arrested. Spiridovich, a gendarme officer from 1899 to 1905, was head of the Okhrana detachment that guarded the Czar from 1906 to 1916.

22. The most exhaustive work on the normal and extraordinary powers of the police is that of V. M. Gessen, *Iskliuchitelnoe polozhenie (The State of Emergency)* (St. Petersburg, 1908). Police arrests are discussed on pp. 27–30. There is useful material on police arrests also in N. M. Korkunov, *Russkoe gosudarstvennoe pravo (Russian State Law)* (7th ed.; St. Petersburg, 1909), I, 477–80, and in V. V. Ivanovsky, *Uchebnik administrativnago prava (Textbook of Administrative Law)* (Kazan, 1907), pp. 155–59.

23. Lopukhin, *op. cit.*, pp. 21–26.

24. Spiridovich, "Pri tsarskom rezhime," in *Arkhiv russkoi revoliutsii*, XV, 137. The activities of the prosecuting attorneys in defense of the accused are also confirmed by Gerasimov, who does not exclude those in the capitals, as does Spiridovich. Gerasimov writes: "Usually the prosecuting attorneys sought to convince (*überführen*) us of unimportant, formal infringements of the law. They hindered our work, yes, sometimes openly defended the interests of the accused." *Op. cit.*, p. 35.

25. The Statute on Measures for the Protection of State Order and Public Peace, approved August 14, 1881, was a temporary law codifying various emergency measures that had been issued by Alexander II toward the close of the 1870's, as the revolutionary movement and terrorist activity reached the climax that was to end in his assassination. The main authority of the emergency laws

is Gessen, *op. cit.*, pp. 160–97. There is an adequate discussion also in Korkunov, *op. cit.*, I, 564–84.

26. *Zhurnaly Komiteta Ministrov po ispolneniiu ukaza 12 dekabria 1904 g.*, pp. 106–7.

27. *Ibid.*, p. 99. See also Gessen, *op. cit.*, p. 195. Police arrest on the basis of "well-founded suspicion" was among the powers exercised in those localities in which emergency rule had not been proclaimed, but for a period of seven days instead of two weeks. The issuance of obligatory decrees was not among the powers exercised.

28. Quoted by Gessen, *op. cit.*, p. 278. The government body concerned was the Special Conference, headed by Count A. P. Ignatiev, set up by the Czar to review the possibility of improved emergency legislation in accordance with point five of the ukase of December 12, 1904. The Committee of Ministers, which initially considered all the points of the ukase, was likewise highly critical.

29. Leroy-Beaulieu, *op. cit.*, II, 565.

30. Gessen writes: "It is not necessary to hide the truth: Police service has been considered by us as shameful; persons possessing the intellectual and moral qualifications necessary for police service do not go into it. Such it will be until the time when the police in general, and the gendarmes in particular, lose their inherently antisocial character." *Op. cit.*, p. 72.

31. *Arkhiv russkoi revoliutsii*, XV, 116.

32. Lopukhin, *op. cit.*, p. 19. See also the testimony of Beletsky, in *Padenie tsarkogo rezhima* . . . , III, 268. Zolotarev has explained how difficult was his position as Assistant Minister of the Interior without at the same time being Commander of the Corps of Gendarmes, in *Padenie tsarkogo rezhima* . . . , V, 129.

33. *Arkhiv russkoi revoliutsii*, XV, 116. Spiridovich sets forth his views on the inadequacies of the Corps of Gendarmes on pages 115–17.

34. I. I. Petrunkevich, "Iz zapisok obshchestvennago dciatelia, vospominaniia," in *Arkhiv russkoi revoliutsii*, XXI, 146–48. Petrunkevich saw to it that the report he wrote was sent to St. Petersburg without changes.

35. Leroy-Beaulieu, *op. cit.*, II, 147–48.

36. Gerasimov, *op. cit.*, pp. 87–88; Nicolaevsky, *op. cit.*, p. 165; Beletsky, in *Padenie tsarkogo rezhima* . . . , III, 265.

37. Spiridovich, in *Arkhiv russkoi revoliutsii*, XV, 116.

38. Beletsky, in *Padenie tsarkogo rezhima* . . . , III, 272.

39. See the article by M. Gubsky, "Smertnaya kazn," *Entsiklopedicheskii Slovar* (Brockhaus and Efron, 1900), XXX, 497; also, N. D. Sergeevsky, *Russkoe ugolovnoe pravo (Russian Criminal Law)* (10th ed.; St. Petersburg, 1913), pp. 117–24; N. S. Tagantsev, *Smertnaya kazn, sbornik statei (Capital Punishment: A Collection of Articles)* (St. Petersburg, 1913), pp. 57–89. Sergeevsky points out that prior to 1754, capital punishment in Russia was not meted out on the same scale as in Western Europe. Furthermore, some methods used in Western Europe to increase the suffering of condemned persons were not resorted to in Russia (pp. 116–17).

40. S. S. Oldenburg (*op. cit.*, I, 24) estimates that 100 people were executed in Russia during the entire nineteenth century (excluding executions in connection with the two Polish rebellions and violations of military discipline). Some such figure may well be accurate. David Footman has pointed out that there was only one executioner in European Russia in 1881. (*Red Prelude* [New Haven, Conn., 1945], p. 166.)

41. Leroy-Beaulieu, *op. cit.*, II, 433.

42. See the memorandum written by Police Chief A. A. Lopukhin in December, 1904, and printed in A. K. Drezen (ed.), *Tsarizm v borbe s revoliutsiei 1905–1907 gg.* (Moscow, 1936), p. 25. According to Lopukhin, at the time of his memorandum the only person ever executed for a state crime under Articles 17–18 of the statute of 1881 was the assassin (Balmashov) of Minister of the Interior Sipiagin, in 1902. Other death sentences had been ordered by military tribunals, but the sentences were subsequently changed to imprisonment at hard labor. There was, of course, no uniformity in the treatment of terrorist acts, and there were instances when cases involving the assassination of high political personages were neither transferred to military tribunals nor punished by execution. For a useful list of political trials between 1901 and 1905, see L. I. Goldman (ed.), *Politicheskie protsessy v Rossii (Political Trials in Russia)* (Moscow, 1932). Materials on this subject published in the Soviet Union must, of course, be treated with the utmost caution, but this list of political trials has been solidly documented and is probably accurate. One execution in 1902, following that of Balmashov, was not taken into account by Lopukhin, but no other execution by sentence of a military tribunal is cited until June, 1905. Many illustrations of acquittals and of drastic reductions in sentences upon appeal or review are given.

43. Political trials were generally held behind closed doors, but the speeches of the defendants nevertheless became known. See, for example, *Osvobozhdenie*, No. 14 (January 2, 1903), pp. 229–39. For an English-language illustration, see the excerpts of Trotsky's speech before the court during the trial of the Executive Committee of the St. Petersburg Soviet in 1906, in Bertram Wolfe, *Three Who Made a Revolution* (New York, 1948), pp. 332–34. There are excellent illustrations of what could be said in the courtroom by defense attorneys in Kucherov, *Courts, Lawyers and Trials Under the Last Three Tsars* (New York, 1953).

44. For figures on executions and the victims of terrorists between 1905 and the first half of 1909, see *Krasnyi Arkhiv*, VIII (1925), 242. No objection to these figures compiled by the Czarist government was made by the Soviet editor, although he did rightly point out that they do not take into account the summary executions performed by the punitive expeditions sent out to restore order in the most disaffected areas. The same, and some alternate, figures are given in Tagantsev, *op. cit.*, pp. 89–93.

45. Maklakov, *Vtoraia Gosudarstvennaia Duma, vospominaniia sovremennika (The Second State Duma, Memoirs of a Contemporary)* (Paris, 1945), pp. 19–21.

46. Petrunkevich, in *Arkhiv russkoi revoliutsii*, XXI, 366–67. Similar incidents are reported by Maklakov, *Vlast i obshchestvennost . . .* , pp. 364, 382–83. According to Maklakov, the picture taken by the photographer was later printed in a well-known illustrated book, *Poslednyi samoderzhets*. See also the letter sent by the bureau of the congress to the governor general of Moscow before the congress convened, in I. P. Belokonsky, *Zemskoe dvizhenie (The Zemstvo Movement)* (2d ed.; Moscow, 1914), pp. 334–38.

47. Isaac Deutscher, *Stalin: A Political Biography* (London and New York, 1949), p. 49.

48. Footman, *op. cit.*, p. 56.

49. *Ibid.*, p. 55.

50. Wolfe, *op. cit.*, pp. 133–46, 621–27; Deutscher, *op. cit.*, pp. 122–28; David Shub, *Lenin, A Biography* (Garden City, N.Y., 1948), pp. 33–39. Lenin was in exile in Siberia from 1897 to 1900; Stalin's longest term was from 1913 to 1917. The description of life under police surveillance in these works should

be compared with the legal provisions governing police surveillance in Gessen, *op. cit.*, pp. 9–17; Korkunov, *op. cit.*, I, 480–82; Ivanovsky, *op. cit.*, pp. 153–55.

51. Leroy-Beaulieu, *op. cit.*, II, 441–65. George Kennan's *Siberia and the Exile System* (New York, 1891), presents a picture of unrelieved suffering and brutality in Siberia, but that picture is not confirmed by the experiences of Lenin and Stalin, or even by those of the Decembrists, to whom much harsher treatment was meted out. Dostoevsky's novel *The House of the Dead* also tends to support Leroy-Beaulieu rather than Kennan.

52. Leroy-Beaulieu has stated that about a third of the exiles escaped, and he cites some supporting statistics. (*Op. cit.*, II, 453–54). According to the Siberian patriot and advocate of regionalism N. M. Iadrintsev, escapes, even among convicts, were once so common that the head of a factory, upon receiving a party of prisoners, would announce: "Those who want to remain, get clothing; but those who want to escape don't need it." *Sibir kak koloniia* (*Siberia as a Colony*) (2d ed.; St. Petersburg, 1892), p. 270.

53. Deutscher, *op. cit.*, p. 124.

54. Gerasimov, *op. cit.*, p. 146.

55. Wolfe, *op. cit.*, p. 476. Wolfe quotes Krupskaya as follows: "At that time the Russian police had decided not to meddle in Finland and we had considerable freedom there. The door of the house was never bolted, a jug of milk and loaf of bread were left in the dining room overnight, and bedding spread on the divan so that in the event of anyone's coming on the night train he could enter without waking anybody, have some refreshments, and lie down to sleep. In the morning we often found comrades in the dining room who had come in the night."

Chapter 4

PRE-REVOLUTIONARY TRENDS IN RUSSIAN SOCIETY

1. This observation has been made by Romanovich-Slavatinsky, *op. cit.*, pp. 73–74. The transfer of the designation "highborn" to the serving nobility and the devising of new forms of reference to the imperial family came about gradually, in imitation of the Western aristocracies, during the course of the eighteenth century. A reference to the nobility as a whole as "highborn" was found by Romanovich-Slavatinsky for the first time in a ukase issued in 1754 (*P.S.Z.*, No. 10,558).

2. See the description of Kliuchevsky, *Istoriia soslovii*, pp. 120–21. Kliuchevsky writes: "The relationship of obligations to benefits in the Moscow state was the reverse of that which existed in other states between political obligations and rights: There the obligations were consequences of the rights; here, conversely, the benefits were political consequences of state obligations."

3. Romanovich-Slavatinsky, *op. cit.*, pp. 504–5.

4. Miliukov, *op. cit.*, I, 238.

5. The first officer's rank in military service and Rank VIII in civilian service. The first upward revision was made in 1845, partly as a result of pressure exerted by the nobles to limit access to the status of hereditary nobility. The qualifications for admission cited in the text were established in 1856. See A. D. Gradovsky, *Sobranie sochinenii* (*Collected Works*) (St. Petersburg, 1901–4), VII, 257; Romanovich-Slavatinsky, *op. cit.*, pp. 27–28.

6. Romanovich-Slavatinsky, *op. cit.*, p. 217. For a more exhaustive descrip-

tion of the personal rights of the nobility before the emancipation of the serfs, see his chap. III, pp. 214–78.

7. E.g., confirmation by the Czar of sentences depriving nobles of their rights and retention of class representatives in certain categories of criminal cases from which the jury was excluded. The influence of class in the courts before and after 1864 has been discussed by P. I. Liublinsky, "Sud i prava lichnosti," in N. V. Davydov and N. N. Poliansky (eds.), *Sudebnaia reforma*, II, 15–16. It is claimed by Liublinsky that judges, on the whole, took an impartial and proper attitude toward all defendants and witnesses and eliminated class differences in dealing with individuals, as required by law.

8. Leroy-Beaulieu, *op. cit.*, II, 384.

9. The ukase of October 5, 1906, "on the abolition of several restrictions on the rights of village inhabitants and persons of the other former taxable classes" (*Polnoe sobranie zakonov* [3d series], XXVI, Nos. 28,392 and 28,393), was adopted by the Stolypin government as an emergency measure, under Article 87 of the Fundamental Laws, between sessions of the Duma. Since the Duma was wholeheartedly in favor of peasant equality, it did not bother to consider the ukase until 1916. The Revolution broke out before a permaid law could be passed by both legislative houses. See Maklakov, *Pervaia Gosudarstvennaia Duma, vospominaniia sovremennika (The First State Duma, Memoirs of a Contemporary)* (Paris, 1945), pp. 140–41.

10. A foreign observer such as Leroy-Beaulieu, who knew the country well, could write even as early as the 1880's: "The nobility has been practically abrogated by the reforms of Alexander II, without even having been mentioned." *Op. cit.*, I, 386.

11. Miliukov quotes official figures showing that the average size of nobles' holdings declined from 538 dessiatines (1 dessiatine equals 2.70 acres), in 1887, to 488, in 1905. In that year, more than half of the nobles' estates (61,000 out of 107,000, or about 57 per cent) represented small holdings (less than 100 dessiatines). *Op. cit.*, I, 236.

12. G. T. Robinson, *Rural Russia Under the Old Regime* (New York, 1932), pp. 130–31; see also Miliukov, *op. cit.*, I, 235–36.

13. Robinson estimates on the basis of incomplete published data that the gentry lost more than 10 million dessiatines of land between 1906–14. Excluding the gentry of the three Baltic provinces, 39.6 million dessiatines remained in their hands, out of a grand total of 387.8 million in forty-seven provinces of European Russia. (*Op. cit.*, Appendix II, pp. 270–72.) A similar figure, with the reservation that it is probably too high, is accepted by A. N. Antsiferov and Others, *Russian Agriculture During the War* (New Haven, 1930), pp. 21–22. It should be added that of those nobles who retained their lands, many were renting them to peasants and many, leaving their estates in the hands of stewards, went to live in the cities. According to Miliukov, only one in three noble families actually remained on the land in 1905. (*Op. cit.*, I, 236.)

14. On the Noble Land Bank and the Special Conference for the Affairs of the Nobility (1897–1902), see Witte, *Vospominaniia*, I, 460–63. Witte, of course, paints himself as the defender of the public treasury against the depredations of the "debt-ridden and artificially supported" nobility.

15. K. P. Pobedonostsev was Chief Procurator of the Holy Synod from 1880 to 1905. His political philosophy, published in a series of essays known as the "Moscow Collection," has been translated under the title *Reflections of a Rus-*

sian Statesman (London, 1898). The Czarist government had no propaganda monopoly and no official ideology. However, Pobedonostsev is known to have had a great influence on Alexander III and Nicholas II, and his views explain many of the reactionary measures adopted by them. His political philosophy seems to have been designed to freeze an outmoded civilization and existing political institutions. Therefore, it commanded little support either inside or outside Russia.

16. A. A. Leontiev, *Krestianskoe pravo* (*Peasant Law*) (St. Petersburg, 1909), pp. 42–46. A peasant who wanted to leave the commune had to renounce his allotment land, pay all state, zemstvo, and communal taxes due from him and his family until January 1 of the following year, get the permission of his parents, prove that all minors and other persons in his family incapable of work were assured of support, pay half of the entire redemption debt due from his allotment, and prove that some other class society had declared its willingness to accept him. If the commune was in arrears on state taxes and redemption payments, and most communes were, the permission of the Provincial Board for Peasant Affairs was required.

17. Control over education was exercised because graduation from secondary school or a university made possible entrance into state service or the acquisition of the status of "honorary citizen." "Honorary citizens" were a kind of intermediate privileged class set up in 1832 by Nicholas I in order to divert those persons of the lower classes from aspiration to the nobility who had acquired wealth or an education and who sought to be relieved from the onerous obligations of the taxable classes. In the words of the distinguished Russian jurist N. M. Korkunov, honorary citizenship, before 1906, "served as a pump to suck out of the peasant medium and peasant institutions the slightest embryos of education . . . and doomed the composition of peasant institutions to complete and unconditional ignorance." For details on honorary citizenship, see Korkunov, *op. cit.*, I, 302–7.

18. A distinction must be drawn between the village society (*selskoe obshchestvo*, translated sometimes as "village community") and the land commune (*pozemelnaia obshchina*). The village society was the class organization of the peasants administering their affairs as a legal class. Most peasants were registered with one or another village society, although a very few without land were registered with a volost. The land commune was the traditional peasant organization through which the land was controlled and cultivated in common, known to the peasants as the *mir*. The two did not always coincide, but no attempt has been made in this study to maintain the distinction. This distinction was not maintained even in Russian law, thereby leading to much confusion. See Robinson, *op. cit.*, pp. 69–71.

19. Lazarevsky, *op. cit.*, II, 273; Leontiev, *op. cit.*, p. 87.

20. For further details on the land captaincy, see Leontiev, *op. cit.*, pp. 144–56, and Lazarevsky, *op. cit.*, II, 274–76. The ukase of October 5, 1906, abolished the right of the land captain to punish ordinary peasants without judicial proceedings. However, he retained the right to punish peasant officials.

21. It had not been the intention of the liberal authors of the Emancipation Act that the peasants should remain thus isolated. While the commune had a firm basis in the traditions of the peasants, the volost was merely an artificial temporary institution created because of the conditions existing at the time of the emancipation. The local administration had not yet been reorganized. The judicial and zemstvo reforms were in preparation, but the authors of the eman-

cipation were not sure that they would be realized. They considered the idea of an all-class volost, but rejected it in favor of a self-governing class unit in order to protect the peasants from the influence of local nobles hostile to the reform and still guided by the traditions of serfdom, as well as from the influence of an admittedly inadequate bureaucracy. See Gradovsky, "Vsesoslovnaia melkaia edinitsa," in *op. cit.*, VIII, 567–69. The real intentions of the authors of the reform on this point are well documented by Witte, *Zapiska po krestianskomu delu (Memorandum on the Peasant Question)* (St. Petersburg, 1904), pp. 10–22. All subsequent attempts to convert the volost into an all-class zemstvo unit or into an all-class administrative unit were blocked by reactionary influences at the Court before 1905 and failed to pass both houses after 1905.

22. Allotment land (*nadel* or *nadelnaia zemlia*) refers to land allotted to the communes at the time of the emancipation and divided equally by the communes among their members. Nonallotment land purchased by a peasant became his private property and was not subject to any of the restrictions discussed in the text.

23. Leontiev, *op. cit.*, pp. 346–50; see also Robinson, *op. cit.*, pp. 118–19. The law of March 18, 1886, was the work of Count D. A. Tolstoy and applied only to repartitional communes.

24. The offenses for which only peasants were punished were the violation of employment agreements (*narushenie dogovora naima*), wastefulness (*motovstvo*), and drunkenness. The ukase of October 5, 1906, ended the punishment of peasants for offenses not included in the penal code or not applicable to all classes. Corporal punishment for peasants was abolished in 1904.

25. A detailed discussion of the changes made in the volost courts by the law of June 15, 1912, may be found in D. Kuzmin-Karavaev, "Volostnoi sud," in *Novyi Entsiklopedicheskii Slovar* (Brockhaus and Efron), XI, 479–82. An improved method of election was established for judges, who were now required to be literate and who were freed from administrative punishment by the land captains. The decisions of the volost courts could now be appealed to a specially constituted superior village court, consisting of a justice of the peace and two chairmen of the volost courts in the district. As before, cases involving allotment land and its inheritance went, in the first instance, exclusively before the volost courts, but other civil suits were subject to their jurisdiction only if they involved a maximum of 100 rubles. Customary law was obligatory only for inheritance cases involving allotment land. In other civil suits its application was optional.

26. Robinson, *op. cit.*, pp. 96–99, 244–45; A. D. Bilimovich, "The Land Settlement in Russia and the War," in A. N. Antsiferov and Others, *op. cit.*, pp. 311–17; G. A. Pavlovsky, *Agricultural Russia on the Eve of the Revolution* (London, 1930), pp. 65–98.

27. There were two types of communes in Russia. In one, the land divided among the households for cultivation was subject to periodic repartition. In the other, the land divided among the households became the permanent possession of the households and was not subject to repartition. In either case, the land was assigned in scattered and intermingled strips. According to Robinson, more than three quarters of the peasant households with allotments belonged, in 1905, to repartitional communes. (*Op. cit.*, p. 211.)

28. For a good summary of the agrarian programs of the various parties, as well as a withering critique, see W. D. Preyer, *Die russische Agrarreform* (Jena, 1914), pp. 117–46. Preyer's study of the Stolypin reforms is one of the most

able and exhaustive available. The opposition parties referred to in the text include the Social Democrats, the Socialist Revolutionaries, and the Constitutional Democrats (Cadets). The most penetrating criticism of the Cadet program has been made by Maklakov, a former Cadet himself. See, for example, *Vlast i obshchestvennost,* pp. 198–222; *Pervaia Gosudarstvennaia Duma,* pp. 138–48; and "The Agrarian Problem in Russia," *Russian Review,* IX (January, 1950), 3–15.

29. See, for example, Robinson, *op. cit.,* pp. 97–98, who points out that the average allotment of a peasant household in European Russia in 1877 was about 35½ acres, while in France, in 1884, the average size of all holdings, great and small, peasant and nonpeasant, was less than 9 acres. Even within Russia, the size of the average allotments in a given region and the severity of the crisis there was disproportionate. See Brutzkus, *Agrarnyi vopros i agrarnaia politika (The Agrarian Problem and Agrarian Policy)* (Petrograd, 1922), pp. 55–60, 103, on this point.

30. Preyer, *op. cit.,* pp. 331–32.

31. Brutzkus, *op. cit.,* pp. 104–5; Preyer, *op. cit.,* p. 143.

32. Preyer, *op. cit.,* pp. 143–44.

33. Antsiferov and Others, *op. cit.,* pp. 15–23. Robinson's figures for the forty-seven provinces of European Russia (i.e., excluding the three Baltic provinces) at the end of 1914 are roughly comparable. (*Op. cit.,* pp. 270–72). Gsovski (*Soviet Civil Law,* I, 662–63, note 6) has marshaled the results of a series of investigators, Soviet and non-Soviet, who have made similar calculations of the proportion of land actually under cultivation owned by the peasants in 1917. The lowest figure is that of the Soviet investigators, 73.3 per cent. Figures on the actual distribution of land per peasant after the Revolution are cited by S. N. Prokopovich, *Narodnoe khoziaistvo SSR (The National Economy of the U.S.S.R.)* (New York, 1952), I, 132–34. Because large numbers of peasants who had been working in factories and were entitled to share in expropriated land returned to the villages after the Revolution, the accretion cited per peasant for most of the provinces of European Russia was half a dessiatine or less.

34. See Witte's long letter on the peasant question sent to the Czar in October, 1898. (*Vospominaniia,* I, 467–73.) Witte did not, however, recommend the liquidation of the commune; neither did the Special Conference of which he was chairman.

35. From the middle of the nineteenth century, the commune was widely revered in Russian society as an institution unique to the Slavs, or, in any case, as an institution having untold advantages for the population. Actually, the commune has been associated with the open-field system in many parts of the world and was liquidated by irresistible economic pressure in advancing economies some time ago. The extensive cultivation of the land associated with communal farming is appropriate for a natural economy in which land is relatively plentiful and the main objective is furnishing subsistence for the entire population. With the development of an exchange economy and a large urban market, and with the growth of the population, the land increases in value and the restrictions of scattered-strip farming become obsolete. Consolidation then takes place, making possible intensified cultivation of the available arable land and the production of diversified crops suitable for a large urban market. There is a long, theoretical treatment of the commune and its place in economic history in Brutzkus, *Agrarnyi vopros . . . ,* pp. 133–62.

36. On November 16, 1907, Stolypin told the Third Duma: "As long as the peasant is poor, does not possess individual landed property, and is held by force within the vise of the commune, he will remain a slave, and no written law will give him the benefits of civil liberty. . . . The small landed proprietor . . . is industrious, possesses a feeling of his own dignity, and will introduce into the village culture, enlightenment, and prosperity. Only then will paper freedom be transformed into real freedom, which is, of course, made up of civil liberties, a grasp of the significance of the state [in Russian, *chuvstvo gosudarstvennosti*], and a feeling of patriotism." *Stenograficheskie otchety* (III sozyv, pervaia sessiia), Part 1, p. 351; quoted by Maklakov, *Vtoraia Gosudarstvennaia Duma*, p. 35.

37. Robinson, *op. cit.*, pp. 208–42; Bilimovich, in *loc. cit.*; Pavlovsky, *op. cit.*, pp. 115–45.

38. Robinson, *op. cit.*, pp. 214–16. The cited figure concerns only repartitional communes. There were about 3 million additional households that had already been assigned their land in perpetuity. Under Article 3 of the ukase of November 9, the ownership of these lands was transferred from the commune to the head of the household. There were, therefore, more than 7 million households whose land had been converted to private property.

39. *Ibid.*, p. 225. All of the above figures apply to the fifty provinces of European Russia. By the end of 1916, the Land Settlement Commissions had received 6.5 million applications for some type of physical adjustment of land ownership. About half of them, according to Robinson, were requests for individual farms; but all could be expected to contribute to increased productivity. Apart from individual requests for consolidation, the law provided for the consolidation of whole communes by a two-thirds vote in most cases, by a simple majority in others. According to Brutzkus, two thirds of the consolidations involved whole communes. (*Agrarnyi vopros* . . . , pp. 94, 195.)

40. On the pressures exerted, see Preyer, *op. cit.*, pp. 334–38; and Brutzkus, *Agrarnyi vopros* . . . , pp. 117–21, 190–201. Both writers agree that the reforms met peasant needs and were proving successful. A. Lositsky, writing late in 1914, points out that some critics who had previously argued that the decline of the commune was due to administrative pressure were now admitting that the decline was caused by economic forces within the villages. ("Raspadenie obshchiny," *Sovremennyi Mir* [November, 1914], Section II, pp. 1–4.) It is worthy of note that, from 1907 to 1914, Czarist Russia was both expanding its heavy industry and improving the standard of living of the peasants. See A. Gerschenkron, "The Rate of Industrial Growth in Russia Since 1885," *Journal of Economic History*, Supplement VII (1947), pp. 154–55.

41. Bertram Wolfe, *Three Who Made a Revolution*, pp. 359–62.

42. An extensive description of state service by the merchants may be found in Kliuchevsky, *Istoriia soslovii* . . . , pp. 170–76. See also Miliukov, *op cit.*, I, 247–48.

43. The memoirs of Kizevetter, *Na rubezhe dvukh stoletii* (*On the Boundary of Two Centuries*) (Prague, 1929), pp. 16–17, contain a graphic description of the old and the new merchants. Kizevetter arrived in Moscow in the middle eighteen-eighties, and there he later witnessed the appearance of the telephone and automobile as well as the emergence of the new merchant, "a gentleman (*dzhentlmen* in Russian), patron of the arts, political oppositionist, bibliophile, and decadent." See also Peter I. Lyashchenko, *History of the National Economy of Russia to the 1917 Revolution* (New York, 1949), p. 416. Peter Struve, in

his uncompleted memoirs, argues that the Russian bourgeoisie constituted a well-defined social type, with a mental and spiritual caste of their own, detectable even among intellectuals of bourgeois origin. ("M. V. Chelnokov and D. N. Shipov," *Novyi Zhurnal*, No. 22 [1949], p. 241.)

44. Some comparative figures for the years 1890–1900 are given by A. Finn-Enotaevsky, *Kapitalizm v. Rossii* (*Capitalism in Russia*) (Moscow, 1925), pp. 78–79. These and other comparative figures used to be mentioned in Soviet propaganda publications (including their English translations) and are cited by Wolfe, *op. cit.*, pp. 268–69.

45. V. I. Grinevetsky, *Poslevoennye perspektivy russkoi promyshlennosti* (*The Postwar Perspectives of Russian Industry*) (2d ed.; Moscow, 1922), pp. 15–22.

46. A. Ermansky, "Krupnaia burzhuaziia do 1905 goda," in L. Martov, P. Maslov, and A. Potresov (eds.), *Obshchestvennoe dvizhenie v Rossii v nachale XX-go veka* (St. Petersburg, 1909–14), I, 313–48; Ermansky, "Krupnaia Burzhuaziia," *ibid.*, II, Part 2, 30–100; F. Dan, "Ocherk politicheskoi evoliutsii burzhuaznykh elementov gorodskogo naseleniia," *ibid.*, II, Part 2, 101–45; M. Pokrovsky, "Burzhuaziia v Rossii," in *Bolshaia Sovetskaia Entsiklopediia*, I (1927), 182–94; P. A. Berlin, *Russkaia burzhuaziia v staroe i novoe vremia* (*The Russian Bourgeoisie in Old and New Times*) (Moscow, 1922), pp. 283–307.

47. Pokrovsky, *op. cit.*, p. 188. Although there appears to be no reason to question Pokrovsky on this point, it should be noted that the bulk of the funds for the financing of *Osvobozhdenie* is known to have come from wealthy landowners.

48. Wolfe, *op. cit.*, pp. 266–67.

49. This subject has been treated at length in the writer's "The Attitude of the Tsarist Government Toward the Labor Problem," *American Slavic and East European Review*, XIII (April, 1954), 163–84. The documentation for the remainder of this section may be found in that article.

50. One of the best studies of pre-Revolutionary working-class life has been made by Gerhart Schulze-Gaevernitz, *Volkswirtschaftliche Studien aus Russland* (*Economic Studies from Russia*) (Leipzig, 1899), pp. 129–71. S. N. Prokopovich, "Krestianstvo i poreformennaia fabrika," in A. K. Dzhivelegov and Others, *Velikaia Reforma* (Moscow, 1911), VI, 268–77, offers supporting statistical data. Useful also is a study made by a Social Democrat, K. A. Pazhitnov, *Polozhenie rabochago klassa v Rossii* (*The Position of the Working Class in Russia*) (St. Petersburg, 1906). There is a brief description available in English in Margaret S. Miller, *The Economic Development of Russia, 1905–1914* (London, 1926), pp. 224–26.

51. Further details on Russian schools during the Czarist period, including relevant statistics, may be found in P. N. Ignatiev, D. M. Odinets, and P. J. Novgorotsev, *Russian Schools and Universities in the World War* (New Haven, 1929); Nicholas Hans, *History of Russian Educational Policy (1701–1917)* (London, 1931); Miliukov, *op. cit.*, II, Part 2; and Olga Kaidanova, *Ocherki po istorii narodnogo obrazovaniia v Rossii . . .* (*Essays on the History of Education for the People in Russia . . .*) (Berlin, 1938).

52. N. S. Timasheff, "Overcoming Illiteracy: Public Education in Russia, 1880–1940," *Russian Review*, II (Autumn, 1942), 80–88. See also Timasheff, *The Great Retreat* (New York, 1946), pp. 34–36.

53. This very point came up at the Peterhof Conference in July, 1905, when

the Czar and his advisers were considering whether the Duma, soon to be opened, should be elected and organized on class lines. N. S. Tagantsev, the well-known criminologist and Senator, pointed out to the Conference that 75 per cent of the lawyers were nobles. (*Petergofskoe soveshchanie o proekte Gosudarstvennoi Dumy*, p. 130.) Tagantsev cited the figure as an argument against those who persisted in regarding the nobility as a united class, unswervingly devoted to the autocracy.

54. Ivanov-Razumnik, *Istoriia russkoi obshchestvennoi mysli* (*History of Russian Social Thought*) I, 5–7.

55. D. N. Ovsianiko-Kulikovsky, *Sobranie sochinenii* (*Collected Works*) (St. Petersburg, 1914), VIII (Vol. II of *Istoriia russkoi intelligentsii*), 94–96. Ovsianiko-Kulikovsky refers to the "movement to the people" on the part of the nobility as a "mass" movement.

56. *Ibid.*, VIII, 94.

57. Cf. on this point Leroy-Beaulieu: "The students who love to mirror before the eyes of the ignorant a coming golden age, free of property and family, are, for the most part, nobles; the young people who distribute revolutionary catechisms to the peasants and the workers are almost all nobles. The émigrés or refugees who, in clandestine newspapers appearing in Russia or in the Russian journals abroad, preach revolution and socialism to their compatriots are noblemen. At home and abroad, nobles of either sex constitute most of the advocates of demagogy and apostles of nihilism." (*Op. cit.*, I, 373–74.)

Chapter 5
CENSORSHIP AND THE PRESS

1. The two chief reactionary papers before 1905 were *Moskovskiia Vedomosti* (*Moscow News*) and *Grazhdanin* (*Citizen*). Of these, Gurko has written: "He [Plehve] was closely associated with such publications as *Moskovskiia Vedomosti* and *Grazhdanin;* these, however, were not only without influence but were even despised in large public circles. The support of these publications only served to harm his public position and the measures he undertook." (*Op. cit.*, p. 166.) Witte mentions that as Prime Minister he founded *Russkoe Gosudarstvo* to counteract the influence of the antigovernment newspapers. Because Stolypin found it useless, he subsidized the already existing *Rossiia* instead. But, says Witte, everybody knew that *Rossiia* was government-subsidized. (*Vospominaniia*, II, 276–77.)

2. This attempt has been described at length by S. E. Kryzhanovsky, Assistant Minister of the Interior from 1906 to 1911, who was initially in charge of the venture. (See his *Vospominaniia*, pp. 100–4, 142–44, 153–59; also his testimony before the Extraordinary Commission of the Provisional Government, in *Padenie tsarskogo rezhima* . . . , V, 403–16.)

3. Harold Williams, *Russia of the Russians* (New York, 1918), p. 114. For an illustration of the seamier side of Meshchersky's treatment of government ministers, see Kokovtsov, *op. cit.*, II, 199–201. Kokovtsov, when Prime Minister, was severely abused by *Grazhdanin* for his "parliamentarism," but the favor Meshchersky enjoyed with the Czar made it impossible to punish him.

4. See Kryzhanovsky, *op. cit.*, pp. 153–56; Kryzhanovsky, in *Padenie tsarkogo rezhima* . . . , V, 406; and Kokovtsov, *op. cit.*, II, 111.

5. In December, 1916, the Empress wrote to the Czar: "Why on earth won't the Generals allow 'Russkoe Znamia' . . . to be sent to the army,

Dubrovin finds it a shame (I agree) and they can read any proclamations. Our chiefs are really idiots." *Letters of the Tsaritsa to the Tsar, 1914–1916* (New York, 1924), p. 457. (The letters of the Empress were written in faulty English.) Dubrovin, an extreme reactionary, was a leader of the Union of Russian People, which published *Russkoe Znamia*.

6. On the law concerning censorship and the press from 1865 to 1905, see "Ustav o tsenzure i pechati," as issued in 1890, in *Svod zakonov*, XIV. There are legal commentaries by Deriuzhinsky, *Politseiskoe pravo (Police Law)*, (St. Petersburg, 1908), pp. 206–23; Korkunov, *Russkoe gosudarstvennoe pravo*, I, 498–512; and V. V. Ivanovsky, *Uchebnik administrativnago prava*, pp. 196–203.

7. For further details on this subject, see *Zhurnaly Komiteta Ministrov*, pp. 496–98, and Gurko, *Features and Figures of the Past*, p. 32.

8. Kizevetter, *Na rubezhe dvukh stoletii*, p. 160.

9. In his memoirs, the editor of *Pravo*, I. V. Gessen, describes a curious interview with Minister of the Interior Plehve in 1904, during which Plehve, while acknowledging that he had no grounds for prosecution, nevertheless called *Pravo* a subsidiary of the illegal publication *Osvobozhdenie*, and warned Gessen to change its "direction" if he wanted to stay in St. Petersburg. "For the first time," writes Gessen, "in the office of the Minister of the Interior, I spontaneously and distinctly felt that the regime was powerless and left the notorious house on the Fontanka with the feeling of a conqueror." "V dvukh vekakh," in *Arkhiv russkoi revoliutsii*, XXII, 174–75.

10. "Karl Marx i tsarskaia tsenzura," *Krasnyi Arkhiv*, LVI (1933), 7. The censorship authorities passed the third volume in 1896, because it was "a serious economic treatise," and the views of Marx "have entered now into all courses being read on political economy."

11. "Marksistskaia periodicheskaia pechat 1896–1906 gg," in *Krasnyi Arkhiv*, IX (1925), 226–68, and XVIII (1926), 163–94.

12. For a brief survey of the revolutionary press, see K. Novitsky, "Pechat revoliutsionnaia v Rossii," *Malaia Sovetskaia Entsiklopediia* (Moscow, 1928–31), VI, 503–8. Two of the most influential nonrevolutionary organs, printed abroad and smuggled into Russia, were *Kolokol* (1857 to about 1865) and *Osvobozhdenie* (1902–5). Censorship was not effective in keeping forbidden books out of Russia. As Korkunov has pointed out: "Often a prohibition of the censors serves only as an excellent advertisement, guaranteeing the wide circulation of the book." (*Russkoe gos. pravo*, I, 485.)

13. Details are given in V. Obolensky, "Vospominaniia o golodnom 1891 gode," *Sovremennyia Zapiski*, No. 7 (1921), p. 263.

14. *Zhurnaly Komiteta Ministrov*, p. 502. Similar ideas had been expressed in government circles after the death of Nicholas I. See V. F. Deriuzhinsky, *Politseiskoe pravo*, pp. 204–12.

15. E. Maevsky, "Obshchaia kartina dvizheniia," in Martov, Maslov, and Potresov (eds.), *op. cit.*, II, Part 1, 62–63, 108–9; B. Gorev, "Tsenzura," in *Bolshaia Sovetskaia Entsiklopediia*, LX, 473–74; Witte, *Vospominaniia*, I, 488–89, II, 55–57; Kizevetter, *Na rubezhe dvukh stoletii*, pp. 397–98; Harold Williams, *op. cit.*, pp. 100–101. The movement to end all censorship restrictions began with the St. Petersburg Soviet, which, in conjunction with the union of printing workers, decided not to set type for any publication that submitted to the censorship. Thereupon almost all the editors of St. Petersburg

newspapers and magazines organized a "Union for the Defense of Freedom of the Press," which willingly agreed to ignore the censorship and projected common measures of defense against any attempt to punish any one of them. Included in the Union were such conservative publications as *Novoe Vremia* and *Svet*.

16. Miliukov, *op. cit.*, II, 861; Kaidanova, *op. cit.*, I, 104. Both quote N. A. Rubakin as their source.

17. For further details and the documentation, see the writer's article "Government Controls Over the Press in Russia, 1905–1914," in the *Russian Review*, XIII (July 1954), pp. 203–9.

18. Bernard Pares, *Fall of the Russian Monarchy* (New York, 1939), p. 105. On the censorship of Duma proceedings during World War I, see the testimony of the President of the Fourth Duma, M. V. Rodzianko, before the Extraordinary Commission. (*Padenie tsarskogo rezhima* . . . , VII, 172.)

19. "Pamiatnaia zapiska o rabochikh gazetakh v Peterburge," *Krasnyi Arkhiv*, X, 290.

20. The importance of this change is well reflected in the difference between the two programs of *Russkiia Vedomosti* drawn up in 1888 and 1906, respectively. They are reprinted in V. A. Rosenberg, *Iz istorii russkoi pechati* . . . (*From the History of the Russian Press* . . .) (Prague, 1924), pp. 77–87. One is long and cautious, built largely around the great reforms; the other is a short, sharp statement of democratic principles, similar to those that would be espoused by any Western newspaper. It was, of course, now possible to demand the civil liberties granted to Russian subjects by Articles 72–81 of the Fundamental Laws of 1906. However, the new Russian "bill of rights" was defectively drawn. Article 79 stated, for example: "Each person may, *within limits established by law*, express his thoughts orally and in writing, as well as disseminate them via the press or other means." (Italics added.)

21. Rosenberg estimates that by the end of 1912, the committees had confiscated about 2,000 books and pamphlets, with the approval of the courts. See *Letopis russkoi pechati 1907–1914 gg.* (*A Chronicle of the Russian Press, 1907–1914*) (Moscow, 1914), p. 61. A list of titles of both books and journals for the period October, 1905–January, 1909, is available in an unofficial publication by P. I. Bernov (ed.), *Spravochnyi ukazatel knig i zhurnalov arestovannykh s 17 oktiabria 1905 g. po 1 ianvaria 1909 g.* (*Reference Index of Books and Journals Confiscated Between October 17, 1905, and January 1, 1909*) (Moscow, 1909).

22. The content of the revolutionary publications of the period is analyzed in the government memorandum printed in *Krasnyi Arkhiv*, X, 286–99. There is an account of the revival of a legal Bolshevik press by S. Chernomordik, "Bolshevistskaia pechat," in *Bolshaia Sovetskaia Entsiklopediia*, VII (1927), 53–55. The story of *Pravda* is told in some detail by Wolfe, *op. cit.*, pp. 559–66.

23. The "thick journals" were soft-cover books of several hundred pages issued once a month. They featured articles on a wide variety of topics, including politics, history, art, literature, science, and philosophy, the emphasis varying with the publication. This form of periodical publication, represented now in the United States by *Novyi Zhurnal*, is likely to remain a permanent feature of the Russian periodical press. There is a more detailed discussion in Williams, *op. cit.*, pp. 119–23.

24. K. Novitsky, "Pechat v Rossii," in *Malaia Sovetskaia Entsiklopediia*, VI (1930), 500. In Alex Inkeles' *Public Opinion in Soviet Russia* (Cambridge,

Mass., 1949), p. 144, the figure of 859 newspapers is given for 1913. This figure, drawn from a Soviet publication, refers only to the pre-1939 boundaries of the Soviet Union. (See *Tsifry o pechati SSSR* [2d ed.; Moscow, 1939], p. 10.)

25. On the provincial press before 1905, see K. K. Arseniev, *Zakonodatelstvo o pechati* (*Legislation on the Press*) (St. Petersburg, 1903), pp. 227–31. The situation after 1905 is well described by Williams, *op. cit.*, pp. 104–7.

26. On the situation before 1905, see Miliukov, *Russia and Its Crisis* (Chicago, 1905), pp. 198–203. On the situation after 1905, see K. Ilinsky, *Chastnyia obshchestva . . .* (*Private Societies . . .*) (Riga, n.d.), pp. 574–81, 601–2; and G. G. Savich, *Novyi Gosudarstvennyi stroi Rossii . . .* (*The New State Order of Russia . . .*) (St. Petersburg, 1907), p. 495. There is also some information on the situation before and after 1905 in V. I. Charnolusky, "Zemstvo i vneshkolnoe obrazovanie," in B. B. Veselovsky and Z. G. Frankel (eds.), *Iubileinyi zemskii sbornik, 1864–1914* (*Jubilee Symposium on the Zemstvo, 1864–1914*) (St. Petersburg, 1914), pp. 370–90.

27. Kizevetter, *Na rubezhe dvukh stoletii*, pp. 24–25; see also his long and interesting account of the establishment and operation of one of the best-known of the people's universities, the Shaniavsky University of Moscow (opened 1908), pp. 470–95.

28. Figures for 1908 to 1916 are given by Miliukov, *Ocherki . . .*, II, 862. Book production reached its peak in 1912, when 34,630 titles and more than 133 million copies were printed. It declined slightly in 1913, and then fell rapidly during World War I.

29. Cf. the statement of Pares on the censorship under Nicholas I: "Journalistic failures were due quite as much to the indifference of the public as to the persecutions of the censorship; in fact it was precisely because the public was indifferent that the censorship was free to do as it pleased." (*Russia and Reform*, p. 272.)

30. Nicholas repeatedly demanded, without success, that his ministers stop the discussion of Rasputin in the press; he then told Kokovtsov that he was dismissing Minister of the Interior Makarov (1911–12) for his failure to draw up a new press law. (Kokovtsov, *op cit.*, II, 19–21, 84–85.) Makarov's successor, N. A. Maklakov, drafted a new and more restrictive press law, but nothing ever came of it.

Chapter 6

THE ROLE OF VOLUNTARY ASSOCIATIONS IN CZARIST RUSSIA

1. Korkunov, *op. cit.*, I, 458. Under the quaint laws that survived into the nineteenth century (Articles 140 and 141 of the "Ustav o preduprezhdenii i presechenii prestuplenii," as issued in 1890, *Svod zakonov*, XIV), the police even had to observe the clothing worn by those present at home meetings. For illustrations of the sweeping powers of local administrations to prohibit societies endangering "public security and morality," see the decree of July 22, 1866, Sec. IV, *Polnoe sobranie zakonov*, 2d series, XLI, No. 43,501, and the decree of March 27, 1867, 2nd series, XLII, No. 44,402.

2. For the temporary laws of March 4, 1906, see *Polnoe sobranie zakonov*, 3d series, XXVI, No. 27,479 (societies and unions) and No. 27,480 (public meetings). For an interpretation of the laws, see the deliberations of the State Council prior to their promulgation, summarized in *Otchet po deloproizvodstvu Gosudarstvennago Soveta za sessiiu 1905–1906 gg.*, pp. 570–637. The best of

the legal commentaries is Gessen's "Obshchestva i Soiuzy," in *Novyi Entsiklopedicheskii Slovar*, XXIX, 161–68. See also Deriuzhinsky, *op. cit.*, pp. 101–15, and Korkunov, *op. cit.*, I, 458–62. There is a wealth of interesting material, including direct quotes from the deliberations of the State Council, in V. Sviatlovsky's discussion of the rules of March 4 as applied to trade unions, *Professionalnoe dvizhenie v Rossii (The Trade-Union Movement in Russia)* (St. Petersburg, 1907), pp. 348–66.

3. Paul Miliukov, in *Outlines of Russian Culture*, ed. M. Karpovich (Philadelphia, 1942), Part I, "Religion and the Church"; John S. Curtiss, *Church and State in Russia; the Last Years of the Empire, 1900–1917* (New York, 1940); Donald Mackenzie Wallace, *Russia* (rev. and enl. ed.; London, 1912), chaps. 4, 17, 18, and 19. Miliukov's work is an abridged translation of Volume II of *Ocherki po istorii russkoi kultury*. Unfortunately, all the references other than those on religion made here to *Ocherki* concern those parts that have not been translated.

4. Cf. on this point Miliukov: "We agree with Professor E. W. Golubinsky that the mass of the population in ancient Russia of the pre-Mongol period had not the time to assimilate anything—either the external form or the inner meaning of the Christian faith. The people, as before, remained pagan, and the proper exercise of Christian rites—churchgoing, the discharge of church ceremonies, and the partaking of the Holy Sacrament—were still questions for the future. It required almost the entire length of Russian history for the people to attain this stage." (*Outlines . . .* , I, 7.) See also Wallace, *op. cit.*, pp. 65–66. While all this is true, the depth of the feeling engendered by Christianity should not be minimized. It is necessary only to recall that the Church has survived the entire period of Communist rule. It could not have passed a more rigorous test.

5. Miliukov, *Outlines . . .* , I, 132–34. According to Miliukov, church organization was an important problem in the West, because upon it depended the location of the supreme authority concerned with the development and the interpretation of dogma. In the East, national churches had no power to make changes in the universal doctrine of the Eastern Church. Their organization was of the purely executive type, which could come under the control of the state without the obvious infringement of Church rights.

6. Miliukov, *Outlines . . .* , I, 122–23. On the organization of the parish before and after Peter, see N. Suvorov, *Uchebnik tserkovnago prava (Textbook of Church Law)* (5th ed.; Moscow, 1913), pp. 125–34. The most active and aggressive Orthodox congregations were in those parts of the Ukraine and Belorussia not annexed until the Polish partitions toward the end of the eighteenth century. See the article "Tserkovnyia bratstva," in *Entsiklopedicheskii Slovar*, XXXVIII, 95–99.

7. Unlike the West, where it was common for younger sons of the nobility to enter the Church, in Russia there were no family ties between the nobility and the clergy. On the whole, the Russian clergy was an isolated class, recruited from and marrying within its own ranks. As for the nobility, it regarded entry into the Church as degrading. However, the situation in the Ukraine was different, because of Polish influence, and it was by no means uncommon to find Ukrainian priests who were also serf-owning nobles. (See Gradovsky, *op. cit.*, VII, 246; Romanovich-Slavatinsky, *op. cit.*, pp. 152–54.)

8. Wallace, *op. cit.*, pp. 58–62; John S. Curtiss, *op. cit.*, pp. 62–70, 79–86, 276–83, 357–65, and *passim*. See also W. H. Chamberlin's comments on

the Church during and after the Revolution of 1917. (*The Russian Revolution* [New York, 1935], II, 355–56.) It is hardly necessary to point out that the intelligentsia as a group was notoriously indifferent to religion.

9. Curtiss, *op. cit.*, pp. 201–2, 209–10. According to Curtiss, most of the lower clergy appear to have been politically neutral during the years of the revolutionary disturbances (pp. 275–76). Liberalism apparently was rare among the upper clergy. For some comments on the intellectual awakening affecting the clergy as well as other elements of society in the last years of the Empire, see V. Weidlé, *Russia: Absent and Present* (London, 1952), p. 83.

10. Curtiss, *op. cit.*, pp. 211–27, and chaps. VII and IX.

11. N. P. Anufriev, "Pravitelstvennaia reglamentatsiia obrazovaniia chastnykh obshchestv v Rossii," in A. I. Elistratov (ed.), V*oprosy administrativnago prava (Problems of Administrative Law)* (Moscow, 1916), I, 16.

12. *Ibid.*, pp. 19–20.

13. *Polnoe sobranie zakonov*, 1st series, XXXVIII, No. 29,151. The wave of reaction in Russia that led to the closing of the Masonic lodges was, in part, the result of a wave of reaction that swept Europe. The Masonic movement in Russia started under European influence in the second quarter of the eighteenth century.

14. Kornilov, *Kurs istorii Rossii XIX veka (Course on Russian History in the Nineteenth Century)* (2d ed.; Moscow, 1918), I, 134–35, 225–26; Deriuzhinsky, *op. cit.*, (3d ed.; St. Petersburg, 1911), p. 408. All future references to Deriuzhinsky are to the third edition, and not, as heretofore, to the second edition (1908).

15. Anufriev, *op. cit.*, p. 24. There is an interesting account of the fate of one society under Nicholas in Deriuzhinsky, *op. cit.*, pp. 515–16.

16. Nicholas Berdyaev, *The Russian Idea* (London, 1947), p. 105.

17. Anufriev, in V*oprosy administrativnago prava*, pp. 25–26; see also the article "Obshchestva," in *Entsiklopedicheskii Slovar* (Brockhaus and Efron, 1897), XXI, 610.

18. Anufriev, *op. cit.*, pp. 27–28; *Entsiklopedicheskii Slovar*, XXI, 610.

19. Deriuzhinsky, *op. cit.*, p. 523. The figures cited by Deriuzhinsky were compiled by the Department of the Institutions of Empress Marie and may well be exaggerated. Some of the societies were undoubtedly supported and dominated by the government.

20. V. Rudakov, "Uchenyia uchrezhdeniia," in the section "Rossiia," in *Entsiklopedicheskii Slovar*, XXVII, 413–14.

21. Anufriev, *op. cit.*, pp. 29–30.

22. On the law of 1884, see *Polnoe sobranie zakonov*, 3d series, IV, No. 2,404. There are comments by Deriuzhinsky on all the university statutes. (*Op. cit.*, pp. 406–15.)

23. For extracts from the official "rules for students" issued by the Ministry of Education, see T. Darlington, "Education in Russia" (*Special Reports on Educational Subjects*, British Board of Education) (London, 1909), XXIII, 445–46. Pares points out that association in any form, whether for amusement or study, was also forbidden to high-school students. "It is sure to be political," he was told by an official. Between 1896 and 1904, according to Pares, not more than two or three boys were allowed to walk together in the street. (*Russia and Reform*, p. 209.)

24. Kizevetter, *Na rubezhe dvukh stoletii*, p. 48. At the first lecture of Kliu-

chevsky attended by Kizevetter in 1884, the students involuntarily broke into applause, whereupon several were placed in the detention house. However, this measure was enforced only at the height of the reaction in the 1880's.

25. On student organizations, see N. Cherevanin, "Dvizhenie intelligentsii," in Martov and Others, *Obshchestvennoe dvizhenie*, I, 293–94; V. A. Maklakov, *Vlast i obshchestvennost*, pp. 86–87; Kizevetter, *Na rubezhe dvukh stoletti*, p. 245. The most common form of student association was the *zemliachestvo*, a society of students from the same province or city organized for the purpose of mutual aid and friendship. *Zemliachestva* were declared illegal in 1884, after it was found that they were being used for political purposes.

26. N. Cherevanin, "Dvizhenie intelligentsii," in Martov and Others, *op. cit.*, I, 275. A striking illustration of the students' aversion to politics in the late 1880's is given by Maklakov, *Vlast i obshchestvennost* . . . , pp. 87–89.

27. The strike movement is discussed in detail by Cherevanin, *op. cit.*, p. 275. The effectiveness of the illegal student organization is underscored by the fact that the strike spread from St. Petersburg to other university centers within a few days, although the press was forbidden to discuss it. See Oldenburg, *op. cit.*, I, 146.

28. Vannovsky's concessions are listed in Cherevanin, *op. cit.*, pp. 279–80. See also Oldenburg, *op. cit.*, I, 163–64.

29. The various student congresses are discussed from a strictly Marxist point of view by G. Engel and V. Gorokhov, *Iz istorii studencheskago dvizheniia, 1899–1906*, pp. 73, 89–92, 103–4, 110. A wider view of the course of the student movement from 1900 to 1904 is given by Cherevanin, *op. cit.*, I, 276–83.

30. *Polnoe sobranie zakonov*, 3d series, XXV, No. 26,692. There is a discussion of the new legal status of the universities in Deriuzhinsky, *op. cit.*, pp. 411–12, and in Maklakov, *Vlast i obshchestvennost* . . . , pp. 394–95. The inspectors, at first subordinated to the rectors (now again elected by the Academic Senate), were abolished entirely in September, 1906. New rules allowing the students to organize were issued in the ukase of June 11, 1907. (*Polnoe sobranie zakonov*, 3d series, XXVII, No. 29,274.) The law of March 4, 1906, applied neither to students nor to cooperatives.

31. Maklakov, *Vlast i obshchestvennost* . . . , pp. 185–87, 395–96. For a more detailed survey of the role of the universities in 1905, see Cherevanin, *op. cit.*, II, Part 2, 185–90; and E. Maevsky, "Obshchaia kartina dvizheniia," Martov and Others, *op. cit.*, II, Part 1, 73–74, 80. An interesting firsthand account of what was going on inside the University of St. Petersburg has been given by W. Woytinsky, *Der erste Sturm, Erinnerungen aus der russischen Revolution 1905* (*The First Storm, Reminiscences from the Russian Revolution of 1905*) (Berlin, 1931), pp. 7–56.

32. P. J. Novgorotsev, "Russian Universities and Higher Technical Schools During the War," in Ignatiev, Odinetz, and Novgorotsev, *op. cit.*; and Nicholas Hans, *History of Russian Educational Policy, 1701–1917* (London, 1931), pp. 196–206.

33. D. Richter, "Volnoe Ekonomicheskoe Obshchestvo," in *Novyi Entsiklopedicheskii Slovar*, XI, 537–43; N. Kuliabko-Koretsky, "Volnoe Ekonomicheskoe Obshchestvo," in *Bolshaia Sovetskaia Entsiklopediia*, XIII (1929), 51–53. There is a brief summary of the history and activity of the Free Economic Society available in English in the appendix of Alfred Levin, *The Second Duma* (New Haven, Conn., 1940), pp. 371–72.

34. Kizevetter, *Na rubezhe dvukh stoletii*, pp. 25–28, 241–44. See also Belokonsky, "Zemskoe dvizhenie," in *Byloe*, No. 6 (June, 1907), pp. 233–34.

35. As of 1899, there were law societies at the universities of St. Petersburg, Kiev, Kazan, and Odessa, and in such nonuniversity provincial cities as Tiflis, Kursk, Yaroslav, and Ekaterinoslav. See the article on learned societies by Rudakov in the Brockhaus encyclopedia, XXVII, 413.

36. M. P. Chubinsky, "Sudba sudebnoi reformy v poslednei treti XIX-go veka," in *Istoriia Rossii v XIX veke* (Granat), VI, 218–20. Gessen in his *Advokatura, obshchestvo i gosudarstvo* (*The Bar, Society, and the State*) (Moscow, 1914), pp. 229–30, points out that during the eight years of the operation of the Petersburg council of barristers, the Judicial Board increased the punishment inflicted by the council only once. An official document shows that the real reasons for suspending the opening of the councils were in part "special considerations of a political character" and in part the insignificant number of lawyers in the districts still without councils. On the qualifications for admission to the bar, see G. B. Sliozberg, *Dorevoliutsionnyi stroi Rossii*, pp. 161–63.

37. Gessen, *Advokatura, obshchestvo, i gosudarstvo*, pp. 442–47. The newly opened councils (in the Novocherkassk, Kazan, Odessa, Saratov, Irkutsk, and Omsk judicial districts) subsequently experienced great difficulty in obtaining quorums for their sessions and in collecting the necessary fees from their members.

38. For examples, see Gessen, *Advokatura . . .*, pp. 447–51.

39. Kizevetter, *Na rubezhe dvukh stoletti*, pp. 28–29. Gurko mentions a series of monthly economic banquets in St. Petersburg organized by a group of members of the State Council interested in economic questions, but attended also by liberals other than chinovniks. The speeches were invariably critical of Witte's economic policy. These banquets gave even high-ranking chinovniks an opportunity to make critical remarks that they could not otherwise make or print. (*Op. cit.*, pp. 169–71, 232.)

40. There is a detailed discussion of the banquet campaign by Cherevanin, *op. cit.*, II, Part 2, 146–63.

41. *The Secret Letters of the Last Tsar*, p. 261. While the funeral itself was orderly, Tolstoy's death did touch off the first street demonstrations by students since 1905. There are descriptions in Oldenburg, *op. cit.*, II, 62–64, and Kizevetter, *Na rubezhe dvukh stoletii*, pp. 511–12. See also Kizevetter's descriptions of the funeral of Turgenev (1883) and that of Saltykov (1889) (pp. 152–54), of the opening of a memorial to Pushkin in Moscow in 1880 (pp. 154–55), the commemoration of the fiftieth anniversary of Pushkin's death (1887) (pp. 155–56), and the burial of Muromtsev (1910) (pp. 510–11).

42. Gurko, *op. cit.*, pp. 229–33.

43. Belokonsky, "Zemskoe dvizhenie," in *Byloe*, No. 5 (May, 1907), pp. 68–71. There is a brief excerpt in Miliukov, *Russia and Its Crisis*, pp. 324–25. Neither Kaidanova nor Kizevetter refers to the letter.

44. V. I. Charnolusky, "Nachalnoe obrazovanie vo vtoroi polovine XIX stoletiia," in *Istoriia Rossii v XIX veke* (Granat), VII, 158. Like Kaidanova and Kizevetter, Charnolusky was an active participant in the movement for the education of the people. Neither Kaidanova nor Kizevetter mentions the steps taken by the government in 1902.

45. Kaidanova, *op. cit.*, I, 517.

46. Kizevetter, *Na rubezhe dvukh stoletii*, pp. 286–99. The use made here of branches of a society, opened without the special permission of the authorities, probably explains why certain sensitive organizations were forbidden to open branches, and why the temporary rules of 1906 gave the Minister of the Interior the right to close associations with branches any time he wished.

47. *Ibid.*, pp. 299–309. Kizevetter cites some amusing instances of the ignorance shown by some governors and of the peculiar reception given the visiting professors by some rather provincial local citizens. He himself was for a time head of the lecture bureau.

48. Deriuzhinsky, *op. cit.*, p. 435; see also the article by V. Nabokov, "O sezde russkikh iuristov," in *Pravo*, No. 1 (January 4, 1904), pp. 7–11. After 1875, only congresses of separate juridical groups, e.g., the criminologists, were authorized.

49. "Iz obshchestvennoi khroniki," *Vestnik Evropy*, March, 1898, p. 446; see also Belokonsky, "Zemskoe dvizhenie," in *Byloe*, No. 6 (June, 1907), pp. 216–17. Since the elementary-school teachers were in direct contact with the peasant population, they were subject to especially rigorous supervision by the government. The result, of course, was the opposite of that intended: the teachers were, as one Marxist puts it, "the most democratic element of the intelligentsia." Like most of the intellectual professions, the teachers were permitted to have relief societies, and a congress was authorized at the end of 1902. For an interesting summary of the professional and political demands made by the teachers at this congress, see Cherevanin, *op. cit.*, I, 288–89.

50. The first two all-Russian congresses of writers furnished the occasion for a lively press discussion on their utility. See, for example, the articles by V. Miakotin in *Russkoe Bogatstvo*, No. 8 (August, 1908), pp. 108–25; N. Yordansky, *Sovremennyi Mir*, No. 3 (March, 1910), pp. 125–35; and A. Peshekhonov in *Russkoe Bogatstvo*, No. 5 (May, 1910), pp. 180–212. According to Yordansky, the government originally gave its permission to the 1910 congress to discuss the legal position of the press, but withdrew it when leftist elements won out over the middle and right at another congress taking place at the same time.

51. The cooperative congresses are discussed by Antsiferov, "Credit and Agricultural Cooperation," in E. M. Kayden and A. N. Antsiferov, *The Cooperative Movement in Russia During the War* (New Haven, Conn., 1929) pp. 410–16.

52. Contrasting descriptions are given of the teachers' congress by Miliukov, *Ocherki* . . . , II, 866–68; Kaidanova, *op. cit.*, I, 528–30; and Oldenburg, *op. cit.*, II, 117–19.

53. *Otchet po deloproizvodstvu Gosudarstvennago Soveta za sessiiu 1905–1906 gg.*, p. 571.

54. E. S. Lurye, "Organizatsiia i organizatsii torgovopromyshlennykh interesov v Rossii" ("The Organization and Organizations of Commercial-Industrial Interests in Russia") (see Bibliography for series title), pp. 81–82.

55. *Ibid.*, pp. 103–5; A. Ermansky, "Krupnaia burzhuaziia do 1905 goda," in Martov and Others, *op. cit.*, I, 315, 334. Ermansky was a doctrinaire Marxist who persisted in viewing Russia as just another capitalist state dominated by the industrialists, and his two chapters on the bourgeoisie, though full of excellent material, must be read with caution. The best known of the above congresses was the Congress of the South-Russian Mining Industry. Indicative of the semi-

official character of these congresses is the fact that several of them had the right
to impose taxes on their members. Their organization was provided for by laws
included in various volumes of the *Svod zakonov*.

56. "Vnutrennee obozrenie," *Russkaia Mysl*, No. 2 (February, 1897), p. 115;
Lurye, *op. cit.*, pp. 80–81.

57. On the three all-Russian congresses before 1905, see Ermansky, *op. cit.*,
I, 341–47, and Berlin, *op. cit.*, pp. 216–22.

58. As early as the second all-Russian congress held at Moscow in 1882, the
Moscow manufacturer Krestovnikov protested against the "desires, often emanating from above, destroying whole branches of industry," and rightly pointed out
that "one stroke of the pen from St. Petersburg can ruin production." Ermansky,
op. cit., I, 342.

59. Witte, *Vospominaniia*, I, 451–52.

60. "Dnevnik A. A. Polovtseva," *Krasnyi Arkhiv*, XLVI, (1931), 129. Polovtsev made this entry in his diary while recording a conversation with Witte
(April, 1900), who explained that State Comptroller Lobko insisted that oil
resources should be given to the poor, not to the rich, as Witte was doing. See
also Polovtsev's discussion with Count D. M. Solsky (later Chairman of the
State Council) in 1894 on the baneful effects of Witte's unlimited interference
with private industrial activity and its similarity to state socialism. Polovtsev was
evidently nonplused when Solsky answered: "Yes, it is true that socialism everywhere makes such rapid strides forward that it remains for us merely to submit
to the movement." (*Krasnyi Arkhiv*, LVII, 177.)

61. See Ermansky, *op. cit.*, II, Part 2, 30–100, especially 30–50.

62. Sviatlovsky, *op. cit.*, pp. 363–64. The trade associations are discussed by
Braikevitch, in *The Russian Economist*, I, No. 3 (April, 1921), 684–85. In
granting the industrialists a privilege not given the workers, the government
promptly violated its intention of granting capital and labor equal opportunity
to organize.

63. Ermansky, *op. cit.*, II, Part 2, 79–80. Ermansky here describes the refusal of the St. Petersburg Association of Manufacturers to fill out forms on a
business tax required by a government board in 1906. He cites also two other
instances in which the Association urged its members to refuse to furnish information asked of them. The activities of the St. Petersburg Association, about
which the most information was available, were, he claims, typical of all the
associations.

64. The Congress is discussed in detail by Ermansky, *op. cit.*, II, Part 2,
86–97. See also Lurye, *op. cit.*, pp. 89–95. There was another all-Russian congress of lesser importance, representing the exchange merchants, called the Congress of the Representatives of Exchange Trade and Agriculture.

65. See the decree of August 24, 1906, *Polnoe sobranie zakonov*, 3d series,
XXVI, No. 28,265. There were few, if any, other groups that enjoyed the privilege of a permanent all-Russian congress with a permanent council and executive
committee. However, it would be a grave error to suppose that the industrialists
had acquired the influence on the government that their power and importance
justified.

66. Pares, *The Fall of the Russian Monarchy* (New York, 1939), pp. 115–16.

67. Berlin, *op. cit.*, pp. 296–300.

68. The most authoritative account of the mutual-aid societies among the
workers has been given by S. N. Prokopovich, *K rabochemu voprosu v Rossii*

(*On the Labor Problem in Russia*) (St. Petersburg, 1905), pp. 1–44. There are accounts also by D. Koltsov, "Rabochie v 1890–1904 gg.," in Martov and Others, *op. cit.*, I, 191–93; and Sviatlovsky, *op. cit.*, pp. 21–52. The most active organizers of mutual-aid societies among the workers were the sales clerks (*prikazchiki*), who, in 1898, had seventy-four societies (excluding Poland, the Baltic states, and Finland), and who were permitted to hold congresses. Mutual-aid societies in Russia proper originated in the second half of the nineteenth century.

69. On the unions up to 1907, see D. Koltsov, "Rabochie v 1905–7 gg.," in Martov and Others, *op. cit.*, II, Part 2, 248–53, 282–88, 294–96, 302–14, 331–33, 337–41. The attitude of the government toward the unions both before and after 1907 has been described by Sviatlovsky in *Istoriia professionalnogo dvizheniia v Rossii* (*History of the Trade-Union Movement in Russia*) (2d ed.; Leningrad, 1925), pp. 172–88, a revised version of his *Professionalnoe dvizhenie v Rossii*. The best analysis of the unions after 1907 is V. Grinevich, *Die Gewerkschaftsbewegung in Russland* (*The Trade-Union Movement in Russia*) (Berlin, 1927), Part 2, which is available only in German. Grinevich is the pseudonym of M. G. Kogan.

70. On the apathy of the workers after 1907 and the tilts of the unions with the administration, see Grinevich, *Die Gewerkschaftsbewegung . . .*, pp. 196, 212–28, 261–86. In addition to the legal means available for reconstituting dissolved unions and the procedure, constantly invoked, of appeal to the Senate, the Social Democratic members of the Duma were demanding explanations from the ministers regarding persecution of the unions. Judging from the available documents, the government's unwillingness to permit the free development of the trade unions was based on the Police Department's concern that the Social Democrats and other revolutionary groups desired to use the unions to promote maximum disorders and to prepare for armed revolt. See the Police Department circular quoted by Sviatlovsky, *Professionalnoe dvizhenie*, pp. 364–65, and the reports of the head of the St. Petersburg Okhrana written in 1913, "Uchet departamentom politsii opyta 1905 goda," in *Krasnyi Arkhiv*, XVIII (1926), 221–26.

71. *Krasnyi Arkhiv*, XVIII, 224. Still active in 1913 and acting as leader of the strike movement was the illegal St. Petersburg Central Bureau of Trade Unions, founded in 1905.

72. M. Bernatsky, "Russkie zakony o strakhovanii rabochikh," *Sovremennyi Mir*, January, 1913, Section 2, p. 91; Grinevich, *Die Gewerkschaftsbewegung . . .*, pp. 303–19. Some checks on the workers' majority in the insurance committees on the part of the entrepreneur and the administration are explained by Bernatsky. On the dissolution of the trade unions during the war, see Florinsky, *The End of the Russian Empire*, pp. 169–70. This writer cannot, however, agree with Florinsky's estimate of the trade unions before the war.

73. The State Council's deliberations on the law of March 4 as it affected disputes between workers and entrepreneurs have been quoted verbatim by Sviatlovsky, *Professionalnoe dvizhenie v Rossii*, pp. 357–58; see also p. 363, note 2. The provisions of the law concerning strikes have been discussed in detail in the writer's article "The Attitude of the Tsarist Government toward the Labor Problem," *American Slavic and East European Review*, XIII (April, 1954), 163–84.

74. Sviatlovsky, *Istoriia professionalnogo dvizheniia*, p. 137. Some examples of government interference in strikes are cited also by Grinevich, *Professionalnoe*

dvizhenie . . . , pp. 206–11, and *Die Gewerkschaftsbewegung* . . . , pp. 252–55.

75. The artel, which had many forms, was widespread among the lower elements of the population, especially the artisans. It was a voluntary association of individuals organized primarily for economic purposes and managed by an elected head. All its members had equal rights, and all were jointly responsible for the undertaking. An interesting, concrete picture of a form of artel in use among factory workers has been given by Schulze-Gaevernitz, *op. cit.*, pp. 149–54.

76. V. F. Totomiants, *Kooperatsiia v Rossii* (*Cooperation in Russia*) (Prague, 1922), p. 20.

77. Kayden, "Consumers' Cooperation," in Kayden and Antsiferov, *op. cit.*, pp. 37–38, 41.

78. *Ibid.*, pp. 14, 71. With the removal of the check placed on consumer cooperatives by the autocracy, the number reached 30,000 at the beginning of 1918, according to Totomiants, with a membership of more than 12 million, thus exceeding the combined membership in England, Germany, and France. (*Kooperatsiia*, p. 43.)

79. Kayden, *op. cit.*, p. 14. On January 1, 1918, the total was 16,500 (p. 17). Note should also be made of the less spectacular, but not unimportant, growth of agricultural associations and producers' cooperatives. These are discussed by Antsiferov, *op. cit.*, chap. V.

80. The whole cooperative movement spread in the face of formidable difficulties placed in its path by the central and local authorities. This subject has been treated in considerable detail by both Kayden and Antsiferov. See especially pp. 8–13 and 300–02 of their joint volume, although both return to the subject too frequently to list all the page references. On the other hand, the state itself greatly encouraged the cooperative credit movement, and such state institutions as the Board of Small Credit (*Upravlenie po delam melkago kredita*) were most sympathetic toward the cooperative movement.

81. Kayden and Antsiferov, *op. cit.*, pp. 111, 304. After the Revolution had removed the restraints imposed by the autocracy, both types of unions grew rapidly, with 207 consumers' unions being formed in 1917 alone.

82. Kayden, *op. cit.*, pp. 16, 18; Antsiferov, *op. cit.*, p. 301, note 2.

83. "It has been estimated that the credit and consumers' organizations included in their membership one-third of the population, and that their aggregate business turnover in 1917 was about 10 million rubles." (Kayden, *op. cit.*, p. 18.) "Cooperative credit gradually became a permanent and necessary element of peasant farming, the real foundation of the whole economic structure of Russia." (Antsiferov, *op. cit.*, p. 417.)

84. Kaidanova, *op. cit.*, I, 533. During the years of the Revolution, according to Totomiants, the Russian cooperative movement took first place among the movements of the world in its educational activity, replacing the hitherto supreme British cooperative system. (*Kooperatsiia*, p. 127.) According to Antsiferov, no other country could match Russia in the number of journals and newspapers issued by cooperative organizations—more than 100 in 1916–17. (*Op. cit.*, p. 408.)

85. Oldenburg, *op. cit.*, II, 9. See also Maklakov, *Vtoraia Gosudarstvennaia Duma* . . . , pp. 50–51.

86. Samuel N. Harper, *The New Electoral Law for the Russian Duma,*

(Chicago, 1908), pp. 20–21, 30–32; Oldenburg, *loc. cit.*; Maklakov, *Vtoraia Gosudarstvennaia Duma* . . . , pp. 51, 55–63. See also Aleksei Smirnov, *Kak proshli vybory vo Vtoruiu Gosudarstvennuiu Dumu (How the Elections to the Second State Duma Proceeded)* (St. Petersburg, 1907).

87. *Arkhiv russkoi revoliutsii*, XXI, 276. See also V. Obolensky, "Vospominaniia o golodnom 1891 gode," *Sovremennyia Zapiski*, 7 (1921), 263–66, and T. J. Polner, *Zheznennyi put Kniaza G. E. Lvova (The Path of Life of Prince G. E. Lvov)* (Paris, 1932), p. 68.

88. Beletsky, in *Padenie tsarskogo rezhima* . . . , IV, 128. Beletsky had asked the heads of the provincial gendarme administrations to survey the state of the rightist organizations. It was pointed out by a member of the Extraordinary Commission that the subsidies to the rightist organizations and press increased from 600,000 rubles in 1912, to 1.6 million, in 1916. (Testimony of N. A. Maklakov, in *ibid.*, III, 112.)

Chapter 7

THE ZEMSTVOS—LOCAL SELF-GOVERNMENT IN AN AUTOCRATIC STATE

1. The social and state theories of self-government are discussed by Korkunov, *op. cit.*, II, 488–501, and Lazarevsky, *op. cit.*, II, 40–42. There is a systematic survey of the theories of self-government in Russian thought in the chapter by P. P. Gronsky, "Teorii samoupravleniia v russkoi nauke," in B. B. Veselovsky and Z. G. Frankel (eds.), *op. cit.*, pp. 76–85.

2. Kizevetter, *Mestnoe samouplavlenie v Rossii*, p. 144; quoted by Polner, *Russian Local Government during the War and the Union of Zemstvos* (New Haven, 1930), p. 17.

3. The evidence has been marshaled by Witte, *Samoderzhavie i zemstvo*, pp. 66–69. Virtually the same material may be found in Svatikov, *Obshchestvennoe dvizhenie v Rossii*, Part 2, pp. 44–47.

4. Some figures on the class distribution of the elected councilors of the district zemstvo assemblies are cited by Korkunov, *op. cit.*, II, 544. The same official figures (for the years 1883–86) are discussed in detail by S. Y. Tseitlin, "Zemskoe samoupravlenie i reforma 1890 g. (1865–90)," in *Istoriia Rossii v XIX veke* (Granat), V, 84–91.

5. There is a brief survey of the upsurge of noble constitutionalism in M. P. Dragomanov, *Liberalizm i zemstvo v Rossii (Liberalism and the Zemstvo in Russia)* (Geneva, 1889) pp. 1–5. There is a great deal of detail with appropriate verbatim quotations in Svatikov, *Obshchestvennoe dvizhenie v Rossii* Part 2, pp. 3–69. A. A. Kornilov is the author of a separate monograph on the social movement during the reign of Alexander II, but his general history of the nineteenth century, *Kurs istorii*, II, is full of significant detail. The first hundred pages of volume II of the English translation offer an authoritative description.

6. Kornilov, *op. cit.*, II, 218–26 (pp. 70–76 in English translation); Svatikov, *op. cit.*, Part 2, pp. 28–34; Miliukov, *Russia and Its Crisis*, pp. 273–77. Extensive excerpts from the Tver address (adopted by a vote of 109 to 12) are quoted by Kornilov.

7. Svatikov, *op. cit.*, Part 2, pp. 50–51. Valuev acknowledged that the zemstvo reform was introduced "in order to place limits on the unrealizable expectations and free aspirations aroused on the part of various classes on the occasion of the organization of zemstvo institutions."

8. *Ibid.*, pp. 60–61, and note 2, p. 60. There is a detailed discussion of the Valuev project by Tseitlin, "Zemskaia reforma," in *Istoriia Rossii v XIX veka* (Granat), III, 217–20.

9. Svatikov, *op. cit.*, Part 2, pp. 53–59; Dragomanov, *op. cit.*, pp. 12–13. Svatikov cites other evidence from Alexander II's reaction to the Moscow address showing that he was not opposed to constitutional government in principle, but that he was convinced that Russia was not ready for it. A broader right of petition was restored to the provincial societies of the nobility by Alexander III in 1888.

10. The proof of this was undertaken by Witte in a well-known report to the Czar in 1899, which fell into the hands of the editors of *Osvobozhdenie* and was published by them under the title of *Samoderzhavie i zemstvo* (*Autocracy and Zemstvo*) (Stuttgart, 1903). On pages 92–93, Witte specifically absolves the zemstvo men of lack of devotion to the autocracy and calls their constitutional tendencies unconscious. The report was inspired by a project of Minister of the Interior Goremykin in 1899 to introduce the zemstvos into the western provinces of Russia, from which they had originally been excluded because of the presence of non-Russian landlords with separatist tendencies. Witte opposed Goremykin's project on the ground that self-government was inconsistent with autocracy and that, sooner or later, one or the other would have to give way. When Goremykin countered with Slavophile arguments on the uniqueness of Russian development and the supposed traditional place of self-government in the autocracy, Witte commissioned one of his aides to prepare the report. The report was so brilliantly written, and proved its points so effectively, that the liberals decided to publish it, partly because it was obvious that in the long run it was the autocracy and not self-government that would have to go if the two were incompatible. The report created a great stir in intellectual circles and helped fasten on Witte the reputation of an uncompromising reactionary, which, in fact, he was not. Witte won a temporary victory, for Goremykin's project was abandoned, and Goremykin himself was dismissed and replaced as minister by a man friendly to Witte, D. S. Sipiagin.

11. Gradovsky, "Pereustroistvo nashego mestnago upravleniia," in *Sobranie sochinenii*, VIII, 537, 561. During the era of serfdom, and before the rise of the zemstvos, the concept of public welfare was hardly understood in Russia, and welfare functions, on the whole, were neglected.

12. *Ibid.*, VIII, 540.

13. Tseitlin, in *Istoriia Rossii v XIX veke* (Granat), V, 103.

14. *Ibid.*, V, 105–6.

15. D. N. Shipov, *Vospominaniia i dumy o perezhitom* (*Reminiscences and Thoughts About My Past*) (Moscow, 1918), pp. 115–18; Witte, *Samoderzhavie i zemstvo*, p. 147.

16. Shipov, *op. cit.*, pp. 198–203; I. P. Belokonsky, *Zemskoe dvizhenie* (*The Zemstvo Movement*) (2d ed.; Moscow, 1914), p. 146.

17. Witte, *Samoderzhavie i zemstvo*, pp. 148–51.

18. *Ibid.*, pp. 81–82; Tseitlin, in *Istoriia Rossii v XIX veke*, V, 103–4, 106–7. On the structure of the local educational administration, see Korkunov, *op. cit.*, II, 421–22.

19. Witte, *Samoderzhavie i zemstvo*, p. 82.

20. B. B. Veselovsky, "Detsentralizatsiia upravleniia i zadachi zemstva," in *Iubileinyi zemskii sbornik*, pp. 48–49.

21. Witte, *Samoderzhavie i zemstvo*, pp. 74, 83; see also Gradovsky, "Vsesoslovnaia melkaia edinitsa," in *Sobranie sochinenii*, VIII, 570–75.

22. B. B. Veselovsky, the historian of the zemstvos, calculated the number of hired employees (apparently in 1903) at 65,000–70,000. The ratio of the hired employees to the elected representatives was fifty to one. *Istoriia zemstva*, III, 494, quoted by L. D. Brukhatov, "Znachenie 'tretiiago elementa' v zhizni zemstva," in Veselovsky and Frankel (eds.), *op. cit.*, p. 190. On the origin of the term "third element," see Belokonsky, *op. cit.*, pp. 71–72.

23. Cherevanin, in Martov and Others, *op. cit.*, I, 268–73; Shipov, *op. cit.*, pp. 24–26, 183–84; Brukhatov, in Veselovsky and Frankel (eds.), *op. cit.*, p. 205.

24. Witte, *Samoderzhavie i zemstvo*, pp. 85, 152; Polner, *Zhiznennyi put Kniaza G. E. Lvova*, pp. 55–56; Gurko, *op. cit.*, pp. 234–37. Plehve obtained the right to stop statistical surveys by an order of the Czar, March 25, 1904. (*P.S.Z.*, 3d series, XXIV, No. 24,289.)

25. Witte, *Samoderzhavie i zemstvo*, pp. 87–88.

26. See the introduction by the editors of *Iubileinyi zemskii sbornik*, pp. ix–x, and the chapter by N. Avinov, p. 28.

27. Shipov, *op. cit.*, pp. 57–58.

28. On the Tolstoy project and its reception by the ministers and the State Council, see the chapter by Tseitlin in *Istoriia Rossii* (Granat), V, 127–39, and N. N. Avinov, "Glavnyia cherty v istorii zakonodatelstva o zemskikh uchrezhdeniiakh (1864–1913 gg.)," in *Iubileinyi zemskii sbornik*, pp. 20–26. Witte's more general remarks are, as usual, penetrating. (*Samoderzhavie i zemstvo*, pp. 138–45.) Details on government supervision of the zemstvos may be found in Korkunov, *op. cit.*, II, 586–91; Elistratov, *Osnovnyia nachala administrativnago prava*, pp. 220–23; Lazarevsky, *op. cit.*, II, 246–48. Certain decisions of the zemstvo assemblies, including all obligatory decrees, were not effective unless confirmed by the governor or the Minister of the Interior. Certain other decisions did not require confirmation but could, nevertheless, be annulled by the governor because they violated the law, or did not "correspond to general state interests and needs, or manifestly violated the interests of the local population." The chairmen and members of the zemstvo boards all required government confirmation. Members of the third element not only required the confirmation of the governor, but could also be dismissed by him at any time for political unreliability.

29. According to Korkunov, the nobles had a majority in 316 out of 361 districts after 1890. *Op. cit.*, II, 544.

30. N. I. Lazarevsky, "Zemskoe izbiratelnoe pravo," in *Iubileinyi zemskii sbornik*, pp. 68–69. The assignment of seats to the nobility in 1890 naturally was based on the number of nobles in the districts, but the assignment remained constant, while the number of qualified nobles constantly diminished.

31. Shipov, *op. cit.*, p. 131.

32. Polner, *Zhiznennyi put Kniaza G. E. Lvova*, pp. 60, 127.

33. T. J. Polner and Others, *Russian Local Government During the War and the Union of the Zemstvos*, p. 32.

34. Kokovtsov, *op. cit.*, I, 240–44. The outraged Kokovtsov fought this proposal bitterly and would have resigned as Minister of Finance had it been pressed. All but one of the members of the Council of Ministers backed Stolypin in his original insistence on the proposal.

35. Testimony of S. E. Kryzhanovsky, in *Padenie tsarskogo rezhima* . . . , V, 402–3. The Chief Administration for the Affairs of Local Economy was one of Kryzhanovsky's responsibilities as Assistant Minister of the Interior under Stolypin.

36. Some interesting details are given by Kryzhanovsky, *Vospominaniia (Memoirs)* (Berlin, 1935), pp. 105–7.

37. A. N. Yakhontov, "Tiazhelye dni," in *Arkhiv russkoi revoliutsii*, XVIII, 128–29. This passage is quoted also by Polner, *Zhiznennyi put Kniaza G. E. Lvova*, pp. 217–18.

38. Polner, *op. cit.*, p. 212. While there was much discontent in Russia at that time, the Minister's imagination was, as usual, well ahead of reality.

39. See the comments of Gradovsky on this point in *Sobranie sochinenii*, IX, 18–34.

40. This kind of analysis of the total social structure has long been practiced by sociologists and is known as "structural-functional analysis." See, for example, Alex Inkeles' "Understanding a Foreign Society: A Sociologist's View," in *World Politics*, III (January, 1951), 275–79.

41. On the patriarchal foundation of Russian society, see Leroy-Beaulieu, *op. cit.*, II, 9–14. Relevant also are the remarks of Witte, *Po povodu neprelozhnosti zakonov gosudarstvennoi zhizni*, p. 52. This volume is Witte's own reprint (1914) of *Samoderzhavie i zemstvo*.

42. *Ibid.*, pp. 15–16; the subject is treated as a whole on pp. 8–16. Elsewhere Witte added: "For me the truth seems indisputable that the degree of development of individual self-activity among the people determines the degree of power of the state and its place among its neighbors. The more highly developed is the personality, the more firmly rooted in it is the habit of arranging one's well being independently and without outside aid, the more stable are the social order and, behind it, the state order." (p. 195.) To the liberals who first published *Samoderzhavie i zemstvo*, this seemed like hypocrisy, because plainly it controlled neither government policy nor Witte's policy as Minister of Finance. In his introduction, Peter Struve points out that despite Witte's protestations to the contrary, he sought to keep the organizations of the capitalists under firm control (pp. xxiii, xxvii).

43. In 1905, such organizations as the All-Russian Union of Physicians actually argued that it could not heal the sick until a constituent assembly, based on universal, equal, secret, and direct suffrage, without regard to nationality, religion, or sex, had been called. According to Kizevetter, wits were saying that the union of midwives had passed a resolution on the impossibility of delivering children from expectant mothers in the absence of a constitution. (*Na rubezhe dvukh stoletii*, p. 375.)

44. V. Grinevich, *Die Gewerkschaftsbewegung* . . . , pp. 226–28, 263.

Chapter 8
THE REVOLUTION OF 1905 AND THE EMERGENCE OF CONSTITUTIONAL GOVERNMENT

1. Bernard Pares characterized the situation very appropriately when he wrote: "Not even a Napoleon or a Peter the Great can control the whole thought of a nation which is beginning to think, the whole enterprise of a nation which is learning to exert itself. . . ." (*Russia and Reform*, p. 176.)

2. Cited by Maklakov, *Vlast i obshchestvennost*, p. 424.

3. Belokonsky, *op. cit.*, pp. 83–85.

4. See Kryzhanovsky, *op. cit.*, pp. 191–202, and Gurko, *op. cit.*, p. 122. On the views of Plehve, see also his conversation with Polovtsev in January, 1903, as described by the latter. ("Dnevnik A. A. Polovtseva," in *Krasnyi Arkhiv*, III, 168–70.)

5. This is brought out by the Social Democrat D. Koltsov among others, in his chapters on the workers' movement in *Obshchestvennoe dvizhenie*, I, 183–229 and II, Part 1, 185–341. There is a brief summary of the situation by another Social Democrat, N. Cherevanin, "Dvizhenie intelligentsii," in *ibid.*, I, 260–61. Cherevanin writes: "The mass movement of the proletariat which took place before the revolution often acquired enormous political significance, but almost never bore a definite political character. The concrete political demands with which Social Democracy emerged were for the time being only the demands of the organized Social Democratic intelligentsia, and not the demands of the proletarian masses of Russia. In an even lesser degree, of course, did the Socialist Revolutionaries have the right to consider themselves the representatives of the peasant masses. In that ever-increasing attack on the autocracy, which began at the end of the 1890's and ended with the Revolution of 1905, all the classes of the population participated, beginning with the proletariat and ending with the landlords, but the actual political self-determination of the various classes began only at the end of 1904 and reached a significant development only after the revolution. In the pre-revolutionary period, the majority of only one layer of the population was irreconcilably opposed to the autocracy, and consciously and explicitly aspired for a free constitutional order. This layer of the population was the professional intelligentsia."

6. For the text of the program, see Shipov, *op. cit.*, pp. 165–68. On the circumstances surrounding the calling of the meeting and the attitude toward it of Witte and Plehve, see the translation of a part of Shipov's memoirs contained in the appendix of Gurko's *Features and Figures*, pp. 691–703.

7. A detailed survey of the activities of the zemstvo men in the district and provincial committees of the Special Conference has been made by Belokonsky, *op. cit.*, pp. 105–31. The Special Conference was closed suddenly by the Czar in March, 1905, before its work had been completed, partly, it appears, because of the dangerous ideas expressed in the committees.

8. Quoted by Rosenberg, *Iz istorii russkoi pechati* . . . , p. 158. Regardless of whether or not Plehve actually made this statement, there is little doubt that it accurately reflects the spirit of his conflict with the public.

9. Belokonsky, *op. cit.*, pp. 174–75, 191–92.

10. There were ten zemstvo men and ten intellectuals present at the meeting in Germany. Their names are given in the memoirs of Petrunkevich, *Arkhiv russkoi revoliutsii*, XXI, 338. There were six of each group represented in the first council elected in January, 1904. Their names are given in the memoirs of Miliukov, "Rokovye gody," in *Russkiia Zapiski*, No. 12 (December, 1938), p. 121, note. All the zemstvo men, of course, were nobles; it is almost certain that most of the intellectuals were also of noble origin.

11. See Struve's article in *Osvobozhdenie*, No. 7 ("Liberalizm i t. n. revoliutsionnyia napravleniia") and his article "Germanskie vybory," in *ibid.*, No. 25. For contrasting comments, see Maklakov, *Vlast i obshchestvennost* . . . , pp. 176–77, and A. Potresov, "Evoliutsiia obshchestvenno-politicheskoi mysli v predrevoliutsionnuiu epokhu," in Martov and Others, *op. cit.*, I, 636–37.

12. The Paris conference is discussed in detail by Miliukov, *Russia and Its*

Crisis, pp. 523–28; see also his memoirs, "Rokovye gody," in *Russkiia Zapiski,* No. 6 (June, 1938), pp. 122–27.

13. See the comments of Miliukov to the zemstvo constitutionalists in July, 1905, "Rokovye gody," in *Russkiia Zapiski,* No. 12 (December, 1938), p. 124.

14. For a revealing exposition of the temper of the Liberation Movement on its first appearance, see its program in "Ot russkikh konstitutsionalistov," in *Osvobozhdenie,* No. 1 (June 18, 1902), pp. 7–12. According to Miliukov, this article was the work of I. I. Petrunkevich, A. A. Kornilov, Prince D. I. Shakhovskoi, and himself.

15. The expanding activities of the attorneys, as well as their use of the boycott, is discussed by Maklakov, *Vlast i obshchestvennost* . . . , pp. 165–73. The boycott was begun in 1903, in connection with the trials growing out of the 1902 peasant disorders in the provinces of Poltava and Kharkov.

16. Belokonsky, *op. cit.,* pp. 188–91. All of the government's normal measures to compel such congresses to adhere to the approved agenda were now useless.

17. The conference at which the decision to introduce the resolutions was taken is described by Shipov, *op. cit.,* pp. 213–26. Direct quotations from the resolutions are cited by Belokonsky, *op. cit.,* pp. 177–83. According to Shipov, the idea of a national assembly was raised at the conference, but was defeated by a vote of fifteen to thirteen.

18. The standard reference on the attitude of society toward the bureaucracy as news of defeat after defeat poured in from the Far East is E. N. Trubetskoi, "Voina i biurokratsiia," *Pravo,* No. 39 (September 26, 1904), pp. 1,872–75. This article was well publicized and emphasized the government's preoccupation with the "internal" rather than the "external" enemy.

19. Maevsky, "Obshchaia kartina dvizheniia," in Martov and Others, *op. cit.,* II, Part 1, 36–37.

20. The basic source for the November congress is Shipov, *op. cit.,* pp. 241–85. Good also is Belokonsky, *Zemskoe dvizhenie,* pp. 212–38. The memorandum prepared by Prince S. N. Trubetskoi in behalf of the zemstvo men and presented to Sviatopolk-Mirsky to help him explain the zemstvo program to the Czar is worthy of attention. It appears in the appendix to Shipov's memoirs, pp. 581–87.

21. For the text of the ukase, see *Polnoe sobranie zakonov,* 3d series, XXIV, No. 25,495. The ukase promised to take steps to make the peasantry "free rural citizens with full rights," to make chinovniks responsible for their actions, to reform the zemstvos, to guarantee equality before the law for all classes and give to judicial institutions the necessary independence, to introduce state insurance for industrial workers, to amend the emergency laws and limit their application, to grant more religious toleration, to amend the laws limiting the rights of the non-Russians, and to remove unnecessary restrictions on the press. Only a small part of this program was ever carried out (peasants, press, greater toleration for the Old Believers, some relief for non-Russians, and, in 1912, insurance for the industrial workers).

22. For Witte's account of what happened, see *Vospominaniia,* I, pp. 294–301. Mirsky gave his version to Shipov a year and a half later, and the latter wrote a summary in *Vospominaniia,* pp. 286–90.

23. The communiqué was written in the language characteristic of a Pobedonostsev. Among other things, it castigated the zemstvo men for discussing matters outside their sphere of competence, charged that they (as well as others)

were attempting to "bring disorder into social and state life," and threatened new repressive measures. The text of the communiqué has been reproduced by Belokonsky, *op. cit.*, pp. 260–61.

24. For details, see the memoirs of Miliukov, "Rokovye gody," in *Russkiia Zapiski*, No. 15 (March, 1939), pp. 101–12.

25. Mark Vishniak, *Vserossiiskoe uchreditelnoe sobranie* (*The All-Russian Constituent Assembly*) (Paris, 1932), p. 52; F. Dan, "Obshchaia politika pravitelstva i izmeneniia v gosud. organizatsii v period 1905–1907 gg.," in *Obshchestvennoe dvizhenie*, IV, Part 1, 318–19.

26. See the seventh installment of Miliukov's memoirs in *Russkiia Zapiski*, No. 11 (November, 1938), pp. 139–47, and the eleventh installment, in *ibid.*, No. 15 (March, 1939), pp. 109–12. See also Cherevanin, "Dvizhenie intelligentsii," in Martov and Others, *op. cit.*, II, Part 2, 170–83, and Maklakov, *Vlast i obshchestvennost . . .* , pp. 355–68. Since the unions of the intelligentsia were not actually concerned with the advancement of professional interests, they died a natural death after the promulgation of the October Manifesto by the Czar.

27. For the text of the ukase, see *Polnoe sobranie zakonov*, 3d series, XXV, No. 25,853. See also the comments of Maklakov, *Vlast i obshchestvennost . . .* , pp. 357–61, and of Belokonsky, *op. cit.*, pp. 264–70. Maklakov interprets the unions of the intelligentsia as organizations especially created to advance political demands in response to the invitation given in the ukase.

28. Pares, *Russia and Reform*, p. 503; F. Dan, in *Obshchestvennoe dvizhenie*, IV, Part 1, 313–14; Maklakov, *Vlast i obshchestvennost . . .* , pp. 361–66.

29. Gerasimov, *Der Kampf gegen die erste russische Revolution*, pp. 50–51.

30. The text of the zemstvo constitutional project, originally printed in *Russkiia Vedomosti*, No. 180 (July 6, 1905), has been reproduced in Belokonsky, *op. cit.*, pp. 297–314, and in *Russkiia Vedomosti (1863–1913)*, *sbornik statei*, pp. 294–303.

31. These points are clearly brought out by E. Maevsky, "Obshchaia kartina dvizheniia," in Martov and Others, *op. cit.*, II, Part 1, 35–184 (especially 53–55, 64–65, 74–76, 80–82, 83, 88–89). They are confirmed in more detail by the longer chapter of D. Koltsov in the same volume, 185–341. See also M. N. Pokrovsky, *Brief History of Russia* (London, 1933), II, 122–23. For a statistical analysis of the strikes of 1905, including the relative weight of political and economic motives, see the article by I. Larsky, "Russkiia stachki poslednykh let," in *Sovremennyi Mir*, January, 1909, pp. 87–103; see also G. Goldberg, "Stachechnoe dvizhenie rabochykh v Rossii," in *Vestnik Evropy*, July, 1910, pp. 242–52.

32. Woytinsky, *op. cit.*, pp. 44–45.

33. Maevsky, *op. cit.*, p. 93.

34. Koltsov writes: "If the speeches about political freedom, about the kingdom of socialism, were accepted enthusiastically because the masses felt in them something new and bright, then speeches about the economic oppression of capital, about the terrible situation of labor, were for them much more accessible and understandable." "Rabochie v 1905–1907 gg.," in *Obshchestvennoe dvizhenie*, II, Part 1, 248. Pokrovsky, in explaining the "failure" of the mass movement of the workers and peasants, writes: "The working class had not yet entirely got rid of 'Economism' in 1905—the peasants did not even begin to get rid of it in 1906." (*Op. cit.*, II, 238.)

35. On the peasant disturbances, see P. Maslov, "Krestianskoe dvizhenie," in Martov *et al.*, *op. cit.*, II, Part 2, 203–82, and W. D. Preyer, *Die russische*

Agrarreform, pp. 94–114. Both these works have made use of the investigation into the causes of the peasant disturbances of 1905–6 conducted by the Free Economic Society, the result of which was published in its *Trudy*, Nos. 3–5 (1908). See also Pares' report on a political meeting of the peasants he personally attended, in *Russia and Reform*, pp. 446–47, and Maevsky's brief summary in his description of the social movement as a whole, in *Obshchestvennoe dvizhenie*, II, Part 1, 118–26.

36. E. Maevsky, in *Obshchestvennoe dvizhenie*, II, Part 1, 83; N. Cherevanin, "Dvizhenie intelligentsii," in *ibid.*, II, Part 2, 165–66, 190.

37. According to Belokonsky, *Zemskoe dvizhenie*, p. 150, the mass dispatch to *Osvobozhdenie* of secret government documents indicates that toward the end of 1902, the government lacked "not only devoted partisans, but even passive, though loyal, collaborators."

38. F. Dan, "Obshchaia politika pravitelstva," in *Obshchestvennoe dvizhenie*, IV, Part 1, 319–20.

39. N. Cherevanin, in *ibid.*, II, Part 2, 179–80. The bylaws and platform of the two unions are of special interest, and may be consulted in V. Ivanovich, *Rossiiskiia partii, soiuzy i ligi (Russian Parties, Unions, and Leagues)* (St. Petersburg, 1906), pp. 218–20, 229. Note should also be made of the proclamation in June of the bureau of the United Petersburg Chinovniks cited by Cherevanin and printed in No. 26 of *Pravo*. In his *Der erste Sturm*, pp. 107–18, W. Woytinsky described how, as a young Social Democratic agitator, he was called upon to assist a group of Petersburg police officers in organizing a union and formulating demands to be presented to Trepov.

40. Cherevanin, in *Obshchestvennoe dvizhenie*, II, Part 2, 195.

41. Maevsky, in *ibid.*, II, Part 1, 113; see also Wolfe, *op. cit.*, pp. 320–21.

42. The text of the October Manifesto has been translated by Pares, *Fall of the Russian Monarchy*, pp. 503–4. For the Russian text, see *P.S.Z.*, 3d series, XXV, No. 26,803.

43. Maevsky, in *Obshchestvennoe dvizhenie*, II, Part 1, 92–93.

44. Gerasimov, *op. cit.*, pp. 62–63.

45. For a brief general description of the "days of freedom," see E. Maevsky, in *Obshchestvennoe dvizhenie*, II, Part 1, 107–9.

46. A. S. Izgoev, "Obshchestvennoe dvizhenie v Rossii," in *Russkaia Mysl*, January, 1907, pp. 160–61. This essay is included in a collection of Izgoev's writings published under the title *Russkoe obshchestvo i revoliutsiia*. The quotation cited refers only to the years of maximum revolutionary ferment. For a more extended discussion of the influence of such ideas on Russian society, see M. Karpovich, "The Historical Background of Soviet Thought Control," in W. Gurian (ed.), *The Soviet Union: Background, Ideology, Reality* (Notre Dame, Ind., 1951), pp. 26–30.

47. There is a more detailed consideration of the influence of liberalism in the final collapse of the autocracy in Maklakov, *Vlast i obshchestvennost* . . . , pp. 352–55.

48. Cf. the remarks of Pokrovsky: "Those who witnessed the movement with their own eyes will never forget its most striking feature: the growing *fearlessness* of the crowd. Only recently it would have dispersed at the one shout of 'the cossacks,' or the 'dragoons'; it now *attacked* the cossacks and the dragoons. It was no longer the crowd that was afraid of the troops but the troops of the crowd." *Op. cit.*, II, 160–61.

49. E. J. Bing (ed.), *The Secret Letters of the Last Tsar* (New York, 1938), pp. 184–86.

50. A. A. Mosolov, *At the Court of the Last Tsar* (London, 1935), p. 90. Frederichs also explained what happened to Witte, and Witte's account of the Grand Duke's reaction is substantially the same. (*Vospominaniia*, II, 35.)

Chapter 9
WHY THE LIBERALS LOST AND THE BOLSHEVIKS WON IN 1917

1. Maklakov (born 1869) was a practicing attorney and a brilliant orator who served in the Second, Third, and Fourth Dumas as a member of the right wing of the Cadet Party. He was Ambassador of the Provisional Government to France in 1917, and lived in Paris, where he was active in *émigré* affairs, until his death, in 1957. His views were first outlined in detail in *Vlast i obshchestvennost na zakate staroi Rossii* (1936) and were further developed in *Pervaia Gosudarstvennaia Duma* (1939) and *Vtoraia Gosudarstvennaia Duma* (1945). His purpose in writing his memoirs has been explained in an article in *Sovremennyia Zapiski* (in which *Vlast i obshchestvennost* was first serialized), No. 38 (1929), pp. 276–314. He has also stated his point of view briefly in the preface to a collection of documents issued in French, *La chute du régime tsariste* (1927), a condensed translation of *Padenie tsarskogo rezhima*.

Although this chapter is based on ideas first voiced by Maklakov, the writer alone is responsible for its organization and detailed content.

2. The word is taken from the following line in Virgil's *Aeneid*: "*Flectere si nequeo superos, Acheronta movebo*" ("If I cannot budge the gods, I will stir up Acheron"). Maklakov quotes this line because it illustrates the process by which the liberals joined forces with the revolutionaries in the struggle against the autocracy and were therefore deflected from what he regards as the historic mission of liberalism.

3. In view of Witte's critical comments, unusual for a former minister, toward the Czar, as well as toward others whom he evidently regarded as his competitors, his opinion is worth noting. He writes: "I must say that however unalluring was the way out of October 17 for the Emperor, and especially for the whole court clique and that part of the nobility that for a long time constituted a parasite on the fortune of the people, Nicholas II would have fulfilled the promises given October 17, if the cultured classes of the population had shown common sense and immediately cut themselves off from the revolutionary elements. But this did not happen; the cultured classes of the population did not rise to the occasion. The ability to do so, by the way, is acquired by great political and state experience." (*Vospominaniia*, II, 290–91.)

4. Gerasimov's testimony on this point is of great interest. In his only audience with the Czar, in January, 1906, the Czar asked: "Well, what do you think, will we or will the Revolution win?" (*Op. cit.*, p. 147.)

5. The proposed new fundamental laws were considered by a special conference, under the chairmanship of the Czar, in April, 1906. In the discussion, the Czar attached great importance to the question of whether the word "unlimited" should be removed from the reference to "supreme autocratic power" in Article 4. (Article 4 of the new Fundamental Laws was substantially the same as Article 1 of the old laws, quoted at the beginning of Chapter II.) Although he had shown his sympathies to be on the side of the few who argued for the retention of the word, at the very end of the conference he ordered it stricken

out. His remarks in introducing the problem to the conference leave little doubt, as Maklakov has pointed out, that he reluctantly accepted the recommendation of the Council of Ministers because of his feeling that he could not go back on his word. See *Protokoly zasedanii soveschchaniia pod lichnym Ego Imperator-skago Velichestva predsedatelstvom po peresmotru Osnovnykh Gosudarstven-nykh Zakonov, 7, 9, 11 i 12 aprelia 1906 g.*, pp. 28–35, 94. The retention of the title "unlimited autocrat" in Article 222 of the Fundamental Laws (concerned with the imperial family), apparently due to defective drafting, does not alter the significance of the Czar's deliberate exclusion of the word "unlimited" from Article 4.

6. Under the Fundamental Laws of 1906, the electoral law could be changed only by action of the Duma and the State Council, with the approval of the Czar. Since there was no hope that the Duma would pass a new electoral law, and the government could not function, if, as it assumed, the deputies elected under the old law continued to make revolutionary speeches instead of applying themselves to practical legislation, the law was put into effect illegally, as an act of necessity.

7. The most severe critic of Maklakov's views within the Cadet Party was Miliukov, the leader of the Party and the prime example of an intellectual suddenly converted into a political leader without adequate preparation. The writer is assuming that the following are representative of Miliukov's polemics with Maklakov and of his views on the events under dispute: "Sud nad kadetskim 'liberalizmom,'" *Sovremennyia Zapiski*, No. 41 (1930), pp. 347–71; "Liberal-izm, radikalizm, i revoliutsiia," *S.Z.*, No. 57 (1934), pp. 285–315; "V. A. Maklakov mezhdu 'obshchestvennostiu' i 'vlastiu,'" *Poslredniia Novosti*, May 28 and 30, 1937; "Rokovye gody," starting with No. 4 of *Russkiia Zapiski*, April, 1938, and ending with Nos. 20–21, August–September, 1939. All of the foregoing were published in Paris. To Maklakov's basic views, outlined above, this writer can find no answer. One obvious difficulty is that Miliukov refuses to accept Maklakov's assumptions. Miliukov is not alone in this; Maklakov had cast in an unfavorable light the actions of many other former leaders of Russian society. Since, in various ways, they were expressing the mood of that society and are not personally culpable, there is some justification in their refusal to accept proposals which appear to them to be historical monstrosities. At the same time, succeeding generations that may be faced with similar problems need have no interest in the counterargument of some that they made no mistakes whatsoever. Even though the climate of opinion and the actions of a whole generation were determined by events beyond the control of any individual, if that opinion and those actions also led to a great catastrophe that might have been avoided, there is merit in reflecting how they failed to take account of political and social realities.

Miliukov apparently continued to assume that an individual was of necessity on the side either of society or of the state. Part of his case against Maklakov, accordingly, rests on the doubtful proposition that Maklakov was a Cadet in name only because of his connections with the "ruling class." ("The views themselves [Maklakov's] grew too organically out of the medium to which our memoirist belongs. . . . Our author belongs to a medium out of which have come governors and ministers. . . .") Miliukov also claims insight into the "totality of the revolutionary process, a complicated historical process," an understanding denied to Maklakov because he is "too limited by personal experiences and the lack of scientific study." Some of the more naïve aspects of Cadet behavior, such as the belief in the completeness of their victory at the opening of the First Duma, Miliukov denies outright, ignoring the evidence furnished by his own voluminous journalistic writing of the period.

Like many other Cadets, Miliukov changed his views between 1905 and 1917. He is, of course, one of those who fought hard to convince Nicholas' brother, Michael, to accept the throne in March, 1917. Nevertheless, he sees no inconsistency between his stand then and his stand eleven years earlier, when, in advocating the calling of a constituent assembly, he, in effect, assumed the collapse of the monarchy. Events in 1917 further opened his eyes, and he became one of those who called for firm measures against the growing anarchy. He does not, however, admit that the Cadet position toward the same disorders ten years before might have been wrong. He correctly states: "I wrote three volumes of history about this [the failure of the February Revolution], and many of my views coincide with those of Maklakov," ignoring the possibility that while Maklakov was being consistent, he was not. In those same three volumes, he has written: "Absolute principles suitable for all countries and in all circumstances do not exist in politics. It is time to understand that even democratic politics does not constitute an exception from this rule. It is time to grasp that its slogans do not include panaceas and cures for all illnesses."

8. The upper house, the State Council, was not an independent force in the legislative process, since the Czar appointed half its members and consequently dominated it. In any case, it could be bypassed through the use of Article 87 if the Czar and the Duma were agreed on a bill. A decree enacted under Article 87 remained in force as a temporary law, if the Duma chose not to examine it. The State Council could pass on it only if the Duma had done so first.

9. "Work," writes Maklakov, "opened the eyes of the Party workers with more persuasiveness than the leading articles of their newspapers blinded them." (*Vtoraia Gos. Duma*, p. 141.)

10. A. S. Izgoev, "Nasha obshchestvennaia zhizn," in *Ezhegodnik gazety Rech na 1914 god*, pp. 211–12.

11. For a discerning discussion of the impact on the intelligentsia of their work in the peasant cooperative movement, see the article by Prince Eugene Trubetskoi, "Novaia zemskaia Rossiia," *Russkaia Mysl*, December, 1913, Section 2, pp. 1–12. Trubetskoi writes: "The intellectual-demagogue did not introduce his own ideas into peasant consciousness and peasant life, but, rather, was himself guided by the instincts of the masses of people, and lavishly praised them, while adapting to them his Party program and tactics." (P. 8.) Arguing that the democratic peasant movement will sweep away the rightists and transform the leftists, Trubetskoi further writes:

> I do not doubt that now, as before, we have many Social Democrats and Socialist Revolutionaries; but what the content corresponding to these labels may be at the present time we do not know precisely and cannot know, since a new ideology is still in the process of formation and has still not been finally consolidated. However, it will hardly remain as before. Apparently deep and fundamental changes are taking place in the psychology of the contemporary Russian intellectual. . . .
>
> There is no insufficiency of attempts in one way or another to fit the cooperative movement to one or another socialist label in order to justify the left intelligentsia's participation in it. But these justifications produce the impression of a kind of invented *post factum* not corresponding to real life. In reality, the most important of all contemporary social movements—the

cooperative movement—proceeds in our villages without the noticeable participation of socialist propaganda, and, in general, of any propaganda whatsoever—social or political. It has a purely businesslike, practical character. In effect, life is moving with its own swift and full course, and the extreme left tendencies . . . are being directly swept away by it. The intellectual in the village is becoming the involuntary instrument of a process not at all foreseen by those leftist programs advanced up to the present. . . . (Pp. 10–11.)

Until 1905, our peasant mass was unintellectual, and the intelligentsia was without a foundation. Now, on the contrary, in proportion as the peasant mass, acquiring culture, becomes more intellectual, the intelligentsia is becoming better grounded, and healthy, realistic thought is getting the upper hand. (P. 11.)

12. Vladimir Weidlé, *Russia: Absent and Present* (London, 1952), p. 86.

13. George Denicke, *Memoirs* (preliminary draft issued in mimeographed form by the Russian Research Center, Harvard University), pp. 41, 51–52.

14. A police report in October, 1916, states: "The peasants willingly converse on political themes, which, until the beginning of the war, was almost completely unobservable after 1906. . . ." ("Politicheskoe polozhenie Rossii nakanune fevralskoi revoliutsii v zhandarmskom osveshchenii," *Krasnyi Arkhiv*, XVII [1926], 20.)

15. Mark Vishniak, himself an active revolutionary at that time, comments: "It is absurd to say that the revolutionaries made or prepared the Revolution by their 'inflammatory slogans.' . . . The Revolution caught the revolutionaries by surprise, in part because the most active agents of Revolution were not so much they themselves as the excessively complaisant partisans of absolutism." ("Padeni russkago absoliutizma," *Sovremennyia Zapiski*, 18 [1924], 261.)

16. For the complete Russian text, see Miliukov, *Istoriia vtoroi russkoi revoliutsii*, I, Part 1, 104–5. There is an English translation in Alexander F. Kerensky, *The Catastrophe* (New York, 1927), pp. 139–41.

17. "Mart-Mai 1917 g.," *Krasnyi Arkhiv*, XV (1926), 36. This statement follows a discussion in the report of the alarm felt in the provinces over the reports of "dual power" and the weakening of the government it portended. "The farther away from the center, the greater is the faith maintained in a strong government."

18. *Ibid.*, pp. 34, 35, 40, 43.

19. Ariadna Tyrkova-Williams, *From Liberty to Brest-Litovsk* (London, 1919), p. 202.

Critical Bibliography

In any serious study of the internal evolution of Russia, a high place among the sources is necessarily occupied by the legal textbooks of Russian jurists. The quality of the pre-Revolutionary Russian jurists was very high, and their works constitute an inexhaustible storehouse of information not only about the content of the laws, the first essential for an understanding of Russian institutions, but also about the practical effect of the laws and their historical background. The three brightest names in the field of public law were A. D. Gradovsky, N. M. Korkunov, and N. I. Lazarevsky. The use which can be made of them depends upon the period under consideration. Gradovsky (*Sobranie sochinenii*, Vols. VII, VIII, and IX) was the oldest of them, and his analysis does not extend beyond 1880. Korkunov's analysis is good for the period up to 1905; however, his *Russkoe gosudarstvennoe pravo* (2 vols.) was brought up to date after 1905 by several of his students, who, without modifying the original text, inserted summaries of the post-1905 laws in the fields analyzed by him. Lazarevsky did his main work in the period after 1905, and his *Lektsii po russkomu gosudarstvennomu pravu* (2 vols., the first on constitutional law, the second on administrative law) is the most up to date and probably the most valuable. Because his comments are always concise and to the point, his work is especially valuable for foreign scholars studying the era in which he wrote. However, for some subjects, such as the class structure and the zemstvos, he must be supplemented by the detail and historical background provided by Gradovsky and Korkunov. Lazarevsky is, of course, indispensable for an analysis of the constitutional structure after 1905.

Besides these three, there are a number of other legal writers in special fields whose works have been of great value in this study. A. I. Elistratov's *Osnovnyia nachala administrativnago prava* generally follows Lazarevsky closely on the constitutional structure after 1905, but because his volume is devoted exclusively to administrative law, it frequently contains more detail and touches subjects (e.g., the background of the "police state" in Russia and

Europe) not covered by Lazarevsky. The second edition of Elistratov's text was published in 1917, and it includes the most recent
developments not available elsewhere. In the field of the police,
the most important work is, of course, V. M. Gessen's *Iskliuchitelnoe polozhenie*. Because the emergency laws were Gessen's main
concern, his volume is excellently supplemented by A. A. Lopukhin's *Nastoiashchee i budushchee russkoi politsii*, which, so far as
is known to the writer, is the only available general treatise on the
police. Since Lopukhin was formerly chief of the Police Department, his analysis is especially authoritative. V. F. Deriuzhinsky's
Politseikoe pravo is concerned not with the police, but with the
functional activity of internal administration (e.g., censorship, education, public health, social welfare, etc.). In this study, it has been
used primarily for its detailed comments on the censorship. A. A.
Leontiev's *Krestianskoe pravo* is a standard work on the legal status
of the peasants. Although not immediately apparent, A. Romanovich-Slavatinsky's *Dvorianstvo v Rossii* is the work of a legal scholar
and is based primarily on *Polnoe sobranie zakonov*. It is, however,
a many-sided study of the development of the nobility, the best
among the very few works available in this field.

These legal writers must, of course, be studied in conjunction
with the laws themselves. The text of the laws are available in
Polnoe sobranie zakonov, a chronological tabulation of all laws
passed since 1649, published in three collections, each consisting of
many volumes. Equally valuable is the digest of the main laws currently in force, the *Svod zakonov*, arranged by subject and published in sixteen volumes. The *Svod zakonov* was periodically reis-
sued to include the changes made since the date of last publication.
Since many basic changes were made in the years 1905–6, editions
published before and after those years must be used.

It should be noted that in the study of the law in pre-Revolutionary Russia, the comparative method was used. Consequently, most
of the legal treatises gave considerable attention to the relevant
laws of other countries, principally England, France, and Germany.
The principal sources for these countries were mastered by Russian
scholars in the original languages, and their legal works were, in
effect, treatises on comparative government—treatises, moreover, of
very high caliber, unknown in the West only because of the language barrier.

Aside from the laws and the treatises on the laws, which have

formed the backbone of virtually every chapter, the main sources
for this study consist of government documents, the memoirs of
prominent figures, a series of treatises on various subjects written
by contemporaries, some of them after the Revolution, and the
encyclopedias. Among the government documents, a very high
place is occupied by the testimony given before the Extraordinary
Investigating Commission of the Provisional Government, subsequently published in seven volumes by the Soviet Government
under the title *Padenie tsarskogo rezhima*. Some of the questions
asked by the Commission do not seem so important now as they
did then, and some of those questioned undoubtedly held back
information because of the fear of prosecution. Nevertheless, in
the seven volumes may be found the direct testimony on important
problems of many high government officials, accompanied, in some
cases, by a searching examination undertaken by the Commission,
and these volumes are an indispensable source of information on
the circumstances surrounding the fall of the monarchy and, in
general, on developments between the two revolutions. The Commission, it should be noted, had a full array of documents in its
possession, and many of them were quoted verbatim by the chairman during the course of the questioning. Also very important are
the stenographic reports of the State Duma (*Stenograficheskie
otchety*) and the summaries of the proceedings of the State Council (*Otchet po deloproizvodstvu Gosudarstvennago Soveta*), both
issued in many large volumes. The review by the Committee of
Ministers in 1905 of the problems connected with the fulfillment
of the ukase of December 12, 1904, touches directly on some of the
issues treated in this study, but the eight points reviewed in the
journals of the Committee (*Zhurnaly Komiteta Ministrov po
ispolneniiu ukaza 12 dekabria 1904 g.*) did not, in all cases, elicit
equally frank statements from the members of the committee. The
writer has used most extensively the review of Point 5 on the emergency legislation, and the review of Point 8 on censorship and the
press. Many documents were published in *Osvobozhdenie* by the
editors of that publication, and the writer has found several of
them very useful, but there are many more which should be tapped
by future scholars. A great deal has been published by the Soviet
Government in *Krasnyi Arkhiv*. Of very great value in this connection is A *Digest of the Krasnyi Arkhiv*, the translation and summary
of the materials in that publication undertaken by the Cleveland

296 CRITICAL BIBLIOGRAPHY

Public Library. Only the first thirty volumes have so far been covered.

Of very great importance among government documents is the memorandum by Witte on the zemstvos, *Samoderzhavie i zemstvo*, originally published by the editors (or future editors) of *Osvobozhdenie* in 1901 in Stuttgart. This memorandum, in which Witte undertook to prove that local self-government is incompatible with autocracy, is, in the opinion of the writer, one of the most remarkable political analyses to be found in any language.

For an understanding of why the monarchy fell in 1917, there is no substitute for the *Letters of the Tsaritsa to the Tsar*. Much is revealed about Nicholas in his diary, *Dnievnik Imperatora Nikolaia II*, and he made many interesting comments in the letters to his mother, *The Secret Letters of the Last Tsar*.

Among the memoirs published by government statesmen, the most important are those by Witte, *Vospominaniia* (2 vols.); Kokovtsov, *Iz moego proshlogo* (2 vols.); Kryzhanovsky, *Vospominaniia*; Gurko, *Features and Figures of the Past*; Mosolov, *At the Court of the Last Tsar*; Spiridovich, in *Arkhiv russkoi revoliutsii* (Vol. XV); and Gerasimov, *Der Kampf gegen die erste russische Revolution*. Witte's memoirs are very useful for the period prior to 1905, but must be used with caution, particularly when he discusses his own accomplishments. Kokovtsov offers an interesting picture of developments at the highest levels of the government after 1905. He is, on the whole, reliable, but it is apparent that he was not always as candid as he might have been. Gurko and Kryzhanovsky were both Assistant Ministers of the Interior; both, while conservative, were men of great intelligence, and their comments are often penetrating and fair. Gurko is most valuable for the period up to 1906, Kryzhanovsky for the period from 1906 to 1911. Gurko was much more detailed than Kryzhanovsky, and his memoirs are available in English, but it should be noted that his style of writing presupposes considerable background knowledge on the part of the reader. Mosolov, a high official in the Ministry of the Imperial Court from 1900 to 1917, gives us an interesting, and because of his position, an intimate, picture of the Czar and the imperial family. Spiridovich, a former gendarme officer assigned to Okhrana units, and Gerasimov, former head of the St. Petersburg Okhrana, make very valuable comments on the police. Along with the above, there is the diary of A. A. Polovtsev, printed by the Soviet Government in *Krasnyi Arkhiv*, and full of penetrating comments on high government officials and government policy.

By far the most important of the memoirs of the "public men" are those of V. A. Maklakov, *Vlast i obshchestvennost, Pervaia Gosudarstvennaia Duma*, and *Vtoraia Gosudarstvennaia Duma*. These are, in part, also political treatises, written with the aid of available documents. They are the work of a man of penetrating intellect and extraordinary training in the social sciences, a man, furthermore, who watched the Russian political scene from the vantage point of the Second, Third, and Fourth Dumas, in which he was a Cadet deputy. In combining his personal talents with personal observation to give us his interpretation of the mistakes of the Cadet Party and the "public men" in general, Maklakov has produced works that are certain to rank high in the political literature of Russia. Indeed, the perspective and penetration with which they are written and the important problems of politics discussed give them high rank in the political literature of the world. Whether his views are accepted or not, they must be reckoned with and answered. Another solid work, written from a position to the right of Maklakov's, is Shipov's *Vospominaniia i dumy o perezhitom*. Besides discussing the critical years of the Revolution of 1905 from the point of view of the "public men," Shipov has many comments on the zemstvos and the zemstvo movement. To Western readers, his Slavophile views on politics will seem quaint and naïve. Further to the left, there are the memoirs of Miliukov, published under the title "Rokovye gody" in seventeen installments in the Paris journal *Russkiia Zapiski*. Miliukov has commented on Maklakov's views in two articles in *Sovremennyia Zapiski* (Nos. 41 and 57), and he has commented on Shipov's views in the little volume *Tri popytki* (the latter has not been cited in this work). Another writer to the left of Maklakov and Shipov is Petrunkevich, whose memoirs have been printed in *Arkhiv russkoi revoliutsii* (Vol. XXI). Petrunkevich's memoirs are somewhat less solid than the other three. Also in this group should be listed the memoirs of Kizevetter, *Na rubezhe dvukh stoletii*; Polner's biography of Prince Lvov, *Zhiznennyi put Kniaza G. E. Lvova*; and Kaidanova's work on Russian education, *Ocherki po istorii narodnogo obrazovaniia*. Kizevetter comments on the events of Russian public life through the period from 1884 to 1914, and gives an especially valuable picture of the self-activity of society. Kaidanova depicts self-activity in the field of education, while Polner's biography has been used in this study primarily for the materials given on the zemstvos.

Because of the wide scope of this book, a very large number of contemporary treatises have been consulted. On the weakness of the Russian social tradition, Miliukov's *Ocherki po istorii russkoi kultury* (3 vols.) and *Russia and Its Crisis* have been indispensable. A. A. Kizevetter, whose memoirs have already been cited, wrote a small volume, *Mestnoe samoupravlenie v Rossii*, which ably supplements the works of Miliukov and Witte's *Samoderzhavie i zemstvo* in this field. It throws perspective particularly on the former Slavophile argument that self-government had a traditional place in the structure of the autocracy. Aside from Kliuchevsky's well-known volumes on Russian history, available in English, his *Istoriia soslovii v Rossii* presents an interesting picture of the organization of the Russian legal classes up to the time of Peter the Great. In this field, Leroy-Beaulieu's *L'empire des Tsars et les Russes* is also very useful. Leroy-Beaulieu, it should be noted, is one of a small number of foreigners who learned the language and thoroughly mastered the subject of Russia. His works became standard references for Russian as well as non-Russian scholars. A general history frequently used by the writer is S. S. Oldenburg's study of the reign of Nicholas II, *Tsarstvovanie Imperatora Nikolaia II* (2 vols.). Oldenburg was a strong monarchist and must be read with caution, but he offers much useful material. Also frequently referred to is the four-volume work edited by the Social Democrats Martov, Maslov, and Potresov, *Obshchestvennoe dvizhenie v Rossii*. Despite the prejudices of most of the contributors, the standard of the scholarship is high, and a huge mass of material not otherwise available in the United States was digested by the contributors with astonishing industry only a few years after the events described. The chapters by Maevsky on the social movement as a whole, by Ermansky on the bourgeoisie, by Koltsov on the workers, and by Cherevanin on the intelligentsia have been frequently cited in this study. Another valuable work on the "social movement" is S. G. Svatikov's *Obshchestvennoe dvizhenie v Rossii*. Svatikov's main interest was the constitutional projects drawn up in Russia from 1700 to 1895. Especially relevant to this study are the ups and downs of the social movement from the era of the Great Reforms until 1895, described by Svatikov with great shrewdness. Belokonsky's *Zemskoe dvizhenie* is a standard work on the zemstvo movement, which starts with the 1860's but emphasizes primarily the period from 1894 to 1905. Many documents are quoted verbatim in this work. His *Zemstvo i konstitutsiia* is a shorter work covering the same field, but without the verbatim documents. The book was first issued as a series of articles in 1907 in the historical journal *Byloe*, but these articles include a great deal of material on non-zemstvo self-activity that was omitted from the book. The symposium on the zemstvos edited by Veselovsky and Frankel, *Iubileinyi zemskii sbornik*, is a thorough and up-to-date work, with the contributors, on the whole, maintaining a uniformly high standard.

On the agrarian problem and the Stolypin reforms, aside from the well-known works in English, the writer found Boris Brutzkus's *Agrarnyi vopros i agrarnaia politika* and W. D. Preyer's *Die russische Agrarreform* of great value. Brutzkus was a well-known and able Russian economist. *Die russische Agrarreform* is an outstanding monograph by a German writer who absorbed an unusual amount of Russian source material. The trade-union movement up to 1907 has been thoroughly covered by such works as *Obshchestvennoe dvizhenie*, cited above, Sviatlovsky's *Professionalnoe dvizhenie*, and Grinovich's *Professionalnoe dvizhenie*. For the period after 1907, Sviatlovsky's post-Revolutionary revision of his work *Istoriia professionalnogo dvizheniia* is inadequate and strongly reflects Sviatlovsky's Social Democratic prejudices. The only thorough study available to date is Grinevich's *Die Gewerkschaftsbewegung in Russland*, which also includes an abbreviated translation of Grinevich's earlier work. The German revision has not been published in Russian. The most valuable contribution on the independence movement and organizational activity of the industrialists is to be found in the chapters by Ermansky in *Obshchestvennoe dvizhenie* (edited by Martov *et al.*), but there is much of value also in the volume by P. A. Berlin, *Russkaia burzhuaziia*, and the monograph by E. S. Lurye, "Organizatsiia i organizatsii torgovo-promyshlennykh interesov."

There is a wealth of material available in the Russian encyclopedias, both pre-Revolutionary and Soviet. These include the two published by Brockhaus and Efron, *Entsiklopedicheskii Slovar* and *Novyi E. S.*; the one published by Granat, *E. S.*, the last volumes of which appeared in the Soviet period; and *Bolshaia* and *Malaia Sovetskaia Entsiklopediia*. The articles in the Brockhaus and Efron encyclopedias are generally more scholarly and longer than those in the Granat encyclopedia. The completion of *Novyi Entsiklopedicheskii Slovar* was interrupted by the Revolution, and it does not go beyond the letter "O," but its late publication date gives it special value. The first editions of the two Soviet encyclopedias appeared at a time when scholarship standards were still relatively high and scholars trained in the pre-Revolutionary period were still active. Many fine articles on pre-Revolutionary institutions consequently may be found in them. The encyclopedias were of greatest value for the chapters on society, especially Chapters IV, V, and VI.

Finally, the "thick journals," pre-Revolutionary and *émigré*, should not be overlooked. Of those before the Revolution, *Vestnik Evropy, Russkaia Mysl, Mir Bozhii, Sovremennyi Mir, Russkoe Bogatstvo* were probably best known and had editorial staffs reflecting different shades of political opinion. The importance of the legal weekly *Pravo* has been stressed in the chapter on the press. Historical journals, such as *Byloe* and *Golos Minuvshego*, contain many interesting articles on the Liberation Movement. Among the post-Revolutionary journals, *Sovremennyia Zapiski*, published in Paris, has often been cited in this study, and more recent journals, such as *Novyi Zhurnal*, published in New York, and *Vozrozhdenie*, published in Paris, frequently contain articles on important pre-Revolutionary problems.

Bibliography

ANTSIFEROV, A. N., and Others. *Russian Agriculture During the War.* New Haven, 1930.

ARSENIEV, K. K. *Zakonodatelstvo o pechati (Legislation on the Press).* St. Petersburg, 1903.

BARING, MAURICE. *A Year in Russia.* Rev. ed. London, 1917.

BELOKONSKY, I. P. *Zemskoe dvizhenie (The Zemstvo Movement).* 2d ed. Moscow, 1914.

BERDYAEV, NICOLAS. *The Russian Idea.* London, 1947.

BERLIN, P. A. *Russkaia burzhuaziia v staroe i novoe vremia (The Russian Bourgeoisie in Old and New Times).* Moscow, 1922.

BERNOV, P. I. (ed.). *Spravochnyi ukazatel knig i zhurnalov arestovannykh s 17 oktiabria 1905 g. po 1 ianvaria 1909 g. (Reference Index of Books and Journals Confiscated from October 17, 1905, to January 1, 1909).* Moscow, 1909.

Bolshaia Sovetskaia Entsiklopediia (Great Soviet Encyclopedia). 65 vols. Moscow, 1926–39.

BOWDEN, WITT, KARPOVICH, MICHAEL, and USHER, ABBOTT P. *An Economic History of Europe since 1750.* New York, 1937.

BRUFORD, W. H. *Chekhov and His Russia.* New York, 1948.

BRUTZKUS, BORIS. *Agrarnyi vopros i agrarnaia politika (The Agrarian Problem and Agrarian Policy).* Petrograd, 1922.

CHAMBERLIN, WILLIAM HENRY. *The Russian Revolution, 1917–1921.* 2 vols. New York, 1935.

CHARNOLUSKY, V. I. "Nachalnoe obrazovanie vo vtoroi polovine XIX stoletiia" ("Elementary Education in the Second Half of the Nineteenth Century"), *Istoriia Rossii v XIX veke* (Granat), VII, pp. 109–69. St. Petersburg, n.d.

CHICHERIN, B. N. *Rossiia nakanune dvadtsatago stoletiia (Russia on the Eve of the Twentieth Century).* 3d ed. Berlin, 1901.

CHUBINSKY, M. P. "Sudebnaia reforma" ("Judicial Reform"), *Istoriia Rossii v XIX veke* (Granat), III, pp. 231–68. St. Petersburg, n.d.

———. "Sudba sudebnoi reformy v poslednei treti XIX-go veka" ("The Fate of the Judicial Reform in the Last Third of the Nineteenth Century"), *Istoriia Rossii v XIX veke* (Granat), VI, pp. 200–44. St. Petersburg, n.d.

CURTISS, JOHN S. *Church and State in Russia: the Last Years of the Empire, 1900–1917.* New York, 1940.

DARLINGTON, T. "Education in Russia," *Special Reports on Educational Subjects.* Vol. XXIII. London; Great Britain, Board of Education, 1909.

Davydov, N. V., and Poliansky, N. N. (eds.). *Sudebnaia reforma (Judicial Reform)*. 2 vols. Moscow, 1915.

Denicke, George. *Links with the Past in Soviet Society*. (Department of State, External Research Paper, Series 3, No. 88.) Washington, D.C., 1952.

Deriuzhinsky, V. F. *Politseiskoe pravo (Police Law)*. 2d ed. St. Petersburg, 1908; 3d ed. St. Petersburg, 1911.

Deutscher, Isaac. *Stalin: A Political Biography*. New York, 1949.

Dnevnik Imperatora Nikolaia II (Diary of Emperor Nicholas II). Berlin, 1923.

Dragomanov, M. P., *Liberalizm i zemstvo v Rossii (Liberalism and the Zemstvo in Russia)*. Geneva, 1889.

Dzhivelegov, A. K., and Others (eds.). *Velikaia reforma (The Great Reform)*, Vol. VI. Moscow, 1911.

Elistratov, A. I. *Osnovnyia nachala administrativnago prava (Fundamental Principles of Administrative Law)*. 2d ed. Moscow, 1917.

————. *Voprosy administrativnago prava (Problems of Administrative Law)*, Book I. Moscow, 1916.

Entsiklopedicheskii Slovar (Encyclopedic Dictionary) (Brockhaus and Efron). 41 vols. St. Petersburg, 1890–1904.

Entsiklopedicheskii Slovar (Granat). 41 vols. Moscow, n.d.

Finn-Enotaevsky, A. *Kapitalizm v Rossii, 1890–1917 (Capitalism in Russia)*. Moscow, 1925.

Florinsky, Michael T. *The End of the Russian Empire*. New Haven, 1931.

————. *Toward an Understanding of the USSR*. 1st ed. New York, 1939.

————. *Russia. A History and interpretation*. 2 vols. New York, 1953.

Footman, David. *Red Prelude: The Life of the Russian Terrorist Zhelyabov*. New Haven, 1945.

Fülöp Miller, René. *Rasputin, the Holy Devil*. New York, 1929.

Gerasimov, Alexander. *Der Kampf gegen die erste russische Revolution*. Frauenfeld and Leipzig, 1934.

Gessen, I. V. *Advokatura, obshchestvo i gosudarstvo (The Bar, Society and the State)*. Moscow, 1914.

————. "V dvukh vekakh" ("In Two Centuries"), *Arkhiv russkoi revoliutsii*. Vol. XXII. Berlin, 1937.

Gessen, V. M. *Iskliuchitelnoe polozhenie (The State of Emergency)*. St. Petersburg, 1908.

Goldman, L. I. *Politicheskie protsessy v Rossii (Political Trials in Russia)*. Moscow, 1932.

Gosudarstvennaia Duma. *Stenograficheskie otchety (Stenographic Reports)*. Numerous volumes, 1906–16.

Gosudarstvennyi Sovet. *Otchet po deloproizvodstvu Gosudarstvennago Soveta za sessiiu 1905–1906 gg. (Report of the Proceedings of* the State Council for the Session of 1905–1906). St. Petersburg, 1906.

GRADOVSKY, A. D. Sobranie sochinenii (Collected Works). Vols. VII, VIII, and IX (Nachala russkago gosudarstvennago prava). St. Petersburg, 1901–4.

GRINEVETSKY, V. I. Poslevoennye perspektivy russkoi promyshlennosti (The Postwar Perspectives of Russian Industry). 2d ed. Moscow, 1922.

GRINEVICH, V. Professionalnoe dvizhenie rabochikh v Rossii (The Trade Union Movement of the Workers in Russia). 3d ed. Moscow, 1924.

———. Die Gewerkschaftsbewegung in Russland (The Trade Union Movement in Russia), Vol. I, 1905–14. Berlin, 1927.

GRONSKY, P. P., and ASTROV, N. J. The War and the Russian Government. New Haven, 1929.

GSOVSKI, VLADIMIR. Soviet Civil Law. 2 vols. Ann Arbor, 1948.

GURIAN, WALDEMAR (ed.). The Soviet Union: Background, Ideology, Reality. Notre Dame, 1951.

GURKO, VLADIMIR I. Features and Figures of the Past. Stanford, 1939.

HANS, NICHOLAS. History of Russian Educational Policy (1701–1917). London, 1931.

HARPER, SAMUEL N. The New Electoral Law for the Russian Duma. Chicago, 1908.

IADRINTSEV, N. M. Sibir kak koloniia (Siberia as a Colony). 2nd ed. St. Petersburg, 1892.

IGNATIEV, P. N., ODINETS, D. M., and NOVGOROTSEV, P. J. Russian Schools and Universities in the World War. New Haven, 1929.

ILINSKY, K. Chastnyia obshchestva: sbornik zakonov, rasporiazhenii pravitelstva i reshenii Pravitelstvuiushchago Senata (Private Societies: A Collection of Laws and Orders of the Government and the Decisions of the Ruling Senate). Riga, n.d.

INKELES, ALEX. Public Opinion in Soviet Russia. Cambridge, 1949.

IVANOVICH, V. Rossiiskiia partii, soiuzy i ligi (Russian Parties, Unions and Leagues). St. Petersburg, 1906.

IVANOV-RAZUMNIK. Istoriia russkoi obshchestvennoi mysli (History of Russian Social Thought). 2 vols. 3d ed. St. Petersburg, 1911.

IVANOVSKY, V. V. Uchebnik administrativnago prava (Textbook of Administrative Law). Kazan, 1907.

IZGOEV, A. S. Russkoe obshchestvo i revoliutsiia (Russian Society and the Revolution). Moscow, 1910.

KAIDANOVA, OLGA. Ocherki po istorii narodnogo obrazovaniia v Rossii i SSSR na osnove lichnogo opyta i nabliudenii (Essays on the History of Education for the People in Russian and the USSR on the Basis of Personal Experience and Observation). Vol. I. Berlin, 1938.

KAYDEN, E. M., and ANTSIFEROV, A. N. The Cooperative Movement in Russia during the War. New Haven, 1929.

KENNAN, GEORGE. *Siberia and the Exile System.* 2 vols. New York, 1891.

KERENSKY, ALEXANDER F. *The Catastrophe.* New York, 1927.

KIZEVETTER, A. A. *Na rubezhe dvukh stoletii (On the Boundary of Two Centuries).* Prague, 1929.

———. *Mestnoe samoupravlenie v Rossii, IX–XIX st., istoricheskii ocherk (Local Self-Government in Russia, IX–XIX Centuries, a Historical Outline).* Moscow, 1910.

KLIUCHEVSKY, V. O. *History of Russia.* 5 vols. London, 1911–31.

———. *Istoriia soslovii v Rossii (History of Legal Classes in Russia).* 3d ed. Petrograd, 1918.

KOKOVTSOV, V. N. *Iz moego proshlogo (Out of My Past).* 2 vols. Paris, 1933.

KOMITET MINISTROV. *Zhurnaly Komiteta Ministrov po ispolneniiu ukaza 12 dekabria 1904 g. (Journals of the Committee of Ministers on the Fulfillment of the Ukase of December 12, 1904).* St. Petersburg, 1905.

KORKUNOV, N. M. *Russkoe gosudarstvennoe pravo (Russian State Law).* 2 vols. 7th ed. St. Petersburg, 1909.

KORNILOV, A. A. *Kurs istorii Rossii XIX veka (Course on Russian History in the Nineteenth Century).* 3 vols. 2d ed. Moscow, 1918. English translation, 2 vols. in 1. New York, 1943.

KRYZHANOVSKY, S. E. *Vospominaniia (Memoirs).* Berlin, 1938.

KUCHEROV, SAMUEL. *Courts, Lawyers and Trials under the Last Three Tsars.* New York, 1953.

LATKIN, V. N. *Uchebnik istorii russkago prava perioda imperii, XVIII i XIX st. (Textbook on the History of Russian Law During the Period of the Empire, Eighteenth and Nineteenth Centuries).* 2d ed. St. Petersburg, 1909.

LAZAREVSKY, N. I. *Lektsii po russkomu gosudarstvennomu pravu (Lectures on Russian State Law).* 2 vols. St. Petersburg, 1908–10.

LEONTIEV, A. A. *Krestianskoe pravo (Peasant Law).* St. Petersburg, 1909.

LEROY-BEAULIEU, ANATOLE. *L'empire des Tsars et les Russes.* 3 vols. Paris, 1889–93.

Letters of the Tsaritsa to the Tsar, 1914–1916. With an introduction by SIR BERNARD PARES. New York, 1924.

LEVIN, ALFRED. *The Second Duma.* New Haven, 1940.

LOPUKHIN, A. A. *Nastoiashchee i budushchee russkoi politsii (Present and Future of the Russian Police).* Moscow, 1907.

LURYE, E. S. "Organizatsiia i organizatsii torgovo-promyshlennykh interesov v Rossii" ("The Organization and Organizations of Commercial-Industrial Interests in Russia"), *Trudy studentov ekonomicheskago otdeleniia S-Peterburgskago Politekhnicheskago Instituta Imperatora Petra Velikago (Proceedings of the Students of the Economic Section of the St. Petersburg Polytechnical Institute of Emperor Peter the Great),* No. 11. St. Petersburg, 1913.

LYASHCHENKO, PETER D. *History of the National Economy of Russia*. New York, 1949.

MAKLAKOV, V. A. *Vlast i obshchestvennost na zakate staroi Rossii, vospominaniia* (*State and Society in the Decline of Old Russia, Memoirs*). Paris, 1936.

——. *Pervaia Gosudarstvennaia Duma, vospominaniia sovremennika* (*The First State Duma, Memoirs of a Contemporary*). Paris, 1939.

——. *Vtoraia Gosudarstvennaia Duma, vospominaniia sovremennika* (*The Second State Duma, Memoirs of a Contemporary*). Paris, 1945.

Malaia Sovetskaia Entsiklopediia (*Small Soviet Encyclopedia*). 10 vols. Moscow, 1928–31.

MARTOV, L., MASLOV, P., and POTRESOV, A. (eds.). *Obshchestvennoe dvizhenie v Rossii v nachale XX-go veka* (*The Social Movement in Russia at the Beginning of the Twentieth Century*). 4 vols. St. Petersburg, 1909–14.

MAYER, OTTO. *Deutsches Verwaltungsrecht*, Vol. I. Munich and Leipzig, 1924.

MAZOUR, ANATOLE. *The First Russian Revolution*. Berkeley, 1937.

MELNIK, J. (ed.). *Russen über Russland, ein Sammelwerk*. Frankfurt-am-Main, 1906.

MILIUKOV, P. N. *Istoriia vtoroi russkoi revoliutsii* (*History of the Second Russian Revolution*). 3 vols. Sofia, 1921–24.

——. *Ocherki po istorii russkoi kultury* (*Essays on the History of Russian Culture*). Vols. I and III; 6th ed. St. Petersburg, 1909–13. Vol. II, Jubilee ed. Paris, 1931.

——. *Outlines of Russian Culture*. Vol. I. *Religion and the Church in Russia*. Philadelphia, 1942.

——. *Russia and Its Crisis*. Chicago, 1905.

MILLER, MARGARET S. *The Economic Development of Russia, 1905–1914*. London, 1926.

Ministerstvo Vnutrennykh Del, 1802–1902, istoricheskii ocherk (*The Ministry of the Interior, 1802–1902; a Historical Outline*). St. Petersburg, 1901.

MOSOLOV, A. A. *At the Court of the Last Tsar*. London, 1935.

MUROMTSEV, S. A. *Statii i rechi* (*Articles and Speeches*). 5 vols. Moscow, 1910.

NICOLAEVSKY, BORIS. *Aseff: The Russian Judas*. London, 1934.

Novyi Entsiklopedicheskii Slovar (*New Encyclopedic Dictionary*) (Brockhaus and Efron). 29 vols. St. Petersburg, 1911–16?

OLDENBURG, S. S. *Tsarstvovanie Imperatora Nikolaia II* (*The Reign of Emperor Nicholas II*). 2 vols. Belgrade and Munich, 1939–49.

OSOBOE SOVESHCHANIE O NUZHDAKH SELSKO-KHOZIAISTVENNOI PROMYSHLENNOSTI. *Printsipialnye voprosy po krestianskomu delu s otvetami mestnykh selsko-khoziaistvennykh komitetov* (*Questions of Principle on the Peasant Problem with the Answers of Local Agricultural Committees*). St. Petersburg, 1904.

Ovsianiko-Kulikovsky, D. N. *Sobranie sochinenii (Collected Works)*. Vols. VII, VIII, IX (*Istoriia russkoi intelligentsii*). St. Petersburg, 1914.

Ozerov, I. Kh. *Politika po rabochemu voprosu v Rossii za poslednie gody* (*Recent Policy Concerning the Labor Problem in Russia*.) Moscow, 1906.

Padenie tsarskogo rezhima, stenograficheskie otchety doprosov i pokazanii dannykh v 1917 g. v Chrezvychainoi Sledstvennoi Komissii Vremennago Pravitelstva (*The Fall of the Tsarist Regime, Stenographic Reports of the Interrogations and Testimonies Given in 1917 in the Extraordinary Investigating Commission of the Provisional Government*). 7 vols. Moscow 1924–27. There is an abridged French translation, *La chute du régime tsariste*, with a preface by V. A. Maklakov. Paris, 1927.

Paléologue, Maurice. *An Ambassador's Memoirs*. 3 vols. London, 1923–24

Pares, Bernard. *The Fall of the Russian Monarchy*. New York, 1939.
———. *Russia and Reform*. London, 1907.

Pavlovsky, G. A. *Agricultural Russia on the Eve of the Revolution*. London, 1930.

Pazhitnov, K. A. *Polozhenie rabochago klassa v Rossii* (*The Position of the Working Class in Russia*). St. Petersburg, 1906.

Petergofskoe soveshchanie o proekte Gosudarstvennoi Dumy, pod lichnym Ego Imperatorskago Velichestva predsedatelstvom, sekretnye protokoly, zasedaniia 19-go, 21-go, 23-go, 25-go i 26-go iulia 1905 g. (*The Peterhof Conference on the Project for a State Duma, under the Personal Chairmanship of His Imperial Majesty, Secret Minutes for the Sessions of July 19, 21, 23, 25, and 26, 1905*). Berlin, n.d.

Petrunkevich, I. I. "Iz zapisok obshchestvennago deiatelia, vospominaniia" ("From the Notes of a Public Man, Memoirs"), *Arkhiv russkoi revoliutsii*, Vol. XXI. Berlin, 1934.

Platonov, S. F. *Lektsii po russkoi istorii* (*Lectures on Russian History*). St. Petersburg, 1901.

Pobedonostsev, K. P. *Reflections of a Russian Statesman*. Translated by Robert C. Long. London, 1898.

Pokrovsky, M. N. *Brief History of Russia*. 2 vols. London, 1933.

Polner, T. J., and Others. *Russian Local Government during the War and the Union of Zemstvos*. New Haven, 1930.
———. *Zhiznennyi put Kniaza G. E. Lvova* (*The Path of Life of Prince G. E. Lvov*). Paris, 1932.

Polnoe sobranie zakonov rossiiskoi imperii (*Full Collection of Laws of the Russian Empire*). 3 collections, each consisting of numerous volumes, 1649–1916.

Preyer, W. D. *Die russische Agrarreform*. Jena, 1914.

PROKOPOVICH, S. N. *K rabochemu voprosu v Rossii* (*On the Labor Problem in Russia*). St. Petersburg, 1905.

———. *Narodnoe khoziaistvo SSSR* (*The National Economy of the USSR*). 2 vols. New York, 1952.

Protokoly zasedanii soveshchaniia pod lichnym Ego Imperatorskago Velichestva predsedatelstvom po peresmotru Osnovnykh Gosudarstvennykh Zakonov, 7, 9, 11 i 21 aprelia 1906 g. (*Proceedings of the Conference under the Personal Chairmanship of His Imperial Majesty for the Revision of the Fundamental State Laws, April 7, 9, 11, and 12, 1906*). St. Petersburg, n.d.

RAFFALOVICH, ARTHUR. *Russia: Its Trade and Commerce.* London, 1918.

ROBINSON, GEROLD TANQUARY. *Rural Russia under the Old Régime.* New York, 1932.

RODZIANKO, M. V. *The Reign of Rasputin.* London, 1927.

ROMANOVICH-SLAVATINSKY, A. *Dvorianstvo v Rossii ot nachala XVIII veka do otmeny krepostnogo prava* (*The Nobility in Russia from the Beginning of the Eighteenth Century until the Abolition of Serfdom.*) 2d ed. Kiev, 1912.

ROSENBERG, V. A. *Iz istorii russkoi pechati; organizatsiia obshchestvennago mneniia v Rossii i nezavisimaia bezpartiinaia gazeta "Russkiia Vedomosti"* (1863–1918) (*From the History of the Russian Press; the Organization of Public Opinion in Russia and the Independent Non-Partisan Newspaper "Russkiia Vedomosti"*). Prague, 1924.

———. *Letopis russkoi pechati 1907–1914 gg.* (*A Chronicle of the Russian Press, 1907–1914*). Moscow, 1914.

Russkiia Vedomosti (1863–1913), *sbornik statei.* Moscow, 1913.

SAVICH, G. G. *Novyi gosudarstvennyi stroi Rossii, spravochnaia kniga* (*The New State Order of Russia, a Reference Book*). St. Petersburg, 1907.

SAVINKOV, BORIS. *Memoirs of a Terrorist.* New York, 1931.

SCHULZE-GAEVERNITZ, GERHART. *Volkswirtschaftliche Studien aus Russland.* Leipzig, 1899.

SCHWARZ, SOLOMON. *Labor in the Soviet Union.* New York, 1952.

The Secret Letters of the Last Tsar (Being the confidential correspondence between Nicholas II and his mother, Dowager Empress Maria Feodorovna). Edited by E. J. BING. New York, 1938.

SERGEEVSKY, N. D. *Russkoe ugolovnoe pravo* (Russian Criminal Law). 10th ed. St. Petersburg, 1913.

SHIPOV, D. N. *Vospominaniia i dumy o perezhitom* (*Reminiscences and Thoughts About My Past*). Moscow, 1918.

SHUB, DAVID. *Lenin: A Biography.* Garden City, 1949.

SLIOZBERG, G. B. *Dorevoliutsionnyi stroi Rossii* (*Pre-Revolutionary Regime of Russia*). Paris, 1933.

SMIRNOV, ALEXEI. *Kak proshli vybory vo Vtoruiu Gosudarstvennuiu*

Dumu (How the Elections to the Second State Duma Proceeded). St. Petersburg, 1907.

SPIRIDOVICH, A. I. "Pri tsarskom rezhime" ("Under the Tsarist Regime"), *Arkhiv russkoi revoliutsii*, Vol. XV. Berlin, 1924.

SUVOROV, N. *Uchebnik tserkovnago prava (Textbook of Church Law)*. 5th ed. Moscow, 1913.

SVATIKOV, S. G. *Obshchestvennoe dvizhenie v Rossii (1700–1895) (The Social Movement in Russia)*. Rostov-on-Don, 1905.

SVIATLOVSKY, V. *Professionalnoe dvizhenie v Rossii (The Trade Union Movement in Russia)*. St. Petersburg, 1907.

———. *Istoriia professionalnogo dvizheniia v Rossii (History of the Trade Union Movement in Russia)*. 2d ed. Leningrad, 1925.

Svod zakonov rossiiskoi imperii (Code of Laws of the Russian Empire). 16 vols. as published before and after 1905.

TAGANTSEV, N. S. *Smertnaia kazn: sbornik statei (Capital Punishment: A Collection of Articles)*. St. Petersburg, 1913.

TOTOMIANTS, V. F. *Kooperatsiia v Rossii (Cooperation in Russia)*. Prague, 1922.

TROTSKY, LEON. *Die russische Revolution*. Berlin, 1923.

Tsarizm v borbe s revoliutsiei, 1905–1907 gg. (Czarism in the Struggle with Revolution, 1905–1907). Edited by A. K. DREZEN. Moscow, 1936.

TSEITLIN, S. Y. "Zemskaia reforma" ("The Zemstvo Reform"), in *Istoriia Rossii v XIX veke* (Granat), III, 179–231.

———. "Zemskoe samoupravlenie i reforma 1890 g." ("Zemstvo Self-Government and the Reform of 1890"), in *Istoriia Rossii v XIX veke* (Granat), V, 79–138.

TUGAN-BARANOVSKY, M. I. *Russkaia fabrika v proshlom i nastoiashchem (The Russian Factory in the Past and Present)*. 3d ed. Moscow, 1922.

TYRKOVA-WILLIAMS, ARIADNA. *From Liberty to Brest-Litovsk*. London, 1919.

VASILIEV, A. T. *The Ochrana: The Russian Secret Police*. Philadelphia, 1930.

VESELOVSKY, B. B., and FRANKEL, Z. G. (eds.). *Iubileinyi zemskii sbornik, 1864–1914 (Jubilee Symposium on the Zemstvo, 1864–1914)*. St. Petersburg, 1914.

VISHNIAK, M. *Vserossiiskoe uchreditelnoe sobranie (The All-Russian Constituent Assembly)*. Paris, 1932.

———. *Dan proshlomu (Due the Past)*. New York, 1954.

WALLACE, DONALD MACKENZIE. *Russia*. Revised and enlarged edition, London, 1912.

WEIDLÉ, VLADIMIR. *Russia: Absent and Present*. London, 1952.

WILLIAMS, HAROLD. *Russia of the Russians*. New York, 1918.

WITTE, S. Y. *Po povodu neprelozhnosti zakonov gosudarstvennoi zhizni (On the Immutability of the Laws of State Life)*. St. Petersburg, 1914.

———. *Samoderzhavie i zemstvo* (*Autocracy and Zemstvo*), with two Forewords by PETER STRUVE. Stuttgart, 1903.
———. *Vospominaniia* (*Memoirs*). 2 vols. Berlin, 1922.
———. *Zapiska po krestianskomu delu* (*Memorandum on the Peasant Question*). St. Petersburg, 1904.
WOLFE, BERTRAM D. *Three Who Made a Revolution.* New York, 1948.
WOYTINSKY, W. *Der erste Sturm, Erinnerungen aus der russischen Revolution 1905.* Berlin, 1931.
ZAGORSKY, S. O. *State Control of Industry in Russia during the War.* New Haven, 1928.

Materials from Krasnyi Arkhiv

A *Digest of the Krasnyi Arkhiv.* Compiled, translated, and annotated by LEONID S. RUBINCHEK; edited by LOUISE M. BOUTELLE and GORDON W. THAYER. Cleveland Public Library, 1947.
"A. I. Gertzen i tsenzura v 1890-kh godakh" ("A. I. Hertzen and the Censorship of the 1890's"), III (1923), 223–28.
"Dnevnik A. A. Polovtseva" ("The Diary of A. A. Polovtsev"), III (1923), 75–172.
"Iz dnevnika A. A. Polovtseva" ("From the Diary of A. A. Polovtsev"), XLVI (1931), 110–32; 57 (1933), 168–86.
"Karl Marx i tsarskaia tsenzura" ("Karl Marx and the Czarist Censorship"), LVI (1933), 3–32.
"Marksistskaia periodicheskaia pechat 1896–1906 gg." ("The Marxist Periodical Press of 1896–1906"), IX (1925), 226–68; XVIII (1926), 163–94.
"Mart-Mai 1917 goda" ("March–May, 1917"), XV (1926), 30–60.
"Obuzdanie revoliutsionnoi deiatelnosti stolichnoi i provintsialnoi periodicheskoi pechati 1906 goda" ("Bridling of the Revolutionary Activity of the Capital and Provincial Periodical Press of 1906"), II (1922), 280.
"Pamiatnaia zapiska o rabochikh gazetakh v Peterburge" ("Memorandum on the Labor Press in St. Petersburg"), X (1925), 286–99.
"Politicheskoe polozhenie Rossii nakanune fevralskoi revoliutsii v zhandarskom osveshchenii" ("The Political Situation in Russia on the Eve of the February Revolution as Seen by the Gendarmes"), XVII (1926), 3–35.
"Tsarizm v borbe s revoliutsionnoi pechatiiu v 1905 g." ("Tsarism in the Struggle with the Revolutionary Press in 1905"), CV (1941), 140–55.
"Uchet departamentom politsii opyta 1905 goda" ("The Police Department's Reckoning of the Experience of 1905"), XVIII (1926), 219–27.
"V gody reaktsii" ("In the Years of Reaction"), VIII (1925), 242–43.

Articles

BELOKONSKY, I. P. "Zemskoe dvizhenie do obrazovaniia Partii Narodnoi Svobody" ("The Zemstvo Movement Until the Organization of the Party of People's Freedom"), *Byloe*, April, 1907 through October, 1907.

BERNATSKY, M. "Russkie zakony o strakhovanii rabochikh" ("Russian Laws on the Insurance of Workers"), *Sovremennyi Mir*, January, 1913, Section 2, pp. 76–95.

BRAIKEVITCH, M. V. "Unification of Russian Industry for the Purpose of Its Systematic Reconstruction," *The Russian Economist* (London), I, No. 3 (April, 1921), 655–701.

BRUTZKUS, BORIS. "Die historischen Eigentümlichkeiten der wirtschaftlichen und sozialen Entwicklung Russlands," *Jahrbücher für Kultur und Geschichte der Slaven*, N.F., X, No. 1–2 (1934), 62–99.

GERSCHENKRON, A. "The Rate of Industrial Growth in Russia Since 1885," *Journal of Economic History*, Supplement VII, 1947.

GOLDBERG, G. "Stachechnoe dvizhenie rabochykh v Rossii" ("The Strike Movement of the Workers in Russia"), *Vestnik Evropy*, July, 1910, pp. 242–52.

INKELES, ALEX. "Understanding a Foreign Society: A Sociologist's View," *World Politics*, III (January, 1951), 269–80.

KIZEVETTER, A. "Iz razmyshlenii o revoliutsii" ("From Reflections on Revolution"), *Sovremennyia Zapiski*, XLII (1930), 344–73.

LARSKY, I. "Russkiia stachki poslednykh let" ("Russian Strikes of Recent Years"), *Sovremennyi Mir*, January, 1909, pp. 87–103.

LOSITSKY, A. "Raspadenie obshchiny" ("The Disintegration of the Commune"), *Sovremennyi Mir*, November, 1914, Section 2, pp. 1–24.

MAKLAKOV, V. A. "The Agrarian Problem in Russian," *Russian Review*, IX (January, 1950), 3–15.

———. "Zakonnost v russkoi zhizni" ("Legality in Russian Life"), *Vestnik Evropy*, May, 1909, pp. 238–75.

MIAKOTIN, V. "O pisatelskom sezde" ("On the Writers' Congress"), *Russkoe Bogatstvo*, August, 1908, pp. 108–25.

MILIUKOV, PAUL N. "Rokovye gody" ("Fateful Years"), *Russkiia Zapiski*, in seventeen installments beginning with No. 4 (April, 1938) and ending with Nos. 20–21 (August–September, 1939).

———. "Sud nad kadetskim liberalizmom" ("The Trial of Cadet Liberalism"), *Sovremennyia Zapiski*, No. 41 (1930), 347–71.

———. "Liberalizm, radikalizm i revoliutsiia" ("Liberalism, Radicalism and Revolution"), *Sovremennyia Zapiski*, No. 57 (1934), 285–315.

———. "Novyi kurs" ("The New Course"), *Osvobozhdenie*, No. 57 (October 2, 1904).

NABOKOV, V. "O sezde russkikh iuristov" ("Concerning a Congress of Russian Jurists"), *Pravo*, No. 1 (January 4, 1904), 7–11.

OBOLENSKY, V. "Vospominaniia o golodnom 1891 gode" ("Recollections of the Famine of 1891"), *Sovremennyia Zapiski*, No. 7 (1921), 261–85.

"Ot russkikh konstitutsionalistov" ("From the Russian Constitutionalists"), *Osvobozhdenie*, No. 1 (June 18, 1902), 7–12.

PESHEKHONOV, A. "O nyneshnikh sezdakh voobshche, o pisatelskom v osobennosti" ("On the Current Congresses in General, On the Writers' Congress in Particular"), *Russkoe Bogatstvo*, May, 1910, pp. 180–212.

STRUVE, PETER. "M. V. Chelnokov i D. N. Shipov," *Novyi Zhurnal*, No. 22 (1949), 240–45.

———. "Rossiia pod nadzorom politsii" ("Russia Under the Surveillance of the Police"), *Osvobozhdenie*, Nos. 20, 29, 30, 33, 35, 43.

———. "Liberalizm i t. n. revoliutsionnyia napravleniia" ("Liberalism and the So-Called Revolutionary Tendencies"), *Osvobozhdenie*, No. 7 (September 18, 1902).

———. "Germanski vybory" ("The German Elections"), *Osvobozhdenie*, No. 25 (June 18, 1903).

TIMASHEFF, NICHOLAS. "Overcoming Illiteracy: Public Education in Russia, 1880–1940," *Russian Review*, II (Autumn, 1942), 80–88.

TRUBETSKOI, E. N. "Voina i biurokratiia" ("The War and the Bureaucracy"), *Pravo*, No. 39 (September 26, 1904), 1872–75.

———. "Novaia zemskaia Rossiia" ("The New Russia"), *Russkaia Mysl*, December, 1913, Section 2, pp. 1–12.

VISHNIAK, MARK. "Padenie russkago absoliutizma" ("The Fall of Russian Absolutism"), *Sovremennyia Zapiski*, No. 18 (1924).

WALKIN, JACOB. "The Attitude of the Tsarist Government toward the Labor Problem," *American Slavic and East European Review*, XIII (April, 1954), 163–84.

———. "Government Controls Over the Press in Russia, 1905–1914," *Russian Review*, XIII (July, 1954), 203–9.

YORDANSKY, N. "Vne zakona" ("Beyond the Law"), *Sovremennyi Mir*, March, 1910, pp. 125–35.

Index

DATE DUE

DEC 2 '64	OCT 21 '69		
MAR 11 '65	NOV 7 '69		
MAR 27 '65	NOV 26 '69		
MAY 4 '66	APR 16 '70		
MAR 2 '67	MAR 23 '72		
MAR 18 '67	FEB 19 '75		
APR 8 '67	MAR 28 '73		
APR 27 '67	AP 1 '80		
MAR 13 '68	FE 5 '83		
MAR 25 '68	FE 17 '83		
APR 8 '68	FEB 2 '84		
	FE 28 '84		
APR 22 '68			
NOV 25 '68			
DEC 9 '68			
MAR 12 '69			
JUL 3			
JUL 3 '69			